THE HISTORY OF CHINA

UNDERSTANDING CHINA

THE HISTORY OF CHINA

EDITED BY KENNETH PLETCHER, SENIOR EDITOR, GEOGRAPHY AND HISTORY

Britannica®
Educational Publishing

IN ASSOCIATION WITH

ROSEN
EDUCATIONAL SERVICES

Published in 2011 by Britannica Educational Publishing
(a trademark of Encyclopædia Britannica, Inc.)
in association with Rosen Educational Services, LLC
29 East 21st Street, New York, NY 10010.

First Edition

Britannica Educational Publishing
Michael I. Levy: Executive Editor
J.E. Luebering: Senior Manager
Marilyn L. Barton: Senior Coordinator, Production Control
Steven Bosco: Director, Editorial Technologies
Lisa S. Braucher: Senior Producer and Data Editor
Yvette Charboneau: Senior Copy Editor
Kathy Nakamura: Manager, Media Acquisition
Kenneth Pletcher: Senior Editor, Geography and History

Rosen Educational Services
Alexandra Hanson-Harding: Senior Editor
Nelson Sá: Art Director
Cindy Reiman: Photography Manager
Nicole Russo: Designer
Matthew Cauli: Cover Design
Introduction by Laura La Bella

Library of Congress Cataloging-in-Publication Data

The history of China / edited by Kenneth Pletcher.—1st ed.
   p. cm.—(Understanding China)
"In association with Britannica Educational Publishing, Rosen Educational Services."
Includes bibliographical references and index.
ISBN 978-1-61530-109-6 (library binding)
1. China—History—Juvenile literature. I. Pletcher, Kenneth.
DS735.H56 2010
951—dc22

$4505

2009046655

Manufactured in the United States of America

On the cover: The Great Wall, China's most famous landmark, was built over a period of
more than 2,000 years. © *www.istockphoto.com/Robert Churchill*

Page 14 © www.istockphoto.com/Hanquan Chen.

On page 20: The Hall of Prayer for Good Harvests, part of a large religious complex called
the Temple of Heaven, was built in 1420 in Beijing. © *www.istockphoto.com/Hanquan Chen*

CONTENTS

25

57

59

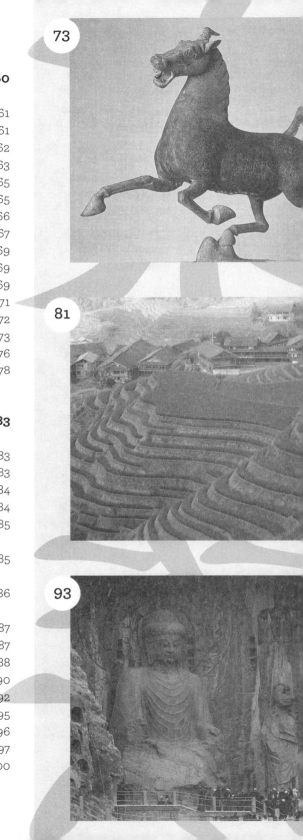

73

81

93

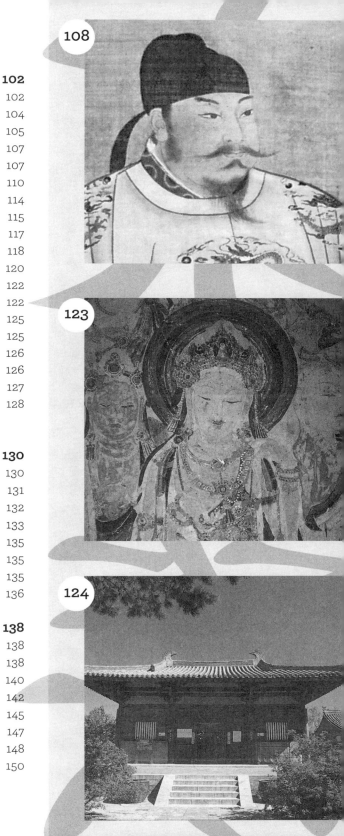
108

123

124

**CHAPTER 12: THE EARLY
REPUBLICAN PERIOD**   **259**

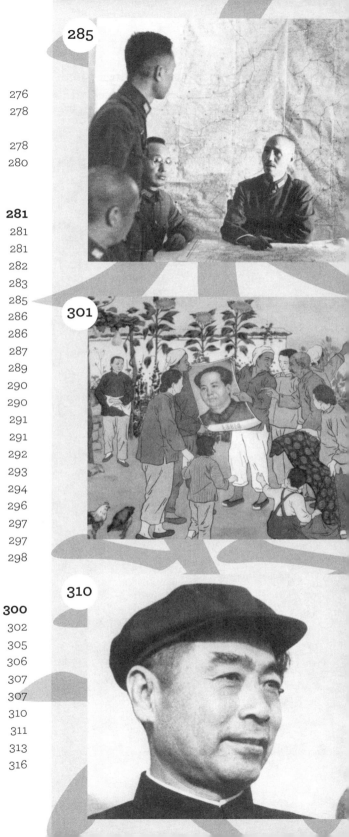

285

301

310

324

326

339

INTRODUCTION

On October 1, 2009, the People's Republic of China celebrated its 60th anniversary with a stunning display of weapons, rumbling tanks, and smartly dressed soldiers under a blue sky in the capital city of Beijing. It was an impressive show of military might that displayed China's rising power in the modern world. From a nation devastated by civil war and the ravages of World War II, China has become the world's third-largest economy and a major player on the world stage. But the ability to renew itself is far from new for China. Despite upheavals that have shattered the country, China is unique among nations: its many cultural and economic accomplishments stretch across a continuous period, from its earliest recorded history, more than 4,000 years ago, to today. This book will reveal much about this exceptional nation and its long, varied history, which reaches back to one of the earliest periods in world civilzation.

China was ruled for centuries by dynasties, each contributing to the country's cultural development. The first Chinese dynasty for which there is archaeological evidence is the Shang dynasty (c. 1600–1046 BC). They left behind beautiful bronze objects, including massive ritual vessels and bronze chariots, which showed that Shang society was sophisticated and organized enough for its people to create large-scale foundries. Eventually, the Shang were conquered by their western neighbours, the Zhou (1046-256 BC). The great philosopher Confucius was born during Zhou times.

The Qin dynasty (221–207 BC) was so influential that the name "China" is derived from Qin. Shihuangdi was its founder and most notable emperor. On the one hand, he was a cruel tyrant. On the other hand, changes he made during his reign helped to define China even today. The boundaries he set during his reign became the traditional territory of China. In later eras China sometimes held other territories, but the Qin boundaries were always considered to embrace the indivisible area of China proper. He developed networks of highways and unified a number of existing fortifications into the Great Wall of China, a UNESCO World Heritage site today. He established a basic administrative system that all succeeding dynasties followed for the next 2,000 years. His tomb near Xi'an contains one of China's most famous treasures—6,000 life-sized terra-cotta statues of warriors.

The Han (202 BC–220 AD), the next great Chinese imperial dynasty established much of Chinese culture, so much so that "Han" became the Chinese word denoting someone who is Chinese. Under its most famous emperor, Han Wudi, China fought against its northern nomad neighbours, the Xiongnu, and took control of the eastern portion of the Silk Road, a trading route that allowed China to sell goods as far away as Rome. He also started China's civil service system in which young men competed through exams for government jobs.

After the Han dynasty fell apart, China was a fractured state. This time was known as the time of the Six Dynasties. Although China was not united in government, it retained its essentially Chinese character. This era was a time of development for two of China's three major religions: Daoism and Buddhism (The other is Confucianism).

The short-lived yet significant Sui dynasty (581–618) unified the country after more than three centuries of fragmentation. One of the greatest accomplishments of the Sui dynasty was building a great waterway, the Bian Canal, which linked north and south China. This system, further enlarged in later times, was a valuable transportation network that proved to be extremely important in maintaining a unified empire.

The Sui set the stage for the succeeding Tang dynasty (618–907), which stimulated a cultural and artistic golden age. Some of China's greatest poets, such as Li Bai and Du Fu, lived and wrote during the Tang dynasty.

Next came another time of political instability (907–960) during which three northern peoples, the Tangut, Khitan, and Juchen, occupied parts of China's traditional territory. The Tangut became middlemen in trade between Central Asia and China. The Khitan founded the Liao dynasty by expanding from the border of Mongolia into southern Manchuria. This area remained out of Chinese political control for more than 400 years and acted for centuries as a centre for the mutual exchange of culture between the Chinese and the northern peoples. The Liao were overthrown by the Juchen.

The Song (960–1279) was one of China's most brilliant dynasties. During the Song period, commerce increased, the widespread printing of literature became popular and a growing number of people became educated. An agricultural revolution, including cultivation of an early ripening strain of rice, produced enough food to feed a population of 100 million people—by far the largest population in the world at the time. Artistically, the Song dynasty marked a high point for Chinese pottery. But militarily, the Song were less powerful. During this dynasty the Juchen continued to control much of China's central plains. This caused a spiritual crisis that led to a new form of Confucianism known as Lixue "School of Universal Principles," which synthesized metaphysics, ethics, and self-cultivation, and became important in China for centuries to come.

In the late 12th and 13th century, Genghis Khan, the great Mongol warrior-ruler, was slashing his way across Asia and Europe. He started the work of conquering the rich prize that was China, and began the Yuan dynasty (1206–1368) but was only partially successful. It wasn't until his grandson, Kublai, took control that the Song dynasty was completely defeated—a fight that took several decades. Being ruled by a foreign invader was difficult for native Chinese, who were not allowed to hold the highest positions in court and were called "southern barbarians." But at the same time, Yuan rule had certain benefits for the Chinese. The Mongols reunited China.

They left religion alone. A large, well-read bourgeoisie enjoyed novels and plays. Because the empire was so vast, China engaged in more extensive foreign trade than ever before, allowing the country to become richer and more stable.

Chinese rulers reclaimed leadership of the country during the Ming dynasty (1368–1644). During the Ming, China exerted immense cultural and political influence on East Asia. This era was famous for its brilliant art, especially craft goods, such as cloisonné and porcelain. The "willow pattern" porcelain wares became a famous export good to Europe.

The Qing dynasty (1644–1911/12) the last of China's imperial dynasties, began when the Manchu, descendants of the Juchen, took over China. From the beginning, the Manchu made efforts to become assimilated into Chinese culture. These efforts bred strongly conservative, Confucian cultural attitudes in official society and stimulated a great period of collecting, cataloging, and commenting upon the traditions of the past. During this time, there was significant trade with other countries—in the 18th century, 10 million Spanish silver dollars a year flowed into China. In its early days, Qing China had a favourable trade balance, but gradually it became weak, and beginning in the 1820s, European powers such as Britain began demanding concessions and other special favours from China (including control of some Chinese territory). The Qing dynasty was not strong enough to resist. A series of brief wars and uprisings took place during the 19th century as Chinese rebelled against both Qing policies and these foreign incursions.

Finally, in 1912, the Qing dynasty abdicated and Yuan Shikai became president of China's new republic. But when the Nationalist Party (Kuomintang, or KMT), made up mostly of former revolutionaries, won a commanding majority of seats in the new legislature and obstructed Yuan's agenda, the president undermined parliament and eventually took on dictatorial powers. He then tried to appoint himself as emperor but died in 1916 before doing so. Still, Yuan managed to leave behind foreign debt, a legacy of brutality, and a country fracturing into warlordism.

On May 4, 1919, students organized protests and riots in the nation's major cities, and waves of workers went on strike to pressure the government to oppose the decisions made at the Paris Peace Conference after World War I ended, especially the decision to allow the Japanese to keep control of valuable Chinese land, resources, and railroads that they had taken in the previous decade. This outburst led to the establishment of the Chinese Communist Party (CCP). After spending several years recruiting new members, the CCP began to compete with the KMT for control of China.

In 1928, the Nationalists formally established a reorganized National Government of the Republic of China. Meanwhile, Japan was moving aggressively to extend its power in Manchuria, and nationalism was growing among the Chinese people.

Throughout most of the 1930s, the KMT clashed with the CCP. The communists established their own rival government in 1931 at several bases in rural areas of central China. In late 1934, the Nationalists forced the communists to abandon their bases. The communists fought their way across western China in what became known as the Long March. By 1936, the remnants of several Red armies had gathered into an impoverished area in northern Shaanxi and reorganized themselves. During the Long March, the communists developed cohesion and discipline. Mao Zedong rose to preeminence as a leader.

The Sino-Japanese War (which later developed into the Pacific theatre of World War II) began in 1937 with Japanese attacks near Beijing. The CCP and KMT formed an alliance (the United Front) to fight against the enemy, but during the war's first year, Japan won victory after victory. By late December, the Japanese had invaded Shanghai and Nanjing. Between 100,000 and 300,000 people were massacred by Japanese soldiers in Nanjing. By mid-1938, Japan controlled the rail lines and major cities of northern China. The next years continued to be a bitter time, and the Chinese suffered terribly. Eventually, the alliance between the CCP and KMT began to fracture, as both sides fought to control territory. The Nationalist government became increasingly corrupt, while the communists, having survived 10 years of civil war, had developed a powerful discipline and sense of camaraderie. After the war ended with Japan's defeat in 1945, the Nationalist government began to deteriorate.

In 1949, the communists took control, establishing the People's Republic of China and installing Mao Zedong, the chairman of the CCP, as its leader. Using the Soviet model, Mao's government wanted to focus on organizing China's industrial workers. But four-fifths of China's people were underemployed, impoverished farmers. To address this problem, Mao came up with the First Five-Year Plan (1953-57), which redistributed land and forced farmworkers into small agricultural collectives. This plan had some success in helping to reduce hunger. However, this success did not carry out in his next large program, the Great Leap Forward (1958–60). During that campaign, the large-scale collectives Mao had envisioned to increase China's food were also pressed to engage in small-scale industrial production. However, agricultural output declined, and this, combined with a series of natural disasters that further ravaged crop production, led to mass starvation in the country.

Indeed, life under Mao was a time of constant social upheaval and uproar. Under his leadership, China went through one kind of social revolution after another. Posters extolling the virtues of the latest propaganda campaigns, with names like "Let a hundred flowers blossom," "The Four Olds," and "Bombard the headquarters," blanketed the country. Often, those who participated in one social movement were attacked in the next.

In 1966, Mao unleashed the most far-reaching of his upheavals: the Great Proletarian Cultural Revolution, a time when many authors, scholars, school-teachers, former party leaders, and other intellectuals were denounced as subversive to the country's cause. Bands of Red Guards (paramilitary units of radical students) roamed the country attacking those whom they deemed unsuitable. Sometimes different Red Guard groups even attacked each other. Students, intellectuals, and party members were encouraged or forced to moved out to the countryside and told to "learn from the poor and middle-class peasants."

The consequences of the 10 years of the Cultural Revolution were severe. In the short run, political instability produced slower economic growth. In the long term, the Cultural Revolution left a severe generation gap in which poorly educated young people only knew how to redress grievances by taking to the streets, an increase in corruption within the CCP, and a loss of legitimacy as China's people became disillusioned by politicians' obvious power plays. Perhaps never before had a political leader unleashed such massive forces against the system that he had created.

After Mao died in 1976 and the Cultural Revolution subsided, China's priorities changed. It began to reach out more to the world, and to develop as an economic powerhouse. In 1978, China formally agreed to establish full diplomatic relations with the United States. In education, top priority was given to raising technical, scientific, and scholarly talent to world-class standards. The collective farming system was gradually dismantled. Private entrepreneurship in the cities increased. It modernized its factories and developed its transportation infrastructure; its cities grew rapidly. China joined the World Trade Organization in 2001.

China faces many problems, among them serious environmental issues, widespread economic inequality, and a sometimes repressive government. Its image was tarnished in 1989, following the deaths of protestors in Tiananmen Square. Still, the world clamours for Chinese goods, and this has led to China becoming a major player on the world stage—it now has the world's third largest economy and is among the top trading countries. China remains cohesive and vital, as it showed when it hosted the glittering 2008 Summer Olympics in Beijing and again demonstrated its ability to reinvent itself and to innovate, even after 4,000 years of history.

What follows is a more detailed narrative of China's vast history with more comprehensive information on the dynasties, movements, and events that account for the nation's rich history.

CHAPTER 1

THE BEGINNINGS OF CHINESE HISTORY

INTRODUCTION

With more than 4,000 years of recorded history, China is one of the few existing countries that also flourished economically and culturally in the earliest stages of world civilization. Indeed, despite the political and social upheavals that frequently have ravaged the country, China is unique among nations in its longevity and resilience as a discrete political and cultural unit. Much of China's cultural development has been accomplished with relatively little outside influence, the introduction of Buddhism from India constituting a major exception. Even when the country was penetrated by such "barbarian" peoples as the Manchu, these groups soon became largely absorbed into the fabric of Han Chinese culture.

This relative isolation from the outside world made possible over the centuries the flowering and refinement of the Chinese culture, but it also left China ill-prepared to cope with that world when, from the mid-19th century, it was confronted by technologically superior foreign nations. There followed a century of decline and decrepitude, as China found itself relatively helpless in the face of a foreign onslaught. The trauma of this external challenge became the catalyst for a revolution that began in the early 20th century against the old regime and culminated in the establishment of a communist government in 1949. This event reshaped

A Chinese scientist holds the unearthed bones of a human who lived 25,000 years ago. AFP/ Getty Images

global political geography, and China has since come to rank among the most influential countries in the world.

PREHISTORY

EARLY HUMANS

The fossil record in China promises fundamental contributions to the understanding of human origins. There is considerable evidence of *Homo erectus* by the time of the Lower Paleolithic (the Paleolithic Period [Old Stone Age] began about 2,500,000 years ago and ended 10,000 years ago) at sites such as Lantian, Shaanxi; Hexian, Anhui; Yuanmou, Yunnan; and, the most famous, that of Peking man at Zhoukoudian, Beijing municipality. The Lower Cave at Zhoukoudian has yielded evidence of intermittent human use from about 460,000 to 230,000 years ago, and fossils of Peking man found in the complex have been dated to about 770,000 years ago. Many caves and other sites in

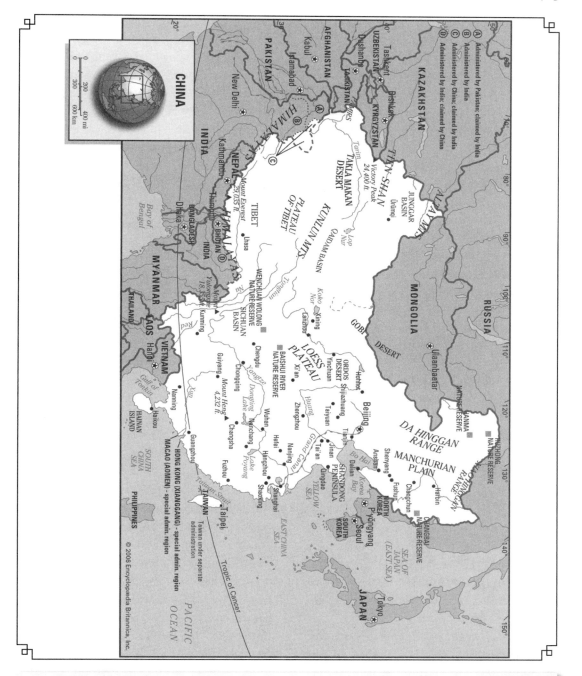

This map shows China and its special administrative regions.

Anhui, Hebei, Henan, Liaoning, Shandong, Shanxi and Shaanxi in northern China and in Guizhou and Hubei in the south suggest that *H. erectus* achieved wide distribution in China. Whether *H. erectus pekinensis* intentionally used fire and practiced ritual cannibalism are matters under debate.

Significant *Homo sapiens* cranial and dental fragments have been found together with Middle Paleolithic artifacts. Such assemblages have been unearthed at Dingcun, Shanxi; Changyang, Hubei; Dali, Shaanxi; Xujiayao, Shanxi; and Maba, Guangdong. Morphological characteristics such as the shovel-shaped incisor, broad nose, and mandibular torus link these remains to modern Asians. Few archaeological sites have been identified in the south.

A number of widely distributed *H. erectus* sites dating from the early Pleistocene Epoch (i.e., about 1.8 million years ago) manifest considerable regional and temporal diversity. Upper Paleolithic sites are numerous in northern China. Thousands of stone artifacts, most of them small (called microliths), have been found, for example, at Xiaonanhai, near Anyang, at Shuoxian and Qinshui (Shanxi), and at Yangyuan (Hebei); these findings suggest an extensive microlith culture in northern China. Hematite, a common iron oxide ore used for colouring, was found scattered around skeletal remains in the Upper Cave at Zhoukoudian (*c.* 10th millennium BC) and may represent the first sign of human ritual.

NEOLITHIC PERIOD

The complex of developments in stone tool technology, food production and storage, and social organization that is often characterized as the "Neolithic Revolution" was in progress in China by at least the 6th millennium BC. Developments during the Chinese Neolithic Period (New Stone Age) were to establish some of the major cultural dimensions of the subsequent Bronze Age.

CLIMATE AND ENVIRONMENT

Although the precise nature of the paleoenvironment is still in dispute, temperatures in Neolithic China were probably some 4 to 7 °F (2 to 4 °C) warmer than they are today. Precipitation, although more abundant, may have been declining in quantity. The Qin (Tsinling) Mountains in north-central China separated the two phytogeographical zones of northern and southern China, while the absence of such a mountain barrier farther east encouraged a more uniform environment and the freer movement of Neolithic peoples about the North China Plain. East China, particularly toward the south, may have been covered with thick vegetation, some deciduous forest, and scattered marsh. The Loess Plateau north and west of the Qin Mountains is thought to have been drier and even semiarid, with some coniferous forest growing on the hills and with brush and open woodland in the valleys.

A farmer in Shaoshan, Hunan province, China, gathers bundles of dried millet stalks. Frederic J. Brown/AFP/Getty Images

Food Production

The primary Neolithic crops, domesticated by the 5th millennium BC, were drought-resistant millet (usually *Setaria italica*), grown on the eolian and alluvial loess soils of the northwest and the north, and glutenous rice (*Oryza sativa*), grown in the wetlands of the southeast. These staples were supplemented by a variety of fruits, nuts, legumes, vegetables, and aquatic plants. The main sources of animal protein were pigs, dogs, fish, and shellfish. By the Bronze Age, millet, rice, soybeans, tea, mulberries, hemp, and lacquer had become characteristic Chinese crops. That most if not all of these plants were native to China indicates the degree to which Neolithic culture developed indigenously. The distinctive cereal, fruit, and vegetable complexes of the northern and southern zones in Neolithic and early historic times suggest, however, that at least two independent traditions of plant domestication may have been present.

The stone tools used to clear and prepare the land reveal generally improving technology. There was increasing use of ground and polished edges and of perforation. Regional variations of shape included oval-shaped axes in central and northwest China, square- and trapezoid-shaped axes in the east, and axes with stepped shoulders in the southeast. By the Late Neolithic a decrease in the proportion of stone axes to adzes suggests the increasing dominance of permanent agriculture and a reduction in the opening up of new land. The burial in high-status graves of finely polished, perforated stone and jade tools such as axes and adzes with no sign of edge wear indicates the symbolic role such emblems of work had come to play by the 4th and 3rd millennia.

MAJOR CULTURES AND SITES

There was not one Chinese Neolithic but a mosaic of regional cultures whose scope and significance are still being determined. Their location in the area defined today as China does not necessarily mean that all the Neolithic cultures were Chinese or even proto-Chinese. Their contributions to the Bronze Age civilization of the Shang, which may be taken as unmistakably Chinese in both cultural as well as geographical terms, need to be assessed in each case. In addition, the presence of a particular ceramic ware does not necessarily define a cultural horizon; transitional phases, both chronological and geographical, are not discussed in detail in the following paragraphs.

INCIPIENT NEOLITHIC

Study of the historical reduction of the size of human teeth suggests that the first human beings to eat cooked food did so in southern China. The sites of Xianrendong in Jiangxi and Zengpiyan in Guangxi have yielded artifacts from the 10th to the 7th millennium BC that include low-fired, cord-marked shards with some incised decoration and mostly chipped stone tools; these pots may have been used for cooking and storage. Pottery and stone tools from shell middens in southern China also suggest Incipient Neolithic occupations. These early southern sites may have been related to the Neolithic Bac Son culture in Vietnam; connections to the subsequent Neolithic cultures of northwestern and northern China have yet to be demonstrated.

6TH MILLENNIUM BC

Two major cultures can be identified in the northwest: Laoguantai, in eastern and southern Shaanxi and northwestern Henan, and Dadiwan I—a development of Laoguantai culture—in eastern Gansu and western Shaanxi. The pots in both cultures were low-fired, sand-tempered, and mainly red in colour, and bowls with three stubby feet or ring feet were common. The painted bands of this pottery may represent the start of the Painted Pottery culture.

SILK

Silk is an animal fibre produced by certain insects as building material for cocoons and webs. In commercial use it refers almost entirely to filament from cocoons produced by the caterpillars of several moth species of the genus Bombyx, commonly called silkworms. Silk is a continuous filament around each cocoon. It is freed by softening the cocoon in water and then locating the filament end; the filaments from several cocoons are unwound at the same time, sometimes with a slight twist, to form a single strand. In the process called throwing, several very thin strands are twisted together to make thicker, stronger yarn. Produced since ancient times, the secret of how silk is made was closely guarded for millennia. Along with jade and spices, silk was the primary commodity traded along the Silk Road beginning about 100 BC. Since World War II, nylon and other synthetic fibres have replaced silk in many applications (e.g., parachutes, hosiery, dental floss), but silk remains an important material for clothing and home furnishings.

Silkworms spin cocoons on a silk farm in Zhejiang province. China is the leader in silk production and trade. China Photos/Getty Images

In northern China the people of Peiligang (north-central Henan) made less use of cord marking and painted design on their pots than did those at Dadiwan I; the variety of their stone tools, including sawtooth sickles, indicates the importance of agriculture. The Cishan potters (southern Hebei) employed more cord-marked decoration and made a greater variety of forms, including basins, cups, serving stands, and pot supports. The discovery of two pottery models of silkworm chrysalides and 70 shuttlelike objects at a 6th-millennium-BC site at Nanyangzhuang (southern Hebei) suggests the early production of silk, the characteristic Chinese textile.

5TH MILLENNIUM BC

The lower stratum of the Beishouling culture is represented by finds along the Wei and Jing rivers; bowls, deep-bodied jugs, and three-footed vessels, mainly red in colour, were common. The lower stratum of the related Banpo culture, also in the Wei River drainage area, was characterized by cord-marked red or red-brown ware, especially round and flat-bottomed bowls and pointed-bottomed amphorae. The Banpo inhabitants lived in partially subterranean houses and were supported by a mixed economy of millet agriculture, hunting, and gathering. The importance of fishing is confirmed by designs of stylized fish painted on a few of the bowls and by numerous hooks and net sinkers.

In the east, by the start of the 5th millennium, the Beixin culture in central and southern Shandong and northern Jiangsu was characterized by fine clay or sand-tempered pots decorated with comb markings, incised and impressed designs, and narrow appliquéd bands. Artifacts include many three-legged, deep-bodied tripods, gobletlike serving vessels, bowls, and pot supports. Hougang (lower stratum) remains have been found in southern Hebei and central Henan. The vessels, some finished on a slow wheel, were mainly red-coloured and had been fired at high heat. They include jars, tripods, and round-bottomed, flat-bottomed, and ring-footed bowls. No pointed amphorae have been found, and there were few painted designs. A characteristic red band under the rim of most gray-ware bowls was produced during the firing process.

Archaeologists have generally classified the lower strata of Beishouling, Banpo, and Hougang cultures under the rubric of Painted Pottery (or, after a later site, Yangshao) culture, but two cautions should be noted. First, a distinction may have existed between a more westerly culture in the Wei valley (early Beishouling and early Banpo) that was rooted in the Laoguantai culture and a more easterly one (Beixin and Hougang) that developed from the Peiligang and Cishan cultures. Second, since only 2 to 3 percent of the Banpo pots were painted, the designation Painted Pottery culture seems premature.

In the region of the lower Yangtze River (Chang Jiang), the Hemudu site in northern Zhejiang has yielded caldrons, cups, bowls, and pot supports made of porous, charcoal-tempered black pottery. The site is remarkable for its wooden and bone farming tools, the bird designs carved on bone and ivory, the superior carpentry of its pile dwellings (a response to the damp environment), a wooden weaving shuttle, and the earliest lacquerware and rice remains yet reported in the world (c. 5000–4750 BC).

The Qingliangang culture, which succeeded that of Hemudu in Jiangsu, northern Zhejiang, and southern Shandong, was characterized by ring-footed and flat-bottomed pots, *gui* (wide-mouthed vessels), tripods (common north of the Yangtze), and serving stands (common south of the Yangtze). Early fine-paste redware gave way in the later period to fine-paste gray and black ware. Polished stone artifacts include axes and spades, some perforated, and jade ornaments.

Another descendant of Hemudu culture was that of Majiabang, which had close ties with the Qingliangang culture in southern Jiangsu, northern Zhejiang, and Shanghai. In southeastern China a cord-marked pottery horizon, represented by the site of Fuguodun on the island of Quemoy (Kinmen), existed by at least the early 5th millennium. The suggestion that some of these southeastern cultures belonged to an Austronesian complex remains to be fully explored.

4TH AND 3RD MILLENNIA BC

A true Painted Pottery culture developed in the northwest, partly from the Wei valley and Banpo traditions of the 5th millennium. The Miaodigou I horizon, dated from the first half of the 4th millennium, produced burnished bowls and basins of fine red pottery, some 15 percent of which were painted, generally in black, with dots, spirals, and sinuous lines. It was succeeded by a variety of Majiayao cultures (late 4th to early 3rd millennium) in eastern Gansu, eastern Qinghai, and northern Sichuan. About one-third of Majiayao vessels were decorated on the upper two-thirds of the body with a variety of designs in black pigment; multiarmed radial spirals, painted with calligraphic ease, were the most prominent. Related designs involving sawtooth lines, gourd-shaped panels, spirals, and zoomorphic stick figures were painted on pots of the Banshan (mid-3rd millennium) and Machang (last half of 3rd millennium) cultures. Some two-thirds of the pots found in the Machang burial area at Liuwan in Qinghai, for example, were painted. In the North China Plain, Dahe culture sites contain a mixture of Miaodigou and eastern, Dawenkou vessel types (*see below*), indicating that a meeting of two major traditions was taking place in this area in the late 4th millennium.

In the northeast the Hongshan culture (4th millennium and probably earlier) was centred in western Liaoning and eastern Inner Mongolia. It was characterized by small bowls (some with red tops), fine redware serving stands, painted pottery, and microliths. Numerous jade amulets in the form of birds, turtles, and coiled dragons reveal strong affiliations with the other jade-working cultures of the east coast, such as Liangzhu.

In east China the Liulin and Huating sites in northern Jiangsu (first half of 4th millennium) represent regional cultures that derived in large part from that of Qingliangang. Upper strata also show strong affinities with contemporary Dawenkou sites in southern Shandong, northern Anhui, and northern Jiangsu. Dawenkou culture (mid-5th to at least mid-3rd millennium) is characterized by the emergence of wheel-made pots of various colours, some of them remarkably thin and delicate; vessels with ring feet and tall legs (such as tripods, serving stands, and goblets); carved, perforated, and polished tools; and ornaments in stone, jade, and bone. The people practiced skull deformation and tooth extraction. Mortuary customs involved ledges for displaying grave goods, coffin chambers, and the burial of animal teeth, pig heads, and pig jawbones.

In the middle and lower Yangtze River valley during the 4th and 3rd millennia, the Daxi and Qujialing cultures shared a significant number of traits, including rice production, ring-footed vessels, goblets with sharply angled profiles, ceramic whorls, and black pottery with designs painted in red after firing. Characteristic Qujialing ceramic objects not generally found in Daxi sites include eggshell-thin goblets and bowls painted with black or orange designs, double-waisted bowls, tall, ring-footed goblets and serving stands, and many styles of tripods. Admirably executed and painted clay whorls suggest a thriving textile industry. The chronological distribution of ceramic features suggests a transmission from Daxi to Qujialing, but the precise relationship between the two cultures has been much debated.

The Majiabang culture in the Lake Tai basin was succeeded during the 4th millennium by that of Songze. The pots, increasingly wheel-made, were predominantly clay-tempered gray ware. Tripods with a variety of leg shapes, serving stands, *gui* pitchers with handles, and goblets with petal-shaped feet were characteristic. Ring feet were used, silhouettes became more angular, and triangular and circular perforations were cut to form openwork designs on the short-stemmed serving stands. A variety of jade ornaments, a feature of Qingliangang culture, has been excavated from Songze burial sites.

Sites of the Liangzhu culture (from the last half of the 4th to the last half of the 3rd millennium) have generally been found in the same area. The pots were mainly wheel-made, clay-tempered gray ware with a black skin and were produced by reduction firing; oxidized redware was less prevalent. Some of the serving stand and tripod shapes had evolved from Majiabang prototypes, while other vessel forms included long-necked *gui* pitchers. The walls of some vessels were black throughout, eggshell-thin, and burnished, resembling those found in Late Neolithic sites in Shandong (*see below*). Extravagant numbers of highly worked jade *bi* disks and *cong* tubes were placed in certain burials, such as one at Sidun (southern Jiangsu) that contained 57 of them. Liangzhu farmers had developed a characteristic triangular shale plow for cultivating the wet soils of the region. Fragments of woven silk from about 3000 BC have been found at Qianshanyang (northern Zhejiang). Along the southeast coast and on Taiwan, the Dapenkeng corded-ware culture emerged during the 4th and 3rd millennia. This culture, with a fuller inventory of pot and tool types than had previously been seen in the area, developed in part from that of Fuguodun but may also have been influenced by cultures to the west and north, including Qingliangang, Liangzhu, and Liulin. The pots were characterized by incised line patterns on neck and rim, low, perforated foot rims, and some painted decoration.

REGIONAL CULTURES OF THE LATE NEOLITHIC

By the 3rd millennium BC, the regional cultures in the areas discussed above showed increased signs of interaction and even convergence. That they are frequently referred to as varieties of the Longshan culture (c. 2500–2000 BC) of east-central Shandong—characterized by its lustrous, eggshell-thin black ware—suggests the degree to which these cultures are thought to have experienced eastern influence. That influence, diverse in origin and of varying intensity, entered

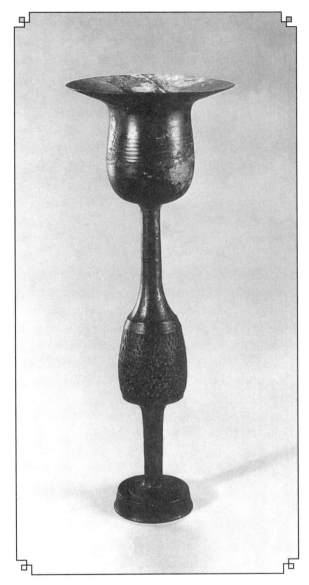

Black pottery stem cup, Neolithic Longshan culture, c. late 3rd millennium BC, from Rizhao, Shandong province, China; in the Shandong Provincial Museum, Jinan. Height 26.5 cm. Wang Lu/ChinaStock Photo Library

the North China Plain from sites such as Dadunzi and Dawenkou to the east and also moved up the Han River from the Qujialing area to the south. A variety of eastern features are evident in the ceramic objects of the period, including use of the fast wheel, unpainted surfaces, sharply angled profiles, and eccentric shapes. There was a greater production of gray and black, rather than red, ware; componential construction was emphasized, in which legs, spouts, and handles were appended to the basic form (which might itself have been built sectionally). Greater elevation was achieved by means of ring feet and tall legs. Ceramic objects included three-legged tripods, steamer cooking vessels, *gui* pouring pitchers, serving stands, fitted lids, cups and goblets, and asymmetrical *beihu* vases for carrying water that were flattened on one side to lie against a person's body. In stone and jade objects, eastern influence is evidenced by perforated stone tools and ornaments such as *bi* disks and *cong* tubes used in burials. Other burial customs involved ledges to display the goods buried with the deceased and large wooden coffin chambers. In handicrafts an emphasis was placed on precise mensuration in working clay, stone, and wood. Although the first, primitive versions of the eastern ceramic types may have been made on occasion in the North China Plain, in virtually every case these types were elaborated in the east and given more-precise functional definition, greater structural strength, and greater

aesthetic coherence. It was evidently the mixing in the 3rd and 2nd millennia of these eastern elements with the strong and extensive traditions native to the North China Plain—represented by such Late Neolithic sites as Gelawangcun (near Zhengzhou), Wangwan (near Luoyang), Miaodigou (in central and western Henan), and Taosi and Dengxiafeng (in southwest Shanxi)—that stimulated the rise of early Bronze Age culture in the North China Plain and not in the east.

RELIGIOUS BELIEFS AND SOCIAL ORGANIZATION

The inhabitants of Neolithic China were, by the 5th millennium if not earlier, remarkably assiduous in the attention they paid to the disposition and commemoration of their dead. There was a consistency of orientation and posture, with the dead of the northwest given a westerly orientation and those of the east an easterly one. The dead were segregated, frequently in what appear to be kinship groupings (e.g., at Yuanjunmiao, Shaanxi). There were graveside ritual offerings of liquids, pig skulls, and pig jaws (e.g., Banpo and Dawenkou), and the demanding practice of collective secondary burial, in which the bones of up to 70 or 80 corpses were stripped of their flesh and reburied together, was extensively practiced as early as the first half of the 5th millennium (e.g., Yuanjunmiao). Evidence of divination using scapulae (shoulder blades) dating from the end of the 4th millennium (from Fuhegoumen, Liaoning) implies the existence of ritual specialists. There was a lavish expenditure of energy by the 3rd millennium on tomb ramps and coffin chambers (e.g., Liuwan [in eastern Qinghai] and Dawenkou) and on the burial of redundant quantities of expensive grave goods (e.g., Dafanzhuang in Shandong, Fuquanshan in Shanghai, and Liuwan), presumably for use by the dead in some afterlife.

Although there is no firm archaeological evidence of a shift from matrilineal to patrilineal society, the goods buried in graves indicate during the course of the 4th and 3rd millennia an increase in general wealth, the gradual emergence of private or lineage property, an increase in social differentiation and gender distinction of work roles, and a reduction in the relative wealth of women. The occasional practice of human sacrifice or accompanying-in-death from scattered 4th- and 3rd-millennium sites (e.g., Miaodigou I, Zhanglingshan in Jiangsu, Qinweijia in Gansu, and Liuwan) suggests that ties of dependency and obligation were conceived as continuing beyond death and that women were likely to be in the dependent position. Early forms of ancestor worship, together with all that they imply for social organization and obligation among the living, were deeply rooted and extensively developed by the Late Neolithic Period. Such religious belief and practice undoubtedly served to validate and encourage the decline of the more egalitarian societies of earlier periods.

THE FIRST HISTORICAL DYNASTY: THE SHANG

THE ADVENT OF BRONZE CASTING

The 3rd and 2nd millennia were marked by the appearance of increasing warfare, complex urban settlements, intense status differentiation, and administrative and religious hierarchies that legitimated and controlled the massive mobilization of labour for dynastic work or warfare. The casting of bronze left the most-evident archaeological traces of these momentous changes, but its introduction must be seen as part of a far-larger shift in the nature of society as a whole, representing an intensification of the social and religious practices of the Neolithic.

A Chalcolithic Period (Copper Age; i.e., transitional period between the Late Neolithic and the Bronze Age) dating to the mid-5th millennium may be dimly perceived. A growing number of 3rd-millennium sites, primarily in the northwest but also in Henan and Shandong, have yielded primitive knives, awls, and drills made of copper and bronze. Stylistic evidence, such as the sharp angles, flat bottoms, and strap handles of certain Qijia clay pots (in Gansu; c. 2250–1900 BC), has led some scholars to posit an early sheet- or wrought-metal tradition

Bronze jia, *Shang dynasty (c. 1600–1046 BC); in the Nelson-Atkins Museum of Art, Kansas City, Mo.* Courtesy of the Nelson Gallery-Atkins Museum, Kansas City, Missouri (Nelson Fund)

possibly introduced from the west by migrating Indo-European peoples, but no wrought-metal objects have been found.

The construction and baking of the clay cores and sectional piece molds employed in Chinese bronze casting of the 2nd millennium indicate that early metalworking in China rapidly adapted to, if it did not develop indigenously from, the sophisticated high-heat ceramic technology of the Late Neolithic potters, who were already using ceramic molds and cores to produce forms such as the hollow legs of the *li* cooking caldron. Chinese bronze casting represents, as the continuity in vessel shapes suggests, an aesthetic and technological extension of that ceramic tradition rather than its replacement. The bronze casters' preference for vessels elevated on ring feet or legs further suggests aesthetic links to the east rather than the northwest.

The number, complexity, and size—the Simuwu tetrapod weighed 1,925 pounds (875 kg)—of the Late Shang ritual vessels reveal high technological competence married to large-scale, labour-intensive metal production. Bronze casting of this scale and character—in which large groups of ore miners, fuel gatherers, ceramists, and foundry workers were under the prescriptive control of the model designers and labour coordinators—must be understood as a manifestation, both technological and social, of the high value that Shang culture placed on hierarchy, social discipline, and central direction in all walks of life. The prestige of owning these metal objects must have derived in part from the political control over others that their production implied.

Chinese legends of the 1st millennium BC describe the labours of Yu, the Chinese "Noah" who drained away the floods to render China habitable and established the first Chinese dynasty, called Xia. Seventeen Xia kings are listed in the *Shiji*, a comprehensive history written during the 1st century BC, and much ingenuity has been devoted to identifying certain Late Neolithic fortified sites—such as Wangchenggang ("Mound of the Royal City") in north-central Henan and Dengxiafeng in Xia county (possibly the site of Xiaxu, "Ruins of Xia"?), southern Shanxi—as early Xia capitals. Taosi, also in southern Shanxi, has been identified as a Xia capital because of the "royal" nature of five large male burials found there that were lavishly provided with grave goods. Although they fall within the region traditionally assigned to the Xia, particular archaeological sites can be hard to identify dynastically unless written records are found. The possibility that the Xia and Shang were partly contemporary, as cultures if not as dynasties, further complicates site identifications. A related approach has been to identify as Xia an archaeological horizon that lies developmentally between Late Neolithic and Shang strata.

THE SHANG DYNASTY

The Shang dynasty—the first Chinese dynasty to leave historical records—is thought to have ruled from about 1600 to 1046 BC. (Some scholars date the Shang from the mid-18th to the late 12th century BC.) One must, however, distinguish Shang as an archaeological term from Shang as a dynastic one. Erlitou, in north-central Henan, for example, was initially classified archaeologically as Early Shang; its developmental sequence from about 2400 to 1450 BC documents the vessel types and burial customs that link Early Shang culture to the Late Neolithic cultures of the east. In dynastic terms, however, Erlitou periods I and II (c. 1900 BC?) are now thought by many to represent a pre-Shang (and thus, perhaps, Xia) horizon. In this view, the two palace foundations, the elite burials, the ceremonial jade blades and sceptres, the bronze axes and dagger axes, and the simple ritual bronzes—said to be the earliest yet found in China—of Erlitou III (c. 1700–1600 BC?) signal the advent of the dynastic Shang.

The archaeological classification of Middle Shang is represented by the remains found at Erligang (c. 1600 BC) near Zhengzhou, some 50 miles (80 km) to the east of Erlitou. The massive rammed-earth fortification, 118 feet (36 metres) wide at its base and enclosing an area of 1.2 square miles (3.2 square km), would have taken 10,000 people more than 12 years to build. Also found were ritual bronzes, including four monumental tetrapods (the largest weighing 190 pounds [86 kg]); palace foundations; workshops for bronze casting, pot making, and bone working; burials; and two inscribed fragments of oracle bones. Another rammed-earth fortification, enclosing about 450 acres (180 hectares) and also dated to the Erligang period, was found at Yanshi, about 3 miles (5 km) east of the Erlitou III palace foundations. These walls and palaces have been variously identified by modern scholars—the identification now favoured is of Zhengzhou as Bo, the capital of the Shang dynasty during the reign of Tang, the dynasty's founder—and their dynastic affiliations are yet to be firmly established. The presence of two large, relatively close contemporary fortifications at Zhengzhou and Yanshi, however, indicates the strategic importance of the area and considerable powers of labour mobilization.

Panlongcheng in Hubei, 280 miles (450 km) south of Zhengzhou, is an example of Middle Shang expansion into the northwest, northeast, and south. A city wall, palace foundations, burials with human sacrifices, bronze workshops, and mortuary bronzes of the Erligang type form a complex that duplicates on a smaller scale Zhengzhou. A transitional period spanning the gap between the Late Erligang phase of Middle Shang and the Yinxu phase of Late Shang indicates a widespread network of Shang cultural sites that were linked by uniform bronze-casting styles and mortuary practices. A relatively homogeneous culture united the Bronze Age elite through much of China around the 14th century BC.

The Late Shang period is best represented by a cluster of sites focused on the village of Xiaotun, west of Anyang in northern Henan. Known to history as Yinxu, "the Ruins of Yin" (Yin was the name used by the succeeding Zhou dynasty for the Shang), it was a seat of royal power for the last nine Shang kings, from Wuding to Dixin. According to the "short chronology" used in this article, which is based on modern studies of lunar eclipse records and reinterpretations of Zhou annals, these kings would have reigned from about 1250 to 1046 BC. (One version of the traditional "long chronology," based primarily on a 1st-century-BC source, would place the last 12 Shang kings, from Pangeng onward, at Yinxu from 1398 to 1112 BC.) Sophisticated bronze, ceramic, stone, and bone industries were housed in a network of settlements surrounding the unwalled cult centre at Xiaotun, which had rammed-earth temple-palace foundations. And Xiaotun itself lay at the centre of a larger network of Late Shang sites, such as Xingtai to the north and Xinxiang to the south, in southern Hebei and northern Henan.

ROYAL BURIALS

The royal cemetery lay at Xibeigang, only a short distance northwest of Xiaotun. The hierarchy of burials at that and other cemeteries in the area reflected the social organization of the living. Large pit tombs, some nearly 40 feet (12 metres) deep, were furnished with four ramps and massive grave chambers for the kings. Retainers who accompanied their lords in death lay in or near the larger tombs, members of the lesser elite and commoners were buried in pits that ranged from medium size to shallow, those of still lower status were thrown into refuse pits and disused wells, and human and animal victims of the royal mortuary cult were placed in sacrificial pits. Only a few undisturbed elite burials have been unearthed, the most notable being that of Fuhao, a consort of Wuding. That her relatively small grave

Ceremonial ivory goblet inlaid with turquoise, c. 12th century BC, Shang dynasty, from the tomb of Lady Fuhao, Anyang, Henan province, China; in the Archaeology Institute, Beijing. Height 30.5 cm. Wang Lu/ChinaStock Photo Library

contained 468 bronze objects, 775 jades, and more than 6,880 cowries suggests how great the wealth placed in the far-larger royal tombs must have been.

THE CHARIOT

The light chariot, with 18 to 26 spokes per wheel, first appeared, according to the archaeological and inscriptional record, about 1200 BC. Glistening with bronze, it was initially a prestigious command car used primarily in hunting. The 16 chariot burials found at Xiaotun raise the possibility of some form of Indo-European contact with China, and there is little doubt that the chariot, which probably originated in the Caucasus, entered China via Central Asia and the northern steppe. Animal-headed knives, always associated with chariot burials, are further evidence of a northern connection.

ART

Late Shang culture is also defined by the size, elaborate shapes, and evolved decor of the ritual bronzes, many of which were used in wine offerings to the ancestors and some of which were inscribed with ancestral dedications such as "Made for Father Ding." Their surfaces were ornamented with zoomorphic and theriomorphic elements set against intricate backgrounds of geometric meanders, spirals, and quills. Some of the animal forms—which include tigers, birds, snakes, dragons, cicadas, and water buffalo—have been thought to represent shamanistic familiars or emblems that ward away evil. The exact meaning of the iconography, however, may never be known. That the predominant *taotie* monster mask—with bulging eyes, fangs, horns, and claws—may have been anticipated by designs carved on jade *cong* tubes and axes from Liangzhu culture sites in the Yangtze delta and from the Late Neolithic in Shandong suggests that its origins are ancient. But the degree to which pure form or intrinsic meaning took priority, in either Neolithic or Shang times, is hard to assess.

Late Shang Divination and Religion

Although certain complex symbols painted on Late Neolithic pots from Shandong suggest that primitive writing was emerging in the east in the 3rd millennium, the Shang divination inscriptions that appear at Xiaotun form the earliest body of Chinese writing yet known. In Late Shang divination as practiced during the reign of Wuding (*c.* 1250–1192 BC), cattle scapulae or turtle plastrons, in a refinement of Neolithic practice, were first planed and bored with hollow depressions to which an intense heat source was then applied. The resulting T-shaped stress cracks were interpreted as lucky or unlucky. After the prognostication had been made, the day, the name of the presiding diviner (some 120 are known), the subject of the charge, the prognostication, and the result might be carved into the surface of the bone. Among the topics divined were sacrifices, campaigns, hunts, the good fortune of the 10-day week or of the night or day, weather, harvests, sickness, childbearing, dreams, settlement building, the issuing of orders, tribute, divine assistance, and prayers to various spirits. Some evolution in divinatory practice and theology evidently occurred. By the reigns of the last two Shang kings, Diyi and Dixin (*c.*

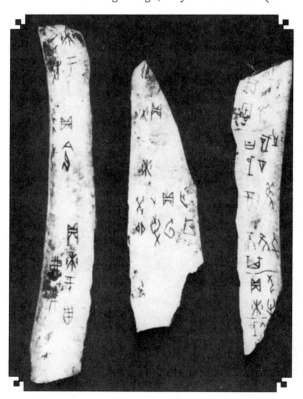

Oracle bone inscriptions from the village of Xiaotun, Henan province, China; Shang dynasty, 14th or 12th century BC. Courtesy of the Syndics of the University Library, Cambridge, Cambridgeshire

1101–1046 BC), the scope and form of Shang divination had become considerably simplified: prognostications were uniformly optimistic, and divination topics were limited mainly to the sacrificial schedule, the coming 10 days, the coming night, and hunting.

STATE AND SOCIETY

The ritual schedule records 29 royal ancestors over a span of 17 generations who, from at least Wuding to Dixin, were each known as *wang* ("king"). Presiding over a stable politico-religious hierarchy of ritual specialists, officers, artisans, retainers, and servile peasants, they ruled with varying degrees of intensity over the North China Plain and parts of Shandong, Shanxi, and Shaanxi, mobilizing armies of at least several thousand men as the occasion arose.

The worship of royal ancestors was central to the maintenance of the dynasty. The ancestors were designated by 10 "stem" names (*jia, yi, bing, ding,* etc.) that were often prefixed by kin titles, such as "father" and "grandfather," or by status appellations, such as "great" or "small." The same stems were used to name the 10 days (or suns) of the week, and ancestors received cult on their name days according to a fixed schedule, particularly after the reforms of Zujia. For example, Dayi ("Great I," the sacrificial name of Tang, the dynasty founder) was worshiped on *yi* days, Wuding on *ding* days. The Shang dynastic group, whose lineage name was Zi (according to later sources), appears to have been divided into 10 units corresponding to the 10 stems. Succession to the kingship alternated on a generational basis between two major groupings of *jia* and *yi* kings on the one hand and *ding* kings on the other. The attention paid in the sacrificial system to the consorts of "great lineage" kings—who were themselves both sons (possibly nephews) and fathers (possibly uncles) of kings—indicates that women may have played a key role in the marriage alliances that ensured such circulation of power.

The goodwill of the ancestors, and of certain river and mountain powers, was sought through prayer and offerings of grain, millet wine, and animal and human sacrifice. The highest power of all, with whom the ancestors mediated for the living king, was the relatively remote deity Di, or Shangdi, "the Lord on High." Di controlled victory in battle, the harvest, the fate of the capital, and the weather, but, on the evidence of the oracle bone inscriptions, he received no cult. This suggests that Di's command was too inscrutable to be divined or influenced; he was in all likelihood an impartial figure of last theological resort, needed to account for inexplicable events.

Although Marxist historians have categorized the Shang as a slave society, it would be more accurate to describe it as a dependent society. The king ruled a patrimonial state in which royal authority, treated as an extension of patriarchal control, was embedded in kinship and kinshiplike ties. Despite the existence of such formal titles as "the many horses" or "the many archers," administration was apparently based primarily on kinship alliances, generational status, and personal charisma. The intensity with which ancestors were worshipped suggests the strength of the kinship system among the living; the ritualized ties of filiation and dependency that bound a son to his father, both before and after death, are likely to have had profound political implications for society as a whole. This was not a world in which concepts such as freedom and slavery would have been readily comprehensible. Everybody, from king to peasant, was bound by ties of obligation—to former kings, to ancestors, to superiors, and to dependents. The routine sacrificial offering of human beings, usually prisoners from the Qiang tribe, as if they were sacrificial animals and the rarer practice of accompanying-in-death, in which 40 or more retainers, often of high status, were buried with a dead king, suggest the degree to which ties of affection, obligation, or servitude were thought to be stronger than life itself. If slavery existed, it was psychological and ideological, not legal. The political ability to create and exploit ties of dependency originally based on kinship was one of the characteristic strengths of early Chinese civilization.

Such ties were fundamentally personal in nature. The king referred to himself as *yu yiren*, "I, the one man," and he was, like many early monarchs, peripatetic. Only by traveling through his domains could he ensure political and economic support. These considerations, coupled with the probability that the position of king circulated between social or ritual units, suggest that, lacking a national bureaucracy or effective means of control over distance, the dynasty was relatively weak. The Zi should above all be regarded as a politically dominant lineage that may have displaced the Si lineage of the Xia and that was in turn to be displaced by the Ji lineage of the Zhou. But the choices that the Shang made—involving ancestor worship, the politico-religious nature of the state, patrimonial administration, the mantic role of the ruler, and a pervasive sense of social obligation—were not displaced. These choices endured and were to define, restrict, and enhance the institutions and political culture of the full-fledged dynasties yet to come.

CHAPTER 2

THE ZHOU AND QIN DYNASTIES

THE HISTORY OF THE ZHOU (1046–256 BC)

The vast time sweep of the Zhou dynasty—encompassing some eight centuries—is the single longest period of Chinese history. However, the great longevity of the Ji lineage was not matched by a similar continuity of its rule. During the Xi (Western) Zhou (1046–771 BC), the first of the two major divisions of the period, the Zhou court maintained

Ceremonial bronze jian, Dong (Eastern) Zhou dynasty (770–256 BC); in the Minneapolis Institute of Arts, Minneapolis, Minn. Courtesy of the Minneapolis Institute of Arts

a tenuous control over the country through a network of feudal states. This system broke down during the Dong (Eastern) Zhou (770–256 BC), however, as those states and new ones that arose vied for power. The Dong Zhou is commonly subdivided into the Chunqiu (Spring and Autumn) period (770–476 BC) and the Zhanguo (Warring States) period (475–221 BC), the latter extending some three decades beyond the death of the last Zhou ruler until the rise of the Qin in 221.

The origin of the Zhou royal house is lost in the mists of time. Although the traditional historical system of the Chinese contains a Zhou genealogy, no dates can be assigned to the ancestors. The first ancestor was Houji, literally translated as "Lord of Millet." He appears to have been a cultural hero and agricultural deity rather than a tribal chief. The earliest plausible Zhou ancestor was Danfu, the grandfather of Wenwang. Prior to and during the time of Danfu, the Zhou people seem to have migrated to avoid pressure from powerful neighbours, possibly nomadic people to the north. Under the leadership of Danfu, they settled in the valley of the Wei River in the present province of Shaanxi. The fertility of the loess soil there apparently made a great impression on these people, who had already been engaged in farming when they entered their new homeland. A walled city was built, and a new nation was formed. Archaeological remains, including ruins of courtyards surrounded by walls and halls on platforms, confirm literary evidence of a Zhou state.

ZHOU AND SHANG

The name Zhou appears often in the oracle bone inscriptions of the Shang kingdom, sometimes as a friendly tributary neighbour and at other times as a hostile one. This pattern is confirmed by records found at the Zhou archaeological site. Marriages were occasionally made between the two ruling houses. The Zhou also borrowed arts such as bronze casting from their more cultivated neighbour. The Zhou royal house, however, had already conceived the idea of replacing Shang as the master of China—a conquest that took three generations. Although the conquest was actually carried out by his sons, Wenwang should be credited with molding the Zhou kingdom into the most formidable power west of the Shang. Wenwang extended the Zhou sphere of influence to the north of the Shang kingdom and also made incursions to the south, thus paving the way for the final conquest by Wuwang.

In Chinese historical tradition Wenwang was depicted as intelligent and benevolent, a man of virtue who won popularity among his contemporaries and expanded the realm of the Zhou. His son Wuwang, though not as colourful as his father, was always regarded as the conqueror. In fact, Wu, his posthumous name, means "Martial." However, the literary records indicate that the Zhou actually controlled two-thirds of all China at the time of Wenwang, who continued to recognize the cultural and political superiority of the Shang out of feudal loyalty. There is not enough evidence either to establish or to deny this. A careful historian, however, tends to take the Zhou subjugation to the Shang as a recognition of Shang strength. It was not until the reign of the last Shang ruler, Zhou, that the kingdom exhausted its strength by engaging in large-scale military campaigns against nomads to the north and against a group of native tribes to the east. At that time Wuwang organized the first probing expedition and reached the neighbourhood of the Shang capital. A full-scale invasion soon followed. Along with forces of the Zhou, the army was made up of the Jiang, southern neighbours of the Zhou, and of eight allied tribes from the west. The Shang dispatched a large army to meet the invaders. The pro-Zhou records say that, after the Shang vanguard defected to join the Zhou, the entire army collapsed, and Wuwang entered the capital without resistance. Yet Mencius, the 4th-century-BC thinker, cast doubt on the reliability of this account by pointing out that a victory without enemy resistance should not have been accompanied by the heavy casualties mentioned in the classical document. One may speculate that the Shang vanguard consisted of remnants of the eastern tribes suppressed by the Shang ruler Zhou during his last expedition and that their sudden defection caught the Shang defenders by surprise, making them easy prey for the invading enemy. The decisive battle took place in 1111 BC

(as tabulated by Dong Zuobin, although it is traditionally dated at 1122; other dates have also been suggested, including 1046, which has been adopted for this article). Wuwang died shortly after the conquest, leaving a huge territory to be consolidated. This was accomplished by one of his brothers, Zhougong, who served as regent during the reign of Wu's son, Chengwang.

The defeated Shang could not be ruled out as a potential force, even though their ruler, Zhou, had immolated himself. Many groups of hostile "barbarians" were still outside the sphere of Zhou power. The Zhou leaders had to yield to reality by establishing a rather weak control over the conquered territory. The son of Zhou was allowed to organize a subservient state under the close watch of two other brothers of Wuwang, who were garrisoned in the immediate vicinity. Other leaders of the Zhou and their allies were assigned lands surrounding the old Shang domain. But no sooner had Zhougong assumed the role of regent than a large-scale rebellion broke out. His two brothers, entrusted with overseeing the activities of the son of Zhou, joined the Shang prince in rebellion, and it took Zhougong three full years to reconquer the Shang domain, subjugate the eastern tribes, and reestablish the suzerainty of the Zhou court.

These three years of extensive campaigning consolidated the rule of the Zhou over all of China. An eastern capital was constructed on the middle reach of the Huang He (Yellow River) as a stronghold to support the feudal lords in the east. Several states established by Zhou kinsmen and relatives were transferred farther east and northeast as the vanguard of expansion, including one established by the son of Zhougong. The total number of such feudal states mentioned in historical records and later accounts varies from 20 to 70; the figures in later records would naturally be higher, since enfeoffment might take place more than once. Each of these states included fortified cities. They were strung out along the valley of the Huang He between the old capital and the new eastern capital, reaching as far as the valleys of the Huai and Han rivers in the south and extending eastward to the Shandong Peninsula and the coastal area north of it. All these colonies mutually supported each other and were buttressed by the strength of the eastern capital, where the conquered Shang troops were kept, together with several divisions of the Zhou legions. Ancient bronze inscriptions make frequent mention of mobilizing the military units at the eastern capital at times when the Zhou feudal states needed assistance.

THE ZHOU FEUDAL SYSTEM

The feudal states were not contiguous but rather were scattered at strategic locations surrounded by potentially dangerous and hostile lands. The fortified city of the feudal lord was often the only area that he controlled directly; the state and the city were therefore identical, both being *guo*, a combination of city wall and weapons. Satellite cities were established at convenient distances from the main city in order to expand the territory under control. Each feudal state consisted of an alliance of the Zhou, the Shang, and the local population. A Chinese nation was formed on the foundation of Zhou feudalism.

The scattered feudal states gradually acquired something like territorial solidity as the neighbouring populations established closer ties with them, either by marriage or by accepting vassal status; the gaps between the fortified cities were thus filled by political control and cultural assimilation. This created a dilemma for the Zhou central court: the evolution of the feudal network buttressed the structure of the Zhou order, but the strong local ties and parochial interests of the feudal lords tended to pull them away from the centre. Each of these opposing forces became at one time or another strong enough to affect the history of the Zhou order.

For about two centuries Zhou China enjoyed stability and peace. There were wars against the non-Zhou peoples of the interior and against the nomads along the northern frontier, but there was little dispute among the Chinese states themselves. The southern expansion was successful, and the northern expansion worked to keep the nomads away from the Chinese areas. The changing strength of the feudal order can be seen from two occurrences at the Zhou court.

In 841 BC the nobles jointly expelled Liwang, a tyrant, and replaced him with a collective leadership headed by the two most influential nobles until the crown prince was enthroned. In 771 BC the Zhou royal line was again broken when Youwang was killed by invading barbarians. The nobles apparently were split at that time, because the break gave rise to two courts, headed by two princes, each of whom had the support of part of the nobility. One of the pretenders, Pingwang, survived the other (thus inaugurating the Dong [Eastern] Zhou period), but the royal order had lost prestige and influence. The cohesion of the feudal system had weakened. Thereafter, it entered the phase traditionally known as Chunqiu (Spring and Autumn).

The familial relationship among the nobles gradually was diluted during the Chunqiu period. A characteristic of the Zhou feudal system was that the extended family and the political structure were identical. The line of lordship was regarded as the line of elder brothers, who therefore enjoyed not only political superiority but also seniority in the family line. The head of the family not only was the political chief but also had the unique privilege of offering sacrifice to and worshipping the ancestors, who would bestow their blessings and guarantee the continuity of the mandate of heaven. After the weakening of the position of the Zhou king in the feudal structure, he was not able to maintain the position of being the head of a large family in any more than a normal sense. The

feudal structure and familial ties fell apart, continuing in several of the Chunqiu states for various lengths of time, with various degrees of modification. Over the next two centuries the feudal-familial system gradually declined and disappeared.

In the first half of the Chunqiu period, the feudal system was a stratified society, divided into ranks as follows: the ruler of a state; the feudal lords who served at the ruler's court as ministers; the *shi* (roughly translated as "gentlemen") who served at the households of the feudal lords as stewards, sheriffs, or simply warriors; and, finally, the commoners and slaves. The state ruler and the ministers were clearly a superior class, and the commoners and slaves were an inferior class; the class of *shi* was an intermediate one in which the younger sons of the ministers, the sons of *shi*, and selected commoners all mingled to serve as functionaries and officials. The state rulers were, in theory, divided into five grades; in reality, the importance of a ruler was determined by the strength of his state. The ministerial feudal lords, however, often had two or three grades among themselves, as determined by the lord-vassal relationship. In general, each state was ruled by a group of hereditary feudal lords who might or might not be of the same surname as the state ruler. The system was not stable in the Chunqiu period, and everywhere there were changes.

The first important change occurred with the advent of interstate leadership. For several decades after 722 BC, the records chiefly show battles and diplomatic maneuvers among the states on the central plain and in the middle and lower reaches of the Huang He valley. These states, however, were too small to hold the leadership and too constricted in the already crowded plain to have potentiality for further development. The leadership was soon taken over by states on the peripheral areas.

The first to achieve this leadership was Huangong (reigned 685–643 BC), the ruler of the state of Qi on the Shandong Peninsula. He successfully rallied around him many other Chinese states to resist the pressure of non-Chinese powers in the north and south. While formally respecting the suzerainty of the Zhou monarchy, Huangong adopted a new title of "overlord" (ba). He convened interstate meetings, settled disputes among states, and led campaigns to protect his followers from the intimidation of non-Chinese powers.

After his death the state of Qi failed to maintain its leading status. The leadership, after a number of years, passed to Wengong of Jin (reigned 636–628 BC), the ruler of the mountainous state north of the Huang He. Under Wengong and his capable successors, the overlordship was institutionalized until it took the place of the Zhou monarchy. Interstate meetings were held at first during emergencies caused by challenges from the rising southern state of Chu. States answering the call of the overlord were expected to contribute and maintain a certain number of war chariots. Gradually

the meetings became regular, and the voluntary contribution was transformed into a compulsory tribute to the court of the overlord. The new system of states under the leadership of an overlord developed not only in northern China under Jin but also in the south under Chu. Two other states, Qin and Qi, though not commanding the strength of the formidable Jin and Chu, each absorbed weaker neighbours into a system of satellite states. A balance of power thus emerged among the four states of Qi, Qin, Jin, and Chu. The balance was occasionally tipped when two of them went to war, but it was subsequently restored by the transference of some small states from one camp to another.

A further change began in the 5th century BC, when the states of Wu and Yue far to the south suddenly challenged Chu for hegemony over the southern part of China, at a time when the strong state of Jin was much weakened by an internecine struggle among powerful magnates. Wu got so far as to claim overlordship over northern China in an interstate meeting held in 482 BC after defeating Chu. But Wu's hegemony was short-lived; it collapsed after being attacked by Yue. Yue held the nominal overlordship for only a brief period; Jin, Qin, and Qi were weakened by internal disturbances (Jin split into three contending powers) and declined; and a series of defeats paralyzed Chu. Thus, the balance-of-power system was rendered unworkable.

A half century of disorder followed. Small states fell prey to big ones, while in the big states usurpers replaced the old rulers. When the chaos ended, there were seven major powers and half a dozen minor ones. Among the seven major powers, Zhao, Han, and Wei had formerly been parts of Jin; the Qi ruling house had changed hands; and Qin was undergoing succession problems. The only "old" state was Chu. Even Chu, a southern state, had become almost completely assimilated to the northern culture (except in art, literature, and folklore). The minor powers also changed: some had retained only small portions of their old territories, some had new ruling houses, and some were new states that had emerged from non-Chinese tribes. The long interval of power struggle that followed (475–221 BC) is known as the Zhanguo (Warring States) period.

SOCIAL, POLITICAL, AND CULTURAL CHANGES

The years from the 8th century BC to 221 BC witnessed the painful birth of a unified China. It was a period of bloody wars and also of far-reaching changes in politics, society, and intellectual outlook.

THE DECLINE OF FEUDALISM

The most obvious change in political institutions was that the old feudal structure was replaced by systems of incipient bureaucracy under monarchy. The decline of feudalism took its course in the Chunqiu period, and the rise of the new order may be seen in the Zhanguo period.

The Zhou feudalism suffered from a continual dilution of authority. As a state expanded, its nobility acquired vassals, and these in turn acquired their own vassals. The longer this went on, the more diluted the family tie became and the more dependent the ruler became on the combined strength of the vassals. At a certain point, the vassals might acquire an advantageous position, and the most dominant figures among them might eclipse the king. The Zhou royal house perhaps reached the turning point earlier than the other feudal states. As a result, the Zhou royal domain and its influence shrank when Pingwang moved his court to the east. The ruling houses of other states suffered the same fate. Within a century after the Zhou court had moved to the east, the ruling houses in most of the feudal states had changed. In some cases a dominating branch replaced the major lineage, and in others a powerful minister formed a strong vassaldom and usurped the authority of the legitimate ruler. Bloody court intrigues and power struggles eliminated many established houses. The new power centres were reluctant to see the process continue and therefore refused to allow further segmentation and subinfeudation. Thus, the feudal system withered and finally collapsed.

URBANIZATION AND ASSIMILATION

Simultaneous with the demise of feudalism was a rise in urbanization. Minor fortified cities were built, radiating out from each of the major centres, and other towns radiated from the minor cities. From these cities and towns orders were issued, and to them the resources of the countryside were sent. The central plain along the Huang He was the first to be saturated by clusters of cities. This is probably the reason why the central states soon reached the maximum of their influence in the interstate power struggle: unlike the states in peripheral areas, they had no room to expand.

The period of urbanization was also a time of assimilation. The non-Zhou population caught in the reach of feudal cities could not but feel the magnetic attraction of the civilization represented by the Zhou people and Zhou feudalism. The bronze inscriptions of the Xi Zhou period (1046–771 BC) refer to the disturbances of the barbarians, who could be found practically everywhere. They were the non-Zhou groups scattered in the open spaces. The barbarians in inland China were forced to integrate with one or another of the contenders in the interstate conflicts. Their lands were annexed, and their populations were moved or absorbed. The strength of the large states owed much to their success at incorporating these non-Chinese groups. By the time of the unification of China in the 3rd century BC, there was virtually no significant concentration of non-Chinese groups north of the Yangtze River valley and south of the steppe. Bronze pieces attributable to non-Zhou chiefs in the late Chunqiu period show no significant

difference in writing system and style from those of the Chinese states.

Zhou civilization was not assimilated so easily in the south, where the markedly different Chu culture flourished. For some centuries, Chu was the archenemy of the Chinese states, yet the nobles of the Chu acquired enough of the northern culture to enable their envoy to the courts of the north to cite the same verses and observe the same manners. The Chu literature that has survived is the fruit of these two distinctive heritages.

To the north were the nomadic peoples of the steppe. As long as they remained divided, they constituted no threat; however, when they were under strong leaders, able to forge a united nomadic empire challenging the dominance of the Chinese, there were confrontations. The "punitive" action into the north during the reign of Xuanwang (827–782 BC) does not seem to have been very large in scope; both sides apparently had little ambition for territorial aggrandizement. Cultural exchange in the northern frontier region was far less than the assimilation that occurred in the south along the Yangtze valley, and it was mainly concerned with techniques of cavalry warfare.

THE RISE OF MONARCHY

Internal political changes also took place as states grew in population and area. The most basic of these was in the pattern of power delegation. Under feudalism, authority had been delegated by the lord to the vassal. The new state rulers sought ways of maintaining and organizing their power.

In the state of Jin the influence of kinsmen of the ruling house had been trimmed even before Wengong established his overlordship. Wengong reorganized the government, installing his most capable followers in the key posts. He set up a hierarchical structure that corresponded to the channels of military command. Appointments to these key positions came to be based on a combination of merit and seniority, thus establishing a type of bureaucracy that was to become traditional in Chinese government.

The Chu government was perhaps the oldest true monarchy among all the Chunqiu states. The authority of the king was absolute. Chu was the only major state in which the ruling house survived the chaotic years of the Zhanguo period.

Local administration went through a slow evolution. The prefecture system developed in both Jin and Chu was one innovation. In Jin there were several dozen prefects across the state, each having limited authority and tenure. The Jin prefect was no more than a functionary, in contrast to the feudal practice. Similar local administrative units grew up in Chu. New lands taken by conquest were organized into prefectures governed by ranking officials who were evidently appointed by the king. The prefecture system of Jin and Chu was to become the principal form of local administration in the Zhanguo period.

By that time, practically all the major states had chancellors, who acted as leaders of the courts, which were composed of numerous officials. Whereas in the feudal state the officials had been military officers, the more functionally differentiated court of the Zhanguo period usually had a separate corps of civil service personnel. Local administration was entrusted to prefects, who served limited terms. Prefects were often required to submit annual reports to the court so that the ruler could judge their performance. Regional supervisors were sometimes dispatched to check the work of the prefects, a system developed by the later Chinese imperial government into the "censor" system. Fiefs of substantial size were given to only a few people, usually close relatives of the ruler. There was little opportunity for anyone to challenge the sovereignty of the state. The majority of government employees were not relatives of the ruler, and some of them might not even have been citizens of the state. Officials were paid in grain or perhaps in a combination of cash and grain. Archives were kept by scribes on wooden blocks and bamboo strips. These features combined indicate the emergence of some form of bureaucracy.

The new pattern was the result of the efforts of many reformers in different states. Both practical men and theoreticians helped to form the emerging structure, which, though still crude, was the forerunner of the large and complex bureaucracy of later Chinese dynasties.

Military technique also underwent great changes in the Zhanguo period. In the feudal era, war had been a profession of the nobles. Lengthy training was needed to learn how to drive and shoot from a chariot drawn by horses. There was also an elaborate code of behaviour in combat. The nature of war had already changed by the late Chunqiu period, as the nobility had given way to professional warriors and mercenaries. In some states, special titles of nobility were created for successful warriors, regardless of their origin. Foot soldiers were replacing war chariots as the main force on the battlefield: the expansion of the major states into mountainous areas and the rise of the southern powers in an area of swamps, lakes, and rivers increased the importance of the infantry.

Battles were fought mostly by hordes of foot soldiers, most of them commoners, aided by cavalry units; war chariots apparently served only auxiliary roles, probably as mobile commanding platforms or perhaps as carriers. All of the Zhanguo powers seem to have used conscription systems to recruit able-bodied male citizens. The organization, training, and command of the infantry required experts of a special type, and professional commanders emerged who conducted battles involving several thousand men along lines extending hundreds of miles. A few treatises on the principles of warfare still survive, including *Bingfa* (*The Art of War*) by Sunzi. Cavalry warfare developed among the northern states, including Qin, Zhao, and Yan. The Qin cavalrymen were generally drawn from the northern and northwestern border areas, where there were constant contacts with the steppe peoples. The rise of Yan from a rather obscure state to a major power probably owed much to its successful adoption of cavalry tactics, as well as to its northern expansion.

ECONOMIC DEVELOPMENT

Important changes occurred in agriculture. Millet had once been the major cereal crop in the north, but wheat gradually grew in importance. Rice, imported from the south, was extended to the dry soil of the north. The soybean, in a number of varieties, proved to be one of the most important crops. Chinese farmers gradually developed a kind of intensive agriculture. Soil was improved by adding manure and night soil. Planting fields in carefully regulated rows replaced the fallow system. Great importance was placed on plowing and seeding at the proper time (especially in the fine-grained loess soil of northern China). Fields were weeded frequently throughout the growing season. Farmers also knew the value of rotating crops to preserve the fertility of the soil, and soybeans were often part of the rotation. Although iron was used to cast implements in the 5th century BC (probably even as early as the 8th century BC), those early examples discovered by archaeologists are of rather inferior quality.

Irrigation became necessary as population pressure forced cropland to be expanded, and irrigation works were constructed in many states beginning in the late Chunqiu period. These projects were built to drain swampy areas, leach out alkaline soil and replace it with fertile topsoil, and, in the south and in the Sichuan Basin, to carry water into the rice paddies. The irrigation systems unearthed by archaeologists indicate that these were small-scale works carried

Wood bowl decorated in red and black lacquer with stylized birds and animals, from Changsha, Hunan province, China, late Zhou dynasty, 3rd century BC; in the Seattle Art Museum, Washington. Diameter 25 cm (10 in). Courtesy of the Seattle Art Museum, Washington

out for the most part by state or local authorities.

Another significant change in the economic sphere was the growth of trade among regions. Coins excavated in scattered spots show by their great variety that active trade had expanded into all parts of Zhou China. Great commercial centres had arisen, and the new cities brought a demand for luxuries. The literary records as well as the archaeological evidence show that wealthy persons had possessions made of bronze and gold, silver inlays, lacquer, silk, ceramics, and precious stones. The advancement of ferrous metallurgy led to the earliest recorded blast furnace and the earliest steel. The Chinese had been casting bronze for more than a millennium; turning to iron, they became highly skilled at making weapons and tools. The Han historian Sima Qian (writing c. 100 BC) told of individuals making fortunes in the iron industry.

As the old feudal regimes collapsed and were replaced by centralized monarchies during the Zhanguo period, the feudal nobility fell victim to power struggles within the states and to conquest by stronger states. During the Chunqiu period these parallel processes drastically reduced the numbers of the nobility.

A new elite class arose in the late Chunqiu, composed of the former *shi* class and the descendants of the old nobility. The members of this class were distinguished by being educated, either in the literary tradition or in the military arts. The *shi* provided the administrators, teachers, and intellectual leaders of the new society. The philosophers Confucius (551–479 BC), Mencius (c. 372–289 BC), Mozi (Mo-tzu; 5th century BC), and Xunzi (Hsün-tzu; c. 300–c. 230 BC) were members of the *shi* class, as was also a large proportion of high-ranking officials and leaders of prominence. The interstate competition that drove rulers to select the most capable and meritorious individuals to serve in their courts resulted in an unprecedented degree of social mobility.

The populace, most of whom were farmers, also underwent changes in status. In feudal times the peasants had been subjects of their lords. They owned no property, at most being permitted to till a piece of the lord's land for their own needs. The ancient texts tell of the "wellfield" system, under which eight families were assigned 100 *mu* (15 acres, or 6 hectares) each of land to live on while collectively cultivating another 100 *mu* as the lord's reservation. Individual ownership grew as farming became more intensive, and, increasingly, farmers were taxed according to the amount of land they "owned." The land tax had become a common practice by Zhanguo times. By paying taxes, the tiller of the field acquired the privilege of using the land as his own possession, which perhaps was the first step toward private ownership. As states expanded and new lands were given to cultivation, an increasing number of "free" farmers were to be found tilling land that had never been part of a lord's manor. With the collapse of the feudal structure, farmers in general gradually ceased to be subjects of a master and became subjects of a state.

A similar transformation occurred among the merchants and artisans, who gradually passed from being household retainers of a lord to the status of independent subjects. Thus, the feudal society was completely reshaped in the two centuries preceding the Qin unification.

CULTURAL CHANGE

These great political and socioeconomic changes were accompanied by intellectual ferment, as the people tried to adjust themselves to a rapidly changing world. Ideas about the proper relationships between members of society were naturally questioned when the old feudal order was shaken, and in that period the great teacher Confucius elaborated the social concepts that henceforth became normative for Chinese civilization. In place of rigid feudal obligations, he posited an order based on more-universal human relationships (such as that between father and son) and taught that ability and moral excellence rather than birth were what fitted a person for leadership.

The great thinkers who came after Confucius, whether or not they agreed with his views, were conditioned by his basic assumptions. Mozi, originally a Confucian, based his system on a concept of universal love that was largely an extension of the Confucian idea of humanity; the "worthy man" Mozi recommended as the ideal leader was a development of Confucius's notion of excellence, combining virtue and ability. Even the individualist thinkers known as Daoists (Taoists), who did not follow Confucius, formulated their teachings as a rebuttal to the Confucian system.

Confucius and other pre-Qin thinkers viewed the traditional political institutions of China as bankrupt and tried to devise a rationale for something to replace them. Some, such as Confucius, put their main emphasis on the quality of the ruling elite group; others, such as Shang Yang (died 338 BC) and Hanfeizi (died 233 BC), regarded a well-organized governing mechanism as the only way to an orderly society. The development of the new centralized monarchical state after the middle of the Chunqiu period is not only the embodiment of the ideas of these various thinkers but also the working premise in the context of which they elaborated their theories. The high degree of social and political consciousness that characterized most of the pre-Qin philosophical schools set the pattern for the close association of the intellectual with government and society in later China.

The burgeoning commercial life of the period also influenced other spheres, especially in the prevalence of contractual relationships. Thus, a minister would roam from one court to another, "selling" his knowledge and service to the most accommodating prince, and the quality of his service was determined by the treatment he received. This kind of contractual relationship remained common in China until the tide of commercialism was ended by the restriction of commercial activity under the Han emperor Wudi in the 2nd century BC.

The local cultures of China were blended into one common civilization during Chunqiu times. Through contacts and interchanges, the gods and legends of one region became identified and assimilated with those of other regions. Local differences remained, but, from that time on, the general Chinese pantheon took the form of a congregation of gods with specific functions, representing a celestial projection of the unified Chinese empire with its bureaucratic society.

Bold challenges to tradition have been rare in Chinese history, and the questioning and innovating spirit of the Chunqiu period was to have no parallel until the ferment of the 20th century, after two millennia had elapsed under the domination of Confucian orthodoxy.

THE QIN EMPIRE (221–207 BC)

The history of the Qin dynasty may be traced to the 8th century BC. According to the Qin historical record, when the Zhou royal house was reestablished at the eastern capital in 770 BC, the Qin ruling house was entrusted with the mission of maintaining order in the previous capital. This may be an exaggeration of the importance of the Qin rulers, and the Qin may have been only one of the ruling families of the old states that recognized Zhou suzerainty and went to serve the Zhou court. The record is not clear. In the old annals Qin did not appear as a significant power until the time of Mugong (reigned 659–621 BC), who made Qin the main power in the western part of China.

THE QIN STATE

Although Qin attempted to obtain a foothold in the central heartland along the Huang He, it was blocked by the territories of Jin. Qin failed several times to enter the eastern bloc of powers and had to limit its activities to conquering, absorbing, and incorporating the non-Chinese tribes and states scattered within and west of the big loop of the Huang He. Qin's success in this was duly recognized by other powers of the Chunqiu period, so that the two superpowers Chu and Jin had to grant Qin, along with Qi, the status of overlord in its own region. The eastern powers, however, regarded Qin as a barbarian state because of the non-Chinese elements it contained.

Qin played only a supporting role in the Chunqiu power struggle; its location made it immune to the cutthroat competition of the states in the central plain. Qin, in fact, was the only major power that did not suffer battle within its own territory. Moreover, being a newly emerged state, Qin did not have the burden of a long-established feudal system, which allowed it more freedom to develop its own pattern of government. As a result of being "underdeveloped," it offered opportunity for eastern-educated persons; with the infusion of such talent, it was able to compete well with the eastern powers, yet without the overexpanded ministerial apparatus that embarrassed other rulers. This may be one reason why Qin was one of the handful of ruling houses that survived the great turmoil of the late Chunqiu period.

A period of silence followed. Even the Qin historical record that was adopted by the historian Sima Qian yields almost no information for a period of some 90 years in the 5th century BC. The evidence suggests that Qin underwent a period of consolidation and assimilation during the years of silence. When it reemerged as an important power, its culture appeared to be simpler and more martial, perhaps because of the non-Chinese tribes it had absorbed.

STRUGGLE FOR POWER

Until the 5th century BC, China was dominated by the central-plain power Wei, a successor to Jin, and by the eastern power Qi, a wealthy state with a new ruling house. Qin remained a secondary power until after the great reforms of Xiaogong (361–338 BC) and Shang Yang (Wei Yang).

Shang Yang, a frustrated bureaucrat in the court of Wei, went westward seeking a chance to try out his ideas. In the court of Qin he established a rare partnership with the ruler Xiaogong and created the best-organized state of their time. Shang Yang first took strong measures to establish the authority of law and royal decree. The law was to be enforced impartially, without regard to status or position. He convinced Xiaogong that the rank of nobility and the privileges attached to it should be awarded only to those who rendered good service to the state, especially for valour in battle. This deprived the existing nobility of their titles and privileges, arousing much antagonism in the court.

One of his most influential reforms was that of standardizing local administration. It was a step toward creating a unified state by combining various localities into counties, which were then organized into prefectures under direct supervision of the court. This system was expanded to all of China after unification in 221 BC.

Another measure taken by Shang Yang was that he encouraged production, especially in agriculture. Farmers were given incentive to reclaim wasteland, and game and fishing reserves were also opened to cultivation. A shortage of labour was met by recruiting the able-bodied from neighbouring states, especially from Han, Zhao, and Wei. This policy of drawing workers to Qin had two consequences: it increased production in Qin, and manpower was lost in the neighbouring states. In order to increase incentives, the Qin government levied a double tax on any male citizen who was not the master of a household. The result was a breakdown of the extended-family system, since younger children were forced to move out and establish their own households. The nuclear family became the prevalent form in Qin thereafter. As late as the 2nd century BC, Han scholars were still attacking the Qin family structure as failing to observe the principle of filial piety, a cardinal virtue in the Confucian moral code. Shang Yang also standardized the system of weights and measures, a reform of some importance for the development of trade and commerce.

Qin grew wealthy and powerful under the joint labours of Xiaogong and Shang Yang. After Xiaogong's death, Shang Yang was put to death by enemies at the Qin court. Tablets of the Qin law substantiate the survival of Shang Yang's policies after his death.

What remained of the Zhou royal court still survived, ruling over a fragmentary domain—poor, weak, and totally at the mercy of the contending powers. It was commonly felt that China ought to be unified politically, although the powers disagreed as to how it was to be done and who would be the universal king. Huiwang, son of Xiaogong, claimed the royal title in 325 BC. The adoption of the royal title by Qin was of course a challenge to Qi and Wei. Qin pursued a strategy of dividing its rivals and individually defeating them. Qin appealed to the self-interest of other powers in order to keep them from intervening in any military action it was taking against one of its neighbours. It befriended the more distant states while gradually absorbing the territories of those close to it.

Within half a century, Qin had acquired undisputed predominance over the other contending powers. It continued maneuvering in order to prevent the others from uniting against it. A common topic of debate in the courts of the other states was whether to establish friendly relations with Qin or to join with other states in order to resist Qin's expansion. The Qin strategists were ruthless: all means, including lies, espionage, bribery, and assassination, were pressed into the service of their state.

For a time, the eastern power Qi had seemed the most likely to win. It defeated Wei, crushed Yan in 314 BC, and annexed Song in 286 BC. But Qi was overturned by an allied force of five states, including Qin. Zhao, the power with extensive territory in the northern frontier, succeeded Qi as the most formidable contender against Qin. In 260 BC a decisive battle between Qin and Zhao destroyed Zhao's military strength, though Qin was not able to complete its conquest of Zhao for several decades.

The Empire

When Qin succeeded in unifying China in 221 BC, its king claimed the title of "First Sovereign Emperor," Shihuangdi. He was a strong and energetic ruler, and, although he appointed a number of capable aides, the emperor remained the final authority and the sole source of power.

Shihuangdi made a number of important reforms. He abolished the feudal system completely and extended the administration system of prefectures and counties, with officials appointed by the

GREAT WALL OF CHINA

The Great Wall of China (Chinese: Wanli Changcheng; "10,000-Li Long Wall") consists of a series of defensive structures built across northern China. One of the largest building-construction projects ever carried out, it runs (with all its branches) about 4,500 miles (7,300 km) east to west. Large parts of the fortification date from the 7th to the 4th century BC. In the 3rd century BC the emperor Shihuangdi connected existing defensive walls into a single system fortified by watchtowers. These served both to guard the rampart and to communicate with the capital, Xianyang (near modern Xi'an) by signal—smoke by day and fire by night. Originally constructed partly of masonry and earth, it was faced with brick in its eastern portion. It was rebuilt in later times, especially in the 15th and 16th centuries. The basic wall is about 23 to 26 feet (7 to 8 metres) high; at intervals towers rise above it to varying heights. It was designated a UNESCO World Heritage site in 1987.

The Great Wall of China covered in winter snow. China Photos/Getty Images

central government sent into all of China. Circuit inspectors were dispatched to oversee the local magistrates. China was divided into some 40 prefectures. The empire created by Shihuangdi was to become the traditional territory of China. In later eras China sometimes held other territories, but the Qin boundaries were always considered to embrace the indivisible area of China proper. In order to control this vast area, Shihuangdi constructed a network of highways to facilitate moving his troops. Several hundred thousand workers were conscripted to connect and strengthen the existing walls along the northern border. The result was a complex of fortified walls, garrison stations, and signal towers extending from near the Bo Hai (Gulf of Chihli) westward across the pastureland of what is today Inner Mongolia and through the fertile loop of the Huang He to what is now northwestern Gansu province. This defense line, known as the Great Wall, marked the frontier where the nomads of the great steppe and the Chinese farmers on the loess soil confronted each other. Yet the emperor failed in another great project: digging a canal across the mountains in the south to link the southern coastal areas with the main body of China. Shihuangdi, with his capable chancellor Li Si, also unified and simplified the writing system and codified the law.

All of China felt the burden of these 11 or 12 years of change. Millions of people were dragooned to the huge construction jobs, many dying on the long journey to their destination. Wealthy and influential men in the provinces were compelled to move to the capital. Weapons were confiscated. Hundreds of intellectuals were massacred for daring to criticize the emperor's policies. Books dealing with subjects other than law, horticulture, and herbal medicine were kept out of public circulation because the emperor considered such knowledge to be dangerous and unsettling. These things have contributed to make Shihuangdi appear the arch tyrant of Chinese history.

Some of the accusations leveled against him by historians are perhaps exaggerated, such as the burning of books and the indiscriminate massacre of intellectuals. Shihuangdi himself claimed in the stone inscriptions of his time that he had corrected the misconduct of a corrupted age and given the people peace and order. Indeed, his political philosophy did not deviate much from that already developed by the great thinkers of the Zhanguo period and adopted later by the Han emperors, who have been generally regarded as benevolent rulers.

Shihuangdi was afraid of death. He did everything possible to achieve immortality. Deities were propitiated, and messengers were dispatched to look for an elixir of life. He died in 210 BC while on a tour of the empire. Excavation of his tomb, near modern Xi'an (ancient Chang'an), revealed more than 6,000 life-size statues of soldiers still on guard.

His death led to the fall of his dynasty. The legitimate heir was compelled to

Some of the army of terra-cotta warriors that have been excavated at the Qin tomb near Xi'an, Shaanxi province, China. In all, some 8,000 pottery soldiers, horses, and chariots were buried there, only a portion of which have been unearthed. Eric Feferberg/AFP/Getty Images

commit suicide when his younger brother usurped the throne. Capable and loyal servants, including Li Si and Gen. Meng Tian, were put to death. Ershidi, the second emperor, reigned only four years. Rebellion broke out in the Yangtze River area when a small group of conscripts led by a peasant killed their escort officers and claimed sovereignty for the former state of Chu.

The uprising spread rapidly as old ruling elements of the six states rose to claim their former titles. Escaped conscripts and soldiers who had been hiding throughout the land emerged in large numbers to attack the imperial armies. The second emperor was killed by a powerful eunuch minister, and in 206 BC a rebel leader accepted the surrender of the last Qin prince.

CHAPTER 3

THE HAN DYNASTY

The Han dynasty was founded by Liu Bang (best known by his temple name, Gaozu), who assumed the title of emperor in 202 BC. Eleven members of the Liu family followed in his place as effective emperors until AD 6 (a 12th briefly occupied the throne as a puppet). In AD 9 the dynastic line was challenged by Wang Mang, who established his own regime under the title of Xin. In AD 25 the authority of the Han dynasty was reaffirmed by Liu Xiu (posthumous name Guangwudi), who reigned as Han emperor until 57. Thirteen of his descendants maintained the dynastic succession until 220, when the rule of a single empire was replaced by that of three separate kingdoms. While the entire period from 206 (or 202) BC to AD 220 is generally described as that of the Han dynasty, the terms Xi (Western) Han (also called Former Han) and Dong (Eastern) Han (also called Later Han) are used to denote the two subperiods. During the first period, from 206 BC to AD 25, the capital city was situated at Chang'an (modern Xi'an), in the west; in the second period, from AD 25 to 220, it lay farther east at Luoyang.

The four centuries in question may be treated as a single historical period by virtue of dynastic continuity, for, apart from the short interval of 9–25, imperial authority was unquestionably vested in successive members of the same family. The period, however, was one of considerable changes in imperial, political, and social development. Organs of government were established, tried, modified, or replaced, and new social distinctions were brought into being. Chinese prestige among other peoples varied with the political stability and military strength of the Han house, and the extent of territory that was subject to the jurisdiction of Han officials varied with the success of Han arms. At the same time, the example of the palace, the activities of government, and the growing luxuries of city life gave rise to new standards of cultural and technological achievement.

China's first imperial dynasty, that of Qin, had lasted barely 15 years before its dissolution in the face of rebellion and civil war. By contrast, Han formed the first long-lasting regime that could successfully claim to be the sole authority entitled to wield administrative power. The Han forms of government, however, were derived in the first instance from the Qin dynasty, and these in turn incorporated a number of features of the government that had been practiced by earlier kingdoms. The Han empire left as a heritage a practical example of imperial government and an ideal of dynastic authority to which its successors aspired. But the Han period has been credited with more success than is its due; it has been represented as a period of 400 years of effective dynastic rule, punctuated by a short period in which a pretender to power usurped authority, and it has been assumed that imperial unity and effective administration advanced steadily with each decade. In fact, there were only a few short periods marked by dynastic strength, stable government, and

intensive administration. Several reigns were characterized by palace intrigue and corrupt influences at court, and on a number of occasions the future of the dynasty was seriously endangered by outbreaks of violence, seizure of political power, or a crisis in the imperial succession.

DYNASTIC AUTHORITY AND THE SUCCESSION OF EMPERORS

XI (WESTERN) HAN

Since at least as early as the Shang dynasty, the Chinese had been accustomed to acknowledging the temporal and spiritual authority of a single leader and its transmission within a family, at first from brother to brother and later from father to son. Some of the early kings had been military commanders, and they may have organized the corporate work of the community, such as the manufacture of bronze tools and vessels. In addition, they acted as religious leaders, appointing scribes or priests to consult the oracles and thus to assist in making major decisions covering communal activities, such as warfare and hunting expeditions. In succeeding centuries the growing sophistication of Chinese culture was accompanied by demands for more-intensive political organization and for more-regular administration; as kings came to delegate tasks to more officials, so was their own authority enhanced and the obedience that they commanded the more widely acknowledged. Under the kingdoms of Zhou, an association was deliberately fostered between the authority of the king and the dispensation exercised over the universe by heaven, with the result that the kings of Zhou and, later, the emperors of Chinese dynasties were regarded as being the sons of heaven.

PRELUDE TO THE HAN

From 403 BC onward seven kingdoms other than Zhou constituted the ruling authorities in different parts of China, each of which was led by its own king or duke. In theory, the king of Zhou, whose territory was by now greatly reduced, was recognized as possessing superior powers and moral overlordship over the other kingdoms, but practical administration lay in the hands of the seven kings and their professional advisers or in the hands of well-established families. Then in 221 BC, after a long process of expansion and takeover, a radical change occurred in Chinese politics: the kingdom of Qin succeeded in eliminating the power of its six rivals and established a single rule that was acknowledged in their territories. According to later Chinese historians, this success was achieved and the Qin empire was thereafter maintained by oppressive methods and the rigorous enforcement of a harsh penal code, but this view was probably coloured by later political prejudices. Whatever the quality of Qin imperial government, the regime

scarcely survived the death of the first emperor in 210 BC. The choice of his successor was subject to manipulation by statesmen, and local rebellions soon developed into large-scale warfare. Gaozu, whose family had not thus far figured in Chinese history, emerged as the victor of two principal contestants for power. Anxious to avoid the reputation of having replaced one oppressive regime by another, he and his advisers endeavoured to display their own empire—of Han—as a regime whose political principles were in keeping with a Chinese tradition of liberal and beneficent administration. As yet, however, the concept of a single centralized government that could command universal obedience was still subject to trial. In order to exercise and perpetuate its authority, therefore, Gaozu's government perforce adopted the organs of government, and possibly many of the methods, of its discredited predecessor.

The authority of the Han emperors had been won in the first instance by force of arms, and both Gaozu and his successors relied on the loyal cooperation of military leaders and on officials who organized the work of civil government. In theory and to a large extent in practice, the emperor remained the single source from whom all powers of government were delegated. It was the Han emperors who appointed men to the senior offices of the central government and in whose name the governors of the commanderies (provinces) collected taxes, recruited men for the labour corps and army, and dispensed justice. And it was the Han emperors who invested some of their kinsmen with powers to rule as kings over certain territories or divested them of such powers in order to consolidate the strength of the central government.

THE IMPERIAL SUCCESSION

The succession of emperors was hereditary, but it was complicated to a considerable extent by a system of imperial consorts and the implication of their families in politics. Of the large number of women who were housed in the palace as the emperor's favourites, one was selected for nomination as the empress; while it was theoretically possible for an emperor to appoint any one of his sons heir apparent, this honour, in practice, usually fell on one of the sons of the empress. Changes could be made in the declared succession, however, by deposing one empress and giving the title to another favourite, and sometimes, when an emperor died without having nominated his heir, it was left to the senior statesmen of the day to arrange for a suitable successor. Whether or not an heir had been named, the succession was

Funerary banner from the tomb of Lady Dai (Xin Zhui), Mawangdui, Hunan province, ink and colours on silk, c. 168 BC, Western Han dynasty; in the Hunan Provincial Museum, Changsha, China. Wang Lu/ChinaStock Photo Library

often open to question, as pressure could be exerted on an emperor over his choice. Sometimes a young or weak emperor was overawed by the expressed will of his mother or by anxiety to please a newly favoured concubine.

Throughout the Xi Han and Dong Han periods, the succession and other important political considerations were affected by the members of the imperial consorts' families. Often the father or brothers of an empress or concubine were appointed to high office in the central government; alternatively, senior statesmen might be able to curry favour with their emperor or consolidate their position at court by presenting a young female relative for the imperial pleasure. In either situation the succession of emperors might be affected, jealousies would be aroused between the different families concerned, and the actual powers of a newly acceded emperor would be overshadowed by the women in his entourage or their male relatives. Such situations were particularly likely to develop if, as often happened, an emperor was succeeded by an infant son.

The imperial succession was thus frequently bound up with the political machinations of statesmen, particularly as the court grew more sophisticated and statesmen acquired coteries of clients engaged in factional rivalry. On the death of the first emperor, Gaozu (195 BC), the palace came under the domination of his widow. Outliving her son, who had succeeded as emperor under the title of Huidi (reigned 195–188), the empress dowager Gaohou arranged for two infants to succeed consecutively. During that time (188–180 BC) she issued imperial edicts under her own name and by virtue of her own authority as empress dowager. She set a precedent that was to be followed in later dynastic crises—e.g., when the throne was vacant and no heir had been appointed. In such cases, although statesmen or officials would in fact determine how to proceed, their decisions were implemented in the form of edicts promulgated by the senior surviving empress.

Gaohou appointed a number of members of her own family to highly important positions of state and clearly hoped to substitute her own family for the reigning Liu family. But these plans were frustrated on her death (180) by men whose loyalties remained with the founding emperor and his family. Liu Heng, better known as Wendi, reigned from 180 to 157. He soon came to be regarded (with Gaozu and Wudi) as one of three outstanding emperors of the Xi Han. He was credited with the ideal behaviour of a reigning monarch according to later Confucian doctrine; i.e., he was supposedly ready to yield place to others, hearken to the advice and remonstrances of his statesmen, and eschew personal extravagance. It can be claimed that his reign saw the peaceful consolidation of imperial power, successful experimentation in operating the organs of government, and the steady growth of China's material resources.

FROM WUDI TO YUANDI

The third emperor of the Xi Han to be singled out for special praise by traditional Chinese historians was Wudi (reigned 141–87 BC), whose reign was the longest of the entire Han period. His reputation as a vigorous and brave ruler derives from the long series of campaigns fought chiefly against the Xiongnu (Hsiung-nu; northern nomads) and in Central Asia, though Wudi never took a personal part in the fighting. The policy of taking the offensive and extending Chinese influence into unknown territory resulted not from the emperor's initiative but from the stimulus of a few statesmen, whose decisions were opposed vigorously at the time. Thanks to the same statesmen, manpower was more intensively

WUDI

Wudi (b. 156 BC—d. March 29, 87 BC) is the posthumous name given to Liu Che, the sixth emperor of the Xi (Western) Han dynasty. He is noted for vastly increasing the Han's authority and influence abroad and for making Confucianism China's state religion. Under Wudi, China's armies drove back the nomadic Xiongnu tribes that plagued the northern border, incorporated southern China and northern and central Vietnam into the empire, and reconquered Korea. Their farthest expedition was to Fergana (in modern Uzbekistan). Wudi's military campaigns strained the state's reserves; seeking new income, he decreed new taxes and established state monopolies on salt, iron, and wine.

Drawing of the Wudi emperor (lower right) *of the Xi (Western) Han dynasty, receiving a letter.* Snark/Art Resource, NY

The Wudi emperor is best remembered for his military conquests; hence, his posthumous title, Wudi, meaning "Martial Emperor." His administrative reforms left an enduring mark on the Chinese state, and his exclusive recognition of Confucianism had a permanent effect on subsequent East Asian history.

used and natural resources more heavily exploited during Wudi's reign, which required more active administration by Han officials. Wudi participated personally in the religious cults of state far more actively than his predecessors and some of his successors. And it was during his reign that the state took new steps to promote scholarship and develop the civil service.

From about 90 BC it became apparent that Han military strength had been overtaxed, leading to a retrenchment in military and economic policies. The last few years of the reign were darkened by a dynastic crisis arising out of jealousies between the empress and heir apparent on the one hand and a rival imperial consort's family on the other. Intense and violent fighting erupted in Chang'an in 91, and the two families were almost eliminated. A compromise was reached just before Wudi's death, whereby an infant—known by his posthumous name Zhaodi (reigned 87–74)—who came from neither family was chosen to succeed. The stewardship of the empire was vested in the hands of a regent, Huo Guang, a shrewd and circumspect statesman who already had been in government service for some two decades; even after Huo's death (68 BC), his family retained a dominating influence in Chinese politics until 64 BC. Zhaodi had been married to a granddaughter of Huo Guang; his successor, who was brought to the throne at the invitation of Huo and other statesmen, proved unfit and was deposed after a reign of 27 days. Huo, however, was able

to contrive a replacement candidate (posthumous name Xuandi) whom he could control or manipulate. Xuandi (reigned 74–49/48), who began to take a personal part in government after Huo Guang's death, had a predilection for a practical rather than a scholastic approach to matters of state. While his reign was marked by a more rigorous attention to implementing the laws than had heretofore been fashionable, his edicts paid marked attention to the ideals of governing a people in their own interests and distributing bounties where they were most needed. The move away from the aggressive policies of Wudi's statesmen was even more noticeable during the next reign (Yuandi; 49/48–33).

FROM CHENGDI TO WANG MANG

In the reigns of Chengdi (33–7 BC), Aidi (7–1 BC), and Pingdi (1 BC–AD 6) the conduct of state affairs and the atmosphere of the court were subject to the weakness or youth of the emperors, the lack of an heir to succeed Chengdi, and the rivalries between four families of imperial consorts. It was also a time when considerable attention was paid to omens. Changes that were first introduced in the state religious cults in 32 BC were alternately countermanded and reintroduced in the hope of securing material blessings by means of intercession with different spiritual powers. To satisfy the jealousies of a favourite, Chengdi went so far as to murder two sons born to him by other women. Aidi took steps to control the growing monopoly exercised by other families over state affairs. It was alleged at the time that the deaths of both Chengdi, who had enjoyed robust health, and Pingdi, not yet 14 years old when he died, had been arranged for political reasons.

In the meantime the Wang family had come to dominate the court. Wang Zhengjun, who had been the empress of Yuandi and mother of Chengdi, exercised considerable powers not only in her own capacity but also through several of her eight brothers. From 33 to 7 BC five members of the family were appointed in succession to the most powerful position in the government, and the status of other members was raised by bestowing titles of nobilities. The empress dowager lived until AD 13, surviving the decline of the family's influence under Aidi, who sought to restore a balance at court by honouring the families of other consorts (the Fu and Ding families). Wang Mang, nephew of the empress dowager Wang, restored the family's position during the reign of Pingdi. After the latter died and an infant succeeded to the throne, Wang Mang was appointed regent, but in AD 9 he assumed the imperial position himself, under the dynastic title of Xin. Insofar as he took imperial power from the Liu family, Wang Mang's short reign from 9 to 23 may be described as an act of usurpation. His policies were marked by both traditionalism and innovation. In creating new social distinctions, he tried to revert to a system allegedly in operation before the imperial age, and some of his changes in the structure of government were similarly related to precedents of the dim past. He appealed to the poorer classes by instituting measures of relief, but his attempts to eliminate private landholding and abolish private slaveholding antagonized the more wealthy members of society. Experiments in new types of coinage and in controlling economic transactions failed to achieve their purpose of increasing state resources, which were depleted by enormously costly preparations for campaigns against the Xiongnu. The last years of his reign were dislocated by the rise of dissident bands in a number of provinces; several leaders declared themselves emperor in different regions, and, in the course of the fighting, Chang'an was entered and damaged. Later it was captured by the Red Eyebrows, one of the most active of the robber bands, and Wang Mang was killed in a scene of violence played out within the palace buildings.

DONG (EASTERN) HAN

The Han house was restored by Liu Xiu, better known as Guangwudi, who reigned from AD 25 to 57. His claim had been contested by another member of the Liu house—Liu Xuan, better known as Liu Gengshi—who had been actually enthroned for two years, until his death in the course of turbulent civil fighting. Chang'an had been virtually destroyed by warfare, and Guangwudi established his capital at Luoyang.

The new emperor completed defeating rival aspirants to the throne in 36. As had occurred in Xi Han, dynastic establishment was followed by a period of internal consolidation rather than expansion. Guangwudi resumed the structure of government of the Xi Han emperors, together with the earlier coinage and system of taxation. The palace once more promoted the cause of scholarship. Eunuchs had come to the fore in the Han palace during Yuandi's reign, and several had succeeded in reaching powerful positions. Guangwudi's policy was to rid the government of such influences, together with that of the families of imperial consorts. Under Mingdi (57–75) and Zhangdi (75–88), China was once more strong enough to adopt a positive foreign policy and set Chinese armies on the march against the Xiongnu. To prevent incursions by the latter, and possibly to encourage the growth of trade, Han influence was again brought to bear in Central Asia. Chinese prestige reached its zenith around 90 and fell markedly after 125.

Dynastic decline can be dated from the reign of Hedi (88–105/106), when the court once more came under the influence of consorts' families and eunuchs. The succession of emperors became a matter of dexterous manipulation designed to preserve the advantages of interested parties. The weakness of the throne can be judged from the fact that, of the 14 emperors of Dong Han, no less than 8 took the throne as boys aged between 100 days and 15 years. Factions gradually increased in number, and their members, like the families of imperial consorts and like the eunuchs, tended to

place their own interests above those of the state.

During the last 50 years of Dong Han, northern China became subject to invasion from different sides, and, as was observed by several philosopher-statesmen, the administration became corrupt and ineffective. Powerful regional officials were able to establish themselves almost independently of the central government. Rivalry between consorts' families and eunuchs led to a massacre of the latter in 189, and the rebel bands that arose included the Yellow Turbans, who were fired by beliefs in supernatural influences and led by inspired demagogues. Soldiers of fortune and contestants for power were putting troops in the field in their attempts to establish themselves as emperors of a single united China. By 207 the great Han general Cao Cao had gained control over the north, and, had he not been defeated by Sun Quan at the battle of the Red Cliff, which later became famous in Chinese literature, he might well have succeeded in establishing a single dynastic rule. Other participants in the fighting included Dong Zhou, Liu Bei, and Zhuge Liang. The situation was resolved in 220 when Cao Pi, son of Cao Cao, accepted an instrument of abdication from Xiandi, last of the Han emperors (acceded 189). Cao Pi duly became emperor of a dynasty styled Wei, whose territories stretched over the northern part of China and whose capital was at Luoyang. A year later, in 221, Liu Bei was declared emperor of the Shu-Han dynasty, thereby maintaining the fiction that as a member of the Liu family he was continuing its rule of the Han dynasty, albeit in the restricted regions of Shu in the southwest (capital at Chengdu). In the southeast there was formed the third of the Sanguo (Three Kingdoms), as the period from 220 to 280 has come to be described. This was the kingdom of Wu, with its capital at Jianye, under the initial dispensation of Sun Quan.

THE ADMINISTRATION OF THE HAN EMPIRE

One of the main contributions of the Han dynasty to the future of imperial China lay in the development of the civil service and the structure of central and provincial government. The evolutionary changes that subsequently transformed Han polity beyond recognition were not directed at altering the underlying principles of government but at applying them expediently to the changing dynastic, political, social, and economic conditions of later centuries.

THE STRUCTURE OF GOVERNMENT

THE CIVIL SERVICE

One of the main contributions of the Han dynasty to the future of imperial China lay in the development of the civil service and the structure of central and provincial government. The evolutionary changes that subsequently transformed Han polity beyond recognition were not directed at

altering the underlying principles of government but at applying them expediently to the changing dynastic, political, social, and economic conditions of later centuries. One of the problems faced by Han governments was recruiting able and honest men to staff the civil service of an empire; those individuals eventually became known in the West as mandarins. Although the Chinese writing system had recently been reformed, which facilitated drafting documents, officials still needed considerable training before they attained sufficient competence. Much of the training occurred in local-level bureaus, where aspirants for imperial appointments served the equivalent of apprenticeships. Meritorious young men advanced from clerical positions to head various local bureaus. Having proved themselves in these positions, they were then eligible for recommendation or sponsorship, the standard means by which civil servants were recruited. Officials were invited to present candidates who possessed suitable qualities of intelligence and integrity, usually established in their service in local bureaus, and at certain regular intervals provincial units were ordered to send a quota of men to the capital. At times candidates were required to submit answers on questions of policy or administration. They might then be kept at the palace to act as advisers in attendance, or they might be given appointments in the central government or in the provinces, depending on their success. However, at that time there was no regular system of examination and appointment akin to what evolved during the Sui and Tang dynasties.

The recruitment system was important for two reasons directly related to the nature and development of Han society. First, the apprenticeship system assured that entry into the imperial bureaucracy was based on administrative merit. Thus, men of little wealth could enter clerical positions and support themselves while preparing for higher-level careers. (This recruitment system differed strikingly from the later examination system that often required years of study in order to master the Confucian Classics and to develop writing skills.) Second, powerful families, increasingly in the Dong Han period, were able to dominate the clerical and other positions in the local bureaus, thereby limiting to those powerful families the candidates for imperial bureaucratic service. Control of local positions in turn strengthened the powerful families by allowing them to manipulate tax and census registers. Such families created the social milieu from which the aristocratic families of the post-Han period were to emerge.

There was a total of 12 grades in the Han civil service, ranging from that of clerk to the most senior minister of state. No division in principle existed between men serving in the central offices or the provincial units. Promotion could be achieved from one grade of the service to the next, and in theory a man could rise from the humblest to the highest post. In theory and partly in practice, the structure of Han government was marked by an adherence to regular hierarchies of authority, by the division of specialist responsibilities, and by a duplication of certain functions. It was hoped that these measures would keep individual officials from accumulating excessive amounts of power. The uppermost stratum of officials or statesmen comprised the chancellor, the imperial counselor, and, sometimes, the commander in chief. These men acted as the emperor's highest advisers and retained final control over the activities of government. Responsibility was shared with nine ministers of state, who cared for matters such as religious cults, security of the palace, adjudication in criminal cases, diplomatic dealings with foreign leaders, and the collection and distribution of revenue. Each minister of state was supported by a department staffed by directors and subordinates. There were a few other major agencies, which ranked slightly below the nine ministries and were responsible for specialist tasks. Functions were duplicated so as to check the growth of power. Occasionally, for example, two chancellors were appointed concurrently. Similarly, financial matters were controlled by two permanent ministries: the Department of Agriculture and Revenue and the Privy Treasury.

The foregoing structure of regular organs of government was known as the Outer Court. With the passage of time, it became balanced by the growth of a secondary seat of power known as the Inner Court. This grew up from members of the secretariat and had started as a subordinate agency in the Privy Treasury. The secretariat officials had acquired direct access to the emperor and could thus circumvent the more formal approaches that protocol required of other officials. The secretariat rose to prominence during the latter part of the 1st century BC and was at times staffed by eunuchs. Its members were sometimes distinguished by receiving privileged titles that conveyed a mark of imperial favour without specific administrative responsibility. The highest of these titles was that of supreme commander, and, when this title was accompanied by the right or the imperial instruction to assume leadership of the secretariat, the powers of the incumbent outweighed those of the highest ministers of the Outer Court. An official thus named could effectively control decisions of state, to the discomfiture of senior officials such as the chancellor. It was in this capacity that Wang Mang and his four predecessors had been able to assert their power without fear of check.

PROVINCIAL GOVERNMENT

At the outset of the Han dynasty, vast areas were entrusted as kingdoms to the emperor's kinsmen, while the central government administered the interior provinces as commanderies. But by about 100 BC the imperial government had deprived the kingdoms of their strength, and most of their lands had been incorporated as commanderies under the central government. Although the kingdoms survived in a much-reduced form until the end of the period, their administration came to differ less and less from that of the commanderies, which formed the regular provincial units. Each commandery was controlled by two senior officials, the governor and the commandant, who were appointed by the central government. Commanderies could be established at will: by dividing larger into smaller units, by taking over the lands of the kings, or by establishing organs of government in regions only recently penetrated by Chinese officials. Provincial government was not necessarily pervasive throughout the lands where commandery offices existed, but there was a steady advance in provincial government during the Han period. During Gaozu's reign 16 commanderies existed, but by the end of the Xi Han there were 83 commanderies and 20 kingdoms.

Each of the commanderies consisted of some 10 or 20 prefectures, the size of which corresponded to that of English counties. The prefect's headquarters were situated in a walled town, from which his administration was extended and his officials were sent to collect taxes, settle disputes, or recruit able-bodied men for service. The prefectures were themselves subdivided into districts. The commanderies included a number of nobilities, the holders of which enjoyed a noble title and income from the taxes collected in them by central government officials. The nobles exercised no administrative, judicial, or other power over their nobilities. The number of nobilities varied considerably, sometimes totaling several hundred. The system was used as a political instrument for reducing the power of the kings, rewarding military officers and civil officials, and treating surrendered enemy leaders. Special arrangements were instituted for provincial government at the periphery of the empire. Agencies of a specialist nature were set up both there and in the provinces of the interior, with responsibilities for such matters as supervision of the salt and iron industries, manufacture of textiles, fruit growing, and sponsored agriculture, as well as control of passage in and out of the frontier.

From 106 BC the government tried to supervise the work of provincial officials more directly. A total of 13 regional inspectors were appointed, with orders to visit the commanderies and kingdoms of a specified area and to report to the central government on the efficiency of officials, the degree of oppression or corruption, and the state of popular affection or disaffection. Although the arrangement was not yet tantamount to the creation of a limited number (about 20) of large provinces, such as came about from about the 13th century, it may have facilitated the establishment of separatist provincial regimes at times of dynastic decline.

THE ARMED FORCES

The command of the armed forces was also arranged so as to avoid giving excessive powers to a single individual. Officers equivalent to generals were usually appointed in pairs, and, in times of emergency or when a campaign was being planned with a defined objective, those officers were appointed for a specific task; when their mission was fulfilled, their commands were brought to a close. Beneath that level was a complement of colonels whose duties consisted of smaller-scale activities. In addition, the governors and commandants of the commanderies were sometimes ordered to lead forces. The commandants were also responsible for training conscript soldiers and setting them to maintain internal discipline and to man the static lines of defense in the north and northwest.

The Han armies drew their recruits from conscripts, volunteers, and convicts. Conscripts, who formed the majority, were obliged to serve for two years, either under training or on active service. This duty devolved on all able-bodied males other than those who had acquired privileges of rank or those who could pay for substitutes. The latter practice was probably rare. In addition, men were liable for recall to the armed forces in times of emergency. Volunteers were the sons of privileged families and probably served as cavalrymen, and convicts were sometimes drafted to work out their terms of sentence in the army. There is ample evidence to show that Han commanders used to draw on Central Asian tribesmen as recruits, and the tribesmen were particularly valuable as skilled cavalrymen. A number of foreigners also served with distinction as officers. While little is known of the organization of armies on campaign, garrison forces were divided

Horse and Swallow, *bronze sculpture from the tomb of General Chang, Leitai, Wuwei county, Gansu province, 2nd century AD, Dong (Eastern) Han dynasty; in the Gansu Provincial Museum, Lanzhou, China. Height 32.4 cm.* Robert Harding Picture Library

into separate commands consisting of perhaps four companies. Each company had a strength of some 40 or 50 sections, each of which comprised one officer and up to five men.

THE PRACTICE OF GOVERNMENT

As the final arbiter of power, the emperor—and at times the empress dowager—issued edicts declaring the imperial will. Such instructions often took the form of repeating officials' proposals with a note of approval. Some edicts were couched as comments on the current situation and called in general terms for an improvement in the quality of government or for more-vigorous attempts to achieve a just administration. The emperor also issued formal deeds of investiture to kings or noblemen and letters of appointment for senior officials. Edicts were circulated to the relevant authorities for action, together with books of other regulations such as the statutes and ordinances, laying down entitlements for services rendered to the state and penalties for infringing its prohibitions. Officials could suggest methods of government by submitting written memorials, and there were occasions when an emperor called a conference of senior statesmen and asked their views on topical problems.

The Han governments regularly issued calendars to enable the court to follow a cosmically correct ritual schedule and officials to maintain their records correctly. Regular means of transport were kept for the use of officials traveling on business and for the conveyance of official mail from one office to another. Provincial and local officials were responsible for two regular counts without which government could not proceed: the census of the population and the register of the land and its production. Returns, which were submitted for the number of households and individuals and for land under cultivation, eventually found their way to the capital. One count that has been preserved records the existence of some 12,233,000 households and 59,595,000 individuals in AD 2. Two other main forms of revenue collection were the land tax and the poll tax. The land tax was levied in kind at a 30th (sometimes a 15th) part of the produce, the assessment depending partly on the quality of the land. Poll tax was usually paid in cash and

varied with the age and sex of the members of the household. Other taxes were levied in respect to wealth and by means of property assessments.

In addition to service in the army, able-bodied males were expected to provide one month's service annually in the state labour corps; tasks included building palaces and imperial mausoleums, transporting staple goods such as grain and hemp, and constructing roads and bridges. Sometimes conscript labour was used to repair breaches in riverbanks or dikes, and men were sent to work in the salt and iron industries after these were taken over by the state.

The establishment of state monopolies for salt and iron was one of several measures taken in Wudi's reign to bring China's resources under the control of the government. Agencies were set up about 117 BC to supervise mining, manufacturing, and distribution and to raise revenue in the process. The measure was criticized on the grounds of both principle and expedience and was withdrawn for three years from 44 BC, and by the mid-1st century AD the industries had in practice reverted to private hands. Final measures to standardize the coinage and to limit minting to state agencies were taken in 112 BC, and, with the exception of Wang Mang's experiments, the copper coin of a single denomination, minted from Wudi's reign onward, remained the standard medium of exchange. Little is known of the work of other agencies established in Xi Han to stabilize the prices of staple commodities and to regulate their transport. Such measures had been the answer of Wudi's government to the problem of moving goods from an area of surplus to one of shortage.

The government ordered migrations of the population for several reasons. At times, such a migration was intended to populate an area artificially—the city of Xianyang during the Qin dynasty, for example, and the state-sponsored farms of the borderlands. Alternatively, if the defense of the periphery was impractical, the population was sometimes moved away from danger, and distressed folk were moved to areas where they could find a more prosperous way of life.

From about 100 BC it was evident to some statesmen that great disparities of wealth existed and that this was most noticeable in respect of landownership. Some philosophers looked back nostalgically to an ideal state in which land was said to have been allotted and held on a basis of equality, thereby eliminating the wide differences between rich and poor. It was only in Wang Mang's time that an attempt was made to abolish private landownership and private slaveholding. But the attempt failed because of powerful economic and social opposition, and the accumulation of land continued during Dong Han. In the last half century or so of the dynasty, country estates acquired retainers and armed defenders, almost independently of the writ of government. The great families thus came to exercise more power than appointed officials of state.

The Han government, like the Qin, ruled by dispensing rewards for service and exacting punishment for disobedience and crime. Rewards consisted of exemptions from tax; bounties of gold, meat, spirits, or silk; amnesties for criminals; and orders of honour. The latter were bestowed either individually or to groups. There was a ranked scale of 20 degrees, and, after receiving several of these awards cumulatively, one could rise to the eighth place in the scale. The more-senior orders were given for specified acts of valour, charity, or good administration, usually to officials, and the highest order was the rank of nobility. In addition to conferring social status, the orders carried with them legal privileges and freedom from some tax and service obligations.

In theory, the laws of Han were binding on all members of the population, and some incidents testify to the punishment of the highest in the land. But some privileged persons were able to get their sentences mitigated. Nobles, for example, could ransom themselves from most punishments by forfeiting their nobilities. Han laws specified a variety of crimes, including those of a social nature such as murder or theft, those that infringed the imperial majesty, and those that were classed as gross immorality. There was a regular procedure for impeachment and trial, and some difficult cases could be referred to the emperor for a final decision. The punishments to which criminals were sentenced included exile, hard labour, flogging, castration, and death. In the most heinous cases the death sentence was carried out publicly, but senior officials and members of the imperial family were usually allowed to avoid such a scene by committing suicide. When the death penalty was invoked, a criminal's goods, including members of his family, were confiscated by the state. Such persons then became slaves of the state and were employed on menial or domestic tasks in government offices. Government slaves were sometimes given as rewards to meritorious officials.

RELATIONS WITH OTHER PEOPLES

Simultaneously with the rise of the Qin and Han empires, some of the nomadic peoples of Central Asia, known as the Xiongnu, succeeded in achieving a measure of unity under a single leader. As a result, while the Chinese were consolidating their government, the lands lying to the north of the empire—and the northern provinces themselves—became subject to incursion by Xiongnu horsemen. One of the achievements of the Qin dynasty had been the unification of the several lines of defense into a single system of fortification, the Great Wall. By keeping that wall, or line of earthworks, manned, the Qin dynasty had been free of invasion. With the fall of Qin and China's subsequent weakness, the wall fell into a state of disrepair and lacked a garrison. Until about 135 BC, Han governments were obliged to seek peaceful

relations with the Xiongnu at the price of gold, silk, and even the hand of a Chinese princess. However, as Wudi's governments began establishing strong policies, China took the offensive in an attempt to throw back the Xiongnu to Central Asia and to free the northern provinces from the threat of invasion and violence. By 119 BC, campaigns fought to the north of Chinese territory had attained this objective, and after a short interval it was possible to send Han armies to advance in the northeast (present-day North Korea), the south (present-day Vietnam), and the southwest. As a result of the campaigns fought from 135 BC onward, 18 additional commanderies were founded, and organs of Han provincial government were installed as outposts among peoples who were unassimilated to a Chinese way of life.

Chinese government was by no means universally accepted in those outlying regions. But despite large losses and expenditures incurred in fighting the Xiongnu, the Chinese were able to mount expeditions into Central Asia from about 112 BC. The defensive walls were repaired and remanned, and by about 100 they were extended to the northwest as far as Dunhuang. Chinese travelers, whether diplomats or merchants, were thus protected as far as the Takla Makan Desert. It was at about that time that trade routes skirting the desert were established and came to be known collectively as the Silk Road.

The success of Chinese arms in those remote areas was short-lived. Long lines of communication made it impossible to set up garrisons or colonies in the forbidding country to the west of Dunhuang. Diplomatic moves were made to implant Chinese prestige more firmly among the communities that were situated around the Takla Makan Desert and that controlled the oases; it was necessary for the Chinese to win those peoples' support, thus denying it to the Xiongnu. In a few cases the Chinese resorted to violence or plots to remove a leader and to replace him with a candidate known to favour the Han cause. More commonly, one of the alien leaders was married to a Chinese princess, with the intention that he should in time be succeeded by an heir who was half-Chinese. These endeavours and the military ventures met with partial success. While the Chinese position in Central Asia was subject to question, relations with the Xiongnu leaders varied. The visit of a Xiongnu leader to Chang'an in 51 BC was hailed as a mark of Chinese success, but the ensuing decades were not free from fighting. Chinese prestige declined toward the end of the Xi Han and recovered only during the reigns of Mingdi and Zhangdi, when the Han government was once more strong enough to take the field. Ban Chao's campaigns in Central Asia (from AD 94) reestablished the Chinese position, but again the full strength of Chinese prestige lasted for only a few decades. During the Dong Han, China suffered invasion from the northeast as well as from the north. The settlement of Xiongnu peoples south of the wall was a disruptive factor in the 2nd and 3rd centuries, to the detriment of imperial unity.

The Han expansion into Central Asia has been represented by the Chinese as a defensive measure designed to weaken the Xiongnu and to free China from invasion. Allowance must also be made for commercial motives. Some of Wudi's statesmen were well aware of the advantages of exporting China's surplus products in return for animals and animal products from Central Asia, and there is evidence that Chinese silk was exported at this time. No attempt can be made to estimate the volume of trade, and, as the transactions were conducted through Parthian middlemen, no direct contact was made by this means between Han China and the world of Rome and the Mediterranean. China's export trade was sponsored by the government and not entrusted to private merchants.

The Great Wall formed a boundary separating the Chinese provinces from the outside world. Traffic was controlled at points of access, not only to check incoming travelers to China but also to prevent the escape of criminals or deserters. At the same time, a ban was imposed on the export of certain goods such as iron manufactures and weapons of war. The wall also formed a protected causeway for travelers to the west. Watch stations were erected in sight of each other to signal the approach of the enemy, and the garrison troops were highly trained and disciplined. Meticulous records were kept to show how government stores were expended and rations

Tourists travel by carriage through the ruins of the ancient capital of the Gaochang empire, Uygur Autonomous Region of Xinjiang, China. The city lay on the famous Silk Road at the foot of Huoyan ("Flaming") Mountain, noted for the Bezeklik Thousand Buddha caves. China Photos/Getty Images

issued; routine signals were relayed along the line and daily patrols were sent out to reconnoitre.

As a result of the campaigns and diplomatic activity, China's immediate contacts with other peoples grew more brisk. Many of the Xiongnu and other neighbouring leaders who had surrendered to Han arms were given nobilities and settled in the interior of the empire. Zhang Qian was a pioneer who had set out about 130 BC to explore the routes into Central Asia and northern China, and, as a result of his report and

observations, Han advances were concentrated in the northwest. In AD 97 Chinese envoys were frustrated in an attempt to visit the western part of the world, but a mission from Rome reached China by ship in 166. The first record of official visitors arriving at the Han court from Japan is for the year AD 57.

CULTURAL DEVELOPMENTS

The Han emperors and governments posed as having a temporal dispensation that had received the blessing of heaven together with its instructions to spread the benefits of a cultured life as widely as possible. By a cultured life the Chinese had in mind a clear distinction between their own settled agriculture and the delights of the cities, as opposed to the rough and hardy life spent in the saddle by the nomads of Central Asia. The growth of Han government both depended on and encouraged the development of literary accomplishment, scholastic competence, religious activity, scientific discovery, and technological achievement.

Han administration required detailed record keeping, which generated a proliferation of documents. Official returns were sometimes kept in duplicate, and each agency kept running files to record its business. Following a reform of the script that had evolved before the Han period, a new style of writing was developed that was suited to compiling official documents. These were written mostly on bulky and fragile wooden strips; silk was also used as a writing medium. A major development in world history occurred in China in AD 105 when officials reported to the throne the manufacture of a new substance. Although archaeological evidence indicates the existence of paper for more than a century before this incident, the earlier materials were not completely superseded until some three or four centuries later. In the meantime, the written vocabulary of the Chinese had increased in response to the demands of a growing civilization. The first Chinese dictionary, completed in AD 121, included more than 9,000 separate ideograms (characters), with explanations of their meanings and the variant forms used in writing.

In an attempt to break with earlier tradition, the Qin government had taken certain steps to proscribe literature and learning. Han governments stressed their desire to promote these causes as part of their mission. In particular, they displayed a veneration for works with which Confucius had been associated, either as a collector of texts or as an editor, and these works became known as the *Wujing*, or the Confucian Classics. Beginning during the reign of Wendi, orders were given to search for books lost during the previous dynasty. Knowledge of texts such as the *Shijing* ("Classic of Poetry"), the *Shujing* ("Classic of History"), the *Yijing* ("Classic of Changes"), and the *Chunqiu* ("Spring and Autumn") annals became a necessary accomplishment for officials and candidates for the civil service. To support an argument laid before the throne, statesmen would find a relevant quotation from these works; already in the 1st century BC the tradition was being formed whereby the civil service of imperial China was nurtured on a Classical education. On two occasions (51 BC and AD 79) the government ordered official discussions about interpreting texts and the validity of differing versions; in AD 175 work was completed on a project that inscribed an approved version on stone tablets, so as to allay scholastic doubts in the future. In the meantime—and still before the invention of paper—a collection of literary texts had been made for the imperial library. The catalog of this collection, which dates from the early 1st century AD, was prepared after comparing different copies and eliminating duplicates. The list of titles has been preserved and constitutes China's first bibliographical list. The works are classified according to subject, but many have been lost. The importance of these measures lies both in their intrinsic achievement and in the example they set for subsequent dynasties.

The prose style of Han writers was later taken as a model of simplicity, and, as a reaction to the literary embellishments and artificialities introduced in the 5th and 6th centuries, deliberate attempts were made to revert to its natural elegance. Examples of this direct prose may be seen in the imperial edicts, the memorials ascribed to statesmen, and, above all, the text of the standard histories themselves, in which such documents of state were incorporated. Compiling the standard histories was a private undertaking in Han times, but it already received imperial patronage and assistance. History was written partly to justify the authority and conduct of the contemporary regime and partly as a matter of pride in Chinese achievement. Further examples of prose writing are the descriptions of protocol for the court. One of the earliest acts of the Han government (c. 200 BC) had been to order the formulation of such modes of behaviour as a means of enhancing the dignity of the throne, and one of the latest compilations (c. AD 175) that still survives is a list of such prescriptions, drawn up at a time when the dynasty was manifestly losing its majesty and natural authority. Some of the emperors were themselves composers of versified prose; their efforts have also been preserved in the standard histories.

The emperor was charged with the solemn duty of securing the blessings of spiritual powers for mankind. One of the nine ministries of state existed to assist in this work of mediation, but from the time of Wudi onward the emperor himself began to play a more active part in worship and sacrifice. The cults were initially addressed to the Five Elements (fire, water, earth, wood, and metal), to the Supreme Unity, and to the Lord of the Soil. In 31 BC these cults were replaced by sacrifices dedicated to heaven and earth. The sites of worship were transferred to the southern and northern outskirts of Chang'an, and a new series of altars and shrines was inaugurated. The Han emperor occasionally paid his respects to supreme powers and reported on the state of the dynasty at the summit of Mount Tai. Wudi's desire for immortality

Terraced rice fields near Longsheng, Guangzi province, nicknamed the "Dragon's Backbone."
Christian Kober/Robert Harding World Imagery/Getty Images

and for quickening his deceased favourites led him to patronize a number of intermediaries who claimed to possess the secret of making contact with the world of the immortals. From such beliefs and from a fear of the malevolent influences that the unappeased souls of the dead could wreak on humanity, a few philosophers such as Wang Chong (AD 27–c. 100) reacted by propounding an ordered and rational explanation of the universe. But their skepticism received little support. Sometime during the 1st century AD, Buddhism reached China, propagated in all probability by travelers who had taken the Silk Road from northern India. Shortly thereafter Buddhist foundations were established in China, as well as the first official patronage of the faith. From the 2nd century AD there arose a variety of beliefs, practices, and disciplines from which alchemy and scientific experiment were to spring and which were to give rise to Daoism.

Most of the cultural attainments of the Han period derived from imperial encouragement and the needs of officials. A textbook of mathematical problems was probably compiled to assist officials in work such as land assessment; fragments of a medical casebook were concerned with the care of troops and horses serving on the northwestern frontier. Water clocks and sundials were used to enable officials to complete their work on schedule. The palace demanded the services of artists and craftsmen to decorate imperial buildings with paintings and sculptures and to design and execute jades, gold and silver wares, and lacquer bowls for use at the imperial table. Intricate patterns in multicoloured silks were woven on looms in the imperial workshops. On a more mundane level, technology served the cause of practical government. The state's ironwork factories produced precision-made instruments and weapons of war, and the state's agencies for the salt industry supervised the recovery of brine from deep shafts cut in the rocks of western China. Water engineers planned the construction of dikes to divert the flow of excess waters and the excavation of canals to serve the needs of transport or irrigation, and in many parts of the countryside there could be seen a sight that remained typical of the Chinese landscape up to the 20th century—a team of two or three peasants sitting astride a beam and pedaling the lugs of the "dragon's backbone" that raised water from the sluggish channels below to the upper levels of the cultivated land.

CHAPTER 4

THE SIX DYNASTIES AND THE SUI DYNASTY

POLITICAL DEVELOPMENTS DURING THE SIX DYNASTIES

B y the end of the 2nd century AD the Han empire had virtually ceased to exist. The repression of the Daoist rebellions of the Yellow Turbans and related sects marked the beginning of a period of unbridled warlordism and political chaos, from which three independent centres of political power emerged.

THE DIVISION OF CHINA

In the north all authority had passed into the hands of the generalissimo and "protector of the dynasty," Cao Cao; in AD 220 the last puppet emperor of the Han officially ceded the throne to Cao Cao's son, who thereby became the legitimate heir of the empire and the first ruler of the Wei dynasty. Soon afterward, two competing military leaders proclaimed themselves emperor, one in the far interior (Shu-Han dynasty, in the present-day Sichuan province) and one in the south, behind the formidable barrier of the Yangtze River (the empire of Wu, with its capital at Jianye, present-day Nanjing). The short and turbulent period of these "Three Kingdoms" (Sanguo), filled with bloody warfare and diplomatic intrigue, has ever since been glorified in Chinese historical fiction as an age of chivalry and individual heroism.

SANGUO (THREE KINGDOMS; AD 220–280)

In fact, even Wei, the strongest of the three Sanguo kingdoms, hardly represented any real political power. The great socioeconomic changes that had started in the Dong (Eastern) Han period had transformed the structure of society to such an extent that all attempts to reestablish the centralized bureaucratic state—the ideal of the Qin and Han dynasties—were doomed to failure. While central authority declined, the great families—aristocratic clans of large landowners—survived the decades of civil war on their fortified estates under the protection of their private armies of serfs and clients and even increased their power. These conditions were to remain characteristic of medieval China. The Han system of recruiting officials on the basis of talent was replaced by a network of personal relations and patronage. The hierarchy of state officials and government institutions was never abolished, but it became monopolized by a few aristocratic clans who filled the highest offices with their own members and the minor posts with their clients.

Wei succeeded in conquering Shu-Han in 263/264, but two years later a general of the dominant Sima clan overthrew the house of Wei (265/266) and in 265 founded the first of two dynasties under the name Jin: the Xi (Western) Jin. Wu, however, was able to maintain itself until 280, when it was overrun by the Jin armies.

The role of Wu was extremely important: it marked the beginning of the progressive Sinicization of the region south of the Yangtze River, which before that time had been a frontier area inhabited mainly by non-Chinese tribal peoples. The rise of Jianye (renamed Jiankang during Jin times) as a great administrative and cultural centre on the lower Yangtze paved the way for future developments: after the north was lost to barbarian invaders (311), it was to become the capital of Chinese successor states and an important locus of Chinese culture for more than 250 years.

THE XI (WESTERN) JIN (AD 265–316/317)

In addition to restoring order, The Xi Jin renewed contacts with the oasis kingdoms of Central Asia and the Indianized states of the far south (Funan and Champa), and in 285 the Jin court even sent an envoy to distant Fergana in Central Asia to confer the title of king on its ruler—a grand imperial gesture reminiscent of the great days of Han. But this ghost of the Han empire disappeared almost as soon as it had been evoked. Within two decades the Jin disintegrated through the struggles of rival clans. There followed an internecine war between the various Sima princes, collapse of the central government, decentralized military control of the provinces, famine, large-scale banditry, and messianic peasant movements.

THE ERA OF BARBARIAN INVASIONS AND RULE

For the first time the power vacuum was filled by non-Chinese forces. In 304 a Sinicized Xiongnu chieftain, Liu Yuan, assumed the title of king of Han and started the conquest of northern China. Operating from bases in western and southern Shanxi, the Xiongnu armies, supported by local Chinese rebels, conquered the ancient homeland of Chinese civilization; the fall and destruction of the two capitals, Luoyang (311) and Chang'an (316), ended Chinese dynastic rule in the north for centuries. Although in the far northeast, in present-day Gansu, and in the inaccessible interior (Sichuan), Chinese local kingdoms did occasionally succeed in maintaining themselves for some time, the whole North China Plain itself became the scene of a bewildering variety of barbarian states, collectively known in Chinese historiography as the Shiliuguo (Sixteen Kingdoms).

THE DONG (EASTERN) JIN (317–420) AND LATER DYNASTIES IN THE SOUTH (420–589)

During the entire medieval period the lower Yangtze region—the former territory of Wu—remained the stronghold of a series of "legitimate" Chinese dynasties, with Jiankang as their capital. In 317 a member of the Jin imperial family had set up a refugee regime at Jiankang, consisting mainly of members of the exiled northern aristocracy. From the beginning the Jin court was completely at the mercy of the great landowning families. Government in the Chinese south became a kind of oligarchy exercised by ever-changing groups and juntas of aristocratic clans. The so-called Six Dynasties were politically and militarily weak and constantly plagued by internal feuds and revolts. (The six were actually five—Dong Jin, 317–420; Liu-Song, 420–479; Nan [Southern] Qi, 479–502; Nan Liang, 502–557; and Nan Chen, 557–589—and all but Dong Jin are also known as Nanchao [Southern Dynasties] in Chinese history; the earlier kingdom of Wu, 222–280, is counted as the sixth dynasty.) Their annihilation (in 589) was postponed only by the internal division of the north and by the protection afforded by the Yangtze. To the very end, their opposition to the north remained alive, but occasional attempts to reconquer the ancient homeland were doomed to failure. The final reunification of China was to start from the northern plains, not from Jiankang.

Although politically insecure, these dynasties were characterized by cultural brilliance: in literature, art, philosophy, and religion, they constituted one of the most creative periods in Chinese history. They reached their highest flowering under the long and relatively stable reign of the great protector of Buddhism, Wudi (reigned 502–549), the first emperor of the Nan Liang dynasty.

THE SHILIUGUO (SIXTEEN KINGDOMS) IN THE NORTH (303–439)

The term Sixteen Kingdoms traditionally denotes the plethora of short-lived non-Chinese dynasties that from 303 came to rule the whole or parts of northern China. Many ethnic groups were involved, including ancestors of the Turks (such as the Xiongnu, possibly related to the Huns of late Roman history, and the Jie), the Mongolians (Xianbei), and the Tibetans (Di and Qiang). Most of these nomadic peoples, relatively few in number, had to some extent been Sinicized long before their ascent to power. Some of them—notably the Qiang and the Xiongnu—actually had been allowed to live in the frontier regions within the Great Wall since late Han times.

The barbarian rulers thus set up semi-Sinicized states, in which the foreign element constituted a military aristocracy and the nucleus of the armed forces. Since they lacked experience in administrative matters and since their own tribal institutions were not adapted to the complicated task of ruling a large agrarian society, they had to make use of traditional Chinese ways of government. In doing so, they faced the dilemma that has ever since confronted foreign rulers on Chinese soil: the tension that existed between the need to preserve their own ethnic identity (and their position as herrenvolk) on the one hand and on the other the practical necessity of using Chinese literati and members of prominent Chinese families in order to rule at all. In spite of various and sometimes highly interesting experiments, most of these short-lived empires did not survive this tension. Significantly, the only one that proved to have more lasting power and that was able to unify the whole of northern China—the Tuoba, or Bei (Northern) Wei (386–534/535)—was largely Sinicized within a century. In the late 5th century the court even forbade the use of the original Tuoba language, dress, customs, and surnames. This policy of conscious acculturation was further symbolized by the transfer of the Bei Wei capital from the northern frontier region to the ancient imperial residence of Luoyang.

Thus, toward the end of the period of division, the north had become more homogeneous as the result of a long process of adaptation. The most important factor in this process may have been the rehabilitation of the Chinese agrarian economy under the Bei Wei, stimulated by fiscal reform and redistribution of land (c. AD 500). The landed gentry again became the backbone of society, and the rulers of nomadic origin simply had to conform to their way of life. Another factor was the perceived intrinsic superiority of Chinese upper-class culture: in order to play the role of the "son of heaven," the leaders of the barbarian court had to adopt the complicated rules of Chinese ritual and etiquette. Likewise, in order to surround themselves with an aura of legitimacy, the foreign conquerors had to express themselves in terms of Chinese culture. In doing so, they invariably lost their own identity. History has constantly repeated itself: in this respect the 4th- and 5th-century Jie and Tuoba were but the forerunners of the Qing, or Manchu, rulers in the 19th century.

In the early 6th century the Wei was divided between the Sinicized court and a faction of the nobility desperate to preserve its Tuoba identity. Soon after 520 the Wei empire disintegrated into rival northeastern and northwestern successor states. Northern China again became a battlefield for several decades. The Bei (Northern) Zhou (557–581), strategically based in the rich basin of the Wei River, reunified the north (577). Four years later Yang Jian (better known by his posthumous name, Wendi), a general of mixed Chinese and barbarian descent (but claiming to be a pure-blooded Chinese), usurped the throne and founded the Sui dynasty. In 589, having consolidated his regime, he crossed the Yangtze River and overthrew the last of the Chinese dynasties at Jiankang. After almost four centuries of division and political decay, China was again united under one central government, which, in spite of its short duration, would lay the foundation of the great Tang empire.

INTELLECTUAL AND RELIGIOUS TRENDS DURING THE SIX DYNASTIES

CONFUCIANISM AND PHILOSOPHICAL DAOISM

The social and political upheaval of the late 2nd and the 3rd century AD was accompanied by intense intellectual activity. During the Han period, Confucianism had been slowly adopted as an ideology and had gradually come to provide the officially accepted norms, morals, and ritual and social behaviour regulating the relations between ruler and subject.

By the beginning of the 3rd century, however, Confucianism had lost its prestige: it had obviously failed to save the empire from disintegration or to safeguard the privileges of the ruling elite. Disappointed members of the scholar-official class started to look elsewhere. Thus, various all-but-forgotten schools of thought were revived in the 3rd century: Legalism, with its insistence on harsh measures, intended to reestablish law and order; Mohism and the ancient school of Logicians (Dialecticians); and, above all, a renewed interest in Daoism and its earliest philosophers, Laozi and Zhuangzi. In general, this movement did not mean a return to ancient Daoist quietism and consequently a rejection of Confucianism. With the breakdown of the elaborate scholastic doctrine that had formed the official Han ideology, Confucianism had been deprived of its metaphysical superstructure, and this vacuum was now filled by a whole set of philosophical ideas and speculations, largely of Daoist provenance.

Within this movement, two trends came to dominate the intellectual life of the cultured minority. One of these was closely related to the practical affairs of government and stressed the importance

CONFUCIUS

Confucius (Chinese: Kongfuzi; b. 551 BC—d. 479 BC) was the renowned teacher, philosopher, and political theorist of ancient China. Born into a poor family, he managed stables and worked as a bookkeeper while educating himself. Mastery of the six arts—ritual, music, archery, charioteering, calligraphy, and arithmetic—and familiarity with history and poetry enabled him to begin a brilliant teaching career in his thirties. Confucius saw education as a process of constant self-improvement and held that its primary function was the training of noblemen (junzi). He saw public service as the natural consequence of education and sought to revitalize Chinese social institutions, including the family, school, community, state, and kingdom. He served in government posts, eventually becoming minister of justice in Lu, but his policies attracted little interest. After a 12-year self-imposed exile during which his circle of students expanded, he returned to Lu at age 67 to teach and write. His life and thoughts are recorded in the Lunyu (Analects).

Drawing depicting the Chinese ethicist and philosopher Confucius. Hulton Archive/ Getty Images

of social duties, ritual, law, and the study of human characteristics. This mixture of Confucian and Legalist notions was called *mingjiao*, "the doctrine of names" ("names" in ancient Confucian parlance designating the various social functions—father, ruler, subject, etc.—that an individual could have in society). The other trend was marked by a profound interest in ontological and metaphysical problems: the quest for a permanent substratum (called *ti*, "substance") behind the world of change (called *yong*, "function"). It started from the assumption that all temporally and spatially limited phenomena—anything "nameable"; all movement, change, and diversity; in short, all "being"—is produced and sustained by one impersonal principle, which is unlimited, unnameable, unmoving, unchanging, and undiversified. This important movement, which found its scriptural support both in Daoist and in drastically reinterpreted Confucian sources, was known as Xuanxue ("Dark Learning"); it came to reign supreme in cultural circles, especially at Jiankang during the period of division, and represented the more abstract, unworldly, and idealistic tendency in early medieval Chinese thought.

The proponents of Xuanxue undoubtedly still regarded themselves as true Confucians. To them, Confucius was not simply the great teacher who had fixed the rules of social behaviour for all time but was the enlightened sage who had inwardly recognized the ultimate reality but had kept silent about it

in his worldly teachings, knowing that these mysteries could not be expressed in words. Hence, his doctrine was supposed to be an expedient, a mere set of ad hoc rules intended to answer the practical needs of the times. This concept of "hidden saintliness" and the "expedient" character of the canonical teachings came to play a very important role in upper-class Buddhism.

Xuanxue is sometimes referred to by the term Neo-Daoism, but this confuses the issue. It was both created by and intended for literati and scholar-officials—not Daoist masters and hermits. The theories of such thinkers as Ji Kang (224–262)—who, with their quest for immortality and their extreme antiritualism, were much nearer to the spirit of Daoism—hardly belong to the sphere of Xuanxue, and the greatest Daoist author of this period, Ge Hong (c. 283–343), was clearly opposed to these mystic speculations.

The popularity of Xuanxue was closely related to the practice of "pure conversation" (*qingtan*), a special type of philosophical discourse much in vogue among the cultured upper class from the 3rd century onward. In the earliest phase, the main theme of such discussion—a highly formalized critique of the personal qualities of well-known contemporaries—still had a concrete function in political life ("characterization" of persons was the basis of recommendation of clients for official posts and had largely taken the place of the earlier methods of selection of officials by court examinations). By the 4th century, however, *qingtan* meetings had evaporated into a refined and highly exclusive pastime of the aristocratic elite, a kind of salon in which "eloquent gentlemen" expressed some philosophical or artistic theme in elegant and abstruse words. It is obvious that much of Xuanxue had become divorced from the realities of life and afforded an escape from it.

True Confucianism had thus lost much of its influence. In the north the not-yet-Sinicized barbarian rulers were interested in Confucianism mainly as a system of court ritual; ideologically, they were more attracted by the magical powers of Buddhist and Daoist masters. In the south the disillusioned aristocratic exiles, doomed by circumstances to lead a life of elegant inactivity, had little use for a doctrine that preached the duties of government and the regulation of human society as its highest goals, although many families preserved Confucian learning and clung to Confucian mores. In this period of internal division and political weakness, Confucianism had to hibernate; soon after the Sui had reunited the empire, it would wake up again.

DAOISM

The suppression of the Yellow Turbans and other Daoist religious movements in AD 184 had left Daoism decapitated. With the elimination of its highest leadership, the movement had fallen apart into many small religious communities, each led by a local Daoist master (*daoshi*), assisted by a council of wealthy Daoist laity. Under such circumstances, local Daoist masters could easily become leaders of independent sectarian movements. They could also, in times of unrest, use their charismatic power to play a leading part in local rebellions. In the early medieval period, Daoism at the grassroots level continued to play this double role: it had an integrating function by providing spiritual consolation and ritualized forms of communal activity, but it could also be a disintegrating factor as a potential source of subversive movements. The authorities naturally were well aware of this. Daoist rebellions periodically broke out during this time, and, although some masters occasionally became influential at court, the governments, both northern and southern, maintained a cautious reserve toward the Daoist religion. It was never stimulated and patronized to an extent comparable to Buddhism.

It would be wrong to speak of Daoism as a popular religion. Daoism counted its devotees even among the highest nobility. In view of the expensive ceremonies, the costly ingredients used in Daoist alchemy (notably cinnabar), and the almost unlimited amount of spare time required from the serious practitioner, one may assume that only the well-to-do were able to follow the road toward salvation. But they were mostly individual seekers; in the 3rd and 4th centuries a distinction gradually grew between individual (and mainly upper-class) Daoism and the popular, collective creed of the simple devotees. In fact, Daoism has always been a huge complex of many different beliefs, cults, and practices. Most of these can be traced to Dong Han times, and after the 3rd century they were influenced increasingly by Buddhism.

The basic ideal of Daoist religion—the attainment of bodily immortality in a kind of indestructible "astral body" and the realization of the state of *xian*, or Daoist "immortal"—remained alive. It was to be pursued by a series of individual practices: dietary control, gymnastics, good deeds, and meditation and visualization of the innumerable gods and spirits that were supposed to dwell inside the microcosmos of the body. Renowned literati, such as the poet Ji Kang and the calligrapher Wang Xizhi (*c.* 303–*c.* 361), devoted much of their lives to such practices. They combined various methods, ranging from mystic self-identification with the all-embracing Dao to the use of charms and experiments in alchemy.

The development of Daoism seems to have reached a new stage during the 4th century. An ancient school of esoteric learning already existed at that time in southern China, exemplified by Ge Hong. The retreat of the Jin to southern China in the early 4th century brought to that region the organized religion and priesthood that had arisen in the north and west during the Dong Han. In that context, new priestly cults arose in the south. Their teachings were connected with a series of revelations, the first through Yang Xi, which led to the formation first of the Shangqing sect and later to the rival Lingbao sect. By the end of the period of division, Daoism had its own canons of scriptural writings, much influenced by Buddhist models but forming a quite independent religious tradition.

The other, collective, and more popular form of Daoism, practiced in the communities throughout the country, was characterized by communal ceremonies (*zhai*, "fasting sessions," and *chu*, "banquets") held by groups of Daoist families under the guidance of the local master, both on fixed dates and on special occasions. The purpose of such meetings was to collectively eliminate sins (evil deeds being considered as the main cause of sickness and premature death) through incantations, deafening music, fasting, and by displaying penance and remorse. The gatherings sometimes lasted several days and nights, and, according to the indignant reports of their Buddhist adversaries, they were ecstatic and sometimes even orgiastic. The allegation of sexual excesses and promiscuity may have been stimulated by the fact that both men and women took part in Daoist meetings, a practice unknown in Confucian and Buddhist ritual.

The Daoist community as an organization and the *daoshi* who led it relied on two sources of income: the gifts made by devotee families at ceremonial gatherings and the regular "heavenly tax," or yearly contribution of five bushels of rice, which every family was expected to pay on the seventh day of the seventh month. The office of *daoshi* was hereditary, within one family; in the early centuries

Daoist priests usually married. Because Buddhist influence also increased at this humble level, however, the *daoshi* increasingly came to resemble the Buddhist clergy, especially since most Daoist priests, at least from the 5th century onward, went to live in Daoist monasteries with their wives and children. In the 6th century, when Buddhism became paramount, some Daoist leaders introduced celibacy; in Sui times the unmarried state had become general, and the Daoist clergy with its monks and nuns had evolved into a counterpart of the Buddhist *sangha*. Unlike Buddhist monasteries, the Daoist monasteries and clergy never developed great economic power.

In spite of their resemblance to each other—or perhaps because of it—the two creeds were bitterly opposed throughout the period. Daoist masters were often involved in anti-Buddhist propaganda and persecution. As an answer to Buddhist claims of superiority, Daoist masters even developed the curious theory that the Buddha had been only a manifestation of Laozi, who had preached to the Indians a debased form of Daoism, which naturally should not be reintroduced into China; this theme can be traced in Buddhist and Daoist polemic literature from the 4th to the 13th century.

BUDDHISM

The Buddhist age of China began in the 4th century. Several factors contributed to the extraordinary expansion and absorption of the foreign religion after about 300, both in the Chinese south and in the occupied north. A negative factor was the absence of a unified Confucian state, which naturally would have been inclined to suppress a creed whose basic tenets (notably, the monastic life and the pursuit of individual salvation outside family and society) were clearly opposed to the ideals of Confucianism. The popularity of Xuanxue was a positive and powerful factor. Especially in the south, Mahayana Buddhism, thoroughly amalgamated with Xuanxue, was preached by cultured monks in the circles of the Jiankang aristocracy, where it became extremely popular.

Another stimulus for the growth of Buddhism was the relative security and prosperity of monastic life. In a countryside devastated by war and rebellion, innumerable small peasants preferred to give up their independence and to avoid the scourges of heavy taxation, forced labour, and deportation by joining the large estates of the nobility as serfs, where they would get at least a minimum of protection. This process of tax evasion that consequently extended the manorial system also stimulated the growth of Buddhist monasteries as landowning institutions, peopled with both monks and families of hereditary temple serfs. By the beginning of the 6th century, the monasteries had become an economic power of the first order, which, moreover, enjoyed special privileges (e.g., exemption from taxes). This, indeed, became a main source of tension

These giant Buddhist sculptures are located at Longmen Grottoes in the outskirts of Luoyang, Henan province. The site features more than 110,000 Buddhist images and 2,800 inscribed tablets. China Photos/Getty Images

between clergy and government and occasionally led to anti-Buddhist movements and harsh restrictive measures imposed on Buddhism (446–452 and again in 574–578).

The monastic life attracted many members of the gentry as well. In these times of turmoil, the official career was beset with dangers, and the monastery offered a hiding place to literati who tried to keep clear of the intrigues and feuds of higher official circles; thus, the ancient Chinese ideal of the retired scholar merged with the new Buddhist ideal of the monastic life. Many large monasteries thereby became centres of learning and culture and so became even more attractive to members of minor gentry families, for whom the higher posts in government in any event would be unattainable. Buddhist institutions offered a kind of "internal democracy"—a fact of great social importance in the history of class-ridden medieval China.

Finally, Buddhism was patronized by most of the barbarian rulers in the north.

At first they were attracted mainly by the pomp and magical power of Buddhist ritual. Later other motivations were added to this. Unwilling to rely too much on Chinese ministers, with their following of clan members and clients, they preferred to make use of Buddhist masters, who as unmarried individuals totally depended on the ruler's favour. Ideologically, Buddhism was less "Chinese" than Confucianism, especially in the north, where the connections with Central Asia constantly reinforced its international and universalistic character. This peculiar "Sino-barbarian" nature of northern Buddhism, with its foreign preachers and its huge translation projects, strongly contrasts with the south, where Buddhism in the 4th century was already fully domesticated.

Because of all these circumstances, the large-scale development of Chinese Buddhism started only after the barbarian invasions of the early 4th century. In the 3rd century the picture basically was not any different from Han times—there are indications that Buddhism was still largely a religion of foreigners on Chinese soil (apart from some activity involving the translation of Buddhist scriptures)— but by the 4th century the situation was changing. At the southern Chinese court in Jiankang a clerical elite was forming of Chinese monks and propagators of a completely Sinicized Buddhism, strongly amalgamated with Xuanxue, and their sophisticated creed was being spread among the southern gentry. Starting at Jiankang and in northern Zhejiang (the Hangzhou region), this trend was further developed in the late 4th and the early 5th century in other centres throughout the middle and lower Yangtze basin. The highest flowering of this uniquely "Chinese" type of Buddhism took place in the early 5th century.

In the north the climax of Buddhist activity and imperial patronage occurred under the Wei, especially after the beginning of their policy of conscious Sinicization. The Tuoba court and the great families vied with each other in building temples and granting land and money to the monasteries; the monumental cave temples at Yungang and Longmen are lasting proof of this large-scale imperial protection. There was also a dark side: in the north the Buddhist clergy became closely tied with secular government, and the government's lavish treatment of the temples was counterbalanced by repeated attempts at government control. It may also be noted that the north remained open to influences brought by traveling monks from Central Asia, and an enormous body of Indian Buddhist texts of all schools and eras was translated.

Little is known of the beginnings of popular Buddhism. Among the masses there was, to judge from Daoist materials, an intense mingling of Buddhist and popular Daoist notions and practices, such as communal festivals and the worship of local Daoist and Buddhist saints. At that level, simple devotionalism was no doubt far more influential than the scriptural teachings. It is also possible that the oral recital of Buddhist scriptures (mainly edifying tales) had already inspired the development of vernacular literature. In any event, the constant amalgamation of Buddhism, Daoism, and the innumerable local cults whose history dated to high antiquity continued for centuries, eventually producing an amorphous mass of creeds and practices collectively known as Chinese popular religion.

THE SUI DYNASTY

The Sui dynasty (581–618), which reunified China after nearly four centuries of political fragmentation during which the north and south had developed in different ways, played a part far more important than its short span would suggest. In the same way that the Qin rulers of the 3rd century BC had unified China after the Zhanguo (Warring States) period, so the Sui brought China together again and set up many institutions that were to be adopted by their successors, the Tang. Like the Qin, however, the Sui overstrained their resources and fell. And also as in the case of the Qin, traditional history has judged the Sui somewhat unfairly, stressing the harshness of the Sui regime and the megalomania of its second emperor and giving too little credit for its many positive achievements.

Wendi (reigned 581–604), the founder of the Sui dynasty, was a high-ranking official at the Bei (Northern) Zhou court, a member of one of the powerful northwestern aristocratic families that had taken service under the successive non-Chinese royal houses in northern China and had intermarried with the families of their foreign masters. In 577 the Bei Zhou had reunified northern China by conquering the rival northeastern dynasty of Bei Qi. However, political life in the northern courts was extremely unstable, and the succession of an apparently deranged and irresponsible young emperor to the Zhou throne in 578/579 set off a train of court intrigues, plots, and murders. Wendi was able to install a child as puppet emperor in 579 and seize the throne for himself two years later.

In control of all of northern China and in command of formidable armies, he immediately set about establishing order within his frontiers. He built himself a grand new capital, Daxing, close to the site of the old Qin and Han capitals, a city erected quickly with a prodigal use of compulsory labour. This great city remained (later under the name Chang'an) the capital of the Sui and Tang dynasties and the principal seat of government until the beginning of the 10th century.

Wendi also took quick action to protect the frontiers of his new state. China during the 6th century had a formidable northern neighbour in the Turks (Tujue), who controlled the steppe from the borders of Manchuria to the frontiers of the Byzantine and Sāsānian empires. At the time of Wendi's seizure of power, the Turks were splitting into two great empires, an eastern one dominating the Chinese northern frontier from Manchuria to Gansu and a western one stretching in a vast arc north of the Tarim Basin into Central Asia. Wendi encouraged this split by supporting the khan (ruler) of the western Turks, Tardu. Throughout his reign Wendi also pursued a policy of encouraging factional strife among the eastern Turks. At the same time, he strengthened his defenses in the north by repairing the Great Wall. In the northwest in the area around the Koko Nor (Qinghai Hu; "Blue Lake"), he defeated the Tuyuhun people, who from time to time raided the border territories.

By the late 580s Wendi's state was stable and secure enough for him to take the final step toward reunifying the whole country. In 587 he dethroned the emperor of the Hou (Later) Liang, the state that had ruled the middle Yangtze valley as a puppet of the Bei Zhou since 555. In 589 he overwhelmed the last southern dynasty, the Chen, which had put up only token resistance. Several rebellions against the Sui regime subsequently broke out in the south, but these were easily quelled. Wendi now ruled over a firmly reunited empire.

WENDI'S INSTITUTIONAL REFORMS

Wendi achieved much more than strengthening and reunifying the empire. He provided it with uniform institutions and established a pattern of government that survived into the Tang dynasty and beyond. A hardworking administrator, he employed a number of extremely able ministers who combined skill in practical statecraft with a flexible approach to ideological problems. They revived the Confucian state rituals to win favour with the literati and to establish a link with the empire of the Han, and, at the same time, they fostered Buddhism, the dominant religion of the south, attempting to establish the emperor's image as an ideal Buddhist saint-king.

Wendi's lasting success, however, was in practical politics and institutional reforms. In the last days of the Bei Zhou, he had been responsible for a revision of the laws, and one of his first acts on becoming emperor was to promulgate a penal code, the New Code of 581. In 583 his ministers compiled a revised code, the Kaihuang code, and administrative statutes. These were far simpler than the laws of the Bei Zhou and were more lenient. Considerable pains were taken to ensure that local officials studied and enforced the new laws. Toward the end of Wendi's reign, when neo-Legalist political advisers gained ascendancy at court, the application of the laws became increasingly strict. The Kaihuang code and statutes have not survived, but they provided the pattern for the Tang code, the most influential body of law in the history of East Asia.

The central government under Wendi developed into a complex apparatus of ministries, boards, courts, and directorates.

The conduct of its personnel was supervised by another organ, the censorate. The emperor presided over this apparatus, and all orders and legislation were issued in his name. He was assisted by the heads of the three central ministries who acted as counselors on state affairs (*yiguozheng*). That system later provided the basic framework for the central government of the early Tang.

Even more important, he carried out a sweeping reform and rationalization of local government. The three-level system of local administration inherited from Han times had been reduced to chaos during the 5th and 6th centuries by excessive subdivision; there were innumerable local districts, some of them extremely small and dominated by single families. Wendi created a simplified structure in which a much reduced number of counties was directly subordinated to prefectures. He also rationalized the chaotic rural administrative units into a uniform system of townships (*xiang*). Appointments to the chief offices in prefectures and counties were now made by the central government rather than filled by members of local influential families, as had been the practice. This reform ensured that local officials would be agents of the central government. It also integrated local officials into the normal pattern of bureaucratic promotion and in time produced a more homogeneous civil service.

Since the registration of population had fallen into chaos under the Bei Zhou, a careful new census was carried out during the 580s. It recorded the age, status, and landed possessions of all the members of each household in the empire, and, based on it, the land allocation system employed under the successive northern dynasties since the end of the 5th century was reimposed. The tax system also followed the old model of head taxes levied in grain and silk at a uniform rate. The taxable age was raised, and the annual period of labour service to which all taxpayers were liable was reduced.

Wendi's government, in spite of his frontier campaigns and vast construction works, was economical and frugal. By the 590s he had accumulated great reserves, and, when the Chen territories were incorporated into his empire, he was in a position to exempt the new population from 10 years of taxes to help ensure their loyalty.

The military system likewise was founded on that of the northern dynasties, in which the imperial forces were organized into militias. The soldiers served regular annual turns of duty but lived at home during the rest of the year and were largely self-supporting. Many troops were settled in military colonies on the frontiers to make the garrisons self-sufficient. Only when there was a campaign did the costs of the military establishment soar.

INTEGRATION OF THE SOUTH

The second Sui emperor, Yangdi (reigned 604–617/618), has been depicted as a supreme example of arrogance, extravagance, and personal depravity who squandered his patrimony in megalomaniac construction projects and unwise military adventures. This mythical Yangdi was to a large extent the product of the hostile record written of his reign shortly after his death. His reign began well enough, continuing the trends begun under Wendi; a further revision of the law code that generally reduced penalties was carried out in 607.

Yangdi's principal achievement was the integration of the south more firmly into a unified China. There is little evidence that the south was ever completely brought into line with all the administrative practices of the north; the land allocation system seems unlikely to have been enforced there, and it is probable that the registration of the population, the essential foundation for the whole fiscal and military system, was only incompletely carried out in the old Chen territories. However, Yangdi himself was personally heavily involved with the south. Married to a princess from the southern state of Liang, he had spent 591–600 as viceroy for the southern territories; their successful integration into the Sui empire after the initial wave of risings was largely because of his administration and the generally clement policies employed in the former Chen territories.

His identification with the southern interest was one of the reasons he began establishing an examination system, based upon the Confucian Classical curriculum, as a means of drawing into the bureaucracy scholars from the southern and northeastern elites who had preserved traditions of Confucian learning. Hitherto, the court had been dominated by the generally less cultivated aristocratic families of mixed ancestry from northwestern China.

Yangdi also attempted to weaken the predominance of the northwest by building a second great capital city at Luoyang, on the border of the eastern plains. This capital was not only distant from the home territories of the northwestern aristocrats but also easily provisioned from the rich farmlands of Hebei and Henan. The new city was constructed in a great hurry, employing vast numbers of labourers both in building and in transporting the timber and other materials required. Yangdi also built new palaces and an immense imperial park, again with a prodigal use of labour.

Another grandiose plan aimed at unifying the empire was to develop still further the canal system his father had begun in the metropolitan region and to construct a great waterway, the Bian Canal, linking Luoyang with the Huai River and with the southern capital, Jiangdu (present-day Yangzhou), on the Yangtze. Much of this route followed existing rivers and ancient canals, but it was still an immense undertaking that employed masses of forced labourers working under appalling conditions.

In 605 the canal system was opened between the capital at Luoyang and the

Traditional housing in Wuzhen township, Tongxiang city, Zhejiang province. Wuzhen is a picturesque town on the Grand Canal with a history dating back more than 1,300 years. China Photos/Getty Images

Yangtze, and in 610 it was extended south of the Yangtze to Hangzhou as part of a general effort to rehabilitate and lengthen the Grand Canal. At the same time, in preparation for campaigns in Manchuria and on the Korean frontier, another great canal was built northward from Luoyang to the vicinity of modern Beijing. By 611 the entire eastern plain had a canal system linking the major river systems of northern China and providing a trunk route from the Yangtze delta to the northern frontier. The construction of these waterways was inordinately expensive, caused terrible suffering, and left a legacy of widespread social unrest, but in the long term the transportation system was to be a most important factor for maintaining a unified empire. Further hardship was caused by the mass levies of labour required to rebuild and strengthen the Great Wall in Shanxi in 607 and 608 as a precaution against the resurgent eastern Turks.

FOREIGN AFFAIRS UNDER YANGDI

In addition to these farsighted construction works, Yangdi also pursued an active foreign policy. An expedition to the south established sovereignty over the old Chinese settlement in Tongking and over the Champa state of Lin-yi in central Nam Viet (present-day Vietnam). Several expeditions were sent to Taiwan, and relations with Japan were opened. Tuyuhun people were driven out of Gansu and Qinghai, and Sui colonies were established along the great western trade routes. The rulers of the various petty local states of Central Asia and the king of Gaochang (Turfan) became tributaries. A prosperous trade with Central Asia and the West emerged.

The principal foreign threat was still posed by the Turks. By the early 7th century, these peoples had been completely split into the eastern Turks, who occupied most of the Chinese northern frontier, and the immensely powerful western Turks, whose dominions stretched westward to the north of the Tarim Basin as far as Sāsānian Persia and Afghanistan. During the early part of Yangdi's reign, the western Turks, whose ruler, Chuluo, was half-Chinese, were on good terms with the Sui. In 610, however, Yangdi supported a rival, Shegui, who drove out Chuluo. The latter took service, with an army of 10,000 followers, at Yangdi's court. When Sui power began to wane after 612, the western Turks under Shegui gradually replaced the Sui garrisons in Central Asia and established control over the states of the Tarim Basin. The eastern Turks had remained on good terms with the Sui, their khans being married to Chinese princesses. In 613 Pei Ju, Yangdi's principal agent in dealing with the foreign states of the north, attempted unsuccessfully to dethrone the eastern Turkish khan and split up his khanate. Relations with the Turks rapidly deteriorated, and in the last years of his reign Yangdi had to contend with a hostile and extremely powerful neighbour.

His most costly venture was a series of campaigns in Korea. At that time Korea was divided into three kingdoms, of which the northern one, Koguryŏ, was the most important and powerful. It was hostile to the Chinese and refused to pay homage to Yangdi. Yangdi made careful preparations for a punitive campaign on a grand scale, including construction of the Yongjiqu Canal from Luoyang to Beijing. In 611 the canal was completed; a great army and masses of supplies were collected, but terrible floods in Hebei delayed the campaign.

During 612, 613, and 614 Yangdi campaigned against the Koreans. The first two campaigns were unsuccessful and were accompanied by the outbreak of many minor rebellions in Shandong and southern Hebei. The severe repression that followed led to outbreaks of disorder throughout the empire. In 614 yet another army was sent into Korea and threatened the capital at P'yŏngyang, but it had to withdraw without a decisive victory. These futile campaigns distracted Yangdi's attention from the increasingly vital internal problems of his empire, involved an immense loss of life and matériel, and caused terrible hardships among the civilian population. They left the Sui demoralized, militarily crippled, and financially ruined.

At that point, Yangdi decided to secure his relations with his northern neighbours. His envoy, Pei Ju, had continued to intrigue against the eastern Turkish khan, in spite of the fact that the Sui were no longer in a position of strength. When in the summer of 615 Yangdi went to inspect the defenses of the Great Wall, he was surrounded and besieged by the Turks at Yanmen; he was rescued only after a month of peril.

Rebellions and uprisings soon broke out in every region of the empire. Late in 616 Yangdi decided to withdraw to his southern capital of Jiangdu, and much of northern China was divided among rebel regimes contending with one another for the succession to the empire. Yangdi remained nominally emperor until the spring of 618, when he was murdered by members of his entourage at Jiangdu. However, by 617 the real powers in China had become the various local rebels: Li Mi in the area around Luoyang, Dou Jiande in the northeast, Xue Ju in the far northwest, and Li Yuan (who remained nominally loyal but had established a local position of great power) in Shanxi. At the beginning of 617, Li Yuan inflicted a great defeat on the eastern Turks and thus consolidated his local power in the impregnable mountainous area around Taiyuan. In the summer of 617 he raised an army and marched on the capital with the aid of the Turks and other local forces; Chang'an fell at year's end. Xue Ju's northwestern rebels were crushed, and the armies of Li Yuan occupied Sichuan and the Han River valley. A Sui prince, Gongdi, was enthroned as "emperor" in 617, while Yangdi was designated "retired emperor." In the summer of 618, after Yangdi's death, Li Yuan (known by his temple name, Gaozu) deposed his puppet prince and proclaimed himself emperor of a new dynasty, the Tang, which was to remain in power for nearly three centuries.

CHAPTER 5

THE TANG DYNASTY

EARLY TANG (618–626)

When Gaozu became emperor (reigned 618–626), he was still only one among the contenders for control of the empire of the Sui. It was several years before the empire was entirely pacified. After the suppression of Xue Ju and the pacification of the northwest, the Tang had to contend with four principal rival forces: the Sui remnants commanded by Wang Shichong at Luoyang, the rebel Li Mi in Henan, the rebel Dou Jiande in Hebei, and Yuwen Huaji, who had assassinated the previous Sui emperor Yangdi and now led the remnants of the Sui's southern armies. Wang Shichong set up a grandson of Yangdi at Luoyang as the new Sui emperor. Yuwen Huaji led his armies to attack Luoyang, and Wang Shichong persuaded Li Mi to return to his allegiance with the Sui and help him fight Yuwen Huaji. Li Mi defeated Yuwen Huaji's armies but seriously depleted his own forces. Wang Shichong, seeing the chance to dispose of his most immediate rival, took over Luoyang and routed Li Mi's forces. Li Mi fled to Chang'an and submitted to the Tang. In the spring of 619 Wang Shichong deposed the puppet Sui prince at Luoyang and proclaimed himself emperor.

The Tang armies gradually forced him to give ground in Henan, and by 621 Gaozu's son Li Shimin was besieging him in Luoyang. At that time Wang Shichong attempted to form an alliance with Dou Jiande, the most powerful of all

Ceramic tomb figure decorated in characteristic coloured glazes, Tang dynasty (618–907); in the Victoria and Albert Museum, London. Height 71 cm. Courtesy of the Victoria and Albert Museum, London

the Sui rebels, who controlled much of Hebei and who had completed the defeat of Yuwen Huaji's forces in 619. He held the key area of southern Hebei, where he had successfully resisted both the Tang armies and the forces of Wang and Li Shimin. Dou now agreed to come to the aid of the beleaguered Wang, but in the spring of 621 Li Shimin attacked his army before it could lift the siege, routed it, and captured Dou. Wang then capitulated. The Tang had thus disposed of its two most powerful rivals and extended its control over most of the eastern plain, the most populous and prosperous region of China.

This was not the end of resistance to the Tang conquest. Most of the surrendered rebel forces had been treated leniently, and their leaders were often confirmed in office or given posts in the Tang administration. Dou and Wang, however, were dealt with severely, Dou being executed and Wang murdered on his way into exile. At the end of 621 Dou's partisans in the northeast again rebelled under Liu Heita and recaptured most of the northeast. He was finally defeated by a Tang army under the crown prince Jiancheng at the beginning of 623. The prolonged resistance in Hebei and the comparatively harsh Tang conquest of the region were the beginning of resistance and hostility in the northeast that continued to some degree throughout the Tang dynasty.

Resistance was not confined to the northeast. Liu Wuzhou in far northern Shanxi, who had been a constant threat since 619, was finally defeated and killed by his former Turkish allies in 622. In the south during the confusion at the end of the Sui, Xiao Xian had set himself up as emperor of Liang, controlling the central Yangtze region, Jiangxi, Guangdong, and Annam (Vietnam). The Tang army descended the Yangtze from Sichuan with a great fleet and defeated Xiao Xian's forces in two crucial naval battles. In 621 Xiao Xian surrendered to the Tang, who thus gained control of the central Yangtze and the far south. The southeast was occupied by another rebel, Li Zitong, based in Zhejiang. He too was decisively defeated near present-day Nanjing at the end of 621. As had been the case with Xiao Xian's dominions, the southeast was incorporated into the Tang empire with a minimum of fighting and resistance. A last southern rebellion by Fu Gongtuo, a general who set up an independent regime at Danyang (Nanjing) in 624, was speedily suppressed. After a decade of war and disorder, the empire was completely pacified and unified under the Tang house.

ADMINISTRATION OF THE STATE

The Tang unification had been far more prolonged and bloody than the Sui conquest. That the Tang regime lasted for nearly three centuries rather than three decades, as with the Sui, was largely the result of the system of government imposed on the conquered territories. The emperor Gaozu's role in the Tang conquest was understated in the traditional histories compiled under his successor Taizong (Li Shimin; reigned 626–649), which portrayed Taizong as the prime mover in the establishment of the dynasty. Taizong certainly played a major role in the campaigns, but Gaozu was no figurehead. Not only did he direct the many complex military operations, but he also established the basic institutions of the Tang state, which proved practicable not only for a rapidly developing Chinese society but also for the first centralized states in societies as diverse as those of Japan, Korea,

Vietnam, and the southwestern kingdom of Nanzhao.

The structure of the new central administration resembled that of Wendi's time, with its ministries, boards, courts, and directorates. There was no radical change in the dominant group at court. Most of the highest ranks in the bureaucracy were filled by former Sui officials, many of whom had been the new emperor's colleagues when he was governor in Taiyuan, or by descendants of officials of the Bei Zhou, Bei Qi, or Sui or of the royal houses of the northern and southern dynasties. The Tang were related by marriage to the Sui royal house, and a majority of the chief ministers were related by marriage to either the Tang or Sui imperial family. The emperor's court was composed primarily of men of similar social origins. At that level the Tang in its early years, like the Sui before it, continued the pattern of predominantly aristocratic rule that had dominated the history of the northern courts.

Gaozu also continued the pattern of local administration established under the Sui and maintained the strict control exercised by the central government over provincial appointments. In the first years after the Tang conquest, many prefectures and counties were fragmented to provide offices for surrendered rebel leaders, surrendered Sui officials, and followers of the emperor. But these new local districts were gradually amalgamated and reduced in number, and by the 630s the pattern of local administration closely resembled that under the Sui. The merging of the local officials into the main bureaucracy, however, took time; ambitious men still looked upon local posts as "exile" from the main current of official promotion at the capital. Until well into the 8th century many local officials continued to serve for long terms, and the ideal of a regular circulation of officials prevailed only gradually.

Local government in early Tang times had a considerable degree of independence, but each prefecture was in direct contact with the central ministries. In the spheres of activity that the administration regarded as crucial—registration, land allocation, tax collection, conscription of men for the army and for corvée duty, and maintenance of law and order—prefects and county magistrates were expected to follow centrally codified law and procedure. They were, however, permitted to interpret the law to suit local conditions. Local influences remained strong in the prefectures and counties. Most of the personnel in these divisions were local men, many of them members of families of petty functionaries.

FISCAL AND LEGAL SYSTEM

Gaozu had inherited a bankrupt state, and most of his measures were aimed at simple and cheap administration. His bureaucracy was small, at both the central and local levels. The expenses of government were largely met by land endowments attached to each office, the rents from which paid office expenses and salaries, by interest on funds of money allocated for similar purposes, and by services of taxpayers who performed many of the routine tasks of government as special duties, being exempted from tax in return.

Land distribution followed the equal-allocation system used under the northern dynasties and the Sui. Every taxable male was entitled to a grant of land—part of which was to be returned when he ceased to be a taxpayer at age 60 and part of which was hereditary. The disposal of landed property was hedged around with restrictive conditions. Great landed estates were limited to members of the imperial clan and powerful officials, various state institutions, and the Buddhist foundations. Although some land was hereditary, and more and more passed into the hereditary category with the passage of time, the lack of primogeniture meant that landholdings were fragmented among all the sons in each generation and thus tended to be small. It is unlikely that the system was ever enforced to the letter in any region, and it was probably never enforced at all in the south. But as a legal system governing registration of landed property and restricting its disposal, it remained in force until An Lushan's rebellion in the 8th century.

The tax system based on this land allocation system was also much the same as that under the Sui and preceding dynasties. Every adult male annually paid a head tax in grain and cloth and was liable to 20 days of work for the central government (normally commuted into a payment in cloth) and to a further period of work for the local authorities. Revenues were collected exclusively from the rural population—the trade sector and the urban communities being exempt—and the system bore more heavily on the poor, since it ignored the taxpayer's economic status.

The Sui had made a somewhat desultory attempt to provide China with a unified coinage. Gaozu set up mints and began the production of a good copper currency that remained standard throughout the Tang era. But cash was in short supply during most of the 7th century and had to be supplemented by standard-sized lengths of silk. Counterfeiting was rife, particularly in the Yangtze valley, where the southern dynasties had supported a more highly monetized economy and where the governments had exploited commerce as a source of revenue.

Gaozu also undertook a new codification of all centralized law, completed in 624. It comprised a code that embodied what were considered basic, unchanging normative rules, prescribing fixed penalties for defined offenses; statutes, comprising the general body of universally applicable administrative law; regulations, or codified legislation supplementary to the code and statutes; and ordinances, detailed procedural laws supplementing the statutes and issued by the departments of the central ministries. Under the early Tang this body of codified law was revised every 20 years or so. The systematic effort to maintain a universally applicable codification of law and administrative practice was essential to the uniform system of administration that the Tang succeeded in imposing throughout its diverse empire. The Tang code proved remarkably durable: it was still considered authoritative as late as the 14th century and was used as a model by the Ming. It was also adopted, with appropriate modifications, in Japan in the early 8th century and by the Koreans and the Vietnamese at a much later date.

Gaozu thus laid down, at the outset of the 7th century, institutions that survived until the mid-8th century. These provided strong central control, a high level of administrative standardization, and highly economical administration.

THE PERIOD OF TANG POWER (626–755)

Two of Gaozu's sons were rivals for the succession: the crown prince Jiancheng and Li Shimin, the general who had played a large part in the wars of unification. Their rivalry, and the factional strife it generated, reached a peak in 625–626, when it appeared that Jiancheng was likely to succeed. In a military coup, Li Shimin murdered Jiancheng and another of his brothers and forced his father to abdicate in his favour. He succeeded to the throne in 626 and is known by his temple name, Taizong.

THE "ERA OF GOOD GOVERNMENT"

The reign of Taizong (626–649), known traditionally as the "era of good government of Zhenguan," was not notable for innovations in administration. Generally, his policies developed and refined those of his father's reign. The distinctive element was the atmosphere of his administration and the close personal interplay between the sovereign and his unusually able team of Confucian advisers. It approached the Confucian ideal of a strong, able, energetic, yet fundamentally moral king seeking and accepting the advice of wise and capable ministers, advice that was basically ethical rather than technical. Some important changes in political organization were begun during his reign and were continued throughout the 7th century. The court remained almost exclusively the domain of men of aristocratic birth. But Taizong attempted to balance the regional groups among the aristocracy so as to prevent any single region from becoming dominant. They comprised the Guanlong group from the northwest, the Daibei group from Shanxi, the Shandong group from Hebei, and the southern group from the Yangtze valley. The most powerful Hebei clans were excluded from high office, but Taizong employed members of each of the other groups and of the lesser

Taizong, detail of a portrait; in the National Palace Museum, Taipei. Courtesy of the National Palace Museum, Taipei, Taiwan, Republic of China

northeastern aristocracy in high administrative offices as well as in his consultative group of scholars.

A second change was the use of the examination system on a large scale. The Sui examinations had already been reestablished under Gaozu, who had also revived the Sui system of high-level schools at the capital. Under Taizong the schools were further expanded and new ones established. Measures were taken to standardize their curriculum, notably completing an official orthodox edition of the Classics with a standard commentary in 638. The schools at the capital were mostly restricted to the sons of the nobility and of high-ranking officials. Other examination candidates, however, came from the local schools. The examinations were in principle open to all, but they provided relatively few new entrants to the bureaucracy. Most officials still entered service by other means—hereditary privilege as sons of officials of the upper ranks or promotion from the clerical service or the guards. The examinations demanded a high level of education in the traditional curriculum and were largely used as an alternative method of entry by younger sons of the aristocracy and by members of lesser families with a scholar-official background. Moreover, personal recommendation, lobbying examiners, and often a personal interview by the emperor played a large part. Even in late Tang times, not more than 10 percent of officials were recruited by the examinations. The main effect of the examination system in Tang times was to bring into being a highly educated court elite within the bureaucracy, to give members of locally prominent clans access to the upper levels of the bureaucracy, and in the long term to break the monopoly of political power held by the upper aristocracy. Employing persons dependent for their position on the emperor and the dynasty, rather than on birth and social standing, made it possible for the Tang emperors to establish their own power and independence.

In the early years there was a great debate as to whether the Tang ought to reintroduce the feudal system used under the Zhou and the Han, by which authority was delegated to members of the imperial clan and powerful officials and generals who were enfeoffed with hereditary territorial jurisdictions. Taizong eventually settled on a centralized form of government through prefectures and counties staffed by members of a unified bureaucracy. The Tang retained a nobility, but its "fiefs of maintenance" were merely lands whose revenues were earmarked for its use and gave it no territorial authority.

Taizong continued his father's economic policies, and government remained comparatively simple and cheap. He attempted to cut down the bureaucratic establishment at the capital and drastically reduced the number of local government divisions. The country was divided into 10 provinces, which were not permanent administrative units but "circuits" for occasional regional inspections of the local administrations; these tours were carried out by special commissioners, often members of the censorate, sent out from the capital. This gave the central government an additional means of maintaining standardized and efficient local administration. Measures to ensure tax relief for areas stricken by natural disasters, and the establishment of relief granaries to provide adequate reserves against famine, helped to ensure the prosperity of the countryside. Taizong's reign was a period of low prices and general prosperity.

Taizong was also successful in his foreign policy. In 630 the eastern Turks were split by dissension among their leadership and by the rebellion of their subject peoples. Chinese forces invaded their territories, totally defeated them, and captured their khan, and Taizong was recognized as their supreme sovereign, the "heavenly khan." A large number of the surrendered Turks were settled on the Chinese frontier, and many served in the Tang armies. A similar policy of encouraging internal dissension was later practiced against the western Turks, who split into two separate khanates for a while. In 642–643 a new khan reestablished a degree of unified control with Chinese support and agreed to become a tributary of the Chinese. To seal the alliance, Taizong married him to a Chinese princess.

The eclipse of Turkish power enabled Taizong to extend his power over the various small states of the Tarim Basin. By the late 640s a Chinese military administration had extended westward even beyond the limits of present-day Xinjiang. To the north, in the region of the Orhon River and to the north of the Ordos (Mu Us) Desert, the Tang armies defeated the Xueyantou (Syr Tardush), former vassals of the eastern Turks, who became Tang vassals in 646. The Tuyuhun in the region around Koko Nor caused considerable trouble in the early 630s. Taizong invaded their territory in 634 and defeated them, but they remained unsubdued and invaded Chinese territory several times.

The Chinese western dominions now extended farther than in the great days of the Han. Trade developed with the West, with Central Asia, and with India. The Chinese court received embassies from Sāsānian Persia and from the Byzantine Empire. The capital was thronged with foreign merchants and foreign monks and contained a variety of non-Chinese communities. The great cities had Zoroastrian, Manichaean, and Nestorian temples, along with the Buddhist monasteries that had been a part of the Chinese scene for centuries.

Taizong's only failure in foreign policy was in Korea. The northern state of Koguryŏ had sent tribute regularly, but in 642 there was an internal coup; the new ruler attacked Silla, another Tang vassal state in southern Korea. Taizong decided to invade Koguryŏ, against the advice of most of his ministers. The Tang armies, in alliance with the Khitan in Manchuria and the two southern Korean states Paekche and Silla, invaded Koguryŏ in 645 but were forced to withdraw with heavy losses. Another inconclusive campaign was waged in 647, and the end of Taizong's reign was spent in building a vast fleet and making costly preparations for a final expedition.

Taizong's last years were also marked by a decline in the firm grasp of the emperor over politics at his court. In the 640s a bitter struggle for the succession developed when it became clear that the designated heir was mentally unstable.

The court split into factions supporting various candidates. The final choice, Li Zhi, prince of Jin (reigned 649–683; temple name Gaozong) was a weak character, but he had the support of the most powerful figures at court.

RISE OF THE EMPRESS WUHOU

Gaozong was 21 years old when he ascended the throne. In his first years he was dominated by the remaining great statesmen of Taizong's court, above all by the emperor's uncle Zhangsun Wuji. However, real power soon passed from Gaozong into the hands of the empress Wuhou, one of the most remarkable women in Chinese history. Wuhou had been a low-ranking concubine of Taizong. She was taken into Gaozong's palace and, after a series of complex intrigues, managed in 655 to have the legitimate empress, Wang, deposed and herself appointed in her place. The struggle between the two was not simply a palace intrigue. Empress Wang, who was of noble descent, had the backing of the old northwestern aristocratic faction and of the great ministers surviving from Taizong's court. Wuhou came from a family of lower standing from Taiyuan. Her father had been one of Gaozu's original supporters, her mother a member of the Sui royal family. She seems to have been supported by the eastern aristocracy, by the lesser gentry, and by the lower-ranking echelons of the bureaucracy.

But her success was largely the result of her skill in intrigue, her dominant personality, and her utter ruthlessness. The deposed empress and another imperial favourite were savagely murdered, and the next half century was marked by recurrent purges in which she hounded to death one group after another of real or imagined rivals. The good relationship between the emperor and his court, which had made Taizong's reign so successful, was speedily destroyed. Political life became precarious and insecure, at the mercy of the empress's unpredictable whims. The first victims were the elder statesmen of Taizong's reign, who were exiled, murdered, or driven to suicide in 657–659. In 660 Gaozong suffered a stroke. He remained in precarious health for the rest of his reign, and Wuhou took charge of the administration.

Although utterly unscrupulous in politics, she backed up her intrigues with policies designed to consolidate her position. In 657 Luoyang was made the second capital. The entire court and administration were frequently transferred to Luoyang, thus removing the centre of political power from the home region of the northwestern aristocracy. Ministries and court offices were duplicated, and Luoyang had to be equipped with all the costly public buildings needed for a capital. After Gaozong's death, Wuhou took up permanent residence there.

Gaozong and Wuhou were obsessed by symbolism and religion, with one favourite magician, holy man, or monk following another. State rituals were radically changed. For symbolic reasons the names of all offices were altered, and the emperor took the new title of "heavenly emperor."

The bureaucracy was rapidly inflated to a far-greater size than in Taizong's time, many of the new posts being filled by candidates from the examination system who now began to attain the highest offices and thus to encroach on what had been the preserves of the aristocracy. Another blow at the aristocracy was struck by the compilation in 659 of a new genealogy of all the empire's eminent clans, which ranked families according to the official positions achieved by their members rather than by their traditional social standing. Needless to say, the first family of all was that of Wuhou. The lower ranks of the bureaucracy, among whom the empress found her most-solid support, were encouraged by the creation of new posts, greater opportunities for advancement, and salary increases.

The Chinese were engaged in foreign wars throughout Gaozong's reign. Until 657 they waged continual war against the western Turks, finally defeating them and placing their territories as far as the valley of the Amu Darya under a nominal Chinese protectorate in 659–661. The Tang also waged repeated campaigns against Koguryŏ in the late 650s and the 660s. In 668 the Tang forces took P'yŏngyang (the capital), and Koguryŏ was also placed under a protectorate. However, by 676 rebellions had forced the Chinese to withdraw to southern Manchuria, and all of Korea became increasingly dominated by the rapidly expanding power of the southern Korean state of Silla. The eastern Turks, who had been settled along the northern border, rebelled in 679–681 and were quelled only after they had caused widespread destruction and had inflicted heavy losses on the Chinese forces.

The most serious foreign threat in Gaozong's reign was the emergence of a new and powerful force to the west, the Tibetans (Tubo), a people who had exerted constant pressure on the northern border of Sichuan since the 630s. By 670 the Tibetans had driven the Tuyuhun from their homeland in the Koko Nor basin. The northwest had to be increasingly heavily fortified and garrisoned to guard against their repeated raids and incursions. After a series of difficult campaigns, they were finally checked in 679.

When Gaozong died in 683, he was succeeded by the young Zhongzong, but Wuhou was made empress dowager and immediately took control over the central administration. Within less than a year she had deposed Zhongzong, who had shown unexpected signs of independence, and replaced him with another son and puppet emperor, Ruizong, who was kept secluded in the Inner Palace while Wuhou held court and exercised the duties of sovereign.

In 684 disaffected members of the ruling class under Xu Jingye raised a serious rebellion at Yangzhou in the south, but this was speedily put down. The empress instituted a reign of terror among the members of the Tang royal family and officials, employing armies of agents and informers. Fear overshadowed the life of the court. The empress herself became more and more obsessed with religious symbolism. She manipulated Buddhist scripture to justify her becoming sovereign and in 688 erected a Ming Tang ("Hall of Light")—the symbolic supreme shrine to heaven described in the Classics—a vast building put up with limitless extravagance. In 690 the empress proclaimed that the dynasty had been changed from Tang to Zhou. She became formally the empress in her own right, the only woman sovereign in China's history. Ruizong, the imperial heir, was given her surname, Wu; everybody with the surname Wu in the empire was exempted from taxation. Every prefecture was ordered to set up a temple in which the monks were to expound the notion that the empress was an incarnation of Buddha. Luoyang became the "holy capital," and the state cult was ceremoniously transferred there from Chang'an. The remnants of the Tang royal family who had not been murdered or banished were immured in the depths of the palace.

Destructive and demoralizing as the effects of her policies must have been at the capital and at court, there is little evidence of any general deterioration of administration in the empire. By 690 the worst excesses of her regime were past. In the years after she had proclaimed herself empress, she retained the services and loyalty of a number of distinguished officials. The court was still unstable, however, with unending changes of ministers, and the empress remained susceptible to the influence of a series of worthless favourites. After 700 she gradually began to lose her grip on affairs.

The external affairs of the empire had meanwhile taken a turn for the worse. The Tibetans renewed their warfare on the frontier. In 696 the Khitan in Manchuria rebelled against their Chinese governor and overran part of Hebei. The Chinese drove them out, with Turkish aid, in 697. The Chinese reoccupied Hebei under a member of the empress's family and carried out brutal reprisals against the population. In 698 the Turks in their turn invaded Hebei and were driven off only by an army under the nominal command of the deposed emperor Zhongzong, who had been renamed heir apparent in place of Ruizong. The military crisis had forced the empress to abandon any plan to keep the succession within her own family.

The expenses of the empire made it necessary to impose new taxes. These took the form of a household levy—a graduated tax based on a property assessment on everyone from the nobility down, including the urban population—and a land levy collected on an acreage basis. These new taxes were to be assessed based on productivity or wealth, rather than a uniform per capita levy. Some tried to evade taxes by illegally subdividing their households to reduce their liabilities. There was a large-scale migration of peasant families fleeing from oppression and heavy taxation in the Hebei and Shandong area. This migration of peasants, who settled as unregistered squatters on vacant land in central and southern China and no longer paid taxes, was accelerated by the Khitan invasion in the late 690s. Attempts to stop it were ineffectual.

By 705 the empress, who was now 80 years old, had allowed control of events to slip from her fingers. The bureaucratic faction at court, tired of the excesses of her latest favourites, forced her to abdicate in favour of Zhongzong. The Tang was restored.

Zhongzong, however, also had a domineering wife, the empress Wei, who initiated a regime of utter corruption at court, openly selling offices. When the emperor died in 710, probably poisoned by her, she tried to establish herself as ruler as Wuhou had done before her. But Li Longji, the future Xuanzong, with the aid of Wuhou's formidable daughter, Taiping, and of the palace army, succeeded in restoring his father, Ruizong (the brother of Zhongzong), to the throne. The princess now attempted to dominate her brother, the emperor, and there followed a struggle for power between her and the heir apparent. In 712 Ruizong ceded the throne to Xuanzong but retained in his own hands control over the most crucial areas of government. A second coup, in 713, placed Xuanzong completely in charge and resulted in Ruizong's retirement and the princess Taiping's suicide.

Prosperity and Progress

Xuanzong's reign (712–756) was the high point of the Tang dynasty. It was an era of wealth and prosperity that was accompanied by institutional progress and a flowering of the arts. Political life was at first dominated by the bureaucrats recruited through the examination system who had staffed the central government under Wuhou. But a gradual revival of the power of the great aristocratic clans tended to polarize politics, a polarization that was sharpened by the emperor's employment of a series of aristocratic specialists who reformed the empire's finances from 720 onward, often in the teeth of bureaucratic opposition.

After 720 a large-scale re-registration of the population greatly increased the number of taxpayers and restored state control over vast numbers of unregistered families. The new household and land taxes were expanded. In the 730s

Minghuang's Journey to Shu, *ink and colour on silk hanging scroll, attributed to Li Zhaodao, Tang-dynasty style, possibly a 10th- or 11th-century copy of an 8th-century original; in the National Palace Museum, Taipei.* National Palace Museum, Taipei, Taiwan

the canal system, which had been allowed to fall into neglect under Wuhou and her successors, was repaired and reorganized so that the administration could transport large stocks of grain from the Yangtze region to the capital and to the armies on the northern frontiers. The south was at last financially integrated with the north. By the 740s the government had accumulated enormous reserves of grain and wealth. The tax and accounting systems were simplified, and taxes and labour services were reduced.

Some important institutional changes accompanied these reforms. The land registration, reorganization of transport, and coinage reform were administered by specially appointed commissions holding extraordinary powers, including the authority to recruit their own staff. These commissions were mostly headed by censors, and they and the censorate became centres of aristocratic power. The existence of these new offices reduced the influence of the regular ministries, enabling the emperor and his aristocratic advisers to circumvent the normal channels and procedures of administration.

After 736 the political dominance of the aristocracy was firmly reestablished. An aristocratic chief minister, Li Linfu, became a virtual dictator, his powers increasing as Xuanzong in his later years withdrew from active affairs into the pleasures of palace life and the study of Daoism. In the latter part of his reign, Xuanzong, who had previously strictly circumscribed the power of the palace women to avoid a recurrence of the disasters of Wuhou's time and who had also excluded members of the royal family from politics, faced a series of succession plots. In 745 he fell deeply under the influence of a new favourite, the imperial concubine Yang Guifei. In 751–752 one of her relatives, Yang Guozhong, thanks to her influence with the emperor, rapidly rose to rival Li Linfu for supreme power. After Li's death in 752 Yang Guozhong dominated the court. However, he had neither Li's great political ability nor his experience and skill in handling people.

MILITARY REORGANIZATION

The most important new development in Xuanzong's reign was the growth in the power of the military commanders. During Gaozong's reign the old militia system had proved inadequate for frontier defense and had been supplemented by the institution of permanent armies and garrison forces quartered in strategic areas on the frontiers. These armies were made up of long-service veterans, many of them non-Chinese cavalry troops, settled permanently in military colonies. Although these armies were adequate for small-scale operations, for a major campaign an expeditionary army and a headquarters staff had to be specially organized and reinforcements sent in by the central government. This cumbersome system was totally unsuitable for dealing with the highly mobile nomadic horsemen on the northern frontiers.

At the beginning of Xuanzong's reign, the Turks again threatened to become a major power, rivaling China in Central Asia and along the borders. Kapghan (Mochuo), the Turkish khan who had invaded Hebei in the aftermath of the Khitan invasion in the time of Wuhou and had attacked the Chinese northwest at the end of her reign, turned his attention northward. By 711 he controlled the steppe from the Chinese frontier to Transoxiana and appeared likely to develop a new unified Turkish empire. When he was murdered in 716, his flimsy empire collapsed. His successor, Bilge (Pijia), tried to make peace with the Chinese in 718, but Xuanzong preferred to try to destroy his power by an alliance with the southwestern Basmil Turks and with the Khitan in Manchuria. Bilge, however, crushed the Basmil and attacked Gansu in 720. Peaceful relations were established in 721–722. Bilge's death in 734 precipitated the end of Turkish power. A struggle among the various Turkish subject tribes followed, from which the Uighurs emerged as victors. In 744 they established a powerful empire that was to remain the dominant force on China's northern border until 840. Unlike the Turks, however, the Uighurs pursued a consistent policy of alliance with the Tang. On several occasions Uighur aid, even though offered on harsh terms, saved the dynasty from disaster.

The Tibetans were the most dangerous foe during Xuanzong's reign, invading the northwest annually from 714 on. In 727–729 the Chinese undertook large-scale warfare against them, and in 730 a settlement was concluded. But in the 730s

fighting broke out again, and the Tibetans began to turn their attention to the Tang territories in the Tarim Basin. Desultory fighting continued on the border of Gansu until the end of Xuanzong's reign. From 752 onward the Tibetans acquired a new ally in the Nanzhao state in Yunnan, which enabled them to exert a continuous threat along the entire western frontier.

In the face of these threats, Xuanzong organized the northern and northwestern frontiers from Manchuria to Sichuan into a series of strategic commands or military provinces under military governors who were given command over all the forces in a large region. This system developed gradually and was formalized in 737 under Li Linfu. The frontier commanders controlled enormous numbers of troops: nearly 200,000 were stationed in the northwest and Central Asia and more than 100,000 in the northeast; there were well in excess of 500,000 in all. The military governors soon began to exercise some functions of civil government. In the 740s a non-Chinese general of Sogdian and Turkish origin, An Lushan, became military governor first of one and finally of all three of the northeastern commands, with 160,000 troops under his orders. An Lushan had risen to power largely through the patronage of Li Linfu. When Li died, An became a rival of Yang Guozhong. As Yang Guozhong developed more and more of a personal stranglehold over the administration at the capital, An Lushan steadily built up his military forces in the northeast. The armed confrontation that followed nearly destroyed the dynasty.

During the 750s there was a steady reversal of Tang military fortunes. In the far west the overextended imperial armies had been defeated by the Arabs in 751 on the Talas River. In the southwest a campaign against the new state of Nanzhao had led to the almost total destruction of an army of 50,000 men. In the northeast the Chinese had lost their grip on the Manchuria-Korea border with the emergence of the new state of Parhae in place of Koguryŏ, and the Khitan and Xi peoples in Manchuria constantly caused border problems. The Tibetans in the northwest were kept in check only by an enormously expensive military presence. The principal military forces were designed essentially for frontier defense.

Thus, the end of Xuanzong's reign was a time when the state was in a highly unstable condition. The central government was dangerously dependent on a small group of men operating outside the regular institutional framework, and an overwhelming preponderance of military power was in the hands of potentially rebellious commanders on the frontiers, against whom the emperor could put into the field only a token force of his own and the troops of those commanders who remained loyal.

LATE TANG (755–907)

The rebellion of An Lushan in 755 marked the beginning of a new period. At first the rebellion had spectacular success. It swept through the northeastern province of Hebei, captured the eastern capital, Luoyang, early in 756, and took the main Tang capital, Chang'an, in July of the same year. The emperor fled to Sichuan, and on the road his consort Yang Guifei and other members of the Yang faction who had dominated his court were killed. Shortly afterward the heir apparent, who had retreated to Lingwu in the northwest, himself usurped the throne. The new emperor, Suzong (reigned 756–762), was faced with a desperately difficult military situation. The rebel armies controlled the capital and most of Hebei and Henan. In the last days of his reign, Xuanzong had divided the empire into five areas, each of which was to be the fief of one of the imperial princes. Prince Yong, who was given control of the southeast, was the only one to take up his command; during 757 he attempted to set himself up as the independent ruler of the crucially important economic heart of the empire in the Huai and Yangtze valleys but was murdered by one of his generals.

An Lushan himself was murdered by a subordinate early in 757, but the rebellion was continued, first by his son and then by one of his generals, Shi Siming, and his son Shi Chaoyi; it was not finally suppressed until 763. The rebellion had caused great destruction and hardship, particularly in Henan. The final victory was made possible partly by the employment of Uighur mercenaries, whose insatiable demands remained a drain on the treasury well into the 770s, partly by the failure of the rebel leadership after the death of the able Shi Siming, and partly by the policy of clemency adopted toward the rebels after the decisive campaign in Henan in 762. The need for a speedy settlement was made more urgent by the growing threat of the Tibetans in the northwest. The latter, allied with the Nanzhao kingdom in Yunnan, had exerted continual pressure on the western frontier and in 763 occupied the whole of present-day Gansu. Late in 763 they actually took and looted the capital. They continued to occupy the Chinese northwest until well into the 9th century. Their occupation of Gansu signaled the end of Chinese control of the region.

PROVINCIAL SEPARATISM

The post-rebellion settlement not only pardoned several of the most powerful rebel generals but also appointed them as imperial governors in command of the areas they had surrendered. Hebei was divided into four new provinces, each under surrendered rebels, while Shandong became the province of An Lushan's former garrison army from Pinglu in Manchuria, which had held an ambivalent position during the fighting. The central government held little power within these provinces. The leadership was decided within each province, and the central government in its appointments merely approved faits accomplis. Succession to the leadership was frequently hereditary. For all practical purposes, the northeastern provinces remained semi-independent throughout the later part of the Tang era. They had been among the most populous and productive parts of the empire, and their semi-independence was not only a threat to the stability of the central government but also represented a huge loss of revenue and potential manpower.

Provincial separatism also became a problem elsewhere. With the general breakdown of the machinery of central administration after 756, many of the functions of government were delegated to local administrations. The whole empire was now divided into provinces (*dao*), which formed an upper tier of routine administration. Their governors had wide powers over subordinate prefectures and counties. The new provincial governments were of two main types.

In northern China (apart from the semiautonomous provinces of the northeast, which were a special category) most provincial governments were military, their institutions closely modeled on those set up on the northern frontier under Xuanzong. The military presence was strongest in the small frontier-garrison provinces that protected the capital, Chang'an, from the Tibetans in Gansu and in the belt of small, heavily garrisoned provinces in Henan that protected China—and the canal from the Huai and Yangtze valleys, on which the central government depended for its supplies—from the semiautonomous provinces. Military governments were also the rule in Sichuan, which continued to be menaced by the Tibetans and Nanzhao, and in the far south in Lingnan.

In central and southern China, however, the provincial government developed into a new organ of the civil bureaucracy. The civil governors of the southern provinces were regularly appointed from the bureaucracy, and it became customary to appoint to these posts high-ranking court officials who were temporarily out of favour.

All the new provinces had considerable latitude of action, particularly during the reigns of Suzong and Daizong, when central power was at a low ebb. There was a general decentralization of authority. The new provinces had considerable independence in the fields of finance, local government, law and order, and military matters.

Under Daizong (reigned 762–779) the court was dominated by the emperor's favourite, Yuan Zai, and by the eunuchs who now began to play an increasing role in Tang politics. A succession of eunuch advisers not only rivaled in influence the chief ministers but even exerted influence over the military in the campaigns of the late 750s and early 760s. Under Daizong many of the regular offices of the administration remained unfilled, while the irregularities encouraged by Yuan Zai and his clique in the appointment of officials led to an increasing use of eunuchs in secretarial posts and to their increasing dominance over the emperor's private treasury.

The central government did achieve some success in finance. The old fiscal system with its taxes and labour services had been completely disrupted by the breakdown of authority and by the vast movements of population. The revenues increasingly came to depend on additional taxes levied on cultivated land or on property, and the government attempted to raise more revenue from the urban population. But its survival depended on the revenues it drew from central China, the Huai valley, and the lower Yangtze. Those revenues were sent to the capital by means of a reconstructed and improved canal system maintained out of the new government monopoly on salt. By 780 the salt monopoly was producing a major part of the state's central revenues, in addition to maintaining the transportation system. The salt and transportation administration was controlled by an independent commission centred in Yangzhou, near the mouth of the Yangtze, and this commission gradually took over the entire financial administration of southern and central China.

The weak Daizong was succeeded by a tough, intelligent activist emperor, Dezong (reigned 779–805), who was determined to restore the fortunes of the dynasty. He reconstituted much of the old central administration and decided on a showdown with the forces of local autonomy. As a first step, in 780 he promulgated a new system of taxation, under which each province was assessed a quota of taxes, the collection of which was to be left to the provincial government. This was a radical measure, for it abandoned the traditional concept of head taxes levied at a uniform rate throughout the empire and also began the assessment of taxes in terms of money.

Those in the semi-independent provinces of the northeast saw this as a threat to their independence, and, when it became apparent that Dezong was determined to carry out consistently tough policies toward the northeast—reducing their armies and even denying them the right to appoint their own governors—the Hebei provinces rebelled. From 781 to 786 there was a wave of rebellions not only in the northeastern provinces but also in the Huai valley and in the area of the capital itself. These events brought the Tang even closer to disaster than had the An Lushan rising. The situation was saved because at a crucial moment the rebels fell out among themselves and because the south remained loyal. In the end, the settlement negotiated with the governors of Hebei virtually endorsed the preceding status quo, although the court made some marginal inroads by establishing two small new provinces in Hebei.

After that disaster, Dezong pursued a much more careful and passive policy toward the provinces. Governors were left in office for long periods, and hereditary succession continued. Nonetheless, the latter part of Dezong's reign was a period of steady achievement. The new tax system was gradually enforced and proved remarkably successful; it remained the basis of the tax structure until Ming times. Revenues increased steadily, and Dezong left behind him a wealthy state. Militarily, he was also generally successful: the Tibetan threat was contained, Nanzhao was won from its alliance with the Tibetans, and the garrisons of the northwest were strengthened. At the same time, Dezong built up large new palace armies, giving the central government a powerful striking force—numbering some 100,000 men by the end of his reign. Command was given to eunuchs considered loyal to the throne. The death of Dezong in 805 was followed by the brief reign of Shunzong, an invalid monarch whose court was dominated by the clique of Wang Shuwen and Wang Pei. They planned to take control of the palace armies from the eunuchs but failed.

THE STRUGGLE FOR CENTRAL AUTHORITY

Under Xianzong (reigned 805–820) the Tang regained a great deal of its power. Xianzong, a tough and ruthless ruler who kept a firm hand on affairs, is notable chiefly for his successful policies toward the provinces. Rebellions in Sichuan (806) and the Yangtze delta (807) were quickly put down. After an abortive campaign (809–810) that was badly bungled by a favourite eunuch commander, the court was again forced to compromise with the governors of Hebei. A fresh wave of trouble came in 814–817 with a rebellion in Huaixi, in the upper Huai valley, that threatened the canal route. That uprising was crushed and the province divided up among its neighbours. The Pinglu army in Shandong rebelled in 818 and suffered the same fate. Xianzong thus restored the authority of the central government throughout most of the empire. His success was based largely upon the palace armies. The fact that these were controlled by eunuchs placed a great measure of power in the emperor's hands. Under his weak successors, however, the eunuchs' influence in politics proved a disaster.

Xianzong's restoration of central authority involved more than military dominance. It was backed by a series of institutional measures designed to strengthen the power of the prefects and county magistrates, as against their provincial governors, by restoring to them the right of direct access to central government and giving them some measure of control over the military forces quartered within their jurisdiction. In an important financial reform, the provincial government no longer had first call on all the revenue of the province, as some revenue went directly to the capital. The government also began the policy, continued throughout the 9th and 10th centuries, of cutting down and fragmenting the provinces. It strengthened its control over the provincial administrations through a system of eunuch army supervisors, who were attached to the staff of each provincial governor. These eunuchs played an increasingly important role, not merely as sources of information and intelligence but as active agents of the emperor, able to intervene directly in local affairs.

The balance of power within the central government had also been considerably changed. The emperor Dezong had begun to delegate a great deal of business, in particular the drafting of edicts and legislation, to his personal secretariat, the Hanlin Academy. Although the members of the Hanlin Academy were handpicked members of the bureaucracy, their positions as academicians were outside the regular official establishment. This eventually placed the power of decision and the detailed formulation of policy in the hands of a group that depended entirely on the emperor, thus threatening the authority of the regularly constituted ministers of the court.

The influence of the eunuchs had also begun to be formalized and institutionalized in the palace council; this provided the emperor with another personal secretariat, which controlled the conduct of official business and had close links with the eunuchs' command of the powerful palace armies. The eunuchs' influence in politics steadily increased. Xianzong was murdered by some of his eunuch attendants, and henceforth the chief eunuchs of the palace council and the palace armies were a factor in nearly every succession to the Tang throne; in some cases they had their own candidates enthroned in defiance of the previous emperor's will. The emperor Wenzong (reigned 827–840) sought to destroy the dominance of the eunuchs; his abortive schemes only demoralized the bureaucracy, particularly after the Sweet Dew (Ganlu) coup of 835, which misfired and led to the deaths of several ministers and a number of other officials. But the apogee of the eunuchs' power was brief, ending with the accession of Wuzong in 840. Wuzong and his minister, Li Deyu, managed to impose some restrictions on the eunuchs' power, especially in the military.

In the second half of the 9th century the central government became progressively weaker. During Yizong's reign (859–873) there was a resurgence of the eunuchs' power and a constant fratricidal strife between eunuchs and officials at court. From the 830s onward the first signs of unrest and banditry had appeared in the Huai valley and Henan, and trouble spread to the Yangtze valley and the south beginning in 856. Major uprisings were led by Kang Quantai in southern Anhui in 858 and Qiu Fu in Zhejiang in 859. The situation was complicated by a costly war against the Nanzhao kingdom on the borders of the Chinese protectorate in Annam, which later spread to Sichuan and dragged on from 858 until 866. After the invaders had been suppressed, part of the garrison force that had been sent to Lingnan mutinied and, under its leader, Pang Xun, fought and plundered its way back to Henan, where it caused widespread havoc in 868 and 869, cutting the canal linking the capital to the loyal Yangtze and Huai provinces. In 870 war broke out again with Nanzhao.

Yizong was succeeded by Xizong (reigned 873–888), a boy of 11 who was the choice of the palace eunuchs. Prior to his ascension, Henan had repeatedly suffered serious floods. In addition, a wave of peasant risings began in 874, following a terrible drought. The most formidable of them was led by Huang Chao, who in 878 marched south and sacked Guangzhou (Canton) and then marched to the north, where he took Luoyang in late 880 and Chang'an in 881. Although Huang Chao attempted to set up a regime in the capital, he proved cruel and inept. Hemmed in by loyal armies and provincial generals, in 883 he was forced to abandon Chang'an and withdraw to Henan and then to Shandong, where he died in 884. His forces were eventually defeated with the aid of Shatuo Turks, and the Tang court was left virtually powerless, its emperor a puppet manipulated by rival military leaders. The dynasty lingered on until 907, but the last quarter century was dominated by the generals and provincial warlords. With the progressive decline of the central government in the 880s and 890s, China fell apart into a number of virtually independent kingdoms. Unity was not restored until long after the Song dynasty was established.

CULTURAL DEVELOPMENTS

THE INFLUENCE OF BUDDHISM

The Tang emperors officially supported Daoism because of their claim to be descended from Laozi, but Buddhism continued to enjoy great favour and lavish imperial patronage through most of the period. The famous pilgrim Xuanzang, who went to India in 629 and returned in

645, was the most learned of Chinese monks and introduced new standards of exactness in his many translations from Sanskrit. The most significant development in this time was the growth of new indigenous schools that adapted Buddhism to Chinese ways of thinking. Most prominent were the syncretistic Tiantai school, which sought to embrace all other schools in a single hierarchical system (even reaching out to include Confucianism), and the radically anti-textual, antimetaphysical southern Chan

Guanyin and attendant bodhisattvas, detail of a painted mural, early 8th century, Tang dynasty, from Cave 57, Dunhuang, Gansu province, China. Chen Zhi'an/ChinaStock Photo Library

(Zen) school, which had strong roots in Daoism. The popular preaching of the salvationist Pure Land sect was also important. After the rebellion of An Lushan, a nationalistic movement favouring Confucianism appeared, merging with the efforts of Tiantai Buddhism to graft Buddhist metaphysics onto Classical doctrine and lay the groundwork for the Neo-Confucianism of the Song era.

In 843–845 the emperor Wuzong, a fanatical Daoist, proceeded to suppress Buddhism. One of his motives was economic. China was in a serious financial crisis, which Wuzong and his advisers hoped to solve by seizing the lands and wealth of the monasteries. The suppression was far-reaching: 40,000 shrines and temples—all but a select few—were closed, 260,000 monks and nuns were returned to lay life, and vast acreages of monastic lands were confiscated and sold and their slaves manumitted. The suppression was short-lived, but irreparable damage was done to Buddhist institutions. Buddhism had already begun to lose intellectual momentum, and this attack on it as a social institution marked the beginning of its decline in China.

Several types of monastic communities existed at the time. Official temples set up by the state had large endowments of land and property and large communities of monks who chose their own abbot and other officers. There were vast numbers of small village temples, shrines, and hermitages; these were often privately established, had little property, and were quite vulnerable to state policies. In addition, private temples or "merit cloisters" were established by great families, often to allow the family to donate its property and have it declared tax-exempt.

A monastic community was free of all obligations to the state. It was able to hold property without the process of division by inheritance that made the long-term preservation of individual and family fortunes almost impossible in Tang times. It acquired its wealth from those taking monastic vows, from gifts of pious laypersons, and from grants of lands by the state. The lands were worked by monastic slaves, dependent families, lay clerics who had taken partial vows but lived with their families, and tenants. Monasteries also operated oil presses and mills, and they were important credit institutions, supplying loans at interest and acting as pawnshops. They provided lodgings for travelers, operated hospitals and infirmaries, and maintained the aged. One of their most important social functions was offering primary education. The temples maintained their own

Main hall of Nanchan Temple, Mount Wutai, Shanxi province, China, AD 782 or earlier, Tang dynasty; reconstructed 1974–75. Christopher Liu/ChinaStock Photo Library

schools, training the comparatively large proportion of the male population, which, although not educated to the standards of the Confucian elite or the clergy, was nevertheless literate.

TRENDS IN THE ARTS

In literature the greatest glory of the Tang period was its poetry. By the 8th century, poets had broken away from the artificial diction and matter of the court poetry of the southern dynasties and achieved a new directness and naturalism. The reign of Xuanzong (712–756)—known as Minghuang, the Brilliant Emperor—was the time of such great figures as Li Bai, Wang Wei, and Du Fu. The rebellion of An Lushan and Du Fu's bitter experiences during it brought a new note of social awareness to his later poetry. This appears again in the work of Bai Juyi (772–846), who wrote verse in clear and simple language. Toward the end of the dynasty a new poetic form, the *ci*, in a less regular metre than the five-word and seven-word *lushi* and meant to be sung, made its appearance. The *guwen*, or "ancient style," movement grew up after the rebellion of An Lushan, seeking to replace the euphuistic *pianwen* ("parallel prose") then dominant. It was closely associated with the movement for a Confucian revival. The most prominent figures in it were Han Yu and Liu Zongyuan. At the same time came the first serious attempts to write fiction, the so-called *chuanqi*, or "tales of marvels." Many of these Tang stories later provided themes for the Chinese drama.

The patronage of the Tang emperors and the general wealth and prosperity of the period encouraged the development of the visual arts. Though few Tang buildings remain standing, contemporary descriptions give some idea of the magnificence of Tang palaces and religious edifices and the houses of the wealthy. Buddhist sculpture shows a greater naturalism than in the previous period, but

DU FU

Du Fu (b. 712–d. 770) is often considered the greatest Chinese poet of all time. After a traditional Confucian education, he failed the important civil service examinations and consequently spent much of his life wandering, repeatedly attempting to gain court positions, with mixed success. His early poetry, which celebrates the natural world and bemoans the passage of time, garnered him renown. He suffered periods of extreme personal hardship, and as he matured his verse began to express profound compassion for humanity. An expert in all the poetic genres of his day, he is renowned for his superb classicism and skill in prosody, though many of the subtleties of his art do not survive translation.

there is some loss of spirituality. Few genuine originals survive to show the work of Tang master painters such as Wu Daoxuan, who worked at Xuanzong's court. As a landscape painter, the poet Wang Wei was a forerunner of the *wenren*, or "literary man's," school of mystical nature painting of later times. The minor arts of Tang, including ceramics, metalwork, and textiles, give expression to the colour and vitality of the life of the period. Printing appeared for the first time during Tang. Apparently invented to help disseminate Buddhist scriptures, it was used by the end of the dynasty for such things as calendars, almanacs, and dictionaries.

SOCIAL CHANGE

DECLINE OF THE ARISTOCRACY

By the late Tang period a series of social changes had begun that did not reach their culmination until the 11th century. The most important of these was the change in the nature of the ruling class. Although from early Tang times the examination system had facilitated recruiting into the higher ranks of the bureaucracy of persons from lesser aristocratic families, most officials continued to come from the established elite. Social mobility increased after the An Lushan rebellion: provincial governments emerged, their staffs in many cases recruited from soldiers of lowly social origins, and specialized finance commissions

were established, a large part of their personnel often recruited from the commercial community. The contending factions of the 9th-century court also employed irregular appointments to secure posts for their clients and supporters, many of whom also came from comparatively lowly backgrounds.

Although the old aristocracy retained a grip on political power until very late in the dynasty, its exclusiveness and hierarchical pretensions were rapidly breaking down. It was finally extinguished as a separate group in the Wudai (Five Dynasties) period (907–960), when the old strongholds of aristocracy in the northeast and northwest became centres of bitter military and political struggles. The aristocratic clans that survived did so by merging into the new official-literati class; this class was based not on birth alone but on education, office holding, and the possession of landed property.

At the same time, there was a return to semiservile relationships at the base of the social pyramid. Sheer economic necessity led many peasants either to dispose of their lands and become tenants or hired labourers of rich neighbours or to become dependents of a powerful patron. Tenancy, which in early Tang times had most often been a temporary and purely economic agreement, now developed into a semipermanent contract requiring some degree of personal subordination from the tenant.

The new provincial officials and local elites were able to establish their fortunes as local landowning gentry largely because after 763 the government ceased to enforce the system of state-supervised land allocation. In the aftermath of the An Lushan and later rebellions, large areas of land were abandoned by their cultivators; other areas of farmland were sold off on the dissolution of the monastic foundations in 843–845. The landed estate managed by a bailiff and cultivated by tenants, hired hands, or slaves became a widespread feature of rural life. Possession of such estates, previously limited to the established families of the aristocracy and the serving officials, now became common at less-exalted levels.

POPULATION MOVEMENTS

Censuses taken during the Sui and Tang dynasties provide some evidence as to population changes. Surviving figures for 609 and 742, representing two of the most complete of the earlier Chinese population registrations, give totals of some 9 million households, or slightly more than 50 million persons. Contemporary officials considered that only about 70 percent of the population was actually registered, so the total population may have been as much as 70 million.

Between 609 and 742 a considerable redistribution of population took place. The population of Hebei and Henan fell by almost one-third because of the destruction suffered at the end of the Sui era and in the invasions of the 690s and because of epidemics and natural disasters. The population of Hedong (present-day Shanxi) and of Guanzhong and Longyou (present-day Shaanxi and Gansu, respectively) also fell, though not so dramatically. The population of the south, particularly the southeastern region around the lower Yangtze, took a leap upward, as did that of Sichuan.

Whereas under the Sui the population of the Great Plain (Hebei and Henan) had accounted for more than half of the empire's total, by 742 this had dropped to about one-third. The Huai-Yangtze area, which had contained only about 8 percent of the total in 609, now contained one-fourth of the entire population, and Sichuan's share jumped from 4 percent to 10 percent of the total, exceeding the population of the metropolitan province of Guanzhong. The increase in the south was almost entirely concentrated in the lower Yangtze valley and delta and in Zhejiang.

The revolt of An Lushan and Shi Siming and his son Shi Chaoyi (755–763) precipitated more population movements from north to south, with some of these migrants penetrating into what is now southern Hunan and beyond. These shifts then and later in the Tang considerably redistributed China's population: the south became more populous than the north, and the populations among regions in the south became more balanced.

There are no reliable population figures from the late Tang era, but the general movement of population toward the south certainly continued, notably in the area south of the Yangtze, in present-day Jiangxi and Hunan, and in Hubei. The chaos of the last decades of the Tang dynasty completed the ruin of the northwest. After the destruction of the city of Chang'an in the Huang Chao rebellion, no regime ever again established its capital in that region.

GROWTH OF THE ECONOMY

The 8th and 9th centuries were a period of growth and prosperity. The gradual movement of the population away from the north, with its harsh climate and dry farming, into the more fertile and productive south meant a great proportional increase in productivity. The south still had large areas of virgin land. Fujian, for example, was still only marginally settled along the coastline at the end of Tang times. During the latter half of the Tang, the Huai and lower Yangtze became a grain-surplus area, replacing Hebei and Henan. From 763 to the mid-9th century, great quantities of grain were shipped from the south annually as tax revenue. New crops, such as sugar and tea, were grown widely. The productivity of the Yangtze valley was increased by double-cropping land with rice and winter wheat and by developing new varieties of grain. After the An Lushan rebellion, silk production began to increase rapidly in Sichuan and the Yangtze delta region, whereas in early Tang times the chief silk-producing areas had been in the northeast.

A boom in trade soon followed. The merchant class threw off its traditional legal restraints. In early Tang times there had been only two great metropolitan markets, in Chang'an and Luoyang. Now every provincial capital became the centre of a large consumer population of officials and military, and the provincial courts provided a market for both staple foodstuffs and luxury manufactures. The diversification of markets was still more striking in the countryside. A network of small rural market towns, purely economic in function and acting as feeders to the county markets, grew up. At these periodic markets, held at regular intervals every few days, traveling merchants and peddlers dealt in the everyday needs of the rural population. By the end of the Tang period these rural market centres had begun to form a new sort of urban centre, intermediate between the county town, with its administrative presence and its central market, and the villages.

The growth of trade brought an increasing use of money. In early Tang times silk cloth had been commonly employed as currency in large transactions. When the central government lost control of the major silk-producing region in Hebei and Henan, silk was replaced in this use by silver. The government neither controlled silver production nor minted a silver coinage. Silver circulation and assay were in the hands of private individuals. Various credit and banking institutions began to emerge: silversmiths took money on deposit and arranged for transfers of funds; a complex system of credit transfers arose by which tea merchants would pay the tax quota for a district, sometimes even for a whole province, out of their profits from the sale of the crop at Chang'an and receive reimbursement in their home province.

The increasing use of money and silver also affected official finance and accounting. Taxes began to be assessed in money. The salt monopoly was collected and accounted for entirely in money. The government also began to look to trade as a source of revenue—to depend increasingly on taxes from commercial transactions, levies on merchants, transit taxes on merchandise, and sales taxes.

The most prosperous of the merchants were the great dealers in salt, the tea merchants from Jiangxi, the bankers of the great cities and particularly of Chang'an, and the merchants engaged in overseas trade in the coastal ports. Foreign trade was still dominated by non-Chinese merchants. Yangzhou and Guangzhou had large Arab trading communities. The northern coastal traffic was dominated by the Koreans. Overland trade to Central Asia was mostly in the hands of Sogdian and, later, Uighur merchants. Central Asian, Sogdian, and Persian merchants and peddlers carried on much local retail trade and provided restaurants, wine shops, and brothels in the great cities. Only in the 9th century did the foreign influence in trade begin to recede.

In the late Tang many officials began to invest their money (and official funds entrusted to them) in commercial activities. High officials took to running oil presses and flour mills, dealing in real estate, and providing capital for merchants. The wall between the ruling class and the merchants that had existed since the Han period was rapidly breaking down in the 9th century, and the growth of urbanization, which characterized the Song period (960–1279), had already begun on a wide scale.

CHAPTER 6

POLITICAL DISUNITY BETWEEN THE TANG AND SONG DYNASTIES

THE FIVE DYNASTIES AND THE TEN KINGDOMS

The period of political disunity between the Tang and the Song lasted little more than half a century, from 907 to 960. During that brief era, when China was truly a multistate system, five short-lived regimes succeeded one another in control of the old imperial heartland in northern China, hence the name Wudai (Five Dynasties). During those same years, 10 relatively stable regimes occupied sections of southern and western China, so the period is also referred to as that of the Shiguo (Ten Kingdoms).

Most of the major developments of that period were extensions of changes already under way during the late Tang, and many were not completed until after the founding of the Song dynasty. For example, the process of political disintegration had begun long before Zhu Wen brought the Tang dynasty to a formal end in 907. The developments that eventually led to reunification, the rapid economic and commercial growth of the period, and the decline of the aristocratic clans had also begun long before the first Song ruler, Taizu, reconquered most of the empire, and they continued during the reigns of his successors on the Song throne.

THE WUDAI (FIVE DYNASTIES)

None of the Wudai regimes that dominated northern China ever forgot the ideal of the unified empire. Each sought, with gradually increasing success, to strengthen the power of the central authorities. Even Zhu Wen, who began the Wudai by deposing the last Tang emperor in 907, sought to extend his control in the north. While consolidating his strength on the strategic plains along the Huang He (Yellow River) and connecting them with the vital transportation system of the Grand Canal, he made the significant choice of locating his base at Bian (present-day Kaifeng, in Henan); it later became the Bei (Northern) Song capital. Bian's lack of historical prestige was balanced by its proximity to the ancient capital, Luoyang, a short distance to the west, which was still China's cultural centre.

Zhu Wen's short-lived Hou (Later) Liang dynasty, founded in 907, was superseded by the Hou Tang in 923, by the Hou Jin in 936, by the Hou Han in 947, and by the Hou Zhou in 951. These rapid successions of dynasties came to an end only with the rise in 960 of the Song dynasty, which finally succeeded in establishing another lasting empire and in taking over much, though not all, of the former Tang empire.

Beneath the surface, however, were the continuous efforts to reintegrate the political process that heralded the coming of a new empire and helped to shape its political system. In this respect the successive rulers moved like a relay team along the tortuous road back to unification. These militarists expanded their personal power by recruiting peoples of relatively humble social origins to replace the aristocrats. Such recruits owed personal allegiance to their masters, on whose favours their political positions depended, thus presaging the rise of absolutism.

Rather than being discarded, the Tang administrative form underwent expedient alterations so that the new types of officials, promoted because of merit from regional posts to palace positions, could use the military administration to supervise the nearby provinces and gradually bring them under direct control. Top priority went to securing fiscal resources from the salt monopoly, tribute transport, and in particular new tax revenues, without which military domination would have been hard to sustain and political expansion impossible. Eventually, a pattern of centralizing authority emerged. Fiscal and supply officials of the successive regimes went out to supervise provincial finances and the local administration. The minor militarists, heretofore the local governors in control of their own areas, were under double pressure to submit to reintegrating measures. They faced the inducement of political accommodation, which allowed them to keep their residual power, and the military threat of palace army units commanded by special commissioners, which were sent on patrol duty into their areas. The way was thus

Huang He

The Huang He (or Huang Ho; English: Yellow River) flows through northern, central, and eastern China. The second longest river in China and one of the world's longest, it flows 3,395 miles (5,464 km) from the Plateau of Tibet generally east to the Yellow Sea (Huang Hai). It is sometimes called "The Great Sorrow" for its tendency to overflow its banks in its lower reaches, flooding vast areas of rich farmland. Its outlet has shifted over the years to enter the Yellow Sea at points as far apart as 500 miles (800 km). Irrigation and flood-control works have been maintained for centuries, and dams, begun in the mid-1950s, exploit the river's hydroelectric potential. A stronghold for the Wudai regimes, it has long played a major role in Chinese history.

The icy Huang He (Yellow River) in winter, near Hukou Waterfall, northern China. China Photos/Getty Images

paved, in spite of occasional detours and temporary setbacks, for the ultimate unification.

The seemingly chaotic period was in fact less chaotic than other rebellious times—except from the standpoint of the aristocrats, who lost their preeminent status along with their large estates, which were usually taken over piecemeal by their former managers. The aristocratic era in Chinese history was gone forever; a new bureaucratic era was about to begin.

THE SHIGUO (TEN KINGDOMS)

From the time of the Tang dynasty until the Qing dynasty, which arose in the 17th century, China consisted of two parts: the militarily strong north and the economically and culturally wealthy south. Between 907 and 960, 10 independent kingdoms emerged in China, mainly in the south: the Wu (902–937), the Nan (Southern) Tang (937–975/976), the Nan Ping (924–963), the Chu (927–951), the Qian (Former) Shu (907–925), the Hou (Later) Shu (934–965), the Min (909–945), the Bei (Northern) Han (951–979), the Nan Han (917–971), and the Wu-Yue (907–978), the last located in China's most rapidly advancing area—in and near the lower Yangtze delta.

Some of these separate regimes achieved relative internal stability, although none attained enough strength to strive to unify China. Nonetheless, the regional developments in southern China, in the upper Yangtze region in southwestern China, and in the lower Yangtze region in southeastern China were of great interest. In southern China the Min kingdom in modern Fujian and the Nan Han in present-day Guangdong and Guangxi reflected sharp cultural differences. Along the coast, sea trade expanded, promoting both urban prosperity and cultural diversity. On land, wave after wave of refugees moved southward, settling along rivers and streams and in confining plains and mountain valleys and using a frontier agriculture but with highly developed irrigation and land reclamation. Usually they pushed aside the aboriginal minorities, earlier settlers, and previous immigrant groups. This process turned southern China into a cultural chessboard of great complexity, with various subcultural pieces sandwiched between one another. Many eventually evolved along different lines.

In southwestern China the valley of what is now Sichuan presented a notably different picture of continuous growth. Usually protected from outside disturbances and invasions by the surrounding mountains, it enjoyed peace and prosperity except for one decade of instability between the Qian Shu and Hou Shu. The beautiful landscape inspired poets, who infused a refreshing vitality into old-style poetry and essays. In this region, a stronghold of Daoist religion, the people inserted into Confucian scholarship an admixture of Daoist philosophy. Buddhism also flourished. These intellectual trends in Sichuan foreshadowed an eclectic synthesis of the three major teachings—Confucianism, Daoism, and Buddhism.

The Buddhist monasteries owned large estates and were usually among the first to introduce new and better technology. Growing commerce created a demand for money. The ensuing shortage of copper for coinage was met by an increasing output of iron through more-efficient methods and an elementary division of labour in production. When the limited number of copper coins could no longer meet the growing volume of trade, iron currency briefly went into circulation. With increasing commerce, various paper credit instruments were also developed, the best-known being drafts for transmitting funds called *feiqian* ("flying money"). Somewhat later the private assay shops in Sichuan began to issue certificates of deposit to merchants who had left valuables at the shops for safekeeping. These instruments, which began to circulate, were the direct ancestors of the paper money that emerged in the early 11th century.

During the Wudai, printing became common. The most famous and monumental cultural production of the period was the editing and printing of the Confucian Classics and the Buddhist *Tipitaka*, but a printing industry also emerged during the Wudai that produced works for private buyers. The best printing in the country during the Wudai and the Song dynasty came from the regions of Sichuan and Fujian.

From the Wudai onward, southeastern China, especially its core region of the Yangtze delta, began to lead the country in both economic prosperity and cultural refinement. In this region, fertile soil, irrigation networks, and highly selected crops combined to create the best model of intensive farming. Interlocking streams, rivers, and lakes fed an ever-increasing number of markets, market towns, cities, and metropolitan areas, where many farm products were processed into an ever-expanding variety of consumer goods. Such development enhanced regional trade, stimulated other regions to adopt specialization, and promoted overseas commerce.

The Song conquerors from the north recognized the high level of cultural development in this region. After the surrender of the last Nan Tang ruler, himself a renowned poet, the unexcelled royal library was moved to the north; along with it went many officials who were skilled in art, literature, and bibliography. The surrender of the Wu-Yue kingdom, slightly farther south, followed the same pattern. Moreover, refined culture developed away from the coast in such inland mountainous areas as present-day Jiangxi, which shortly thereafter produced internationally coveted porcelain and where many great artists and scholar-officials attained positions of cultural leadership. Thereafter, southeastern China retained its cultural excellence. At the end of the Bei Song period, the Nan Song based itself in the lower Yangtze delta and located its capital at Lin-an (present-day Hangzhou), the former capital of the Wu-Yue.

As traditional histories stress, this period of disunity definitely had its dark side: militarism, wars, disintegration of the old order, and an inevitable lowering of moral standards. The dark side, however, stemmed largely from underlying changes that were transforming China into a new pattern that would last for nearly a millennium.

BARBARIAN DYNASTIES

On the frontier, the far-reaching influence of Tang culture affected various nomadic, seminomadic, and pastoral peoples. Three groups in the northern areas—the Tangut, Khitan, and Juchen—established their own regimes in the region. Respectively, these were the Xi (Western) Xia, Liao, and Jin dynasties.

The Tangut

In the northwest the Tangut (Pinyin: Dangxiang), a Tibetan-speaking branch of the Qiang, inhabited the region between the far end of the Great Wall in present-day Gansu and the Huang He bend in Inner Mongolia. Their semi-oasis economy combined irrigated agriculture with pastoralism, and, by controlling the terminus of the famous Silk Road, they became middlemen in trade between Central Asia and China. They adopted Buddhism as a state religion, in government and education followed the Tang model, and devised a written script for their own language. This richly mixed culture blossomed, as evidenced by the storing at the Dunhuang caves of an unparalleled collection of more than 30,000 religious paintings, manuscripts, and books in Chinese, Tibetan, Uighur, and other languages. In 1038 the Tangut proclaimed their own kingdom of Xi Xia, which survived for nearly two centuries with remarkable stability despite a series of on-and-off border clashes with the neighbouring states in northern China. The kingdom's end came at the hands of the Mongols, the first nomads to conquer all of China.

The Khitan

To the north at the time of the Wudai rose the seminomadic but largely pastoral Khitan, who were related to the eastern Mongols. The word *Khitan* (or *Khitai*) is the source of Cathay, the name for northern China in medieval Europe (as reported by Marco Polo), and of Kitai, the Russian name for China. The Khitan founded the Liao dynasty (907–1125) by expanding from the border of Mongolia into both southern Manchuria and the 16 prefectures south of the Great Wall. This area below the line of the Great Wall was to remain out of Chinese political control for more than 400 years. Its control by a non-Chinese state posed a dangerous security problem for the Bei (Northern)

Song. More importantly in the long run, this region acted for centuries as a centre for the mutual exchange of culture between the Chinese and the northern peoples.

The Liao made Yanjing (present-day Beijing) their southern capital, thus starting that city's history as a capital, and claimed to be the legitimate successors to the Tang. They incorporated their own tribes under respective chieftains and, with other subdued tribes in the area, formed a confederation, which they then transformed into a hereditary monarchy. Leadership always remained in the hands of the ruling tribe, the Yelü, who for the sake of stability shifted to the Chinese clan system of orderly succession.

The Liao economy was based on horse and sheep raising and on agriculture. Millet was the main crop, and salt, controlled by government monopoly, was an important source of revenue. Other commodities included iron produced by smelters. The Liao employed an effective dual system of administration to guard against the danger of being absorbed by Sinicization. They had one administration for their own people that enforced tribal laws, maintained traditional rites, and largely retained the steppe style of food and clothing. The Liao deliberately avoided the use of Chinese and added to their particular branch of the Mongolian language two types of writing—a smaller one that was alphabetical and a larger one related to Chinese characters. A second administration governed the farming region using the old Tang system, with

Tang official titles, an examination system, Chinese-style tax regulations, and the Chinese language. The laws of the second administration enforced the established way of life, including such practices as ancestral worship among the Chinese subjects. The status of Chinese subjects varied: some were free subjects who might move upward into the civil service, while others might be held in bondage and slavery.

Though honouring the Confucian philosophy, the Liao rulers patronized Chinese Buddhism. Their achievements were generally military and administrative rather than cultural, but they did provide a model for their successors, the Jin, who in turn influenced the Mongols and, through them, succeeding Chinese dynasties.

THE JUCHEN

The Liao were eventually overthrown by the Juchen (Pinyin: Nüchen), another seminomadic and semipastoral people who originated in Manchuria, swept across northern China, ended the Bei Song, and established the Jin dynasty (1115–1234). This new and much larger empire in northern China followed the Liao pattern of dual government and of some acculturation but at a much higher cultural level.

The Juchen, in establishing their Chinese-style Jin empire, occupied a broader geographic region in the farming country than had any previous nomadic or pastoral conquerors. The migration of their own people in large numbers notwithstanding, they were proportionally a smaller minority than were the Khitan, for the Jin ruled a much larger Chinese population. Because they formed a small minority in their own empire, their tribesmen were kept in a standing army that was always prepared for warfare. They were quartered among their farming subjects but were expected to respond to the command of their captains at short notice. In the military service the Juchen language was kept alive, and no Chinese-style names, clothing, or customs were permitted. They realized that protecting their separate ethnic and cultural identity was indispensable to maintaining military superiority.

Politically, however, it was necessary for the Juchen rulers to familiarize themselves with the sophisticated culture of their Chinese subjects in order to manage state affairs. While limiting Chinese participation in the government, they shrewdly deflected the interests of their subjects toward the pursuit of such peaceful arts as printing, scholarship, painting, literature, and, significantly, the development of drama for widespread entertainment. (These trends continued under the Mongols and enriched Chinese culture.) In spite of the Juchen efforts, time was on the side of the majority culture, which gradually absorbed the minority. The transplanted tribesmen, after settling on farmland, could not avoid being affected by the Chinese way of life, particularly during long periods of peace.

Economically, the Juchen were no match for the Chinese. In time a number of Juchen became tenants on Chinese-owned land; some were reduced to paupers. Their economic decline altered social relations. Eventually they were permitted to intermarry, usually with parties wealthier than themselves. Their military strength also declined. It became normal for military units to be undermanned. Captains of "hundreds" often could put no more than two dozen men into the field, and captains of "thousands" had no more than four or five such nominal "hundreds" under them. Their ruling class followed a parallel decline. The interests of the ruling group shifted from government affairs to Confucian studies, Chinese Classics, and Tang- and Song-style poetry. The rulers found little use for the two styles of Juchen script that their ancestors had devised. Eventually the Juchen, much weakened, were brought down by the Mongols, led by Genghis Khan and his successors.

CHAPTER 7

THE SONG DYNASTY

BEI (NORTHERN) SONG (960–1127)

The Bei Song (also known simply as the Song) was the last major Chinese dynasty to be founded by a coup d'état. Its founder, Zhao Kuangyin (known by his temple name, Taizu), the commander of the capital area of Kaifeng and inspector general of the imperial forces, usurped the throne from the Hou (Later) Zhou, the last of the Wudai.

UNIFICATION

Though a militarist himself, Taizu ended militarism as well as usurpation. Even his own coup was skillfully disguised to make it appear that the popular acclaim of the rank and file left him with no choice. Taizu was masterful in political maneuvering, and as emperor (reigned 960–976) he did not destroy other powerful generals as had many previous founding rulers. Instead, he persuaded them to give up their commands in exchange for honorary titles, sinecure offices, and generous pensions—an unheard-of arrangement in Chinese history. The Song founder and his successors reduced the military power of the generals and used a variety of techniques to keep them weak, but Song rulers continued to support their social importance by frequently marrying members of the imperial clan to members of leading military families.

Taizu, founder of the Song dynasty, detail of a portrait; in the National Palace Museum, Taipei. Courtesy of the National Palace Museum, Taipei, Taiwan, Republic of China

With a shrewd appreciation of the war-weariness among the population, Taizu stressed the Confucian spirit of humane administration and the reunification of the whole country. To implement this policy, he took power from the military governors, consolidated it at court, and delegated the supervision of military affairs to able civilians; no official was regarded as above suspicion. A pragmatic civil service system evolved, with a flexible distribution of power and elaborate checks and balances. Each official had a titular office, indicating his rank but not his actual function, a commission for his normal duties, and additional assignments or honours. This seemingly confusing formula enabled the ruler to remove an official to a lower position without demotion of rank, to give an official a promotion in rank but an insignificant assignment, and to pick up a low-ranking talent and test him on a crucial commission. Councillors controlled only the civil administration because the division of authority made the military commissioner and the finance commissioner separate entities, reporting directly to the ruler, who coordinated all important decisions. In decision making, the emperor received additional advice from academicians and other advisers—collectively known as opinion officials—whose function was to provide separate channels of information and to check up on the administrative branches.

Similar checks and balances existed in the diffused network of regional officials. The empire was divided into circuits, which were units of supervision rather than administration. Within these circuits, intendants were charged with overseeing the civil administration. Below these intendants were the actual administrators. These included prefects, whose positions were divided into several grades according to an area's size and importance. Below the prefects there were district magistrates (subprefects) in charge of areas corresponding roughly in size to counties. The duties of these subprefects were catholic, for they were supposed to see to all aspects of the welfare of the people in their area. This was the lowest level of major direct imperial rule (though there were some petty officials on levels below the district). Because the members of the formal civil service level of the government were so few, actual administration in the yamen, or administrative headquarters, depended heavily on the clerical staff. Beyond the yamen walls, control was in the hands of an officially sanctioned but locally staffed sub-bureaucracy.

Following Confucian ideals, the founder of the Song dynasty lived modestly, listened to his ministers, and curbed excessive taxation. The rising prestige of his regime preceded his conquests. He also absorbed the best military units under his own command and disciplined them in the same Confucian style. His superior force notwithstanding, he embarked on a reunification program by mixing war with lenient diplomatic or accommodative terms that assured defeated rivals of generous treatment. A well-planned strategy first took Sichuan in the southwest in 965, the extreme south in 971, and the most prosperous lower Yangtze area in the southeast one year before his death, making the reunification nearly complete. The Wu-Yue, the sole survivor among the Shiguo (Ten Kingdoms) in the south, chose to surrender without a war in 978.

The sudden death of the founder of the Song dynasty left a speculative legend of assassination, though it was probably caused by his heavy drinking. The legend stemmed from the fact that his young son was denied the orderly succession. Instead, the emperor's younger brother, who had acquired much experience at his side, seized the throne. With reunification accomplished in the south, the new emperor, Taizong (reigned 976–997), turned northward to attack and conquer Bei Han (979), the last remaining Shiguo. He continued to fight the Khitan empire in the north, only to suffer a disastrous defeat in 986. Taizong's relative shortage of horses and grazing grounds to breed them, in contrast to the strong Khitan cavalries, was not the only reason for the defeat. It also resulted from a deliberate policy of removing generals from their armies, subordinating officers to civilians, concentrating strength in imperial units, and converting most provincial armies into labour battalions.

The Song never achieved a military prowess comparable to that of the Han or the Tang. Despite the occasional bellicosity of its officials, the Song government failed to penetrate Indochina or to break the power of the Xi Xia of Gansu and Shaanxi. As a result, Song China became increasingly isolated, especially from Central Asia, whence much cultural stimulus had come under preceding dynasties. Combined with a natural pride in internal advancements, China's cultural ethnocentrism deepened.

CONSOLIDATION

The Song achieved consolidation under the third emperor, Zhenzong (reigned 997–1022). A threatening Khitan offensive was directly met by the emperor himself, but a few battles assured neither side of victory. The two empires pledged peaceful coexistence in 1004 through an exchange of sworn documents that foreshadowed modern international treaties. The Khitan gave up its claim to a disputed area it had once occupied south of the Great Wall, and the Song agreed to a yearly tribute: 100,000 units (a rough equivalent of troy ounces) of silver and 200,000 rolls of silk. It was a modest price for the Song to pay for securing the frontier.

The emperor thereafter sought to strengthen his absolutist image by claiming a Daoist charisma. Prompted by magicians and ingratiating high officials, he proclaimed that he had received a sacred document directly from heaven. He ordered a grand celebration with elaborate rites, accompanied by reconstructed music of ancient times, and he made a tour to offer sacrifices at Mount Tai, following precedents of the Qin, Han, and Tang dynasties.

After the emperor's death, friction arose between his widow—the empress dowager, who was acting as regent—and Renzong (reigned 1022–63), Zhenzong's teenage son by a palace lady of humble rank. Following the death of the empress dowager, Renzong divorced his empress, who had been chosen for him by and had remained in sympathy with the empress dowager. However, the divorce was unjustifiable in Confucian morality and damaged the imperial image.

By that time the bureaucracy was more highly developed and sophisticated than it had been in the early Song. Well-regulated civil service examinations brought new groups of excellent scholar-officials who, though a numerical minority, dominated the higher policy-making levels of government. The sponsorship system, which discouraged favouritism by putting responsibility on the sponsors for the official conduct of their appointees, also ensured deserving promotions and carefully chosen appointments. Many first-rate officials—especially those from the south whose families had no previous bureaucratic background—upheld Confucian ideals. These new officials were critical not only of palace impropriety but also of bureaucratic malpractices, administrative sluggishness, fiscal abuses, and socioeconomic inequities. Respecting absolutism, they focused their attacks on a veteran chief councillor, whom the emperor had trusted for years. Factionalism developed because many established scholar-officials, mostly from the north, with long bureaucratic family backgrounds, stood by their leader, the same chief councillor.

A series of crises seems to prove that the complaints of the idealists were justified. After half a century of complacency, peace and prosperity began to erode. This became apparent in the occurrence of small-scale rebellions near the capital itself, in the disturbing inability of local governors to restore order themselves, and in a dangerous penetration of the northwestern border by Xi Xia, which rejected its vassal status and declared itself an independent kingdom. The

Khitan took advantage of the changing military balance by threatening another invasion. The idealistic faction, put into power under these critical circumstances in 1043–44, effectively stopped the Xi Xia on the frontier by reinforcing a chain of defense posts and made it pay due respect to the Song as the superior empire (though the Song no longer claimed suzerainty). Meanwhile, peace with the Khitan was again ensured when the Song increased its yearly tribute to them.

The court also instituted administrative reforms, stressing the need for emphasizing statecraft problems in civil service examinations, eliminating patronage appointments for family members and relatives of high officials, and enforcing strict evaluation of administrative performance. It also advocated reducing compulsory labour, land reclamation and irrigation construction, organizing local militias, and thoroughly revising codes and regulations. Though mild in nature, the reforms hurt vested interests. Shrewd opponents undermined the reformers by misleading the emperor into suspecting that they had received too much power and were disrespectful of him personally. With the crises eased, the emperor found one excuse after another to send most reformers away from court. The more conventionally minded officials were returned to power.

Despite a surface of seeming stability, the administrative machinery once again fell victim to creeping deterioration. Some reformers eventually returned to court, beginning in the 1050s, but

their idealism was modified by the political lesson they had learned. Eschewing policy changes and tolerating colleagues of varying opinions, they made appreciable progress by concentrating on the choice of better personnel, proper direction, and careful implementation within the conventional system, but many fundamental problems remained unsolved. Mounting military expenditures did not bring greater effectiveness, and an expanding and more costly bureaucracy could not reverse the trend of declining tax yields. Income no longer covered expenditures. During the brief reign of Yingzong (1063–67), relatively minor disputes and symbolically important issues concerning ceremonial matters embroiled the bureaucracy in mutual and bitter criticism.

REFORMS

Shenzong (reigned 1067–85) was a reform emperor. Originally a prince reared outside the palace, familiar with social conditions and devoted to serious studies, he did not come into the line of imperial succession until adoption had put his father on the throne before him. Shenzong responded vigorously (and rather unexpectedly, from the standpoint of many bureaucrats) to the problems troubling the established order, some of which were approaching crisis proportions. Keeping above partisan politics, he made the scholar-poet Wang Anshi his chief councillor and gave him full backing to make sweeping reforms. Known as the New Laws, or New Policies, these reform measures attempted drastic institutional changes. In sum, they sought administrative effectiveness, fiscal surplus, and military strength. Wang's famous "Ten Thousand Word Memorial" outlined the philosophy of the reforms. Contrary to conventional Confucian views, it upheld assertive governmental roles, but its ideal remained basically Confucian: economic prosperity would provide the social environment essential to moral well-being.

Never before had the government undertaken so many economic activities. The emperor empowered Wang to institute a top-level office for fiscal planning, which supervised the Finance Commission, previously beyond the jurisdiction of the chief councillor. The government squarely faced the reality of a rapidly spreading money economy by increasing the supply of currency. The state became involved in trading, buying specific products of one area for resale elsewhere (thereby facilitating the exchange of goods), stabilizing prices whenever and wherever necessary, and making a profit itself. This did not displace private trading activities. On the contrary, the government extended loans to small urban and regional traders through state pawnshops—a practice somewhat like modern government banking but unheard-of at the time. Far more important, if not controversial, the government made loans at the interest rate, low for the period, of 20 percent to the whole peasantry during the sowing

season, thus assuring their farming productivity and undercutting their dependency upon usurious loans from the well-to-do. The government also maintained granaries in various cities to ensure adequate supplies on hand in case of emergency need. The burden on wealthy and poor alike was made more equitable by a graduated tax scale based on a reassessment of the size and the productivity of the landholdings. Similarly, compulsory labour was converted to a system of graduated tax payments, which were used to finance a hired-labour service program that at least theoretically controlled underemployment in farming areas. Requisition of various supplies from guilds was also replaced by cash assessments, with which the government was to buy what it needed at a fair price.

Wang's reforms achieved increased military power as well. To remedy the Song's military weakness and to reduce the immense cost of a standing professional army, the villages were given the duty of organizing militias, under the old name of *baojia*, to maintain local order in peacetime and to serve as army reserves in wartime. To reinforce the cavalry, the government procured horses and assigned them to peasant households in northern and northwestern areas. Various weapons were also developed. As a result of these efforts, the empire eventually scored some minor victories along the northwestern border.

The gigantic reform program required an energetic bureaucracy, which Wang attempted to create—with mixed results—by means of a variety of policies: promoting a nationwide state school system; establishing or expanding specialized training in such utilitarian professions as the military, law, and medicine, which were neglected by Confucian education; placing a strong emphasis on supportive interpretations of Classics, some of which Wang himself supplied rather dogmatically; demoting and dismissing dissenting officials (thus creating conflicts in the bureaucracy); and providing strong incentives for better performances by clerical staffs, including merit promotion into bureaucratic ranks.

The magnitude of the reform program was matched only by the bitter opposition to it. Determined criticism came from the groups hurt by the reform measures: large landowners, big merchants, and moneylenders. Noncooperation and sabotage arose among the bulk of the bureaucrats, drawn as they were from the landowning and otherwise wealthy classes. Geographically, the strongest opposition came from the traditionally more conservative northern areas. Ideologically, however, the criticisms did not necessarily coincide with either class background or geographic factors. They were best expressed by many leading scholar-officials, some of whom were northern conservatives while others were brilliant talents from Sichuan. Both the emperor and Wang failed to reckon with the fact that, by its very nature, the entrenched bureaucracy could tolerate no sudden change in the system to which it had

become accustomed. It also reacted against the over concentration of power at the top, which neglected the art of distributing and balancing power among government offices, the overexpansion of governmental power in society, and the tendency to apply policies relatively uniformly in a locally diverse empire.

Without directly attacking the emperor, the critics attacked the reformers for deviating from orthodox Confucianism. It was wrong, the opponents argued, for the state to pursue profits, to assume inordinate power, and to interfere in the normal life of the common people. It was often true as charged that the reforms—and the resulting changes in government—brought about the rise of unscrupulous officials, an increase in high-handed abuses in the name of strict law enforcement, unjustified discrimination against many scholar-officials of long experience, intense factionalism, and resulting widespread miseries among the population—all of which were in contradiction to the claims of the reform objectives. Particularly open to criticism was the rigidity of the reform system, which allowed little regional discretion or desirable adjustment for differing conditions in various parts of the empire.

In essence the reforms augmented growing trends toward both absolutism and bureaucracy. Even in the short run, the cost of the divisive factionalism that the reforms generated had disastrous effects. To be fair, Wang was to blame for his overzealous if not doctrinaire beliefs, his low tolerance for criticism, and his persistent support of his followers even when their errors were hardly in doubt. Nonetheless, it was Shenzong himself who was ultimately responsible. Determined to have the reform measures implemented, he ignored loud remonstrances, disregarded friendly appeals to have certain measures modified, and continued the reforms after Wang's retirement.

The traditional historians, by studying documentary evidence alone, overlooked the fact that scholar-officials rarely openly criticized an absolutist emperor, and they generally echoed the critical views of the conservatives in assigning the blame to Wang—a revisionist Confucian in public, a profound Buddhist practitioner in his old age, and a great poet and essayist.

DECLINE AND FALL

Careful balancing of powers in the bureaucracy, through which the rulers acted and from which they received advice and information, was essential to good government in China. The demonstrated success of this principle in early Bei Song so impressed later scholars that they described it as the art of government. It became a lost art under Shenzong, however, in the reform zeal and more so in the subsequent eagerness to do away with the reforms.

The reign of Zhezong (1085–1100) began with a regency under another empress dowager, who recalled the conservatives to power. An antireform period lasted until 1093, during which time most of the reforms were rescinded or drastically revised. Though men of integrity, the conservatives offered few constructive alternatives. They managed to relax tension and achieve a seeming stability, but this did not prevent old problems from recurring. Some conservatives objected to turning back the clock, especially by swinging to the opposite extreme, but they were silenced. Once the young emperor took control, he undid what the empress dowager had put in place; the pendulum swung once again to a restoration of the reforms, a period that lasted to the end of the Bei Song. In such repeated convulsions, the government could not escape dislocation, and the society became demoralized. Moreover, the restored reform movement was a mere ghost without its original idealism. Enough grounds were found by conservatives out of power to blame the reforms for the fall of the dynasty.

Zhezong's successor, Huizong (reigned 1100–1125/26), was a great patron of the arts and an excellent artist himself, but such qualities did not make him a good ruler. Indulgent in pleasures and irresponsible in state affairs, he misplaced his trust in favourites. Those in power knew how to manipulate the regulatory system to obtain excessive tax revenues. At first, the complacent emperor granted more support to government schools everywhere; the objection that this move might flood the already crowded

閏中秋月

挂彩中秋特地圓況當餘

閏魄澄鮮因懷勝賞祀

經月免使詩人嘆隔年

萬象欽光增浩蕩四溟收

夜助嬋娟麟雲清廓心

田豫兼興能無賦詠篇

Zhenshu ("regular style") calligraphy, written by the emperor Huizong (reigned 1100–1125/26), Bei (Northern) Song dynasty, China; in the National Palace Museum, Taipei. Courtesy of the National Palace Museum, Taipei

bureaucracy was dismissed, seeing the significant gains it would bring in popular support among scholar-officials. The emperor then commissioned the construction of a costly new imperial garden. When his extravagant expenditures put the treasury in deficit, he rescinded scholarships in government schools. Support for him among scholar-officials soon vanished.

More serious was carelessness in war and diplomacy. The Song disregarded the treaty and coexistence with the Liao empire, allied itself with the expanding Juchen from Manchuria, and made a concerted attack on the Liao. The Song commander, contrary to long-held prohibition, was a favoured eunuch; under him and other unworthy generals, military expenditures ran high, but army morale was low. The fall of Liao was cause for court celebration, but because the Juchen had done most of the fighting, they accused the Song of not doing its share and denied it certain spoils of the conquest. The Juchen soon turned on the Song. Huizong chose to abdicate at that point, giving himself the title of Daoist "emperor emeritus" and leaving affairs largely in the unprepared hands of his son, Qinzong (reigned 1125/26–1127), while seeking safety and pleasure himself by touring the Yangtze region.

During that period the government became increasingly ineffective. The reform movement had enlarged both the size and duties of the clerical staff. The antireform period brought a cutback but also a confusion that presented manipulative opportunities to some clerks. Supervision was difficult because officials stayed only a few years, whereas clerks remained in office for long periods. Bureaucratic laxity spread quickly to the clerical level. Bribes for appointments went either to them or through their hands. It was they who made cheating possible at examinations, using literary agents as intermediaries between candidates and themselves.

The Juchen swept across the Huang He plain and found the internally decayed Song an easy prey. During their long siege of Kaifeng (1126), they repeatedly demanded ransoms in gold, silver, jewels, other valuables, and general supplies. The court, whose emergency call for help brought only undermanned reinforcements and untrained volunteers, met the invaders' demands and ordered the capital residents to follow suit. Finally, an impoverished mob plundered the infamous imperial garden for firewood. The court remained convinced that financial power could buy peace, and the Juchen lifted the siege briefly. But once aware that local resources were exhausted and that the regime, even with the return of the emperor emeritus, no longer had the capability of delivering additional wealth from other parts of the country, the invaders changed their tactics. They captured the two emperors and the entire imperial house, exiled them to Manchuria, and put a tragic end to the Bei Song.

NAN (SOUTHERN) SONG (1127–1279)

The Juchen could not extend their conquest south of the Yangtze River. In addition, the Huai River valley, with its winding streams and crisscrossed marshlands, made cavalry operations difficult. Though the invaders penetrated this region and raided several areas below the

Spring Fragrance, Clearing After Rain, *ink and slight colour on silk album leaf by Ma Lin, Nan (Southern) Song dynasty; in the National Palace Museum, Taipei.* National Palace Museum, Taipei, Taiwan, Republic of China

Yangtze, they found the weather there too warm and humid for them. Moreover, the farther they went, the stronger the resistance they met, as they penetrated into areas that had been leading the country in productivity and population and therefore in defense capability. Besides, the Juchen felt concerned about the areas in the rear that they had already occupied: one after another of their puppet rulers there had failed to secure popular support, and the Juchen had been forced to consolidate control by setting up their own administration, following the Liao model of dual government.

SURVIVAL AND CONSOLIDATION

Despite the fall of the Bei Song, the majority of scholar-officials refused to identify themselves with the alien conquerors. The same was generally true at the grass-roots level, among numerous roving bands of former volunteer militias, army units that had disintegrated, and bandits who had arisen during the disorder. As time went on, both civilians and military men turned toward the pretender to the throne, Gaozong. He was the only son of the former emperor Huizong who had been absent from Kaifeng and thus spared captivity.

As the founder of the Nan Song, Gaozong devoted his long reign (1127–62) to the arduous task of putting the pieces together. He rediscovered the lost arts of his ancestors: recruiting bureaucrats, securing fiscal resources, and extending centralized control. Because he started with no more than a few thousand troops, he had to place a much greater reliance on sophisticated politics, which he often artfully disguised. By praising the old, established ways of his predecessors, he pleased the conservatives who remained opposed to the reform system. In reality, he modified the system he had inherited where it had obviously failed and pragmatically retained the parts that were working. He honoured the scholar-officials who had refused to serve under the puppet rulers, but he was also glad to have those who had compromised their integrity in so serving. While he denounced the notorious favourites who had misled his father, he used the excuse of being broad-minded in picking many of their former subordinates for key positions, especially those experienced in raising tax revenues. A new network of officials called the fiscal superintendent generals was set up in each region, but they reported directly to court. Urban taxes were increased; they were easier to collect than rural revenues, and prosperous cities did not suffer much from the imposition. The high priority placed on fiscal matters, though not publicized as in the previous reform period in order to avoid a bad image, persisted throughout the Nan Song, which was a long era of heavy taxation.

Some officials, anxious to recover the central plains, wished to have the capital located in Nanjing, or farther up the Yangtze in central China. Gaozong discreetly declined such advice because these locations were militarily exposed. Instead, he chose Hang (present-day Hangzhou), renaming it Lin'an ("Temporary Safety"), as it occupied a more defensible location. It was popularly referred to as the place of imperial headquarters (Xingzai), later known to Marco Polo as Quinsai. Economically, it had the advantage of being at the corner of the lower Yangtze delta, the wealthy core of the new empire.

The Nan Song, through continuous development, eventually became wealthier than the Bei Song had been. Though its capital was near the sea—the only such instance among the Chinese empires—and international trade increased, the country was not sea-oriented. Gaozong maintained a defensive posture against periodic Juchen incursions from the north and meanwhile proceeded to restore imperial authority in the hinterland as far west as the strategic Sichuan and in parts of Shaanxi to its immediate north.

No less important was the need for adequate military forces. Neither conscription nor recruitment would suffice. Because his position was militarily weak but financially strong, Gaozong adopted the *zhao'an* policy, which offered peace to the various roving bands. The government granted them legitimate status as regular troops, and it overlooked their minor abuses in local matters. Thus, the size of imperial forces swelled, and the problem of internal security was largely settled. The court then turned its attention to the control of these armies, which was inseparable from the issue of war or peace with the Juchen.

Gaozong did not want to prolong the war; he valued most the security of his realm. A few minor victories did not convince him that he could hope to recover northern China. Rather, he saw war as a heavy drain on available resources, with the risk of eventual defeat. Nor did he feel comfortable with the leading generals, on whom he would have to rely in case the war went on. He had to get around the critics at court, however, who found the Juchen peace terms humiliating and unacceptable: in addition to an enormous yearly tribute, the Juchen demanded that the Nan Song formally admit, with due ceremonials, its inferior status as a vassal state. The shrewd emperor found an impeccable excuse for accepting the terms by claiming filial piety: he sought the return of his mother from captivity. To this no Confucian could openly object. Significantly, Gaozong refrained from asking the release of former emperor Qinzong, as such a move would have

called into question the legitimacy of his succession.

A dramatic crisis occurred in 1141. On the eve of concluding peace negotiations, Gaozong decided to strip the three leading generals of their commands. The generals, summoned to the capital on the pretext of rewarding their merits, were promoted to military commissioners, while their units were reorganized into separate entities directly under imperial control. Two of the generals reconciled themselves to the nominal honours and sizable pensions, but the third, Yue Fei, openly criticized the peace negotiations. He was put to death on a trumped-up charge of high treason. He later became the subject of a great legend, in which he was seen as a symbol of patriotism. At the time, however, his elimination signified full internal and external security for the court.

RELATIONS WITH THE JUCHEN

In spite of Gaozong's personal inclination, his artful guiding hand, and the success of his efforts to consolidate the empire, the impulse remained strong among many idealistic Confucians to attempt to recover the central plains. Even when silenced, they were potentially critical of court policies. Gaozong eventually decided to abdicate, leaving the matter to his adopted heir, but he retained control from behind the throne. The new emperor, Xiaozong (reigned

1163–89), sympathetic to the idealists, appointed several of them to court positions and command posts. Information about a Juchen palace coup and alleged unrest in the Juchen empire, particularly in the parts recently occupied, led to a decision to resume the war. An initial Song attack was repulsed with such heavy losses that even regrouping took some time to accomplish. Sporadic fighting went on for nearly two years in the Huai valley, reflecting a military stalemate. The outcome, in 1165, was a significant change in the new peace formula: the vassal state designation was dropped, and the Nan Song attained a nearly equal footing with the Juchen, although it had to defer to the latter empire as the senior one.

After the death of Gaozong in 1187, Xiaozong followed the precedent of abdicating. The international peace was kept during the brief reign of his son, Guangzong (reigned 1190–94), but it was broken again in 1205, during the reign of his grandson, Ningzong (reigned 1195–1224). The 40-year span of continuous peace dimmed the memory of difficulties in waging war. A new generation, nurtured by a flourishing Confucian education, tended to underestimate enemy strength and to think once more about recovering the central plains. The Nan Song again initiated a northward campaign, and again it met with defeat. The event left no doubt that the Juchen empire's hold over northern China was far beyond the military capability of the southern empire alone. It was also obvious that the Chinese population in northern China consisted of new generations brought up under alien domination and accustomed to it.

The Juchen not only retained their military edge over the Nan Song but also revived their ambition of southward expansion. An offer was made to the governor of Sichuan, who decided to turn against the Song court in faraway Lin'an and to become king of a vassal state allied with the Juchen. The civilian officials around him, however, took quick action and ended his separatist rebellion. Though a passing danger, it highlighted the fact that the Nan Song consolidation was not entirely secure; peace was preferred.

THE COURT'S RELATIONS WITH THE BUREAUCRACY

Gaozong set the style for all subsequent Nan Song emperors. The first two emperors in the Bei Song, both strong militarists, had towered above the relatively modest bureaucracy they had created; most of their successors had found little difficulty in maintaining a balance in the bureaucracy. The circumstances under which the Nan Song came into being, however, were quite different. Gaozong faced tough competition in building up a loyal bureaucracy, first with the two puppet rulers in the north and then from the dual administration the Juchen empire had set up. He became keenly aware that a cautious handling of bureaucrats was essential. Later, the attempted rebellion in Sichuan taught his successors the same lesson.

Gaozong was an attentive student of history who consciously emulated the restoration by the Dong (Eastern) Han (AD 25–220) and defined his style as the "gentle approach." This meant using bureaucratic tactics to deal with the bureaucrats themselves. The gentle approach proved helpful in maintaining a balance at court and thus in protecting councillors and imperial favourites from the criticism of "opinion-officials." Absolutism had grown since the middle of the Bei Song; the emperors had delegated much more power than before to a few ranking councillors. Similarly, imperial favourites—e.g., eunuchs, other personal attendants of the emperor, and relatives of the consorts—gained influence.

The opinion-officials by virtue of their rank or conviction wished to speak against those who abused power and influence; as a result of the factionalism that had plagued the late Bei Song, their effectiveness had declined and never recovered. But as long as absolutism was qualified by Confucian values and the monarch cherished a Confucian image, he had to learn to deal with some adverse opinions, and he often resorted to sophisticated delaying tactics. Skilled at bureaucratic manipulation, the Nan Song emperors listened to criticism with ostensible grace, responded appreciatively, and made it known that they had done so, but they did not take concrete action. Sometimes an emperor would either order an investigation or express a general agreement with the criticism, thereby preventing the critics from making an issue of it by repeated remonstrances. On other occasions the emperors would listen to the critics and commend them for their courage, but, to avoid stirring up a storm, the court would explicitly forbid the circulating of private copies of the criticisms among other scholar-officials. More subtly, the court would sometimes announce an official version of such criticism, leaving out the most damaging part. Likewise, rectifying edicts that followed the acceptance of criticism often had little substance. Reconciliation at court was another technique: an emperor would deliberately, if not evasively, attribute criticism to probable misunderstanding, assemble the parties in dispute, ask them to compose their differences, caution those under attack to mend their ways, and suggest to the critics that their opinions, though valid, should be modified. The handling of severe critics who refused to change their stand required different tactics. Seemingly accepting their adverse opinion, the court might reward them by promotion to a higher position, whose functions did not include the rendering of further advice. Rarely did the court demote or punish opinion-officials, especially those with prestige; sometimes it would not even permit them to resign or to ask for a transfer. Any such move tended to damage the court's valuable Confucian image. On sensitive issues the emperors were likely to invoke their absolutist power, but this was usually handled gently, by quietly advising the opinion-officials to refrain from commenting on the issues again.

Under this bureaucratized manipulation by the court, the institution of opinion-officials degenerated. Often the emperors appointed their own friends to such posts, but just as often, when the emperors hinted that they were displeased with certain ministers, the opinion-officials dutifully responded with unfavourable evidence, thus furnishing the court with grounds for dismissals. Such imperial manipulations served manifold purposes: safeguarding absolutist power and its delegation to various individuals, disguising absolutism, and keeping the bureaucracy in balance.

THE CHIEF COUNCILLORS

The later Nan Song emperors preferred not to take on the awesome burden of managing the huge and complex bureaucracy. Most of them were concerned chiefly with security and the status quo. The Nan Song court delegated a tremendous amount of power and thus had a series of dominant chief councillors; none of them, however, ever was a potential usurper. No bureaucrat during the Song era had a political base, a hereditary hold, or a personal following in any geographic area. In addition, the size of the bureaucracy and fluidity of its composition precluded anyone from controlling it. The tenure of chief councillor essentially depended on the sanction of the emperor. At times even the chief councillor had to reaffirm his loyalty along with other bureaucrats. Loyalty in absolutist terms being another name for submission, the court, bureaucratized as it was, retained its supreme position beyond challenge.

Nevertheless, the history of Nan Song politics had much to do with powerful chief councillors, increasingly so as time went on. Gaozong at first had a rapid succession of ranking ministers, but none of them measured up to the difficult task at hand: seeking external security by maintaining peace with the northern empire and maintaining internal security by undermining the power of leading generals. Only the chief councillor Qin Kui did both; moreover, he increased tax revenues, strengthening the fiscal base of the court and enriching the private imperial treasury. For these merits, he was given full support to impose tight control over the bureaucracy as long as he lived. Powerful as he was, he avoided doing anything that might arouse imperial suspicion. He had many dissident scholar-officials banished from court, but only with imperial sanction. He accommodated many bureaucrats, even those who neither opposed nor followed him, but he made many of them jealous of his great power and of the rapid promotions he gave to his son and grandson. Qin Kui failed, however, to properly assess the wiles of his bureaucratized master, who turned out to be the more skillful politician. Upon Qin Kui's death, the emperor shifted all blame to him and recalled from banishment some of his opponents, thus restoring in time a balance in the bureaucracy.

After his voluntary abdication, Gaozong retained his power by using Xiaozong more or less as a chief councillor. Xiaozong subsequently failed to find a firm hand among his successive ministers, and the great burden on himself was probably one reason that he chose to abdicate. His son, Guangzong, was mentally disturbed, unresponsive to bureaucratic consensus, and pathetically dominated by his consort. He turned against Xiaozong and even refused to perform state funeral rites when the retired emperor died—an unprecedented default that shocked the court. The solution was equally unprecedented: the empress dowager, the palace personnel, and the ranking ministers agreed to force his abdication and oversee the accession of Ningzong. Through the crisis, Han Tuozhou, who renewed the war against the Juchen, moved rapidly into power. Related originally to the empress dowager and again to a new consort, he received deferential treatment from Ningzong. He was made chief councillor but found it hard to control many bureaucrats who objected to his lack of scholarly qualifications, questioned his political ability, and criticized his nepotistic appointments. Reacting to the hostility, he made first a crucial mistake and then a fatal one. First, he banned a particular school of Confucian idealists, led by Zhu Xi. This proved unpopular, even among neutral scholar-officials. After he rescinded the ban, he attempted to recruit support and to reunite the bureaucracy by initiating the war against the Juchen. After its defeat in the war, the Song executed him as a sacrifice in its search for peace.

Shi Miyuan emerged as the dominant chief councillor. He came from a bureaucratic family background and understood the gentle approach and the importance of accommodating various kinds of bureaucrats in order to achieve a political balance. Promoting on merit and refraining from nepotism, he restored stability. He also recognized that the ideological prestige the followers of Zhu Xi had won had become a political factor, and he appointed some of their prominent leaders to highly respectable posts but without giving them real power. Like the emperors he served, Shi wanted to have both authority and a good political image. Ningzong had no son, and the chief councillor helped him adopt two heirs. When the emperor died without designating an heir apparent, Shi Miyuan arbitrarily decided in favour of the younger one, which was contrary to the normal order of succession but had the backing of palace-connected personnel.

Both Lizong (reigned 1224/25–1264) and his successor Duzong (reigned 1264/65–1274) indulged excessively in pleasure, though much of it was carefully concealed from the public. Shortly after the death of Shi Miyuan, the role of chief councillor went to Jia Sidao, who, though he was denounced in history, actually deserves much credit. He dismissed many incompetents from the palace, court, bureaucracy, and army and curbed excessive corruption by instituting minor administrative reforms. His strict accounting made the generals personally liable for misappropriation of funds. A system of public fields was introduced, which cut into the concentration of land-ownership by requisitioning at a low price one-third of large estates beyond certain sizes and using the income for army expenditures when the government faced external danger and fiscal deficit. These measures, however, hurt the influential elements of the ruling class, making Jia unpopular. He too had failed to practice the gentle approach. He was denounced by those who had defected to the enemy and later reconciled their guilt by placing the blame on him.

Except in name, the several dominant chief councillors were nearly actual rulers by proxy. They ran the civil administration, supervised both state finance and military affairs, and controlled most scholar-officials by some varying combination of gentle accommodation and high-handed pressure. The emperors, however, kept their separate imperial treasury—from which the government in deficit had to borrow funds—and their private intelligence systems to check on the chief councillors. Moreover, potential competitors always existed in the bureaucracy, ready to criticize the chief councillors whenever state affairs went badly enough to displease or disturb the emperors. The chief councillors had enormous power only by virtue of the imperial trust, and that lasted only as long as things went tolerably well.

THE BUREAUCRATIC STYLE

Regular posts in the Nan Song civil service numbered about 20,000, without counting numerous sinecures, temporary commissions, and a slightly larger number of military officers. Besides eliminating most patronage privileges—by which high officials were entitled to obtain an official title for a son or other family member—the court occasionally considered a general reduction in the size of the bureaucracy, although vested interests always opposed it. Those who entered government service seldom dropped out or were thrown out. Meanwhile, new candidates waiting for offices came in waves from state examinations, extra examinations on special occasions, graduation from the National Academy, and special recommendations and unusual sponsorship; others gained official titles because their families contributed to famine relief or military expenditures. Thus, the ever-increasing supply of candidates far exceeded the vacancies.

According to Confucian theory, any prosperity that made possible more books in print, more schools, and a better-educated elite was all for the good. But the original Confucian ideal intended to have the elite serve the society in general and the community in particular rather than flood the bureaucracy. Rising educational standards made the competition at examinations harder and perhaps raised the average quality of degree holders.

Families with members in the bureaucracy responded in part by successfully increasing the importance of other avenues of entrance into government service, especially the "protection" privilege that allowed high officials to secure official rank for their protégés (usually junior family members). People outside the civil service responded by altering their goals and values and by reducing the stress on the importance of entering the bureaucracy. It was not accidental that Neo-Confucian academies spread during the era, emphasizing moral self-development—not success in examinations—as the proper goal of education.

During the Song period, increased emphasis was placed on morals and ethics and a continuous development of the law. The early Song had adopted a legal code almost wholly traceable to an earlier Tang code, but Song circumstances differed from those of the Tang. As a result,

there was a huge output of legislation in the form of imperial edicts and approved memorials that took precedence over the newly adopted code and soon largely displaced it in many areas of law. Song legal bureaucrats periodically compiled and edited the results of this outpouring of new laws. The new rules not only altered the content of the (largely criminal) sphere covered by the code but also legislated in the areas of administrative, commercial, property, sumptuary, and ritual law. There were literally hundreds of compilations of various sorts of laws.

Perhaps as a result of the growth of this legal tangle from the late Bei Song onward, magistrates made increasing use of precedents, decisions by the central legal authorities on individual cases, in reaching legal decisions. The government sought to help its officials by instituting a variety of devices to encourage officials and prospective officials to learn the law and to certify that those in office did have some familiarity with things legal. There was an increase in the writing and publication of other sorts of works concerned with the law, including casebooks and the world's oldest extant book on forensic medicine. Despite the appearance of such works, which were intended to help them, officials were under strong pressure to rule in a conservative way and to avoid rocking the boat.

Many scholar-officials sought simply to keep things quiet and maintain the appearance that there was no serious trouble. The bureaucratic style was to follow the accustomed ways in accordance with proper procedure, find expedient solutions based upon certain principles in spirit, make reasonable compromises after due consideration of all sides, and achieve smooth reconciliations of divergent views. To protect one's own career record it was essential to engage in time-consuming consultations with all appropriate offices and to report to all concerned authorities so that everyone else would have a share of responsibility. Anyone who criticized the bureaucratic style would be going against the prevalent mode of operation—namely, mutual accommodation. Even the emperor adopted the bureaucratic style.

The picture was not entirely bleak. Evasions and deviations notwithstanding, the letter of the laws and the formalities of procedures had to be fulfilled. Definite limits were set on official negligence and misconduct. For example, suppressing evidence or distorting information were punishable offenses. Minor juggling of accounts went on, but outright embezzlement was never permissible. Expensive gifts were

CHINESE CIVIL SERVICE

The Chinese civil service constituted the administrative system of the traditional Chinese government, the members of which were selected by a competitive examination. The system gave the Chinese empire stability for more than 2,000 years and provided one of the major outlets for social mobility in Chinese society. It later served as a model for the civil-service systems that developed in other Asian and Western countries.

The Qin dynasty established the first centralized Chinese bureaucratic empire in the 3rd century BC and thus created the need for an administrative system to staff it. Succeeding dynasties further refined and expanded the system to what many consider its highest point during the Song dynasty—although the bureaucratic style of mutual favouritism sometimes led to corruption. Public schools were established throughout the country to help the talented but indigent, business contact was barred among officials related by blood or marriage, relatives of the imperial family were not permitted to hold high positions, and promotions were based on a merit system in which a person who nominated another for advancement was deemed totally responsible for that person's conduct.

Almost all Song officials in the higher levels of the bureaucracy were recruited by passing the jinshi examinations (which tested a candidate's knowledge of the Confucian Classics), and the jinshi became regularly established affairs. After 1065 they were held every three years, but only for those who first passed qualifying tests on the local level.

The examination system was finally abolished in 1905 by the Qing dynasty in the midst of modernization attempts. The whole civil-service system as it had previously existed was overthrown along with the dynasty in 1911/12.

customary and even expected, but an undisguised bribe was unacceptable. The refined art of the bureaucratic style was not sophistry and hypocrisy alone; it required a circumspect adherence to the commonly accepted substandard norms, without which the maintenance of government would have been impossible.

THE CLERICAL STAFF

The norms for the clerks were even lower, especially in local government. Some 300 clerks in a large prefecture or nearly 100 in a small one were placed under the supervision of a few officials. The clerks had numerous dealings with various other elements in the community, whereas the officials, being outsiders, rarely had direct contacts. Holding practically lifelong tenure after benefiting from the cumulative experience of their fathers and uncles before them, the clerks knew how to operate the local administrative machinery far better than did the officials, who served only brief terms before moving elsewhere. Clerks often received inadequate salaries and were expected to support themselves with "gifts" from those needing their services. The clerks under honest, strict, and hardworking magistrates would recoil, but only briefly, because such magistrates would soon either gain promotion for their remarkable reputations, or their strict insistence on clean government would become intolerable to their superiors, colleagues, subordinates, and

influential elements in the community who had connections with high circles. Though all bureaucrats complained of clerical abuses, many connived with the clerks, and none had a viable alternative to the existing situation. One significant suggestion was to replace the clerks with the oversupply of examination candidates and degree holders, who presumably had more moral scruples. But that solution had no chance of being considered, because it implied a downgrading of the status of those who considered themselves to be either potential or actual members of the ruling class.

The law did place definite limits on clerical misbehaviour. But when a clerk was caught in his wrongdoing, he knew enough to save himself—taking flight before arrest, getting a similar job elsewhere under a different name, defending himself through time-consuming procedures, appealing for leniency in sentencing, requesting a review, or applying for clemency on the occasion of imperial celebrations. What prevented clerical abuses from getting worse was not so much official enforcement of legal limits as it was the social convention in the community. For themselves as well as for their descendants, the clerks could ill afford to overstep the socially acceptable limits.

The net result of a large bureaucracy and its supporting clerical staff, accommodating one another in various defaults, malfunctions, and misconduct within loose limits, was a declining tax yield, tax evasion by those who befriended colluding officials and clerks, and an undue shift of the tax burden onto those least able to pay.

THE RISE OF NEO-CONFUCIANISM

The rise of the particular school of Neo-Confucianism led by Zhu Xi takes on special meaning in this context. The Neo-Confucian upsurge beginning in the late Tang embraced many exciting extensions of the Classical vision. Noteworthy during the Bei Song was the emergence of a new Confucian metaphysics that was influenced by Buddhism and that borrowed freely from Daoist terminology while rejecting both religions. Of relevance to Nan Song political and social conditions was its continuous growth into a well-integrated philosophical system that synthesized metaphysics, ethics, social ideals, political aspirations, individual discipline, and self-cultivation.

The best thinkers of the early Nan Song were disillusioned by the realization that previous Neo-Confucian attempts had failed. Reforms that had sought to apply statecraft had ended in abuses and controversies. The spread of education had not coincided with an uplifting of moral standards. The loss of the central plains was a great cultural shock, but to talk of recovering the lost territory was useless unless it was preceded by a rediscovery of the true meaning of Confucianism. To Zhu Xi and his followers, a state permeated by true Confucian practices would be so internally strong and would have such an attraction for outsiders that retaking the north would require only a minimal effort; a state lacking true Confucian practices would be so internally weak and unattractive that retaking the lost territories would be quite impossible.

Moreover, threatened by the Juchen adoption of the same heritage, the Song felt driven to make an exclusive claim to both legitimacy and orthodoxy. Such a claim required that the new departures be interpreted as reaffirmation of ancient ideals. Thus, the intellectual trend that developed under Zhu Xi's leadership was referred to first as Daoxue ("School of True Way") and later as Lixue ("School of Universal Principles"). Education, to the thinkers of this school, meant a far-deeper self-cultivation of moral consciousness, the ultimate extent of which was the inner experience of feeling at one with universal principles. These men, who might be described as transcendental moralists in Confucianism, also made a commitment to reconstruct a moral society—to them the only conceivable foundation for good government. With missionary-like zeal, they engaged in propagation of this true way and formed moral-intellectual fellowships. Zhu Xi, the great synthesizer, ranked the Classics in a step-by-step curriculum, interpreted his foremost choices, collectively known as the *Sishu* ("Four Books"), summed up a monumental history in a

宋徽國朱文公遺像

short version full of moralistic judgments, prepared other extensive writings and sayings of his own, and opened the way for an elementary catechism, titled the *Sanzijing* ("Three Character Classics"), that conveyed the entire value system of this school in simple language for what approximated mass education.

Many idealistic scholars flocked to Zhu Xi, his associates, and his disciples. Frustrated and alienated by the prevalent conditions and demoralizing low standards, these intellectuals assumed a peculiar archaic and semireligious lifestyle. Prominent in scholarship, educational activities, and social leadership and filling some relatively minor government posts, they asserted their exclusive ideological authority with an air of superiority, much to the displeasure of many conventional Confucians. Though they were not keen about politics, the prestige they acquired was an implicit threat to those in power. The chief councillor Han Tuozhou was particularly alarmed when he found some of his political adversaries sympathetic to and even supporting this particular school. A number of other bureaucrats at various ranks shared Han's alarm; one after another, they accused the school of being similar to a subversive religious sect, calling it a threat to state security and attacking its alleged disrespect for the court. The school was proscribed as false learning and un-Confucian. Several dozen of its leaders, including Zhu Xi, were banished, some to distant places. Thenceforth, all state examination candidates had to declare that they had no connection with the school.

Most historical accounts follow the view that the controversy was another example of factional strife, but that was not the case. The attackers were not a cohesive group, except for their common resentment toward the school, nor was the school itself an active group in politics. The conflict was in fact one between two polarized levels—political power and ideological authority. The nature of the Confucian state required that the two should converge if not coincide.

The persecution boomeranged by making heroes out of its victims and arousing sympathy among neutral scholar-officials. Realizing his mistake a few years later, Han lifted the ban. Most historical accounts leave an erroneous impression that, once the ban was removed, the Zhu Xi school of Neo-Confucianism by its preeminence soon gained wide acceptance, which almost automatically raised it to the coveted status of official orthodoxy. But in reality the rise to orthodoxy was slow and achieved by political manipulation, occasioned by an internal crisis of imperial succession

Neo-Confucian leader Zhu Xi, ink on paper, by an unknown artist; in the National Palace Museum, Taipei. Courtesy of the National Palace Museum, Taiwan, Republic of China

and then by the external threat of the Mongols. Shi Miyuan, the chief councillor who made Lizong emperor, created circumstances that forced the elder heir of Ningzong to commit suicide. This was damaging to the image of the court and to that of Shi himself. Mending political fences, he placed a few of the school's veteran leaders in prestigious positions in order to redress the balance of the bureaucracy.

In 1233, the year before the Mongol conquest of Juchen, the Mongols honoured Confucius and rebuilt his temple in Beijing. In 1237 their emerging nomadic empire, already occupying a large portion of northern China, reinstituted a civil service examination, thus claiming that it too was a Confucian state. Threatened both militarily and culturally, the Nan Song made Zhu Xi's commentaries official, his school the state orthodoxy, and its claim the accepted version—that the true way of Confucius had been lost for more than a millennium and that the line of transmission was not resumed until, inspired by the early Bei Song masters, Zhu Xi reestablished it. This implied that whatever Confucianism the Mongols took over was but a pale imitation and without legitimacy.

INTERNAL SOLIDARITY DURING THE DECLINE OF THE NAN SONG

Honouring the Zhu Xi school did not reinvigorate the Nan Song administration, but the military, despite some weaknesses, maintained an effective defense against the Mongols for four decades—the longest stand against Mongol invasions anywhere. The final Song defeat came in part because the Mongol forces, frustrated for many years in their attempts to break the main Song line of resistance, drove through territories to the west and outflanked the Song defenders. The Song capital, Lin'an, finally fell in 1276 without much fighting, all the high-ranking officials and officers having already fled. The empire itself came to an end in 1279, after its last fleet had been destroyed near Guangzhou, when a loyal minister with the boy pretender to the throne committed suicide by jumping into the sea.

Later Chinese historians attempted to explain the fall of the Nan Song as the result of internal decay and abuses, and so they stressed the problems of heavy taxation, inflated paper currency, bureaucratic laxity, and clerical abuses. The absence of any large-scale uprisings among the peasantry, however, suggests that they overstated the seriousness of such problems. To explain this lack of popular discord, most historical accounts cite Chinese patriotism, the point being that the war against the Mongols was for cultural rather than merely dynastic survival. Though partly true, this was not the only reason. Other significant factors contributed to this high degree of internal solidarity: (1) the government mobilized the resources of the wealthiest region, that of the lower Yangtze, without overburdening other regions; (2) the tax burden and the emergency requisitions fell mostly on the prosperous urban sectors rather than on rural areas, the backbone of the empire; and (3) scholar-officials in many areas, in spite of their shortcomings, were sophisticated in the art of administration, moving quickly to put down small uprisings before they got larger or offering accommodative terms to induce some rebel leaders to come over while dividing the rest. Finally, the Neo-Confucian values had pervaded the country through more books, more schooling, and greater efforts by Neo-Confucians to promote moral standards, community solidarity, and welfare activities and through widespread Neo-Confucian roots planted at the local levels by half-literate storytellers, makeshift theatres, and traveling companies in various performing arts.

The examination system itself played a major role in the Confucianization of Chinese society. Only a small percentage of the candidates actually passed the degree examinations and entered the civil service. The vast majority, thoroughly imbued with Confucian studies, returned to the larger society, often to serve as teachers to the next generation. Furthermore, the examination system reinforced the deeply Confucian character of the curriculum, from the lowest level of primary education to the highest level in the academies. Children began imbibing Confucian moral precepts when they began to read. These precepts stressed loyalty, and that in turn probably helped bolster the strength of the dynasty in the face of foreign invasion and helped limit internal disloyalty.

SONG CULTURE

The Song was an era of great change in most facets of Chinese life. Some of these developments were the outgrowths of earlier patterns, while others were largely born under that dynasty. These developments often related to or were made possible by major changes in Chinese economic life.

An agricultural revolution produced plentiful supplies for a population of more than 100 million—by far the largest in the world at the time. Acreages under cultivation multiplied in all directions, stretching across sandy lands, climbing uphill, and pushing back water edges. A variety of early ripening rice, imported during the 11th century from Champa (in present-day Cambodia), shortened the growing season to fewer than 100 days, making two crops per year the norm and three crops possible in the warm south. Among other new crops the most important was cotton, which was made into clothing for rich and poor alike; silk and hemp were also important. Improved tools, new implements, and mechanical devices that raised manpower efficiency were widely used and found their way into guidebooks used by the literate community leaders. The production of such minerals as gold, silver, lead, and tin also

Longquan celadon wine jar and cover with light bluish green glaze, Song dynasty, 12th century, Longquan, Zhejiang province, China; in the Victoria and Albert Museum, London. Height 25.4 cm. Courtesy of the Victoria and Albert Museum, London

increased. Consumption of iron and coal grew at a faster rate from 850 to 1050 than it later did in England during the first two centuries of the Industrial Revolution. The Chinese, however, never developed technology that used these two resources to generate power mechanically.

Manufacturing made tremendous headway within the skill-intensive pattern but with the aid of new devices, better processing, a beginning of division of labour, and expertise. Chinese porcelain attained international fame. Though information on ordinary handicrafts was available in handbooks and encyclopaedias, advanced skills were guarded as trade secrets. As production and regional trade became specialized, this stimulated mutual growth.

Transportation facilities improved, allowing production away from the sources of supplies and making products available to distant regions. The state maintained highways, with staffed stations, for official travel and a courier service network, the latter being an index of centralized government control. Along the highways and branching byways stood private hostels and inns frequented by private traders. Rivers carried tribute vessels and barges, private shipping, transfer crafts, fishing boats, and pleasure yachts. Large ships with multiple decks were propelled by fast-moving wheels paddled by manpower; many sailed on the high seas, aided by accurate compasses, charts, and instruments as well as by experience in distant navigation. The expanding sea trade, apart from that with Japan and Korea, moved southward and linked up with merchants from Persia and Arabia. Some Chinese merchants began to settle in Southeast Asia. For the first time in history, Chinese naval forces assumed a vital military role, though China had not become a sea power.

An advanced money economy was everywhere in evidence. Many cultivated lands produced cash crops. By 1065 the Bei Song government was taking in annual cash tax payments that were 20 times what the Tang had received in 749. The income of the Nan Song consisted of more cash revenues than grain and textile receipts. The economy had progressed to such a state that it needed more means of exchange. Merchants used drafts called *feiqian* ("flying money") and certificates of deposits made elsewhere. State monopoly agencies in salt and tea followed with their respective certificates, which were as good as money. The government first permitted printed paper money for limited regional circulation and then authorized it as nationwide legal tender. (China was the first country to do so.)

Busy transactions approached a commercial revolution, carried on by rapid calculations on the abacus, a specialized service skill that remained unmatched until the appearance of adding machines and computers. Cities changed: the Tang pattern of walled-in blocks, each for a particular trade, broke down; stores appeared in various parts of cities; and trade guilds proliferated. Though official documents and scholarly essays adopted a downgrading tone toward commercial activities, Song China became a society of wholesalers, shippers, storage keepers, brokers, traveling salesmen, retail shopkeepers, and peddlers. Urban life reached a new intensity. The populations of several metropolitan areas approached one million.

Crowding was serious in the cities, and houses usually had narrow frontages. Fires were frequent and disastrous. Neighbourhood fire squads, with water containers at hand, could not prevent destruction, and some fires lasted several days. Nonetheless, prosperity was the keynote of urban life. Teahouses, wine shops, exquisite cuisines, and catering services for private parties existed in multitude and variety. Pleasure grounds provided daily amusement and festival merriment with acrobats, jugglers, wrestlers, sword swallowers, snake charmers, fireworks, gambling, performing arts of all sorts, puppet shows, storytellers, singing girls, and professionally trained courtesans. Upper-class families enjoyed higher culture, with diversions such as music, pets, intricate games, hobbies, calligraphy, painting, and poetry. Noticeably declining were hunting, horseback riding, and polo. Gentility displaced sportsmanship. The prosperous cities also provided easy prey for pickpockets and professional thieves. Inasmuch as pauperism appeared in cities, parallel to rural underemployment and unemployment, the government undertook relief and welfare measures such as orphanages, nursing homes for the aged poor, charitable graveyards, and state pharmacies.

Knowledge expanded because of specialization. Medicine embraced skills such as acupuncture, obstetrics, dentistry, laryngology, ophthalmology, and treatment of rheumatism and paralysis. The demand for improved technology, aided by certain concerns of the Neo-Confucian philosophy, helped to promote numerous investigations that approached the use of scientific methods. Literacy spread with printing, which evolved from rubbing through block printing to the use of movable type that facilitated much larger-scale production at reduced cost. A great many scholars achieved high standing through Classical studies, newly developed archaeology, philosophical interpretations, statecraft ideas, Classical forms of poetry, an evolving lyric poetry called *ci*, which had its origin in singing, and written versions of popular songs, called *sanqu*. Of greatest influence on scholar-officials in succeeding generations was a masterly prose style that was original and creative but was always used in the name of reviving ancient models. Diversified and specialized developments widened

knowledge so much that scholars compiled voluminous histories, collected works, comprehensive handbooks, compendiums, and encyclopaedias. Fine arts also reached new heights.

The term *early modern* has often been applied in describing Song culture, because it not only advanced beyond the earlier pattern in China and far ahead of the rest of the world at the time but also had many startlingly new features that approximated later developments in western Europe. This characterization, though helpful to highlight and appreciate the progress during Song times, is somewhat misleading, since this stage of development did not pave the way for more modernity later. On the contrary, the Song pattern attained cultural stability, giving rise to the myth of an unchanging China.

These conflicting images stemmed from the cultural and regional diversity of the Song, in which modern-style advances existed alongside continuing older practices. In some areas, such as the delta lands immediately south of the Yangtze River, sizable estates grew up with a complicated social pattern characterized by tenant farming. Elsewhere, in areas less well-developed, owner-farmers constituted a greater proportion of the population, while in other regions the landlords tried to bind the tillers to the soil. The same confusion was reflected in the status of women. During the Song the notorious practice of foot binding first became common, clearly marking a fall in the status of women, but there is evidence that during the Nan Song (unlike any other Chinese dynasty) daughters as well as sons could inherit property in their own names. Furthermore, Song families tried in various ways to strengthen the ties created by the marriages of their daughters to other families.

The extraordinarily rapid pace of economic and technological change that marked the Bei Song seems to have slowed during the Nan Song. For reasons that are not wholly clear, Chinese society did not break through its inherited patterns in any radically new ways. It may be that, with an abundance of inexpensive labour, economic rationality moved men to produce through increased amounts of labour rather than through innovation or capital investment. This disincentive to investment helped create a relatively stable economic and technological pattern that remained with little change for centuries thereafter. Despite this slowing of economic and technological development, however, the Song did give birth to changes. Not only did a new Confucian synthesis emerge but also the devices that spread the new ideas among the people at large. The urban and urbanized culture that arose in the Song was retained and developed in succeeding dynasties, when the early modern (or neo-traditional) pattern created in the Song provided both the model for and the basis of the gradual transformation of some aspects of Chinese life that belied the image of China as unchanging.

CHAPTER 8

The Yuan, or Mongol, Dynasty

THE MONGOL CONQUEST OF CHINA

Genghis Khan rose to supremacy over the Mongol tribes in the steppe in 1206, and within a few years he attempted to conquer northern China. By securing in 1209 the allegiance of the Tangut state of Xi (Western) Xia in what are now Gansu, Ningxia, and parts of Shaanxi and Qinghai, he disposed of a potential enemy and prepared the ground for an attack against the Jin state of the Juchen in northern China. At that time the situation of Jin was precarious. The Juchen were exhausted by a costly war (1206–08) against their hereditary enemies, the Nan (Southern) Song. Discontent among the non-Juchen elements of the Jin population (Chinese and Khitan) had increased, and not a few Chinese and Khitan nobles defected to the Mongol side. Genghis Khan, in his preparation for the campaign against Jin, could therefore rely on foreign advisers who were familiar with the territory and the conditions of the Jin state.

INVASION OF THE JIN STATE

The Mongol armies started their attack in 1211, invading from the north in three groups; Genghis Khan led the centre group himself. For several years they pillaged the country;

GENGHIS KHAN

Genghis, or Chinggis, Khan (original name Temüjin; b. 1162—d. 1227) was the great Mongolian warrior-ruler of the late 12th and early 13th centuries. Under his leadership, the Mongols consolidated nomadic tribes into a unified Mongolia and fought from China's Pacific coast to Europe's Adriatic Sea, creating the basis for one of the greatest continental empires of all time. The leader of a destitute clan, Temüjin fought various rival clans and formed a Mongol confederacy, which in 1206 acknowledged him as Genghis Khan ("Universal Ruler"). By that year the united Mongols were ready to move out beyond the steppe. He adapted his method of warfare, moving from depending solely on cavalry to using sieges, catapults, ladders, and other equipment and techniques suitable for the capture and destruction of cities. In less than 10 years he took over most of Juchen-controlled China; he then destroyed the Muslim Khwārezm-Shah dynasty while his generals raided Iran and Russia. He is infamous for slaughtering the entire populations of cities and destroying fields and irrigation systems but admired for his military brilliance and ability to learn. He died on a military campaign, and the empire was divided among his sons and grandsons.

The Mongol conqueror Genghis Khan on his deathbed, surrounded by his four sons. Hulton Archive/Getty Images

finally, in 1214 they concentrated on the central capital of the Jin, Zhongdu (present-day Beijing). Its fortifications proved difficult to overcome, so the Mongols concluded a peace and withdrew. Shortly afterward the Jin emperor moved to the southern capital at Bianjing (present-day Kaifeng). Genghis Khan considered this a breach of the armistice, and his renewed attack brought large parts of northern China under Mongol control and finally resulted in 1215 in the capture of Zhongdu (renamed Dadu in 1272). The Mongols had had little or no experience in siege craft and warfare in densely populated areas; their strength had been chiefly in cavalry attacks. The assistance of defectors from the Jin state probably contributed to this early Mongol success. In subsequent campaigns the Mongols relied even more on the sophisticated skills and strategies of the increased number of Chinese under their control.

After 1215 the Jin were reduced to a small buffer state between the Mongols in the north and Song China in the south, and their extinction was but a matter of time. The Mongol campaigns against Xi Xia in 1226–27 and the death of Genghis Khan in 1227 brought a brief respite for Jin, but the Mongols resumed their attacks in 1230.

The Song Chinese, seeing a chance to regain some of the territories they had lost to the Juchen in the 12th century, formed an alliance with the Mongols and besieged Bianjing in 1232. Aizong, the emperor of Jin, left Bianjing in 1233, just before the city fell, and took up his last residence in Cai prefecture (Henan), but that refuge was also doomed. In 1234 the emperor committed suicide, and organized resistance ceased. The southern border of the former Jin state—the Huai River—now became the border of the Mongol dominions in northern China.

INVASION OF THE SONG STATE

During the next decades an uneasy coexistence prevailed between the Mongols in northern China and the Song state in the south. The Mongols resumed their advance in 1250 under the grand khan Möngke and his brother Kublai Khan—grandsons of Genghis Khan. Their armies outflanked the main Song defenses on the Yangtze River and penetrated deeply into southwestern China, conquered the independent Dai (Tai) state of Nanzhao (in what is now Yunnan), and even reached present-day northern Vietnam. Möngke died in 1259 while leading an army to capture a Song fortress in Sichuan, and Kublai succeeded him. Kublai sent an ambassador, Hao Jing, to the Song court with an offer to establish peaceful coexistence. Hao did not reach the Song capital of Lin'an (now Hangzhou), however, but was interned at the border and regarded as a simple spy. The Song chancellor, Jia Sidao, considered the Song position strong enough to risk this affront against Kublai; he thus ignored the chance for peace offered by

A Mongol encampment, detail from the Cai Wenji *scroll, a Chinese hand scroll of the Nan (Southern) Song dynasty.* Courtesy of Asia House Gallery, New York

Kublai and instead tried to strengthen the military preparations against a possible Mongol attack. Jia secured military provisions by a land reform that included confiscating land from large owners, but this alienated the greater part of the landlord and official class. The Song generals, whom Jia distrusted, also had grievances, which may explain why a number of them later surrendered to the Mongols without fighting.

From 1267 onward the Mongols, this time assisted by numerous Chinese auxiliary troops and technical specialists, attacked on several fronts. The prefectural town of Xiangyang (present-day Xianfan) on the Han River was a key fortress, blocking the access to the Yangtze River, and the Mongols besieged it for five years (1268–73). The Chinese commander finally surrendered in 1273, after he had obtained a solemn promise from the Mongols to spare the population, and he took office with his former enemies.

Kublai Khan's warning to his forces not to engage in indiscriminate slaughter seems to have been heeded to a certain extent. Several prefectures on the Yangtze River surrendered; others were taken after brief fighting. In January 1276,

Mongol troops reached Lin'an. Last-minute attempts by the Song court to conclude a peace failed, and the Mongol armies took Lin'an in February. The reigning Song empress dowager and the nominal emperor—a boy—were taken to Dadu and granted an audience by Kublai Khan.

National resistance in the Song state continued, however, and loyalists retreated with two imperial princes into the southern province of Fujian and from there to the region of Guangzhou (Canton). In 1277 the last remnants of the court left Guangzhou and eventually fled the mainland by boat. A faithful minister drowned himself and the last surviving imperial prince in the ocean in March 1279. When organized resistance ceased soon afterward, foreign invaders controlled the whole Chinese empire for the first time in history.

CHINA UNDER THE MONGOLS

MONGOL GOVERNMENT AND ADMINISTRATION

After their initial successes in northern China in 1211–15, the Mongols faced the problem of how to rule and extract material benefits from a largely sedentary population. They were assisted by Khitan and Chinese and even Juchen renegades; these defectors were treated as "companions" (nökör) of the Mongols and were given positions similar to the higher ranks of the steppe aristocracy. Their privileges included the administration and exploitation of fiefs considered as their private domain.

EARLY MONGOL RULE

The government system during the early years of the Mongol conquest was a synthesis of Mongol military administration and a gradual return to Chinese traditions in those domains ruled by former subjects of the Jin state. The most important office or function in Mongol administration was that of the *darughatchi* (seal bearer), whose powers were at first all-inclusive; only gradually were subfunctions entrusted to specialized officials in accordance with Chinese bureaucratic tradition. This re-feudalization of northern China, along Mongol lines with a slight understructure of Chinese-type bureaucrats, lasted for many years.

The central administration of Mongol China was largely the creation of Yelü Chucai, originally a Jin state official of Khitan extraction who had acquired a profound Chinese scholarship and who had become one of Genghis Khan's trusted advisers. Yelü continued to serve under Ögödei, who became grand khan in 1229, and persuaded him to establish a formal bureaucracy and to replace indiscriminate levies with a rationalized taxation system along Chinese lines. An important part of Yelü's reforms was the creation of the Central Secretariat (Zhongshu Sheng), which centralized the civilian administration and achieved some continuity. The territory was divided into provinces, and the provincial administrations were responsible for regularized taxation. The people had to pay a land tax and a poll tax, either in kind (textiles and grain) or in silver. Merchants had to pay a sales tax. Monopolies on wine, vinegar, salt, and mining products were also introduced. All this enabled the treasuries of the Mongol court to accumulate considerable wealth.

In spite of the success of his economic policy, Yelü's influence decreased during his later years. One reason was bitter opposition from the Mongol feudatories and from those Chinese, Juchen, and Khitan nobles who were used to ruling independently in their appanages, which they exploited at will. Also, Ögödei himself apparently lost interest in the internal conditions of the Mongol dominion in China. During the 1230s Muslims from the Middle East had already begun to fill the higher positions at the Mongol court, and their ruthless exploitation of the Chinese created widespread resentment of Mongol rule. A relapse into feudal anarchism seemed inevitable, and Yelü's reforms fell into temporary abeyance. China was ruled more or less like a colony by the foreigners and their allies.

CHANGES UNDER KUBLAI KHAN AND HIS SUCCESSORS

Kublai Khan's ascendancy in 1260 marked a definite change in Mongol government practice. Kublai moved the seat of Mongol government from Karakorum in Mongolia to Shangdu ("Upper Capital"), near present-day Dolun in Inner Mongolia. In 1267 the official capital was transferred to Zhongdu, where Kublai ordered the construction of a new walled city, replete with grand palaces and official quarters, that was renamed Dadu ("Great Capital") before its completion. Under its Turkicized name, Cambaluc (Khan-baliq, "The Khan's Town"), the capital became known throughout Asia and even Europe. But, true to nomad traditions, the Mongol court continued to move between these two residences—Shangdu in summer and Dadu in winter. With the establishment of Dadu as the seat of the central bureaucracy, Mongolia and Karakorum no longer remained the centre of the Mongol empire. Mongolia began to fall back to the status of a northern borderland, where a nomadic way of life continued and where Mongol grandees, dissatisfied with the growing Sinicization of the court, repeatedly engaged in rebellions.

Kublai, who even prior to 1260 had surrounded himself with Chinese advisers such as the eminent Buddho-Daoist Liu Bingzhong and several former Jin scholar-officials, was still the nominal overlord of the other Mongol dominions (ulus) in Asia. By then, however, his Chinese entourage had persuaded him to accept the role of a traditional Chinese emperor. A decisive step was taken in 1271 when the Chinese dominion was given a Chinese dynastic name—Da Yuan, the "Great Origin." Before this the Chinese name for the Mongol state was

Kublai Khan, grandson of Genghis Khan founded the Yuan (Mongol) dynasty in China.
Hulton Archive/Getty Images

Da Chao ("Great Dynasty"), introduced about 1217. It was a translation of the Mongol name Yeke Mongghol Ulus ("Great Mongol Nation") adopted by Genghis Khan about 1206. The new name, however, was a departure from Chinese traditions. All earlier Chinese dynasties were named for ancient feudal states or geographic terms; even the Khitan and the Juchen had followed this tradition by naming their states Liao (for the Liao River in Manchuria) and Jin ("Gold," for a river in Manchuria that had a Juchen name with that meaning). Yuan was the first nongeographic name of a Chinese dynasty since Wang Mang established the Xin dynasty (AD 9–25).

During the 1260s the central bureaucracy and the local administration of the Chinese empire were remodeled on Chinese lines, with certain alterations introduced by the Jin state. The Central Secretariat remained the most important civilian authority, with specialized agencies such as the traditional six ministries of finance, war, officials, rites, punishments, and public works. The Shumiyuan (Military Council) was another institution inherited from previous dynasties. A Yushitai (Censorate) was originally created for remonstrations against the emperor and criticism of policies, but increasingly it became an instrument of the court itself and a tool to eliminate other members of the bureaucracy. In the main the territorial divisions followed Chinese models, but the degree of local independence was much smaller than it had been under the Song; the provincial administrations were actually branches of the Central Secretariat. The structures of the various provincial administrations throughout China were smaller replicas of the Central Secretariat. According to Chinese sources, in 1260–61 the lower echelons in the Central Secretariat were mostly Chinese; the high offices, however, even if they had traditional Chinese names, were reserved for non-Chinese. Surprisingly, Kublai Khan had few Mongols in high administrative positions; apparently suspicious of some of his tribal leaders, he preferred absolute foreigners. The military sphere was affected least by the attempts to achieve a synthesis between Chinese and native ways of life; there the Mongol aristocracy remained supreme.

Too many antagonistic social and ethnic groups existed within the Yuan government to secure a stable rule. The traditional Chinese value system had largely disappeared, and no political ethics had replaced it. While personalized loyalty focused on the ruler, the companionship of *nökör* relations was not enough to amalgamate the heterogeneous ruling group into a stable body. This unbalanced system of government could function only under a strong ruler; under a weak or incompetent emperor, disintegration was certain, and a decline in efficiency resulted.

The former scholar-officials of China remained to a great extent outside the governmental and administrative structure; only minor positions were open to them. The Mongols never made full use of the administrative potential of the scholar-officials, fearing their competence and abilities. The ruling foreign minority in China was more an elite of the colonialist type than a part of the Chinese social system.

The unwillingness of the Mongols to assimilate with the Chinese is shown by their attempts to cement the inequalities of their rule. After the Song empire had been conquered, the population of China was divided into four classes. The first class was the Mongols themselves, a tiny but privileged minority. Next came the semuren ("persons with special status"), confederates of the Mongols such as Turks or Middle Eastern Muslims. The third group was called the hanren (a term that generally means Chinese but that was used to designate the inhabitants of only northern China); this class included the Chinese and other ethnic groups living in the former Jin state, as well as Xi Xia, Juchen, Khitan, Koreans, Bohai, and Tangut, who could be employed in some functions and who also formed military units under Mongol leadership. The last group was the nanren, or manzi, pejorative terms in Chinese, meaning "southern barbarian," which designated the former subjects of Song China (about three-fourths of the Chinese empire). The lowest stratum in Yuan China was occupied by the slaves, whose numbers were quite considerable. Slave status was hereditary, and only under certain conditions could a slave be freed.

More than four-fifths of the taxpayers came from the nanren group, which was generally barred from holding higher office (only rarely would one of them rise to some prominence). The Mongols and the semuren were tax-exempt and enjoyed the protection of the law to a higher degree than did the hanren and nanren.

The formal distinction between various ethnic groups and the corresponding graded status was not a Mongol invention but a social differentiation inherited from the Jin state. In the same way, many institutions were taken over from the Jin. Law in Yuan China was based partly on the legislation of the Jin and partly on traditional Chinese law; Mongol legal practices and institutions also played a great role, particularly in penal law. The Yuan legal code has been preserved in the dynastic history, Yuanshi, as well as other sources. In addition, many rules, ordinances, and decisions of individual cases are collected in compilations such as Yuandianzhang, which throw much light not only on the legal system but also on social conditions in general.

Mongol and Chinese dualism is also reflected in the problem of administrative documents and languages. Few of the ruling Mongols, even in the later years of the Yuan, knew Chinese, and the number who mastered the Chinese script was still smaller. On the other hand, only a few Chinese bothered to learn the language of their conquerors. Administration and jurisdiction therefore had to rely largely on interpreters and translators. Mongol was the primary language; most decisions, ordinances, and decrees were originally drafted in

Mongol, and a Chinese interlinear version was added. This Chinese version was in the colloquial language instead of the formal documentary style, and it followed the Mongol word order so that it must have seemed barbaric to the native literati. Many of these Chinese versions have survived in collections such as *Yuandianzhang*.

ECONOMY

The Mongol conquest of the Song empire had, for the first time since the end of the Tang, reunified all of China. Song China had traded with its neighbours, the Liao and the Jin, but trade had been strictly controlled and limited to authorized border markets. The Mongol conquest therefore reintegrated China's economy. The Mongol administration, in its desire to utilize the resources of the former Song territory, the most prosperous part of China, tried to promote internal trade and aimed at a fuller integration of north and south. The region around the capital was dependent on grain transports from the south, and large quantities of food and textiles were needed to keep the Mongol garrisons. The Grand Canal, which had linked the river systems of the Yangtze, the Huai, and the Huang since the early 7th century, was repaired and extended to Dadu in 1292–93 with the use of corvée (unpaid labour) under the supervision of a distinguished Chinese astronomer and hydraulic engineer, Guo Shoujing—an action entirely within Chinese tradition. This was preceded, however, by another measure in the field of economic communications that was unorthodox in Chinese eyes: about 1280, concessions for grain transport overseas were granted to some private Chinese entrepreneurs from the southeastern coastal region (some Chinese government officials were traditionally antagonistic toward private trade and enterprise, an attitude that the ruling Mongols did not share). These private shipowners transported in their fleets grain from the lower Yangtze region to northern Chinese harbours and from there to the capital. Early in the 14th century, however, these private fleet owners, who had made huge fortunes, were accused of treason and piracy, and the whole action was abolished. The Mongol government never replaced them with government fleets.

Another factor that contributed to the flourishing internal trade in China was standardized currency. The Song and Jin had issued paper money but only in addition to bronze coins, which had remained the basic legal tender. The Yuan government was the first to make paper money the only legal currency throughout the empire (1260). This facilitated financial transactions in the private sector as well as in the state treasuries. As long as the economy as such remained productive, the reliance on paper money as the basic currency had no detrimental effects. Only when the economy began to disintegrate under the last Mongol ruler did the paper money become gradually valueless and inflation set in. One reason for the paper currency might have been that much bronze and copper was used for the Buddhist cult and its statues, another that metal ores in China proper were insufficient to supply enough coins for some 80 million people.

RELIGIOUS AND INTELLECTUAL LIFE

The Mongols did not try to impose their own religion (a cult of heaven, the forces of nature, and shamanistic practices) on their subjects. This gave comparative freedom to the existing religions in China, including what the Mongol rulers considered to be the *sanjiao* ("three teachings"): Daoism, Buddhism, and Confucianism. Both Daoism and Buddhism retained their distinctive identities and organizations; although they often rivaled each other, they were not mutually exclusive. The Neo-Confucianism of the Zhu Xi school enjoyed orthodox status after the 1310s, but adherents of the three teachings interacted philosophically and intellectually in a way that popularized the "amalgamation" of the three schools among the common people and the literati, if not the foreign residents, of China.

DAOISM

Under the Jin dynasty several popular Daoist sects had flourished in northern China, and Genghis Khan had apparently been impressed by the Daoist patriarch Changchun. In 1223 Genghis Khan granted to Changchun and his followers full exemption from taxes and other duties demanded by the government; this was the first of a series of edicts granting special privileges to the clergy of the various religions in China.

For some time it seemed as if Chinese Daoism would win favour with the Mongol rulers at the expense of Chinese Buddhism. The Buddhists, however, also profited from the open-minded attitude at the court; they tried to win influence within the imperial family, prompted by the fact that many Buddhist institutions had been occupied by the Daoists, who relied on Mongol favour. Under the grand khan Möngke, several discussions were held between the Daoist and Buddhist clergy (1255–58), ending in a ruling that the former Buddhist temples should be returned to their original purpose. Imperial orders also outlawed some apocryphal Daoist texts, in which Buddhism was presented as a branch of Daoism and the Buddha as a reincarnation of Laozi, the founder of Daoism. But Daoism as such continued to exist under the Yuan, and the fiscal privileges originally granted to the Daoist followers of Changchun were extended on principle to all clergies.

Timber pagoda of the Fogong Temple, 1056, Song dynasty; at Yingxian, Shanxi province, China. Christopher Liu/ChinaStock Photo Library

BUDDHISM

The spokesmen of Chinese Buddhism under the early Mongol rulers came from the Chan (Zen) sect (a discipline focused on meditation). Their high intellectuality and refined aestheticism, however, did not appeal to the Mongols, who felt more attracted by the mixture of magic practices, rather nebulous metaphysics, and impressive symbolism in the visual arts of Tibetan Buddhism. Kublai Khan appointed a young Tibetan lama known by the honorific name of 'Phags-pa as imperial preceptor (*dishi*); 'Phags-pa became the head of the Buddhist faith in all Mongol dominions, including China. A special government agency was established in 1264 to deal with Buddhism and served as a sort of bureau for the imperial preceptor; it was in charge not only of Buddhist affairs in general but also of Tibetan affairs, although Tibet remained outside the administration of China proper, and no Mongol garrisons were ever established in Tibet. Tibetan politicians had thus succeeded in winning over the Mongol court and in retaining a more-than-nominal independence.

After the conquest of Song China, a special agency for the supervision of Buddhism in southern China was established and placed under the control of another Tibetan lama. There thus existed two supervisory offices for Buddhism—one in Dadu for northern China and Tibet and one in Lin'an for southern China. The southern office caused great resentment among Chinese Buddhists and the population at large by its brutal and avaricious procedures, property seizures, and extortions from the population. Throughout the Yuan dynasty, complaints continued against the arrogant behaviour of Tibetan lamas. (Under the last emperor, Togon-temür, Tibetan clerics introduced the court to sexual rites calling for intercourse with consecrated females—practices not unfamiliar in Indian and Tibetan cultures but shocking to the Chinese elite.)

Although Buddhism had won a victory among the ruling minority of China, it was a foreign rather than a Chinese Buddhism. The national varieties of Buddhism, especially Chan Buddhism, continued to exist, and monasteries in southern China sometimes became islands of traditional civilization where monks and lay Buddhists alike cultivated poetry, painting, and all the intellectual pastimes of the Chinese literati class, but, on the whole, Chinese Buddhism suffered from the general conditions in the Yuan empire. The exemption from taxes and corvée attracted many persons to monastic life for purely utilitarian reasons; the more society disintegrated, the more people sought refuge behind the monastery walls. About 1300 the number of monks throughout China was estimated at 500,000, and it must have grown during the last decades of Mongol rule. Monks played a great role in the rebellions to which the Yuan empire eventually succumbed; also, the first Ming emperor had been a monk for some time.

FOREIGN RELIGIONS

Tibetan Buddhism always remained outside Chinese civilization, as did other imported religions. A certain number of Muslims came to China, all from the Middle East or from Central Asia. The Turkic Öngüt tribe was largely Nestorian Christian. Many tombstones with a bilingual Turkic and Chinese inscription have been preserved, but none of these believers seems to have been Chinese by origin; a census taken about 1300 in Zhenjiang (in the present-day province of Jiangsu) lists the Nestorians together with foreign nationalities. The number of Nestorian Christians in China was so great that in 1289 a special agency for their supervision was established in Dadu. Manichaeism, which had spread to China under the Tang, became extinct as an organized religion under the Yuan, but some Manichaean communities were probably absorbed by messianic Buddhist sects, such as the White Lotus sect, a group that attracted many followers among the Chinese lower classes.

CONFUCIANISM

Confucianism was perceived by the Mongols as a Chinese religion, and it had mixed fortunes under their rule. The teachings of the Neo-Confucian school of Zhu Xi from the Song period were introduced to the Mongol court at Zhongdu in the late 1230s but were confined to limited circles there and in northern China. Confucian scholars enjoyed the benefits extended to the clergy of all religions, but they were dealt a strong blow when the literary examinations were discontinued following the Mongol conquest. For many centuries the examinations, based on Confucian texts, had been the basis for the selection of officials and for their privileged position within the state and society. After Kublai's accession, Confucianism had a more cordial reception at the Mongol court through the efforts of Chinese advisers such as Liu Bingzhong and the great Confucian master Xu Heng. Under their stewardship a certain Confucianization took place in government and education. Chinese rituals were performed for a while in the dynastic temple (*taimiao*), erected in Zhongdu in 1263. State sacrifices were offered to Confucius, and the study of the Classics was encouraged. However, many of the rites observed at the court that were either Tibetan Buddhist or inherited from the Mongol nomadic past were continued. The emperor Buyantu (reigned 1311–20), one of the most Sinicized Mongol rulers, reintroduced the examination system in 1313, but it remains doubtful how well the examinations functioned. They certainly did not guarantee an official career, as those under the Song and, to a certain extent, under the Jin had done.

The system of the Yuan, as introduced in 1313, provided different types of curricula for Mongols, other foreigners (*semuren*), and Chinese; also, the requirements were different: Chinese had to show their complete mastery of the curriculum, whereas Mongols and other foreigners had to give only a mediocre performance. This inequality was even formalized for the candidates who were to be admitted to the state academy (*guozijian*). The first examinations were held in the presence of the emperor in 1315, and, of the 300 persons granted the title of doctor (*jinshi*), 75 were Mongols, 75 were other foreigners, 75 were northern Chinese (*hanren*), and 75 came from southern China; they all received official positions within the bureaucracy, Mongols the higher and Chinese the lower posts. The positions of power within the hierarchy remained in the hands of the Mongols and other foreigners.

Under Buyantu, for the first time the interpretation and commentaries of the Neo-Confucian school were made obligatory. This cemented Neo-Confucian ideology not only among the Chinese literati who wished to pass an examination but also for future generations. Chinese Confucian orthodoxy from the 14th to the 19th century therefore rested largely on the foundations it had received under the Yuan. In spite of all this, Classical scholarship under the Yuan did not produce a single remarkable work but struggled under an adverse political and intellectual climate. Striving to preserve their sacred tradition, the Confucian scholars were content with expounding the doctrines laid down by the Song philosophers, seeking to harmonize the different philosophical issues and points of view rather than exploring new horizons.

LITERATURE

Chinese literature of the period also showed conservative tendencies. Poetry composition remained a favourite pastime of the educated class, including the Sinicized scholars of Mongol, Central Asian, and western Asian origins, but no great works or stylistic innovations were created. During the last chaotic decades of the Yuan, some notable poets emerged, such as the versatile Yang Weizhen and the bold and unconventional Gao Qi. Many prose works dealing with contemporary events and persons were written under the Yuan, but these are notable for their content, not their literary merit. Surprisingly harsh criticism and satire against the Mongols and also undisguised Song loyalism found open expression, presumably because the Mongols were uninterested in what the Chinese wrote in Chinese and, moreover, were mostly unable to read it. Some writers collected rare or interesting and piquant items and transmitted many aspects of Song culture to future generations. The lament for the refinement and grandeur of the Song is a constant theme in Yuan writings.

During the early Yuan period, the traditional Chinese official historiography was restored under the charge of the Hanlin Academy, which sponsored the compilation of the official dynastic histories of the Song, Liao, and Jin states conquered by the Mongols and undertook the compilation of the reign chronicles (*shilu*) and other governmental compendiums. The major achievement of official historiography was the compilation (1329–33) of the *Jingshi dadian*, a repository of 800 *juan* (chapters) of official documents and laws; the text is now lost. Private historiography, especially works on the events of the Song, fared rather poorly under the Yuan because of the adverse political and intellectual climate. The most-distinguished contribution was written by Ma Duanlin and titled *Wenxian tongkao* ("General Study of the Literary Remains"): an encyclopaedic documentary history of Chinese institutions from the earliest times to the middle reign of the Nan Song dynasty.

In urban society a literature in the vernacular language began to flourish, untrammeled by rigid norms of formalistic or ideological orthodoxy. Novels and stories were written for the amusement of a wide-reading public, and dramatic literature reached such a peak in Yuan China that later literary criticism regarded the Yuan as the classical age for operatic arias, or *qu* (a word that is also used for a full opera, with arias and chanted recitatives). The collection *Yuanquxuan* ("Selection from Yuan Operas"), with 100 opera librettos, and the storyteller "prompt books" for dramatized historical romances such as *Sanguo* ("Three Kingdoms") give ample evidence for the creativity and vitality of Chinese dramatic literature. This phenomenon may perhaps be considered as evidence that under the Yuan a certain urbanization took place and something like a bourgeoisie emerged, because dramatic literature and colloquial novels found their clientele chiefly among the merchant and artisan classes.

Foreigners, chiefly of Turkic or Persian origin, also contributed to Chinese literature under the Yuan. They wrote poetry and painted in the Chinese way in order to distinguish themselves in fields where they could gain prestige among the educated Chinese. All the foreigners who wrote in Chinese seem to have avoided any reference to their foreign origin or creed. Nothing, in fact, could be more Chinese than their productions. Even foreigners who, like the Persians, came from a country with a considerable literary tradition of its own never attempted to introduce their native forms, subject matter, or religions. No literary symbiosis seemed possible, and, although China was exposed to more external influences under the Yuan than ever before, Chinese literature shows little effect from such contacts with the outside world. It is perhaps symptomatic that under the Yuan no literary works from other civilizations were translated into Chinese and that practically no translations of Chinese Classical and historical works into Mongol have survived. There seemed to be only the alternatives of complete rejection of Chinese civilization, as practiced by most Mongols, or wholesale absorption by Chinese culture.

THE ARTS

Conservatism played a dominant role in the arts during the Mongol period. In sponsored arts such as sculpture and ceramics, the Mongols' desire to lay claim to the Chinese imperial heritage was not complemented by any strong

Example of xingshu *by Zhao Mengfu, Yuan dynasty; in the National Palace Museum, Taipei.* Courtesy of the National Palace Museum, Taipei, Taiwan, Republic of China

artistic vision of their own, and conservatism meant mere perpetuation. Song, Liao, and Jin ceramic types were continued, often altered only by increased bulk, while the great artistic achievement of the era, blue-and-white ware, probably derived from non-imperial sources. Government-sponsored Buddhist sculpture often attained high artistic standards, preserving the realism and powerful expression of Tang and Song traditions, while in the finest sculpture of the time, such as the reliefs at Juyong Pass north of Dadu (1342–45), this was combined with a flamboyant surface decor and a striking dramatization better suited to foreign taste than to the increasingly restrained Chinese aesthetic.

Conservatism also tempered the private arts of calligraphy and painting: the scholar-amateurs who produced them felt impelled to preserve their heritage against a perceived barbarian threat. Conservatism, however, often took the form of a creative revival that combed the past for sources of inspiration and then artistically transformed them into a new idiom. In calligraphy, Zhao Mengfu gave new impetus to the 4th-century style of Wang Xizhi, which then became a standard for Chinese writing and book printing for centuries. In painting, Zhao and his contemporary Qian Xuan helped to complete the development of a distinctively amateur style that ushered in a new phase in the history of Chinese painting. Their work did not continue that of the previous generation but ranged widely over the available past tradition, and past styles rather than observed objects became the subject of artistic interpretation. The naturalism of Song painting gave way to calligraphically inspired abstractions. Paintings became closely linked in style to the written inscriptions that appeared upon them with increasing frequency and prominence. Skillful professional techniques and overt visual attractiveness were avoided, replaced by deliberate awkwardness and an intellectualized flavour. Their works were done for private purposes, often displaying or concealing personal and political motives, to be understood only by fellow literati through the subtle allusions of their subject matter, stylistic references, or inscriptions.

Naturalistic painting styles also contnued in popularity throughout the first two-thirds of the period, painted by such important artists as Li Kan and Ren Renfa. Perpetuating northern traditions of the Tang and Song periods, these styles were practiced chiefly by scholar-officials associated with the court at the capital. Several members of the Mongol royal family became major patrons or collectors of such conservative styles, although imperial patronage remained slight in comparison with earlier periods.

In the latter third of the dynasty, with a sharp decline in the practice of painting by scholar-officials and northerners, Yuan painting was increasingly represented by

Nine Horses, *detail of a hand scroll by Ren Renfa, ink and colours on silk, 1324, Yuan dynasty; in the Nelson-Atkins Museum of Art, Kansas City, Mo., U.S.* The Nelson-Atkins Museum of Art, Kansas City, Missouri; purchase Nelson Trust (72-8)

the innovative approach of Zhao Mengfu as practiced by reclusive scholars from the Suzhou-Wuxing area. Four of these—the landscape painters Huang Gongwang, Wu Zhen, Ni Zan, and Wang Meng—transformed and blended certain elements from the past into highly personal, easily recognizable styles and later came to be known as the Four Masters of the Yuan dynasty. In the early Ming period the Hongwu emperor decimated the Suzhou literati and with it Suzhou painting; by the end of the 15th century, however, Suzhou artists once again dominated Chinese painting, and the styles of the Four Masters became the most influential of all painting models in later Chinese history.

YUAN CHINA AND THE WEST

As has been mentioned, Mongol rulers favoured trade in all their dominions. In China too they eliminated state trade controls that had existed under the Song and Jin, so that internal and external trade reached unprecedented proportions. It seems, however, that China's transcontinental trade with the Middle East and Europe was in the hands of non-Chinese (mainly Persians, Arabs, and Syrians). Silk, the Chinese export commodity par excellence, reached the Middle East and even Europe via the caravan routes across Asia; Chinese ceramics were also exported, chiefly into the Islamic countries. The Asian countries concentrated their European trade largely with the Italian republics (e.g., Genoa, Venice). To the Italians, trade with the East was so important that the *Practica della mercatura*, a handbook on foreign trade, included the description of trade routes to China.

Direct contacts between China and Europe were insignificant, however, even though China was part of an empire stretching from Dadu to southern Russia. Chinese historical and geographic literature had little to say about the European parts of the Mongol empire; in the official dynastic history of the Yuan, references to foreign countries are limited to countries such as Korea, Japan, Nam Viet, Myanmar (Burma), and Champa, with which China had carried on trade or tributary relations for centuries, and there are some scattered data on Russia. For some time a Russian guards regiment existed in Dadu, and some Russian soldiers were settled in military colonies in eastern Manchuria. As a whole, however, the civilizations of Europe and China did not meet, although contacts were made easy; Europe remained for the Chinese a vague region somewhere "beyond the Uighur."

More important were the contributions from the Islamic countries of the Middle East, chiefly in the fields of science and technology. During the reign of Kublai Khan, Arab-Persian astronomy and astronomical instruments were introduced into China, and the Chinese astronomer Guo Shoujing operated an observatory. Nevertheless, the basic conceptions of astronomy remained Chinese, and no attempt was made to adopt the Middle Eastern mathematical and theoretical framework. Similarly, Middle Eastern physicians and surgeons practiced successfully in China, but Chinese medical theory remained uninfluenced by Western practices. In geography a Chinese world map of the 14th century incorporates Arabic geographical knowledge into the Chinese worldview. It shows not only China and the adjacent countries but also the Middle East, Europe, and Africa; the African continent is already given in its actual triangular shape. But this knowledge probably never spread beyond a limited circle of professional geographers, and it is certain that the Sino-centric world conception continued unchallenged under the Yuan dynasty; no curiosity of what lay beyond the Chinese borders was aroused. For the countries to be reached by sea (such as Southeast Asian countries and India), Chinese works of the Yuan offer only a poor extract from the Song work *Zhufanzhi* (c. 1225; "Description of the Barbarians").

The situation was different regarding European knowledge of China. The Mongol advance into eastern Europe had given Europeans an acute awareness that actual people lived in regions hitherto shrouded in vague folkloric legends and myths. The Islamic world had similarly become a reality to Europeans with the first Crusades. It was, therefore, only natural that the Roman Catholic Church looked for potential converts among non-Muslim people of Asia. After Franciscan envoys brought back information on what was known as Cathay (northern China) in the mid-13th century, Pope Nicholas IV, a former Franciscan, dispatched a Franciscan mission to the court of the grand khan in Dadu (known in Europe as Cambaluc). The missionaries formed the nucleus of a Catholic hierarchy on Chinese soil: Cambaluc became the seat of an archbishopric, and in 1323 a bishopric was established in Quanzhou. A renowned Franciscan missionary was Odoric of Pordenone, who traveled in China in the 1320s; his reports, together with letters written by other Catholic missionaries, brought firsthand information on China to medieval Europe and today throw some light on the earliest missionary work in China. The Franciscan mission, which had to compete with the Nestorian clergy, was carried on more by the foreigners in China than by the Chinese themselves. The friars preached in Tatar (i.e., either Mongol or Turkic) and apparently won no Chinese converts. Significantly, no Chinese source mentions the activities of these missionaries; the Chinese probably regarded the Franciscans as one of the many strange, foreign sects, perhaps an outlandish variety of Buddhism. Archaeological evidence of the presence of Europeans and of Roman Catholicism has been discovered only in modern times; one example is from Yangzhou (in present-day Jiangsu), where the Latin inscription on a tombstone dated 1342 is a record of the death of an Italian lady whose name suggests some relation to a Venetian family engaged in trade with Asia.

Only the last direct contact between the papal see and Yuan China can be corroborated by both Western and Chinese sources. In 1336 a group of Alani Christians in Dadu sent a letter to Pope Benedict XII, who sent John of Marignola with a mission to the Mongol court. The mission reached the summer capital, Shangdu, in 1342. Chinese sources recorded the date of its audience as Aug. 19, 1342. The country the envoys came from is given by the Chinese source as Fulang, a Chinese version of the name Farang (Franks), which was used in the Middle East as a general term for Europeans. The arrival of envoys from what must have seemed the end of the world so impressed the court that an artist was commissioned to paint a portrait of the battle horse that Marignola had brought as a present; this portrait was still extant in the 18th century but is now lost. Chinese literati wrote many eulogies on the portrait of the horse; the country of Fulang, however, did not interest the Chinese poets, and the whole embassy of Marignola is invariably described in terms that point to an unbroken Sinocentric attitude. Thus, the contact between the pontiff and the Mongol court remained without further consequence.

The end of Mongol rule over China and the strong nationalism of the Ming dynasty also doomed the Catholic missions of the 14th century. The reports of the Venetian adventurer Marco Polo, on the other hand, inaugurated for Europe the era of discoveries and created a new vision of the world, with China as a part.

Although China as a separate cultural entity was realized only dimly and gradually in the European West, Chinese influences spread under the Yuan dynasty to other parts of Asia. Chinese medical treatises were translated into Persian, and Persian miniature painting in the 13th and 14th centuries shows many influences of Chinese art. Chinese-type administration and chancellery practices were adopted by various Mongol dominions in Central Asia and the Middle East. It has even been suggested that the invention of gunpowder and of printing in Europe was because of a sort of stimulus diffusion from China, although a direct influence from China cannot be proved.

Chinese civilization itself remained very much what it had been before the Yuan dynasty, with a certain cultural isolationism a distinctive element. Neither the self-image of the Chinese nor China's position in the world changed very drastically. The change and challenges to which China was exposed under the Yuan, however, can explain many of the characteristic traits of Ming history.

THE END OF MONGOL RULE

The basic dilemma of Mongol rule in China—the Mongols' inability to achieve a durable identification with Chinese civilian institutions and to modify the military and colonialist character of their rule—became more apparent under Kublai's successors and reached a maximum under Togon-temür, the last Yuan ruler. Togon-temür was not unfriendly toward Chinese civilization, but this could not alter the contempt of many leading Mongols for Chinese civilian institutions. For centuries China had known clique factionalism at court, but this was mostly fought with political means; Mongol factionalism usually resorted to military power. Militarization gradually spread from the Mongol ruling class into Chinese society, and not a few dissatisfied Chinese leaders established regional power based on local soldiery. The central administration headed by a weak emperor proved incapable of preserving its supremacy.

Thus, the military character of Mongol rule paved the way for the success of Chinese rebels, some of whom came from the upper class, while others were messianic sectarians who found followers among the exploited peasantry. The Mongol court and the provincial administrations could still rely on a number of faithful officials and soldiers, and so the progress of the rebel movement in the 1350s and 1360s remained slow. But the rebel armies who had chosen what is now Nanjing as their base took Dadu in 1368; the Mongol emperor fled, followed by the remnants of his overthrown government.

The Mongols remained a strong potential enemy of China for the next century, and the Genghis Khan clan in Mongolia continued to regard itself as the legitimate ruler of China. The century of Mongol rule had some undesirable effects on the government of China: imperial absolutism and a certain brutalization of authoritarian rule, inherited from the Yuan, were features of the succeeding Ming government. Yet, Mongol rule lifted some of the traditional ideological and political constraints on Chinese society. The Confucian hierarchical order was not rigidly enforced as it had been under the Tang and Song, and the Mongols thereby facilitated the upward mobility of some social classes, such as the merchants, and encouraged extensive growth of popular culture, which had been traditionally downgraded by the literati.

CHAPTER 9

THE MING DYNASTY

POLITICAL HISTORY

Ineptitude on the throne, bureaucratic factionalism at court, rivalries among Mongol generals, and ineffective supervision and coordination of provincial and local administration had gravely weakened the Yuan government by the 1340s. And in 1351 disastrous flooding of the Huang and Huai river basins aroused hundreds of thousands of long-oppressed Chinese peasants into open rebellion in northern Anhui, southern Henan, and northern Hubei provinces. Rebel movements, capitalizing on the breakdown of Yuan control, spread rapidly and widely, especially throughout central China. By the mid-1360s, large regional states had been created that openly flouted Yuan authority: Song in the Huai basin, under the nominal leadership of a mixed Manichaean-Buddhist secret-society leader named Han Lin'er; Han in the central Yangtze valley, under a onetime fisherman named Chen Youliang; Xia in Sichuan, under an erstwhile general of the rebel Han regime named Ming Yuzhen; and Wu in the rich Yangtze delta area, under a former Grand Canal boatman named Zhang Shicheng. A onetime salt trader and smuggler named Fang Guozhen had simultaneously established an autonomous coastal satrapy in Zhejiang. While Yuan chieftains contended with one another for dominance at the capital, Dadu (present-day Beijing), and in the North China Plain, these rebel states to the south wrangled for survival and supremacy. Out of this turmoil emerged a new native dynasty called Ming (1368–1644).

THE DYNASTY'S FOUNDER

Zhu Yuanzhang, founder of the new dynasty, came from a family originally from northwestern Jiangsu province who by Yuan times had deteriorated into itinerant tenant farmers in northern Anhui province. Orphaned by famine and plague in 1344, young Zhu was taken into a small Buddhist monastery near Fengyang city as a lay novice. For more than three years he wandered as a mendicant through the Huai basin before beginning studies for the Buddhist priesthood in his monastery. In 1352, after floods, rebellions, and Yuan campaigns against bandits had devastated and intimidated the whole region, Zhu was persuaded to join a Fengyang branch of Han Lin'er's uprising. He quickly made himself the most successful general on the southern front of the rebel Song regime, and in 1356 he captured and set up his headquarters in Nanjing, a populous and strategically located city on the Yangtze River. There he began assembling a rudimentary government and greatly strengthened his military power. Between 1360 and 1367, still nominally championing the cause of the Song regime, his armies gained control of the vast central and eastern stretches of the Yangtze valley, absorbing first the Han domain to the west of Nanjing and

then the Wu domain to the east. He also captured the Zhejiang coastal satrap, Fang Guozhen. Zhu then announced his intention of liberating all of China from Mongol rule and proclaimed a new dynasty effective with the beginning of 1368. The dynastic name Ming, meaning "Brightness," reflects the Manichaean influence in the Song-revivalist Han Lin'er regime under which Zhu had achieved prominence. Zhu came to be known by his reign name, the Hongwu ("Vastly Martial") emperor.

The Hongwu emperor, hanging scroll, ink and colour on silk, 14th century; in the National Palace Museum, Taipei. Courtesy of the National Palace Museum, Taipei, Taiwan, Republic of China

HONGWU

Hongwu is the reign name of Zhu Yuanzhang (b. Oct. 21, 1328—d. June 24, 1398), founder of China's Ming dynasty. A poor peasant orphaned at 16, Zhu entered a monastery to avoid starvation. Later, as a rebel leader, he came in contact with educated gentry from whom he received an education and political guidance. He was advised to present himself not as a popular rebel but as a national leader against the foreign Mongols whose Yuan dynasty was on the point of collapse. Defeating rival national leaders, Zhu proclaimed himself emperor in 1368, establishing his capital at Nanjing and adopting Hongwu as his reign title. He drove the last Yuan emperor from China that year and reunified the country by 1382. His rule was despotic: he eliminated the posts of prime minister and central chancellor and had the next level of administration report directly to him. He prohibited eunuchs from participating in government and appointed civilian officials to control military affairs.

Vigorous campaigning in 1368 drove the Mongols out of Shandong, Henan, and Shanxi provinces and from Dadu itself, which was occupied by Ming forces on September 14, and simultaneously extended Ming authority through Fujian and Hunan into Guangdong and Guangxi provinces on the south coast. In 1369–70 Ming control was established in Shaanxi, Gansu, and Inner Mongolia, and continued campaigning against the Mongols thereafter extended northwestward to Hami (1388), northeastward to the Sungari (Songhua) River in Manchuria (1387), and northward into Outer Mongolia beyond Karakorum, almost to Lake Baikal (1387–88). In operations to the west and southwest, Ming forces destroyed the rebel Xia regime in Sichuan in 1371, wiped out major Mongol and aboriginal resistance in Guizhou and Yunnan in 1381–82, and

pacified aboriginal peoples on the border between China and Myanmar in 1398. Thus, by the end of the Hongwu emperor's 30-year reign in 1398, his new dynasty controlled the whole of modern China proper and dominated the northern frontier regions, from Hami through Inner Mongolia and into northern Manchuria.

THE DYNASTIC SUCCESSION

The Ming dynasty, which encompassed the reigns of 16 emperors, proved to be one of the stablest and longest ruling periods of Chinese history. Rulers of Korea, Mongolia, East Turkistan, Myanmar, Siam, and Nam Viet regularly acknowledged Ming overlordship, and at times tribute was received from as far away as Japan, Java and Sumatra, Sri Lanka and South India, the East African coast, the Persian Gulf region, and

Samarkand. Modern Chinese honour the Ming emperors especially for having restored China's international power and prestige, which had been in decline since the 8th century. The Ming emperors probably exercised more far-reaching influence in East Asia than any other native rulers of China, and their attitude toward the representatives of Portugal, Spain, Russia, Britain, and Holland who appeared in China before the end of their dynasty was a condescending one.

For the first time in Chinese history, the Ming rulers regularly adopted only one reign name (*nianhao*) each; the sole exception was the sixth emperor, who had two reigns separated by an interval of eight years. Because of this reign-name practice (which was perpetuated under the succeeding Qing dynasty), modern writers, confusingly but correctly, refer to the Wanli emperor, for example, by his personal name, Zhu Yijun; by his temple name, Shenzong; or sometimes, incorrectly but conveniently, simply as Wanli, as if the reign name were a personal name.

The Ming dynasty's founder, the Hongwu emperor, is one of the strongest and most colourful personalities of Chinese history. His long reign established the governmental structure, policies, and tone that characterized the whole dynasty. After his death in 1398 his grandson and successor, the Jianwen emperor, trying to assert control over his powerful uncles, provoked a rebellion on the part of the prince of Yan and was overwhelmed in 1402. The prince of Yan took the throne as the Yongle emperor (reigned 1402–24) and proved to be vigorous and aggressive. He subjugated Nam Viet, personally campaigned against the reorganizing Mongols in the north, and sent large naval expeditions overseas, chiefly under the eunuch admiral Zheng He, to demand tribute from rulers as far away as Africa. He also returned the empire's capital to Beijing, giving that city its present-day name.

For a century after the Yongle emperor, the empire enjoyed stability, tranquillity, and prosperity. But state administration began to suffer when weak emperors were exploitatively dominated by favoured eunuchs: Wang Zhen in the 1440s, Wang Zhi in the 1470s and 1480s, and Liu Jin from 1505 to 1510. The Hongxi (reigned 1424–25), Xuande (1425–35), and Hongzhi (1487–1505) emperors were nevertheless able and conscientious rulers in the Confucian mode. The only serious disruption of the peace occurred in 1449 when the eunuch Wang Zhen led the Zhengtong emperor (first reign 1435–49) into a disastrous military campaign against the Oyrat (western Mongols). The Oyrat leader Esen Taiji ambushed the imperial army, captured the emperor, and besieged Beijing. The Ming defense minister, Yu Qian, forced Esen to withdraw unsatisfied and for eight years dominated the government with emergency powers. When the interim Jingtai emperor (reigned 1449–57) fell ill in 1457, the Zhengtong emperor, having been released by the Mongols in 1450, resumed the throne as the Tianshun emperor (1457–64). Yu Qian was then executed as a traitor.

The Zhengde (reigned 1505–21) and Jiajing (1521–1566/67) emperors were among the less-esteemed Ming rulers. The former was an adventure-loving carouser, the latter a lavish patron of Daoist alchemists. For one period of 20 years, during the regime of an unpopular grand secretary named Yan Song, the Jiajing emperor withdrew almost entirely from governmental cares. Both emperors cruelly humiliated and punished hundreds of officials for their temerity in remonstrating.

China's long peace ended during the Jiajiang emperor's reign. The Oyrat, under the vigorous new leadership of Altan Khan, were a constant nuisance on the northern frontier from 1542 on; in 1550 Altan Khan raided the suburbs of Beijing itself. During the same era, Japan-based sea raiders repeatedly plundered China's southeastern coast. Such sea raiders, a problem in Yuan times and from the earliest Ming years, had been suppressed during the reign of the Yongle emperor, when Japan's Ashikaga shogunate offered nominal submission to China in exchange for generous trading privileges. However, changes in the official trade system eventually provoked new discontent along the coast, and during the 1550s corsair fleets looted the Shanghai-Ningbo region almost annually, sometimes sending raiding parties

far inland to terrorize cities and villages throughout the whole Yangtze delta. Although coastal raiding was not totally suppressed, it was brought under control in the 1560s. Also in the 1560s Altan Khan was repeatedly defeated, so that he made peace in 1571. For the next decade, during the last years of the Longqing emperor (reigned 1566/67–1572) and the early years of the Wanli emperor (1572–1620), the government was highly stable. The court was dominated by the outstanding grand secretary of Ming history, Zhang Juzheng, and capable generals such as Qi Jiguang restored and maintained effective military defenses.

In 1592, when Japanese forces under Toyotomi Hideyoshi invaded Korea, Ming China was still strong and responsive enough to campaign effectively in support of its tributary neighbour. But the Korean war dragged on indecisively until 1598, when Hideyoshi died and the Japanese withdrew. It made heavy demands on Ming resources and apparently precipitated a military decline in China.

The reign of the Wanli emperor was a turning point of Ming history in other regards as well. Partisan wrangling among civil officials had flared up in the 1450s in reaction to Yu Qian's dominance and again in the 1520s during a prolonged "rites controversy" provoked by the Jiajing emperor on his accession;

One of 36 stone statues (18 pairs) of officials and creatures that guard the route to the tombs of 13 emperors of the Ming dynasty north of Beijing. Richard Nowitz/National Geographic/ Getty Images

after Zhang Juzheng's death in 1582, it became the normal condition of court life. Through the remainder of the Wanli emperor's long reign, a series of increasingly vicious partisan controversies absorbed the energies of officialdom, while the harassed emperor abandoned more and more of his responsibilities to eunuchs. The decline of bureaucratic discipline and morale continued under the Taichang emperor, whose sudden death after a reign of only one month in 1620 fueled new conflicts. The Tianqi emperor (reigned 1620–27) was too young and indecisive to provide needed leadership. In 1624 he finally gave almost totalitarian powers to his favourite, Wei Zhongxian, the most notorious eunuch of Chinese history. Wei brutally purged hundreds of officials, chiefly those associated with a reformist clique called the Donglin party, and staffed the government with sycophants.

A new threat had in the meantime appeared on the northern frontier. The Manchu, quiet occupants of far eastern Manchuria from the beginning of the dynasty, were aroused in 1583 by an ambitious young leader named Nurhachi. During the Wanli emperor's latter years, they steadily encroached on central Manchuria. In 1616 Nurhachi proclaimed a new dynasty, and overwhelming victories over Ming forces in 1619 and 1621 gave him control of the whole northeastern segment of the Ming empire, south to the Great Wall at Shanhaiguan.

The Chongzhen emperor (reigned 1627–44) tried to revitalize the deteriorating Ming government. He banished Wei Zhongxian but could not quell the partisan strife that was paralyzing the bureaucracy. The Manchu repeatedly raided within the Great Wall, even threatening Beijing in 1629 and 1638. Taxes and conscriptions became increasingly oppressive to the Chinese population, and banditry and rebellions spread in the interior. The Ming government became completely demoralized. Finally, a domestic rebel named Li Zicheng captured the capital in April 1644, and the Chongzhen emperor committed suicide. The Ming commander at Shanhaiguan accepted Manchu help in an effort to punish Li Zicheng and restore the dynasty, only to have the Manchu seize the throne for themselves.

Ming loyalists ineffectively resisted the Qing (Manchu) dynasty from various refuges in the south for a generation. Their so-called Nan (Southern) Ming dynasty principally included the prince of Fu (Zhu Yousong, reign name Hongguang), the prince of Tang (Zhu Yujian, reign name Longwu), the prince of Lu (Zhu Yihai, no reign name), and the prince of Gui (Zhu Youlang, reign name Yongli). The loyalist coastal raider Zheng Chenggong (Koxinga) and his heirs held out on Taiwan until 1683.

GOVERNMENT AND ADMINISTRATION

The Ming state system was built on a foundation of institutions inherited from the Tang and Song dynasties and modified by the intervening dynasties of conquest from the north, especially the Yuan. The distinctive new patterns of social and administrative organization that emerged in Ming times persisted, in their essential features, through the Qing dynasty into the 20th century.

LOCAL GOVERNMENT

At local and regional levels, the traditional modes and personnel of government were perpetuated in ad hoc fashion in the earliest Ming years, but, as the new empire became consolidated and stabilized, highly refined control structures were imposed that—in theory and probably also in reality—eventually subjugated all Chinese to the throne to an unprecedented and totalitarian degree. The Ming law code, promulgated in final form in 1397, reinforced the traditional authority and responsibility of the paterfamilias, considered the basis of all social order. Each family was classified according to hereditary status—the chief categories being civilian, military, and artisan—and neighbouring families of the same category were organized into groups for purposes of self-government and mutual help and surveillance. Civilians were grouped into "tithings" of 10 families, and these in turn were grouped into "communities" totaling 100 families, plus 10 additional prosperous households, which in annual rotation provided community chiefs, who were intermediaries between the citizenry at large and the formal agencies of government. This system of social organization, called *lijia* (later replaced by or coexistent with a local defense system called *baojia*), served to stabilize, regulate, and indoctrinate the populace under relatively loose formal state supervision.

Ming provincial governments consisted of three coordinate agencies with specialized responsibilities for general administration, surveillance and judicial affairs, and military affairs. These were the channels for routine administrative contacts between local officials and the central government.

CENTRAL GOVERNMENT

In its early form the Ming central government was dominated by a unitary Secretariat. The senior executive official of the Secretariat served the emperor as a chief counselor, or prime minister. Suspected treason on the part of the chief counselor Hu Weiyong in 1380 caused the Hongwu emperor to abolish all executive posts in the Secretariat, thus fragmenting general administration authority among the six functionally differentiated, formerly subordinate Ministries of Personnel, Revenue, Rites, War, Justice, and Works. This effective abolition of the Secretariat left the emperor as the central government's sole coordinator of any significance, strengthened his control over the officialdom, and, in the view of many later scholars, gravely weakened the Ming state system.

Especially prominent among other agencies of the central government was a Censorate, which was charged with the dual functions of maintaining disciplinary surveillance over the whole of officialdom and remonstrating against unwise state policies and improprieties in the conduct of the emperor. Equally prominent were five chief military commissions, each assigned responsibility, jointly with the Ministry of War, for a geographically defined segment of the empire's military establishment. There was originally a unitary Chief Military Commission paralleling the Secretariat, but in the 1380s its authority was similarly fragmented. The hereditary soldiers, who were under the administrative jurisdiction of the chief military commissions, originated as members of the rebel armies that established the dynasty, as surrendering enemy soldiers, in some instances as conscripts, and as convicted criminals. They were organized and garrisoned principally along the frontiers, near the capital, and in other strategic places but also throughout the interior, in units called guards and battalions. Whenever possible, such units were assigned state-owned agricultural lands so that, by alternating military duties with farm labour, the soldiers could be self-supporting. The military families, in compensation for providing soldiers in perpetuity, enjoyed exemptions from labour services levied by the state on civilian families. Each guard unit reported to its Chief Military Commission at the capital through a provincial-level Regional Military Commission. Soldiers from local guards were sent in rotation to the capital for special training or to the Great Wall or another area of comparable military importance for active patrol and guard duty. At such times, as on large-scale campaigns, soldiers served under tactical commanders who were on ad hoc duty assignments, detached from their hereditary posts in guard garrisons or higher echelons of the military service.

LATER INNOVATIONS

In the 15th century, new institutions were gradually devised to provide needed coordination both in the central government and in regional administration. Later emperors found the Hongwu emperor's system of highly centralized power and fragmented government structure inefficient and inconvenient. Litterateurs of the traditional and prestigious Hanlin Academy came to be assigned to the palace as secretarial assistants, and they quickly evolved into a stable Grand Secretariat (Neige) through which emperors guided and responded to the ministries and other central government agencies. Similarly, the need for coordinating provincial-level affairs led to delegating high-ranking central government dignitaries to serve as regional commanders (*zongbing guan*) and governor-like grand coordinators (*xunfu*) in the provinces. Finally, clusters of neighbouring provinces came under the supervisory control of still-more-prestigious central government officials, known as supreme commanders (*zongdu*), whose principal function was to coordinate military affairs in extended, multi-province areas. As the dynasty grew older, as the population expanded, and as administration became increasingly complex, coordinators proliferated even at sub-provincial levels in the form of circuit intendants (*daotai*), who were delegated from provincial agencies as functionally specialized intermediaries with prefectural administrations.

To an extent unprecedented except possibly in Song times, Ming government was dominated by nonhereditary civil service officials recruited on the basis of competitive written examinations. Hereditary military officers, although granted ranks and stipends higher than their civil service counterparts and eligible for noble titles rarely granted to civil officials, always found themselves subordinate to policy-making civil servants, except in the first years of the dynasty. Members of the imperial clan, except in the earliest and latest years of the dynasty, were forbidden to take active part in administration, and the Ming practice of finding imperial consorts in military families effectively denied imperial in-laws access to positions of significant authority. High-ranking civil officials usually could place one son each in the civil service by hereditary right, and, beginning in 1450, wealthy civilians often were able to purchase nominal civil service status in government fund-raising drives. But those entering the service in such irregular ways rarely had notable, or even active, careers in government. In the early decades of the dynasty, before competitive examinations could provide sufficient numbers of trustworthy men for service, large numbers of officials were recruited directly from government schools or through recommendations by existing officials, and such recruits often rose to eminence. But after about 1400, persons entering the civil service by avenues other than examinations had little hope for successful careers.

In a departure from traditional practices but in accordance with the Yuan precedent, there was only one type of examination given in Ming times. It required a general knowledge of the Classics and history and the ability to relate Classical precepts and historical precedents to general philosophical or specific political issues. As in Yuan times, interpretations of the Classics by the Zhu Xi school of Neo-Confucianism were prescribed. By the end of the Ming dynasty, the writing of examination responses had become highly stylized and formalized in a pattern called "the eight-legged essay" (*baguwen*), which in subsequent centuries became notoriously repressive of creative thought and writing.

Beginning in the Hongwu emperor's reign, the government sponsored district-level schools, in which state-subsidized students prepared for the civil service examinations. Especially talented students could be promoted from such local schools into programs of advanced learning and probationary service at a national university in the capital. Especially after 1500, there was a proliferation of private academies in which scholars gathered to discuss philosophy and students were also prepared for the examinations. Education intendants from provincial headquarters annually toured all localities, examining candidates who presented themselves and certifying those of "promising talent" (*xiucai*) as being qualified to undertake weeklong examination ordeals that were conducted every third year at the provincial capitals. Those who passed the provincial examinations (*juren*) could be appointed directly to posts in the lower echelons of the civil service. They were also eligible to compete in triennial metropolitan examinations conducted at the national capital. Those who passed were given degrees often called doctorates (*jinshi*) and promptly took an additional palace examination, nominally presided over by the emperor, on the basis of which they were ranked in order of excellence. They were registered as qualified officials by the Ministry of Personnel, which assigned them to active-duty posts as vacancies occurred. While on duty they were evaluated regularly by their administrative superiors and irregularly by touring inspectors from the Censorate. It was normally only after long experience and excellent records in low- and middle-grade posts, both in the provinces and in the capital, that an official might be nominated for high office and appointed by personal choice of the emperor.

Although acceptance into, and success in, the civil service were the most highly esteemed goals for all and were nominally determined solely by demonstrated scholastic and administrative abilities, other factors inevitably intruded to prevent the civil service system from being wholly "open." Differences in the economic status of families made for inequalities of educational opportunity and, consequently, inequalities of access to civil service careers. The sons of well-to-do families clearly had advantages, and men of the affluent and cultured southeastern region so threatened to monopolize scholastic competitions that regional quotas for those passing the metropolitan examinations were imposed by the government, beginning in 1397. Once in the service, one's advancement or even survival often depended on shifting patterns of favouritism and factionalism. Present-day scholarship strongly suggests nevertheless that "new blood" was constantly entering the Ming civil service, that influential families did not monopolize or dominate the service, and that men regularly rose from obscurity to posts of great esteem and power on the basis of merit. Social mobility, as reflected in the Ming civil service, was very possibly greater than in Song times and was clearly greater than in the succeeding Qing era.

The Ming pattern of government has generally been esteemed for its stability under civil service dominance, its creativity in devising new institutions to

THE MING DYNASTY | 201

serve changing needs, and its suppression of separatist warlords on one hand and disruptive interference by imperial clansmen and palace women on the other. It suffered, however, from sometimes vicious factionalism among officials, recurrences of abusive influence on the part of palace eunuchs, and defects in its establishment of hereditary soldiers. The military system not only failed to achieve self-support but stagnated steadily, so that from the mid-15th century onward it had to be supplemented by conscripts and, finally, all but replaced by mercenary recruits. Most notoriously, the Ming state system allowed emperors to behave capriciously and abusively toward their officials. Despite their high prestige, officials had to accept being ignored, humiliated, dismissed, and subjected to bodily punishment and to risk being cruelly executed (sometimes in large numbers), as suited the imperial fancy. Power was concentrated in the hands of the Ming emperors to a degree that was probably unparalleled in any other long-lived dynasty of Chinese history, and the Ming emperors often exercised their vast powers in abusive fashion.

FOREIGN RELATIONS

Whereas in Ming times the Chinese organized themselves along wholly bureaucratic and tightly centralized lines, the Ming emperors maintained China's traditional feudal-seeming relationships with foreign peoples. These included the aboriginal tribes of south and southwest China, who often rose in isolated rebellions but were gradually being assimilated. The Chinese took for granted that their emperor was everyone's overlord and that de facto (mostly hereditary) rulers of non-Chinese tribes, regions, and states were properly his feudatories. Foreign rulers were thus expected to honour and observe the Ming ritual calendar, to accept nominal appointments as members of the Ming nobility or military establishment, and, especially, to send periodic missions to the Ming capital to demonstrate fealty and present tribute of local commodities. Tributary envoys from continental neighbours were received and entertained by local and provincial governments in the frontier zones. Those from overseas were welcomed by special maritime trade supervisorates (*shibosi*, often called trading-ship offices) at three key ports on the southeast and south coasts: Ningbo in Zhejiang for Japanese contacts, Quanzhou in Fujian for contacts with Taiwan and the Ryukyu Islands, and Guangzhou (Canton) in Guangdong for contacts with Southeast Asia. The frontier and coastal authorities forwarded foreign missions to the national capital, where the Ministry of Rites offered them hospitality and arranged for their audiences with the emperor. All envoys received valuable gifts in acknowledgement of the tribute they presented. They also were permitted to buy and sell private trade goods at specified, officially supervised markets, both in the capital and on the coasts and frontiers. Thus, copper coins and luxury goods (notably silks and porcelains) flowed out of China, and pepper, other spices, and similar rarities flowed in. On the western and northern frontiers the principal exchange was in Chinese tea and steppe horses. On balance, the combined tribute and trade activities were highly advantageous to foreigners—so much so that the Chinese early established limits for the size and cargoes of foreign missions and prescribed long intervals that must elapse between missions.

The principal aim of Ming foreign policy was political: to maintain China's security and, especially, to make certain the Mongols could not threaten China again. To this end the Hongwu emperor repeatedly sent armies northward and northwestward to punish resurgent Mongol groups and prevent any reconsolidation of Mongol power. The Yongle emperor was even more zealous: he personally campaigned into the Gobi (desert) five times, and his decision to transfer the national capital from Nanjing to Beijing, completed in 1421 after long preparations, was largely a reflection of his concern about the frontier. His successors, though less zealous than he in this regard, were vigilant enough so that the Great Wall was restored and expanded to its present-day extent and dimensions. Frontier defense forces, aligned in nine defense commands stretching from Manchuria to Gansu, kept China free from Mongol incursions, except for occasional raiding forays such as those by Esen Taiji and Altan Khan.

The fact that the Mongols could not reunite themselves was a fortunate circumstance for Ming China. As early as the Yongle emperor's time, the Mongols were divided into three groups that were often antagonistic to one another: the so-called western Mongols or Oyrat (including the Kalmyk), the eastern Mongols or Tatars, and a group in the Chengde area known as the Urianghad tribes. The Urianghad tribes surrendered to the Hongwu emperor and were incorporated into China's frontier defense system under a Chinese military headquarters. Because they served the Yongle emperor as a loyal rear guard during his seizure of the throne, he rewarded them with virtual autonomy, withdrawing the Chinese command post from their homeland beyond the Great Wall. Subsequently, the Xuande emperor similarly withdrew the command post that the Hongwu emperor had established at the Mongols' old extramural capital, Shangdu. These withdrawals isolated Manchuria from China proper, terminated active Chinese military control in Inner Mongolia, and exposed the Beijing area in particular to the possibility of probing raids from the nearby steppes. They reflected an essentially defensive Chinese posture in the north, which by late Ming times allowed the Oyrat to infiltrate and dominate Hami and other parts of the northwestern frontier and the Manchu to rise to power in the northeast.

The Ming attitude toward foreign peoples other than the Mongols was generally unaggressive: so long as they were not disruptive, the Ming emperors left them to themselves. The Hongwu emperor made this his explicit policy. Even though he threatened the Japanese with punitive expeditions if they persisted in marauding along China's coasts, he dealt with the problem by building strong fortresses and coastal defense fleets that successfully repulsed the marauders. He did send an army to subdue Turfan (Turpan) in 1377, when the Turko-Mongol rulers of that oasis region rebelled and broke China's traditional transport routes to the west. But he refused to intervene in dynastic upheavals in Nam Viet and Korea (when Koryŏ was replaced by Chosŏn), and he was unmoved by the rise of the Turko-Mongol empire of Timur (Tamerlane) in the far west at Samarkand, even though Timur murdered Chinese envoys and was planning to campaign against China.

The Yongle emperor was much more aggressive. He sent the eunuch admiral Zheng He on tribute-collecting voyages to Southeast Asia, the Indian Ocean, and the Persian Gulf and as far as East Africa. On one early voyage, Zheng He intervened in a civil war in Java and established a new king there; on another, he captured the hostile king of Sri Lanka and took him prisoner to China. The Yongle emperor also reacted to turbulence in Nam Viet by sending an expeditionary force that incorporated the area into the Ming domain as a province in 1407.

After the Yongle era the Ming government reverted to the founding emperor's unaggressive policy toward foreign states. Nam Viet was abandoned in 1428 after protracted guerrilla-style resistance had thoroughly undermined Chinese control there. A new civil war in Nam Viet provoked the Chinese, after long and agonized discussion, to prepare to intervene there again in 1540, but the offer of ritual submission by a usurper gave the Chinese an opportunity to avoid war, and they welcomed it. On only two other occasions were Ming military forces active outside China's borders: in 1445–46, when Chinese troops pursued a rebellious border chief into Myanmar despite resistance there, and in 1592–98, when the Ming court undertook to help the Chosŏn (Yi) dynasty in Korea repulse Japanese invaders, a long and costly effort.

In order to preserve the government's monopolistic control of foreign contacts and trade and, at least in part, to keep the Chinese people from being contaminated by barbarian customs, the Ming rulers prohibited private dealings between Chinese and foreigners and forbade any private voyaging abroad. The rules were so strict as to disrupt even coastal fishing and trading, on which large populations in the south and southeast had traditionally based their livelihood. Such unrealistic prohibitions were unpopular and unenforceable, and, from about the mid-15th century, Chinese readily collaborated with foreign traders in widespread smuggling, for the most part officially condoned. In addition, by late Ming times, thousands of venturesome Chinese had migrated to become mercantile entrepreneurs in the various regions of Southeast Asia and even in Japan. In efforts to enforce its laws, the Ming court closed all maritime trade supervisorates except the one at Guangzhou early in the 16th century, and by the 1540s it had begun to reinvigorate coastal defenses against marauders throughout the southeast and the south.

These circumstances shaped the early China coast experiences of the Europeans, who first appeared in Ming China in 1514. The Portuguese had already established themselves in southern India and at Malacca, where they learned of the huge profits that could be made in the regional trade between the China coast and Southeast Asia. Becoming involved in what the Ming court considered smuggling and piracy, the Portuguese were not welcomed to China, but they would not be rebuffed, and by 1557 they had taken control of a settlement at the walled-off end of a coastal peninsula (present-day Macau) and were trading periodically at nearby Guangzhou. In 1575 Spaniards from Manila visited Guangzhou in a vain effort to get official trading privileges, and soon they were developing active though illegal trade on the Guangdong and Fujian coasts. Representatives of the Dutch East India Company, after unsuccessfully trying to capture Macau from the Portuguese in 1622, took control of coastal Taiwan in 1624 and began developing trade contacts in nearby Fujian and Zhejiang provinces. In 1637 a squadron of five English ships shot its way into Guangzhou and disposed of its cargoes there. Russia, meanwhile, had sent peaceful missions overland to Beijing, and by the end of the Ming dynasty the Russians' eastward expansion across Siberia had carried them finally to the shores of the Pacific north of the Amur River.

Christian missionaries from Europe were handicapped by the bad reputation their trader countrymen had acquired in China, but the Jesuit tactic of accommodating to local customs eventually got the Jesuits admitted to the mainland. Matteo Ricci was the successful pioneer, beginning his work in 1583 well-trained in the Chinese language and acquainted with Confucian learning. By the time of his death in 1610, despite hostility in some quarters, Jesuit communities were established in many cities of south and central China, a church had been built in Beijing under imperial patronage, and Christianity was known and respected by many Chinese scholar-officials. Before the end of the dynasty, Jesuits had won influential converts at court (notably the grand secretary Xu Guangqi, or Paul Xu), had produced Chinese books on European science as well as theology, and were manufacturing Portuguese-type cannon for Ming use against the Manchu. They also held official appointments in China's Directorate of Astronomy, which had the important responsibility of determining the official calendar. Both European technology and European ideas were beginning to have some effect on China, albeit still very limited.

ECONOMIC POLICY AND DEVELOPMENTS

POPULATION

Ming China's northward orientation in foreign relations was accompanied by a flow of Chinese migrants from the crowded south back into the vast North China Plain and by a concomitant shift in emphasis from an urban and commercial way of life back to a rural and agrarian pattern. Thus, demographic and economic trends that had characterized China for centuries—the southward movement of population and the urbanization and commercialization of life—were arrested or even reversed.

The North China Plain had been neglected since early Song times, and its rehabilitation became a high-priority project of the early Ming emperors. The Ming founder's ancestral home was in northern China, and his son, the Yongle emperor, won the throne from a personal power base in the newly recovered north at Beijing. Securing the northern frontier was the major political goal of both these emperors, and both had reasons for being somewhat suspicious of southerners and hostile toward them. In consequence, both emperors regularly moved well-to-do city dwellers of the Yangtze delta region to northern towns for their cultural adornment, resettled peasants from the overpopulated southeast into the vacant lands of the north for their agrarian redevelopment, and instituted water-control projects to restore the productivity of the Huang and Huai river basins. (Notable among these is the rehabilitation and extension of the Grand Canal, which reopened in 1415.) Colonists were normally provided with seeds, tools, and animals and were exempted from taxes for three years. The numerous army garrisons that were stationed in the north for defense of the frontier and of the post-1420 capital at Beijing were also given vacant lands to develop and were encouraged to become self-supporting. Such government measures were supplemented, following political reunification, by popular migration into the relatively frontierlike and open north. Rehabilitation of northern China was no doubt also facilitated by the new availability of sorghum for dry farming. All these elements produced a substantial revival of the north. In Yuan times, censuses credited the northern provinces with only one-tenth of the total Chinese population, but by the late 16th century they claimed some two-fifths of the registered total. Suspension of government incentives late in the 15th century caused the northwest to enter into agrarian decline, and Shaanxi eventually became impoverished and bandit-infested. Support of the frontier defenses became an increasing burden on the central government.

During the migrations back to northern China, the registered populations of the largest urban centres of the southeast declined. For example, between 1393 and 1578, Nanjing declined from 1,193,000 to 790,000, Zhejiang province from 10,487,000 to 5,153,000, and Jiangxi province from 8,982,000 to 5,859,000. (It should be mentioned, however, that the actual population in cities typically was greater than what was registered.) Despite this leveling trend in the regional distribution of population, southern China—especially the southeast—remained the most populous, the wealthiest, and the most cultured area of China in Ming times. Great southeastern cities such as Nanjing, Suzhou, and Hangzhou remained the major centres of trade and manufacturing, entertainment, and scholarship and the arts. Beijing was their only rival in the north—solely because of its being the centre of political power.

Although official census figures suggest that China's overall population remained remarkably stable in Ming times at a total of about 60 million, modern scholars have estimated that there was in fact substantial growth, probably to a total well in excess of 100 million and perhaps almost as high as 150 million in the early 17th century. Domestic peace and political stability in the 15th century clearly set the stage for great general prosperity in the 16th century. This can be accounted for in part as the cumulative result of the continuing spread of early ripening rice and of cotton production—new elements that had been introduced into the Chinese economy in Song and Yuan times. The introduction in the 16th century of food crops originating in America—peanuts (groundnuts), corn (maize), and sweet potatoes—created an even stronger agrarian basis for rapidly escalating population growth in the Qing period.

Agriculture

Neo-feudal land-tenure developments of late Song and Yuan times were arrested with the establishment of the Ming dynasty. Great landed estates were confiscated by the government, fragmented, and rented out, and private slavery was forbidden. In the 15th century, consequently, independent peasant landholders dominated Chinese agriculture. But the Ming rulers were not able to provide permanent solutions for China's perennial land-tenure problems. As early as the 1420s, the farming population was in new difficulties despite repeated tax remissions and other efforts to ameliorate its condition. Large-scale landlordism gradually reappeared, as powerful families encroached upon the lands of poor neighbours. Song-style latifundia do not seem to have reemerged, but, by the late years of the dynasty, sharecropping tenancy was the common condition of millions of peasants, especially in central and southeastern China, and a new gulf had opened between the depressed poor and the exploitative rich. The later Ming government issued countless pronouncements lamenting the plight of the common man but never undertook any significant reform of land-tenure conditions.

TAXATION

The Ming laissez-faire policy in agrarian matters had its counterpart in fiscal administration. The Ming state took the collection of land taxes—its main revenues by far—out of the hands of civil service officials and entrusted that responsibility directly to well-to-do family heads in the countryside. Each designated tax captain was, on the average, responsible for tax collections in an area for which the land-tax quota was 10,000 piculs of grain (one picul is the equivalent of 3.1 bushels or 109 litres). In collaboration with the *lijia* community chiefs of his fiscal jurisdiction, he saw to it that tax grains were collected and then delivered, in accordance with complicated instructions; some went to local storage vaults under control of the district magistrate and some to military units, which, by means of the Grand Canal, annually transported more than three million piculs northward to Beijing. In the early Ming years, venal tax captains seem to have been able to amass fortunes by exploiting the peasantry. Later, however, tax captains normally faced certain ruin because tax-evading manipulations by large landlords thrust tax burdens increasingly on those least able to pay and forced tax captains to make up deficiencies in their quotas out of their personal reserves.

The land-tax rate was highly variable, depending not on the productivity of any plot but on the condition of its tenure, which might be as freehold or as one of several categories of land rented from the government. The land tax was calculated together with labour levies, or corvée, which, though nominally assessed against persons, were assessed against land in normal practice. Corvée obligations also varied widely and were usually payable in paper money or in silver rather than in actual service. Assessments against a plot of land might include several other considerations as well, so that a farmer's tax bill was a complicated reckoning of many different tax items. Efforts to simplify land-tax procedures in the 16th century, principally initiated by conscientious local officials, culminated in the universal promulgation of a consolidated-assessment scheme called "a single whip" (*yitiaobian*) in 1581. Its main feature was reducing land tax and corvée obligations to a single category of payment in bulk silver or its grain equivalent. This reform was little more than a bookkeeping change at best, and it was not universally applied. Land-tax inequities were unaffected, and assessments rose sharply and repeatedly from 1618 to meet spiraling costs of defense.

Many revenues other than land taxes contributed to support of the government. Some, such as mine taxes and levies on marketplace shops and vending stalls, were based on proprietorship; others, such as salt taxes, wine taxes, and taxes on mercantile goods in transit, were based on consumption. Of all state revenues, more than half seem to have remained in local and provincial granaries and treasuries; of those forwarded to the capital, about half seem normally to have disappeared into the emperor's personal vaults. Revenues at the disposal of the central government were always relatively small. Prosperity and fiscal caution had resulted in the accumulation of huge surpluses by the 1580s, both in the capital and in many provinces, but thereafter the Sino-Japanese war in Chosŏn, unprecedented extravagances on the part of the long-lived Wanli emperor, and defense against domestic rebels and the Manchu bankrupted both the central government and the imperial household.

COINAGE

Copper coins were used throughout the Ming dynasty. Paper money was used for various kinds of payments and grants by the government, but it was always nonconvertible and, consequently, lost value disastrously. It would in fact have been utterly valueless, except that it was prescribed for the payment of certain types of taxes. The exchange of precious metals was forbidden in early Ming times, but gradually bulk silver became common currency, and, after the mid-16th century, government accounts were reckoned primarily in taels (ounces) of silver. By the end of the dynasty, silver coins produced in Mexico, introduced by Spanish sailors based in the Philippines, were becoming common on the south coast.

Because during the last century of the Ming dynasty a genuine money economy emerged and because concurrently some relatively large-scale mercantile and industrial enterprises developed under private as well as state ownership (most notably in the great textile centres of the southeast), some modern-day scholars have considered the Ming age one of "incipient capitalism"; according to this reasoning, European-style mercantilism and industrialization might have evolved had it not been for the Manchu conquest and expanding European imperialism. It would seem clear, however, that private capitalism in Ming times flourished only insofar as it was condoned by the state, and it was never free from the threat of state suppression and confiscation. State control of the economy—and of society in all its aspects, for that matter—remained the dominant characteristic of Chinese life in Ming times, as it had earlier.

CULTURE

The predominance of state power also marked the intellectual and aesthetic life of Ming China. By requiring use of their interpretations of the Classics in education and in the civil service examinations, the state prescribed the Neo-Confucianism of the great Song thinkers Cheng Yi and Zhu Xi as the orthodoxy of Ming times; by patronizing or commandeering craftsmen and artists on a vast scale, it set aesthetic standards for all the minor arts, for architecture, and even for

Poet on a Mountain Top, *ink on paper or ink and light colour on paper, album leaf mounted as a hand scroll, by Shen Zhou, Ming dynasty; in the Nelson-Atkins Museum of Art, Kansas City, Mo., U.S. 38.7 × 60.2 cm.* The Nelson-Atkins Museum of Art, Kansas City, Missouri; purchase Nelson Trust (46–51/2)

painting, and, by sponsoring great scholarly undertakings and honouring practitioners of traditional literary forms, the state established norms in those realms as well. Thus, it has been easy for historians of Chinese culture to categorize the Ming era as an age of bureaucratic monotony and mediocrity, but the stable, affluent Ming society actually proved to be irrepressibly creative and iconoclastic. Drudges by the hundreds and thousands may have been content with producing second-rate imitations or interpretations of Tang and Song masterpieces in all genres, but independent thinkers, artists, and writers were striking out in many new directions. The final Ming century especially was a time of intellectual and artistic ferment akin to the most seminal ages of the past.

PHILOSOPHY AND RELIGION

Daoism and Buddhism by Ming times had declined into ill-organized popular religions, and what organization they had was regulated by the state. State espousal of Zhu Xi thought and state repression of noted early Ming litterateurs, such as the poet Gao Qi and the thinker Fang Xiaoru, made for widespread philosophical conformity during the 15th century. This was perhaps best characterized by the scholar Xue Xuan's insistence that the Daoist Way had been made so clear by Zhu Xi that nothing remained but to put it into practice. Philosophical problems about human identity and destiny, however, especially in an increasingly autocratic system, rankled in many minds, and new blends of Confucian, Daoist, and Buddhist elements appeared in a sequence of efforts to find ways of personal self-realization in contemplative, quietistic, and even mystical veins. These culminated in the antirationalist individualism of the famed scholar-statesman Wang Yangming, who denied the external "principles" of Zhu Xi and advocated striving for wisdom through cultivation of the innate knowledge of one's own mind and attainment of "the unity of knowledge and action." Wang's followers carried his doctrines to extremes of self-indulgence, preached to the masses in gatherings resembling religious revivals, and collaborated with so-called "mad" Chan (Zen) Buddhists to spread the notion that Confucianism, Daoism, and Buddhism are equally valid paths to the supreme goal of individualistic self-fulfillment. Through the 16th century, intense philosophical discussions were fostered, especially in rapidly multiplying private academies (*shuyuan*).

Vase, cloisonné enamel, Ming dynasty, c. *1500; in the British Museum, London. Height 41.5 cm.* Courtesy of the trustees of the British Museum

Rampant iconoclasm climaxed with Li Zhi, a zealous debunker of traditional Confucian morality, who abandoned a bureaucratic career for Buddhist monkhood of a highly unorthodox type. Excesses of this sort provoked occasional suppressions of private academies, periodic persecutions of heretics, and sophisticated counterarguments from traditionalistic, moralistic groups of scholars, such as those associated with the Donglin Academy near Suzhou, who blamed the late Ming decline of political efficiency and morality on widespread subversion of Zhu Xi orthodoxy. The zealous searching for personal identity was only intensified, however, when the dynasty finally collapsed.

FINE ARTS

In the realm of the arts, the Ming period has long been esteemed for the variety and high quality of its state-sponsored craft goods—cloisonné and, particularly, porcelain wares. The sober, delicate monochrome porcelains of the Song dynasty were now superseded by rich, decorative polychrome wares. The best known of these are of blue-on-white decor, which gradually changed from floral and abstract designs to a pictorial emphasis. From that eventually emerged the "willow-pattern" wares that became export goods in great demand in Europe. By late Ming times, perhaps because of the unavailability of the imported Iranian cobalt that was used for the finest blue-on-white products, more-flamboyant polychrome wares of three and even five colours predominated. Painting—chiefly portraiture—followed traditional patterns under imperial patronage, but independent gentlemen painters became the most esteemed artists of the age, especially four masters of the Wu school (in the Suzhou area): Shen Zhou, Qiu Ying, Tang Yin, and Wen Zhengming. Their work, always of great technical excellence, became less and less academic in style, and out of this tradition, by the late years of the dynasty, emerged a conception of the true painter as a professionally competent but deliberately amateurish artist bent on individualistic self-expression. Notably in landscapes, a highly cultivated and somewhat romantic or mystical simplicity became the approved style, perhaps best exemplified in the work of Dong Qichang.

LITERATURE AND SCHOLARSHIP

As was the case with much of the painting, Ming poetry and belles lettres were deliberately composed "after the fashion of" earlier masters, and groups of writers and critics earnestly argued about the merits of different Tang and Song exemplars. No Ming practitioner of traditional poetry has won special esteem, though Ming literati churned out poetry in prodigious quantities. The historians Song Lian and Wang Shizhen and the philosopher-statesman Wang Yangming were among the dynasty's most noted prose stylists, producing expository writings of exemplary lucidity and straightforwardness. Perhaps the most admired master was Gui Youguang, whose most famous writings are simple essays and anecdotes about everyday life—often rather loose and formless but with a quietly pleasing charm, evoking character and mood with artless-seeming delicacy. The iconoclasm of the final Ming decades was mirrored in a literary movement of total individual freedom, championed notably by Yuan Zhongdao, but writings produced during this period were later denigrated as insincere, coarse, frivolous, and so strange and eccentric as to make impossible demands on the readers.

The late Ming iconoclasm did successfully call attention to popular fiction in colloquial style. In retrospect, this must be reckoned the most significant literary work of the late Yuan and Ming periods, even though it was disdained by the educated elite of the time. The late Yuan–early Ming novels *Sanguozhi yanyi* (*Romance of the Three Kingdoms*) and *Shuihuzhuan* (*The Water Margin*, also published as *All Men Are Brothers*) became the universally acclaimed masterpieces of the historical and picaresque genres, respectively. Sequels to each were produced throughout the Ming period. Wu Cheng'en, a 16th-century local official, produced *Xiyouji* (*Journey to the West*, also partially translated as *Monkey*), which became China's most-treasured novel of the supernatural. Late in the 16th century an unidentifiable writer produced *Jinpingmei* (*Golden Lotus*), a realistically Rabelaisian account of life and love among the bourgeoisie, which established yet another genre for the novel. By the end of the Ming period, iconoclasts such as Li Zhi and Jin Shengtan, both of whom published editions of *Shuihuzhuan*, made the then-astonishing assertion that this and other works of popular literature should rank alongside the greatest poetry and literary prose as treasures of China's cultural heritage. Colloquial short stories also proliferated in Ming times, and collecting anthologies of them became a fad of the last Ming century. The master writer and editor in this realm was Feng Menglong, whose creations and influence dominate the best-known anthology, *Jingu qiguan* ("Wonders Old and New"), published in Suzhou in 1624.

Operatic drama, which had emerged as a major new art form in Yuan times, was popular throughout the Ming dynasty, and Yuan masterpieces in the tightly disciplined four-act *zaju* style were regularly performed. Ming contributors to the dramatic literature were most creative in a more-rambling, multiple-act form known as "southern drama" or *chuanqi*. Members of the imperial clan and respected scholars and officials such as Wang Shizhen and particularly Tang Xianzu wrote for the stage. A new southern opera aria form called *kunqu*, originating in Suzhou, became particularly popular and provided the repertoire of women singers throughout the country. Sentimental romanticism was a notable characteristic of Ming dramas.

Perhaps the most representative of all Ming literary activities, however, are voluminous works of sober scholarship in many realms. Ming literati were avid bibliophiles, both collectors and publishers. They founded many great private libraries, such as the famed Tianyige collection of the Fan family at Ningbo. They also began producing huge anthologies (*congshu*) of rare or otherwise interesting books and thus preserved many works from extinction. The example was set in this regard by an imperially sponsored classified anthology of all the esteemed writings of the whole Chinese heritage completed in 1407 under the title *Yongle dadian* ("Great Canon of the Yongle Era"). Its more than 11,000 volumes being too numerous for even the imperial government to consider printing, it was preserved only in manuscript copies; only a fraction of the volumes have survived. Private scholars also produced great illustrated encyclopaedias, including *Bencao gangmu* (late 16th century; "Index of Native Herbs"), a monumental materia medica listing 1,892 herbal concoctions and their applications; *Sancai tuhui* (1607–09; "Assembled Pictures of the Three Realms"), a work on subjects such as architecture, tools, costumes, ceremonies, animals, and amusements; *Wubeizhi* (1621; "Treatise on Military Preparedness"), on weapons, fortifications, defense organization, and war tactics; and *Tiangong kaiwu* (1637; "Creations of Heaven and Human Labour"), on industrial technology. Ming scholars also produced numerous valuable geographical treatises and historical studies. Among the creative milestones of Ming scholarship, which pointed the way for the development of modern critical scholarship in early Qing times, were the following: a work by Mei Zu questioning the authenticity of sections of the ancient *Shujing* ("Classic of History"); a phonological analysis by Chen Di of the ancient *Shijing* ("Classic of Poetry"); and a dictionary by Mei Yingzuo that for the first time classified Chinese ideograms (characters) under 214 components (radicals) and subclassified them by number of brushstrokes—an arrangement still used by most standard dictionaries.

One of the great all-around literati of Ming times, representative in many ways of the dynamic and wide-ranging activities of the Ming scholar-official at his best, was Yang Shen. Yang won first place in the metropolitan examination of 1511, remonstrated vigorously against the caprices of the Zhengde and Jiajing emperors, and was finally beaten, imprisoned, removed from his post in the Hanlin Academy, and sent into exile as a common soldier in Yunnan. However, throughout his life he produced poetry and belles lettres in huge quantities, as well as a study of bronze and stone inscriptions across history, a dictionary of obsolete characters, suggestions about the phonology of ancient Chinese, and a classification of fishes found in Chinese waters.

CHAPTER 10

THE EARLY QING DYNASTY

THE RISE OF THE MANCHU

The Manchu, who ruled China from 1644 to 1911/12, were descendants of the Juchen (Nüzhen) tribes who had ruled northern China as the Jin dynasty in the 12th century. From the 15th century they had paid tribute to the Ming and were organized under the commandery system, so they had long had extensive and regular contact with the Chinese state and, more importantly, with the Chinese military officers stationed in the Ming frontier garrisons. By the 16th century these officers had become a hereditary regional military group in southern Manchuria, the Manchu homeland. Transformed by their long residence on the frontier, the Chinese soldiers mingled with the barbarians, adopting Manchu names and tribal customs. Still other Chinese were in the area as enslaved "bond servants" who worked the land or helped manage the trade in ginseng root, precious stones, and furs with China and Korea. Later, after the conquest of China, many of these bond servants became powerful officials who were sent on confidential missions by the emperor and who staffed the powerful Imperial Household Department.

Under Nurhachi and his son Abahai, the Aisin Gioro clan of the Jianzhou tribe won hegemony among the rival Juchen tribes of the northeast, then through warfare and alliances extended its control into Inner Mongolia and Korea. Nurhachi

Panel from an imperial Chinese silk dragon robe embroidered in silk and gold thread, 17th century, early Qing dynasty; in the Metropolitan Museum of Art, New York City. Lee Boltin

created large, permanent civil-military units called "banners" to replace the small hunting groups used in his early campaigns. A banner was composed of smaller companies; it included some 7,500 warriors and their households, including slaves, under the command of a chieftain. Each banner was identified by a coloured flag that was yellow, white, blue, or red, either plain or with a border design. Originally there were four, then eight, Manchu banners; new banners were created as the Manchu conquered new regions, and eventually there were Manchu, Mongol, and Chinese banners, eight for each ethnic group. By 1648 less than one-sixth of the bannermen were actually of Manchu ancestry. The Manchu conquest was thus achieved with a multi-ethnic army led by Manchu nobles and Han Chinese generals. Han Chinese soldiers were organized into the Army of the Green Standard, which became a sort of imperial constabulary force posted throughout China and on the frontiers.

Modern scholarship on the rise of the Manchu emphasizes the contributions of Chinese collaborators to the Manchu cause. The Manchu offered rewards and high positions to these Chinese, who not only brought military skills and technical knowledge with them but also encouraged the adoption of Chinese institutional models. From Chinese and Korean artisans the Manchu learned iron-smelting technology and acquired the advanced European artillery of the Ming. They created a replica of the Ming central government apparatus in their new capital, Mukden (present-day Shenyang), established in 1625. Whereas Nurhachi had initially based his claim to legitimacy on the tribal model, proclaiming himself khan in 1607, he later adopted the Chinese political language of the Tianming ("Mandate of Heaven") as his reign title and in 1616 proclaimed the Hou (Later) Jin dynasty. Abahai continued to manipulate the political symbols of both worlds by acquiring the great seal of the Mongol khan in 1635, and thus the succession to the Yuan dynasty, and by taking on a Chinese dynastic name, Qing, for his own dynasty the following year.

The downfall of the Ming house was the product of factors that extended far beyond China's borders. In the 1630s and 1640s China's most-commercialized regions, the Yangtze River delta and the southeast coast, suffered an acute economic depression brought on by a sharp break in the flow of silver entering ports through foreign trade from Acapulco (Mexico), Malacca, and Japan. The depression was exacerbated by harvest shortfalls resulting from unusually bad weather during 1626–40. The enervated government administration failed to respond adequately to the crisis, and bandits in the northwest expanded their forces and began invading north and southwest China. One of these bandit leaders, Li Zicheng, marched into Beijing in 1644 unopposed, and the emperor, forsaken by his officials and generals, committed suicide. A Ming general, Wu

DORGON

Dorgon (Chinese temple name: Chengzong; b. Nov. 7, 1612—d. Dec. 31, 1650), prince of the Manchu people, was instrumental in founding the Qing (Manchu) dynasty in China. He joined his former enemy Wu Sangui in driving the Chinese rebel Li Zicheng from Beijing, where Li had already unseated the last Ming-dynasty emperor. Though some wanted to put Dorgon on the throne, he saw to it that his nephew Fulin was proclaimed emperor (Dorgon acted as regent); this loyalty and selflessness won him the high regard of future historians.

Sangui, sought Manchu assistance against Li Zicheng. Dorgon, the regent and uncle of Abahai's infant son (who became the first Qing emperor), defeated Li and took Beijing, where he declared the Manchu dynasty.

It took the Manchu several decades to complete their military conquest of China. In 1673 the conquerors confronted a major rebellion led by three generals (among them Wu Sangui), former Ming adherents who had been given control over large parts of southern and southwestern China. That revolt, stimulated by Manchu attempts to cut back on the autonomous power of these generals, was finally suppressed in 1681. In 1683 the Qing finally eliminated the last stronghold of Ming loyalism on Taiwan.

THE QING EMPIRE

After 1683 the Qing rulers turned their attention to consolidating control over their frontiers. Taiwan became part of the empire, and military expeditions against perceived threats in north and west Asia created the largest empire China has ever known. From the late 17th to the early 18th century, Qing armies destroyed the Oyrat empire based in Dzungaria and incorporated into the empire the region around the Koko Nor (Qinghai Hu, "Blue Lake") in Central Asia. In order to check Mongol power, a Chinese garrison and a resident official were posted in Lhasa, the centre of the Dge-lugs-pa (Yellow Hat) sect of Buddhism that was influential among Mongols as well as Tibetans. By the mid-18th century the land on both sides of the Tien Shan range as far west as Lake Balkhash had been annexed and renamed Xinjiang ("New Dominion").

Military expansion was matched by the internal migration of Chinese settlers into parts of China that were dominated by aboriginal or non-Han ethnic groups. The evacuation of the south and southeast coast during the 1660s spurred a westward migration of an ethnic minority, the Hakka, who moved from the hills of southwest Fujian, northern Guangdong, and southern Jiangxi. Although the Qing dynasty tried to forbid migration into its homeland, Manchuria, in the 18th and 19th centuries Chinese settlers flowed into the fertile Liao River basin. Government policies encouraged Han movement into the southwest during the early 18th century, while Chinese traders and assimilated Chinese Muslims moved into Xinjiang and the other newly acquired territories. This period was punctuated by ethnic conflict stimulated by the Han Chinese takeover of former aboriginal territories and by fighting between different groups of Han Chinese.

POLITICAL INSTITUTIONS

The Qing had come to power because of their success at winning Chinese over to their side; in the late 17th century they adroitly pursued similar policies to win the adherence of the Chinese literati. Qing emperors learned Chinese, addressed their subjects using Confucian rhetoric, reinstated the civil service examination system and the Confucian curriculum, and patronized scholarly projects, as had their predecessors. They also continued the Ming custom of adopting reign names, so that Xuanye, for example, is known to history as the Kangxi emperor. The Qing rulers initially used only Manchu and bannermen to fill the most-important positions in the provincial and central governments (half of the powerful governors-general throughout the dynasty were Manchu), but Chinese were able to enter government in greater numbers in the 18th century, and a Manchu-Han dyarchy was in place for the rest of the dynasty.

The early Qing emperors were vigorous and forceful rulers. The first emperor, Fulin (reign name, Shunzhi), was put on the throne when he was a child of six *sui* (about five years in Western calculations). His reign (1644–61) was dominated by his uncle and regent, Dorgon, until Dorgon died in 1650. Because the Shunzhi emperor had died of smallpox, his successor, the Kangxi emperor, was chosen in part because he had already survived a smallpox attack. The Kangxi emperor (reigned 1661–1722) was one of the most dynamic rulers China has known. During his reign the last phase of the military conquest was completed, and campaigns were pressed against the Mongols to strengthen Qing security on its Central Asian borders. China's literati were brought into scholarly projects, notably the compilation of the Ming history, under imperial patronage.

The Kangxi emperor's designated heir, his son Yinreng, was a bitter disappointment, and the succession struggle that followed the latter's demotion was perhaps the bloodiest in Qing history. Many Chinese historians still question whether the Kangxi emperor's eventual successor, his son Yinzhen (reign title Yongzheng), was truly the emperor's

Imperial Chinese throne of the Qianlong emperor (reigned 1735–96), red lacquer carved in dragons and floral scrolls, Qing dynasty; in the Victoria and Albert Museum, London. Courtesy of the Victoria and Albert Museum, London; photograph, A.C. Cooper Ltd.

deathbed choice. During the Yongzheng reign (1722–35) the government promoted Chinese settlement of the southwest and tried to integrate non-Han aboriginal groups into Chinese culture; it reformed the fiscal administration and rectified bureaucratic corruption.

The Qianlong reign (1735–96) marked the culmination of the early Qing. The emperor had inherited an improved bureaucracy and a full treasury from his father and expended enormous sums on the military expeditions known as the Ten Great Victories. He was both noted for his patronage of the arts and notorious for the censorship of anti-Manchu literary works that was linked with the compilation of the *Siku quanshu* ("Complete Library of the Four Treasuries"; Eng. trans. under various titles). The closing years of his reign were marred by intensified court factionalism centred on the meteoric rise to political power of an imperial favourite, a young officer named Heshen. Yongyan, who reigned as the Jiaqing emperor (1796–1820), lived most of his life in his father's shadow. He was plagued by treasury deficits, piracy off the southeast coast, and uprisings among aboriginal groups in the southwest and elsewhere. These problems, together with new pressures resulting from an expansion in opium imports, were passed on to his successor, the Daoguang emperor (reigned 1820–50).

The early Qing emperors succeeded in breaking from the Manchu tradition of collegial rule. The consolidation of imperial power was finally completed in the 1730s, when the Yongzheng emperor destroyed the power base of rival princes. By the early 18th century the Manchu had adopted the Chinese practice of father-son succession but without the custom of favouring the eldest son. Because the identity of the imperial heir was kept secret until the emperor was on his deathbed, Qing succession struggles were particularly bitter and sometimes bloody.

The Manchu also altered political institutions in the central government. They created an Imperial Household Department to forestall eunuchs from usurping power—a situation that had plagued the Ming ruling house—and they staffed this agency with bond servants. The Imperial Household Department became a power outside the control of the regular bureaucracy. It managed the large estates that had been allocated to bannermen and supervised various government monopolies, the imperial textile and porcelain factories in central China, and the customs bureaus scattered throughout the empire. The size and strength of the Imperial Household Department reflected the accretion of power to the throne that was part of the Qing political process. Similarly, revisions of the system of bureaucratic communication and the creation in 1729 of a new top decision-making body, the Grand Council, permitted the emperor to control more efficiently the ocean of government memorandums and requests.

This 18th-century drawing depicts Qianlong, the fourth emperor of the Qing dynasty. De Agostini Picture Library/Getty Images

FOREIGN RELATIONS

The Manchu inherited the tributary system of foreign relations from previous dynasties. This system assumed that China was culturally and materially superior to all other nations, and it required those who wished to trade and deal with China to come as vassals to the emperor, who was the ruler of "all under heaven." The tributary system was used by the Qing Board of Rites to deal with the countries along China's eastern and southern borders and with the European nations that sought trade at the ports of south and southeast China.

The tributary system operated in its fullest form in the Qing treatment of Korea. The Korean court used the Chinese calendar, sent regular embassies to Beijing to present tribute, and consulted the Chinese on the conduct of foreign relations. The Qing emperor confirmed the authority of the Korean rulers, approved the Korean choice of consorts and heirs, and bestowed noble ranks on Korean kings. The Korean envoy performed the kowtow (complete prostration and knocking of the head on the ground) before the Qing emperor and addressed him using the terms appropriate to someone of inferior status.

Central Asia was another matter. Tribes on the northwestern and western frontiers had repeatedly invaded China, and the Manchu, who had been part of the world of the steppe, were keenly aware of the need to maintain military supremacy on China's northern borders.

Central Asian affairs were handled by a new agency, the Court of Colonial Affairs, that was created before 1644. Qing policies toward Central Asia frequently deviated from the tributary ideal, Chinese relations with Russia being a case in point. The early Qing rulers attempted to check the Russian advance in northern Asia and used the Russians as a buffer against the Mongols. The Sino-Russian Treaty of Nerchinsk (1689), which tried to fix a common border, was an agreement between equals. The Treaty of Kyakhta (1727) extended agreement on the borders to the west and opened markets for trade. When Chinese ambassadors went to Moscow (1731) and St. Petersburg (1732) to request that Russia remain neutral during the Chinese campaigns against the Oyrat in Central Asia, they performed the kowtow before the empress.

Foreign trade was not always restricted to the formal exchanges prescribed by the tributary system. Extensive trading was carried out in markets along China's borders with Korea, at the Russo-Mongolian border town of Kyakhta, and at selected ports along the coast, whence ships traded with Southeast Asia. Perhaps the most striking example of trade taking precedence over tribute was the Qing trade with Japan. The Tokugawa shogunate viewed the Manchu as barbarians whose conquest sullied China's claim to moral superiority in the world order. They refused to take part in the tributary system and themselves issued trade permits (counterparts of the Chinese tributary tallies) to Chinese merchants coming to Nagasaki after 1715. The Qing need for Japanese copper, a money metal in China, required that trade with Japan be continued, and it was.

ECONOMIC DEVELOPMENT

In the 1640s and 1650s the Manchu abolished all late Ming surtaxes and granted tax exemptions to areas ravaged by war. Tax remissions were limited, however, by the urgent need for revenues to carry on the conquest of China. It was not until the 1680s, after the consolidation of military victory, that the Qing began to permit tax remissions on a large scale. The permanent freezing of the *ding* (corvée quotas) in 1712 and the subsequent merger of the *ding* and land tax into a single tax that was collected in silver were part of a long-term simplification of the tax system. The commutation of levies from payment in kind to payment in money and the shift from registering males to registering land paralleled the increasing commercialization of the economy.

A healthy tax base required that land be brought under cultivation. Because more than one-fourth of the total cultivated land had slipped off the tax rolls in the early 17th century, the restoration of agriculture was an important goal. The new dynasty began to resettle refugees on abandoned land with offers of tax exemptions for several years and grants of oxen, tools, seeds, or even cash in some areas. In the late 17th century the resettlement of the Chengdu Basin in western

China and of Hunan, Hubei, and the far southwest proceeded on this basis.

Land reclamation went hand in hand with the construction and reconstruction of water-control projects. This was an activity so characteristic of a new dynasty that one can speak of "hydraulic cycles" moving in tandem with political consolidations in China. These water-control projects varied in scale with terrain and ecology. In central and southern China, irrigation systems were the foundation for rice cultivation and were largely the product of private investment and management. In northern China, control of the heavily silted Huang He (Yellow River), which frequently inundated the eastern portion of the North China Plain, required large-scale state management and coordination with the related water level of the Grand Canal, the major north-south waterway supplying Beijing.

The preferred crops—rice in central and southern China, wheat in northern China—retained their primacy in Qing agriculture. In the course of the dynasty, the cultivation of wheat and other northern staple grains continued to creep southward; rice was transplanted to the best lands on the frontiers, and the cropping cycle gradually intensified. Both on the frontiers and within China proper, new lands were opened for settlement using the New World crops that had been introduced into China in the late 16th century. Corn (maize) and the Irish potato permitted Chinese to cultivate the marginal hilly lands. The sweet potato provided insurance against famine, while peanuts (groundnuts) were a new source of oil in the peasant diet. Tobacco, another 16th-century import, competed with rice and sugarcane for the best lands in southern China and became an important cash crop.

Once the economy had been restored, the Qing state attempted to keep it running smoothly. For the most part, the state did not actively intervene in what was becoming an extremely complex market economy. The major exception was its successful effort to offset regional food shortages in years of crop failure. Every province was supposed to purchase or retain reserves in the "ever-normal" granaries located in each county, so named because they were intended to stabilize the supply, and hence the price, of grain. Even relatively uncommercialized hinterlands were thus armoured against famine. The ability of the government to respond effectively to food scarcity depended on its information gathering. During the 18th century, data on local grain prices became a regular feature of county, prefectural, and provincial reports.

The Qing government played a relatively minor role in the commercial economy. There were state monopolies in salt, precious metals, pearls, and ginseng, but the long-run trend was to reduce the number of monopolies. The state barely began to tap the growing revenue potential of trade, just as it failed to tap the expanding agricultural base. Its rare interventions in trade were motivated by a desire to dampen economic fluctuations in employment. Its major goal was stability, not growth.

And yet the early Qing was a period of economic growth and development. With the imposition of the Qing peace, the economy resumed a commercial expansion that had begun in the 16th century. This expansion in turn stimulated specialization in crops sent to market, which included raw materials to be used in the textile industry as well as consumption goods such as tea, sugar, and tobacco. Profit enticed merchants, landlords, and peasants to buy or rent land to produce cash crops. A new kind of managerial landlord, who used hired labour to grow market crops, emerged in the 18th century.

The tenant's position improved vis-à-vis the landlord's, a wage-labour force arose in agriculture, and land was increasingly used as a marketable commodity. Systems that guaranteed tenants permanent cultivation rights spread in the 18th century through the wet-rice cultivation zone and in some dryland cultivation systems. Multiple layers of rights to the land generally benefited the tenant and improved incentives to maintain the fertility of the soil and to raise output. There was a general shift from servile to contractual labour in agriculture that was part of a long trend toward eliminating fixed status and increasing mobility of labour and land.

Equally important processes of commercialization gained momentum with the recovery of the domestic economy. The 16th-century boom created new layers of rural markets that linked villages more firmly to a market network. Although the majority of economic transactions continued to take place within local and intermediate markets, interregional and national trade in grain, tea, cotton, and silk expanded significantly. In the 18th century, Shanghai became a thriving entrepôt for the coastal trade that extended from Manchuria to southern China.

The most-dramatic economic innovations of the 18th century resulted from the needs of long-distance traders for credit and new mechanisms that would ease the transfer of funds. Native banks, as they were called by foreigners in the 19th century, accepted deposits, made loans, issued private notes, and transferred funds from one region to another. Promissory notes issued by native banks on behalf of merchants facilitated the purchase of large quantities of goods, and money drafts and transfer accounts also helped ease the flow of funds. By the early 19th century, paper notes may have constituted one-third or more of the total volume of money in circulation. The demands of large-scale, long-distance trade had, without government participation, inspired merchants to transform a metallic monetary system into one in which paper notes supplemented copper coins and silver.

Customary law evolved outside the formal legal system to expedite economic transactions and enable strangers to do business with one another. Business partnerships in mining, commerce, and commercial agriculture could be formalized and protected through written contract. Reliance on written contracts for purchasing and mortgaging land, purchasing commodities and people, and hiring wage labourers became commonplace.

The early Qing economy was intimately tied to foreign trade, which consisted of junks trading with ports in Southeast Asia, Japan, and the Philippines and of the expanding trade conducted by Europeans. After 1684, when the ban on maritime trade was lifted, Western traders flocked to Guangzhou (Canton), and foreign commerce was finally confined to this port in 1759. The "Canton system" of trade that prevailed from that year until 1842 specified that Europeans had to trade through the cohong (*gonghang*), a guild of Chinese firms that had monopoly rights to the trade in tea and silk.

From 1719 to 1833 the tonnage of foreign ships trading at Guangzhou increased more than 13-fold. The major export was tea; by 1833, tea exports were more than 28 times the export levels of 1719. Silk and porcelain were also exported in increasing quantities through the early 18th century. Although only a small fraction of total output was exported, the effect of foreign trade on the Chinese economy was direct and perceptible. Its repercussions were not limited to the merchants and producers involved in specific export commodities but also had a general impact on domestic markets through the monetary system.

The Chinese economy had long been based on a metallic currency system in which copper cash was used for daily purchases and silver for large business transactions and taxes. The exchange ratio between silver and copper cash was responsive to fluctuations in the supply of the metals, and changes in the exchange ratio affected all citizens. The economic expansion of the 18th century brought rising demand for silver and copper. Although domestic production of copper increased, silver was primarily obtained from abroad. After 1684 the net balance of trade was consistently in China's favour, and silver flowed into the Chinese economy. Perhaps 10 million Spanish silver dollars per year came into China during the early Qing, and in the 18th century Spanish silver dollars became a common unit of account in the southeast and south.

QING SOCIETY

Chinese society continued to be highly stratified during the early Qing. Hereditary status groups ranged from the descendants of the imperial line down to the "mean people" at the bottom of the social ladder. Many professions were hereditary: bannermen, brewers, dyers, doctors, navigators, and Daoist priests usually passed on their occupations to at least one son in each generation. The mean people included remnants of aboriginal groups who had survived Chinese expansion and settlement and certain occupational groups, including prostitutes, musicians, actors, and local government underlings (e.g., jailers and gatekeepers). Qing laws forbade intermarriage between respectable commoners ("good people") and the mean people, who were also barred from

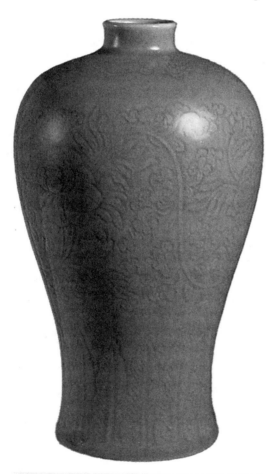

Meiping porcelain vase with a celadon glaze, decorated with incised floral motifs, from the reign of the Yongzhen emperor (1722–35), Qing dynasty; in the Victoria and Albert Museum, London. Courtesy of the Victoria and Albert Museum, London

sitting for the civil service examinations. Despite attempts in the 1720s to return some of these mean people to ordinary commoner status, the social stigma persisted throughout the dynasty.

Servitude was commonplace in Qing society. The Manchu had enslaved prisoners of war, and in China persons could be sold by their families. Many well-to-do households owned some domestic servants. Servants were grouped with the mean people in Qing law, but some of them nonetheless achieved considerable power and authority. Bond servants of the imperial house ran the powerful Imperial Household Department and themselves owned slaves. Servile tenants of the wealthy Huizhou merchants were sometimes raised as companions to the master's son and trusted to help run the long-distance trade on which Huizhou fortunes were based. Servitude in some cases was thus an important avenue for social advancement.

Social mobility increased during the early Qing, supported by a pervasive belief that it was possible for a peasant boy to become the first scholar in the land. An ethic that stressed education and hard work motivated many households to invest their surplus in the arduous preparation of sons for the civil service examinations. Although the most prestigious career in Qing society remained that of the scholar-official, the sharpened competition for degrees in the prosperous 18th century significantly expanded socially acceptable forms of achievement. At one pole, alienated literati deliberately eschewed the morally ambiguous role of official to devote their energies to scholarship, painting, poetry, and the other arts. Others turned to managing their localities and assumed leadership in public welfare, mediation of disputes, and local defense. Families with a long tradition of success in examinations and official service were increasingly preoccupied with strategies for ensuring the perpetuation of their elite status and countering the inexorable division of family estates stemming from the Chinese practice of partible inheritance. Downward mobility was a more general phenomenon than upward mobility in Qing society; those at the bottom of the social scale did not marry and have children, while the wealthy practiced polygyny and tended to have large families.

In China's long-settled and densely populated regions, degree holders who confronted the prospect of downward mobility for their sons were profoundly disturbed by the circumstances that permitted wealthy merchants to mimic their way of life. The money economy and its impersonal values penetrated more deeply into Chinese society than ever before, challenging former indicators of status for preeminence. Alarmed, the Chinese elite joined the Qing state in trying to propagate traditional values and behaviour. Morality books, published in increasing quantities from the late 16th century onward, tied virtuous behaviour to concrete rewards in the form of educational success, high office, and sons. The Qing bestowed titles, gifts, and imperial calligraphy on virtuous widows and encouraged the construction of memorial arches and shrines in their honour to reinforce this female role. Rural lectures (*xiangyue*) were public ceremonies staged for citizens that combined religious elements with reciting the sacred edict promulgated by the emperor.

SOCIAL ORGANIZATION

The basic unit of production and consumption in Chinese society remained the *jia* ("family"), consisting of kin related by blood, marriage, or adoption that shared a common budget and common property. The Chinese family system was patrilineal; daughters married out, while sons brought in wives and shared the residence of their fathers. The head of the family, the patriarch, had the power to direct the activities of each member in an effort to optimize the family's welfare. The family was a metaphor for the state, and family relations were the foundation of the hierarchical social roles that were essential in the Confucian vision of a morally correct society.

In southeastern and southern China during the early Qing, there was an expansion of extended kinship organizations based on descent from a common ancestor. In those areas, lineages became a powerful tool for collective action and local dominance, using revenues from corporate property to support education, charity, and ancestral rites. Other types of lineages, possessing little corporate property, existed in other parts of China.

These lineages seem to have been composed of only the most elite lines within a descent group, who focused their efforts on national rather than local prominence and emphasized their marriage networks rather than ties to poorer kinsmen.

Kinship was of limited use to the increasingly numerous sojourners who were working away from home in the early Qing. Other kinds of organizations emerged to meet the needs of a more mobile population. The share partnership permitted unrelated persons to pool their resources to start a business, and it was used to finance a wide variety of enterprises, including mining ventures, coastal and overseas shipping, commercial agriculture, money shops, and theatres. The trading empires created by the Huizhou and Shanxi merchants were examples of how such partnerships, cemented by kinship and native-place ties, could be used for large-scale business operations.

"Native place" was the principle used to organize the *huiguan* (native-place associations) that spread throughout Qing market centres. Some *huiguan* were primarily intended for officials and examination candidates; these were located in the capitals of provinces and in Beijing. Others, located in the southwest, were for immigrants, but the vast majority were created and used by merchants. The *huiguan* provided lodging and a place to meet fellow natives, receive financial aid, and store goods. In the course of the 18th century, another kind of organization that encompassed all those engaged in a trade, the *gongsuo* (guild), emerged in

China's cities. *Huiguan* frequently became subunits of *gongsuo*, and both groups participated in the informal governance of cities.

New kinds of social organization also emerged on China's frontiers. Native-place ties were frequently expressed in worship of a deity, so that a temple or territorial cult would become a vehicle for collective action. White Lotus sectarianism appealed to other Chinese, most notably to women and to the poor, who found solace in worship of the Eternal Mother, who was to gather all her children at the millennium into one family. The Qing state banned the religion, and it was generally an underground movement. Although the White Lotus faith was practiced by boatmen on the Grand Canal with no attempts to foment uprising, its millenarian message spurred spectacular rebellions; the most-notable was the White Lotus Rebellion at the close of the 18th century.

A new form of social organization, based on sworn brotherhood, emerged among male sojourners in southeast China in the late 18th century. The Triad fraternities built on kinship, native-place, and contractor-worker ties but added special rituals that bound fellow workers together as "brothers" in discipleship to a monk founder. Secret lore, initiation rituals, and an elaborate origin myth evolved, but the fraternities tended to be highly decentralized autonomous units. Appearing first on Taiwan, the Triads expanded with transport workers into southern China and became a powerful organization that dominated the Chinese underworld.

STATE AND SOCIETY

The state barred literati from using the academies and literary societies for explicitly political activities. Scholars in Beijing and in the rich cities of the Yangtze delta turned from politics to the study of texts that marked the empirical school of scholarship (*kaozheng xue*). Influenced by their knowledge of European mathematics and mathematical astronomy, these scholars laid down new rules for verifying the authenticity of the Classical texts and, by revealing flaws in previously accepted canons, challenged the Neo-Confucian orthodoxy. Turning away from the Confucian quest for sagehood, the empirical scholars were increasingly secular and professional in their pursuit of textual studies. Scholarly associations, poetry societies, and academies were the organizational loci for the empirical schools. Great libraries were created, rare texts were reprinted, and compilation projects proliferated, culminating in the great government-sponsored *Siku quanshu* (1772–82), which undertook to collect for reprinting the best editions of the most important books produced in China, using as selection criteria the methods of the empirical school.

A hallmark of Qing society was the expansion and extension of a national urban culture into various parts of the empire. Urban culture circulated through the market network into the hinterland, as sojourners disseminated culture from localities into the cities and back again. The spread of this culture was also supported by increased functional literacy and the expansion of large-scale printing for commercial and scholarly audiences. A wide variety of written materials were available in market towns and cities—collections of winning examination essays, route books for commercial travelers, religious pamphlets and scriptures, novels, short-story collections, jokebooks, and almanacs. Storytelling, puppet plays, and regional drama in rural and urban places provided yet another mode of cultural dissemination. In China's cities, sojourning merchants sponsored visits of drama troupes from their own localities, which facilitated the spread of regional drama forms outside their own territories. Drama was the bridge connecting the oral and written realms, the "living classroom" for peasants who learned about cultural heroes and history through watching plays. The expansion of a national urban culture supported the state's efforts to systematize and standardize Chinese society.

China's non-Han minorities found themselves surrounded by an aggressive, expansionist Han Chinese culture during the early Qing. Attempts by the emperors at that time to protect minorities from the Han onslaught were largely unavailing, and some rulers, such as the Yongzheng emperor, actually tried to hasten the assimilation of aboriginal groups into the Chinese order. The Qing categorized the ethnic minorities into two groups: those who were "raw," or still possessed of their own culture, and those who were "cooked," or assimilated. The ethnic minorities resisted violently, but they were gradually assimilated or pushed farther south and west during the early Qing.

TRENDS IN THE EARLY QING

The tripling of China's population from the beginning of the Qing dynasty to the mid-19th century rested on the economic expansion that followed the consolidation of Manchu rule. This population growth has been frequently cited as the major cause of the decline of China in the 19th century. Certainly, by the year 1800 the Qing state's surpluses—sufficient through the 18th century to pay for numerous military expeditions—were exhausted in the long campaign to quell the White Lotus Rebellion. Whereas fiscal reforms had strengthened the state in the 18th century, fiscal weakness plagued Qing governments thereafter. The vaunted power of the Qing armies also waned after 1800, in part because of new modes of warfare. Increased commercialization had tied more and more Chinese into large market fluctuations. In the 18th century the world market economy into which China was increasingly integrated worked in its favour and stimulated a long period of internal prosperity. But the favourable trend was reversed in the 1820s and 1830s, when rising opium imports altered the net balance of trade against China and ushered in a period of economic depression.

CHAPTER 11

LATE QING

WESTERN CHALLENGE, 1839–60

The opium question, the direct cause of the first Sino-British clash in the 19th century, began in the late 18th century as the British attempted to counterbalance their unfavourable China trade with traffic in Indian opium. After monopolizing the opium trade in 1779, the East India Company's government began to sell the drug at auction to private British traders in India, who shipped it to buyers in China. The silver acquired from the sale of opium in China was sold at Guangzhou for the company's bills of exchange, payable in London, and was used by the company to purchase its large

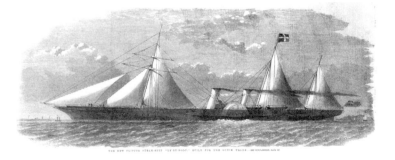

The clipper ship Le-Rye-Moon, *built for the opium trade, 19th-century wood engraving; from the* Illustrated London News. Encyclopædia Britannica, Inc.

annual tea cargo for sale in Europe. This "triangular trade" became a major vehicle for realizing the potential gains from the British conquest of India, providing a means to repatriate the company's Indian revenue in opium in the form of Chinese teas. In 1819 the company began to handle larger amounts of opium. Substantial social and economic disruption followed in China, not only from the effects of the opium habit itself as it spread among the populace but from the corruption it engendered among petty officials and from a fall in the value of copper in China's bimetallic monetary system as silver was drained from the economy. The Beijing court repeatedly banned the opium imports but without success, because the prohibition itself promoted corruption among the officials and soldiers concerned. There was no possibility of the opium question being solved as a domestic affair.

After the turn of the 19th century, the main avenue for opium smuggling was through the designated traders who were allowed only to manage the inter-Asian trade under the company's license. Without protection from the company, they cultivated the opium market in China on their own. They defied the opium ban in China and gradually became defiant toward Chinese law and order in general, having nothing in mind but making money. After Parliament revoked the East India Company's monopoly in 1834, William John Napier was appointed chief superintendent of British trade in China and arrived at Guangzhou. He tried to negotiate with the Guangzhou authorities on equal footing, but the latter took his behaviour as contrary to the established Sino-foreign intercourse. His mission failed, and he was replaced in 1836 by Charles (later Sir Charles) Elliot.

In Beijing a proposal in 1836 to relax the opium restraint acquired much support, but the Daoguang emperor appointed a radical patriot, Lin Zexu, as imperial commissioner for an anti-opium campaign. Chinese anti-opium efforts in fact began to make considerable headway in controlling the Chinese side of the smuggling trade in late 1838 and early 1839. The critical foreign side of the opium trade was, however, beyond Commissioner Lin's direct reach. Arriving at Guangzhou in March 1839, Lin confiscated and destroyed more than 20,000 chests of opium. Skirmishes began after September between the Chinese and the British.

THE FIRST OPIUM WAR AND ITS AFTERMATH

In February 1840 the British government decided to launch a military expedition, and Elliot and his cousin, George (later Sir George) Elliot, were appointed joint plenipotentiaries to China (though the latter, in poor health, resigned in November). In June, 16 British warships arrived in Hong Kong and sailed northward to the mouth of the Bei River to press China with their demands. Charles Elliot entered into negotiations with the

Chinese, and, although an agreement was reached in January 1841, it was not acceptable to either government. In May 1841 the British attacked the walled city of Guangzhou (Canton) and received a ransom of $6 million, which provoked a counterattack on the part of the Cantonese. This was the beginning of a continuing conflict between the British and the Cantonese.

The Qing had no effective tactics against the powerful British navy. They retaliated merely by setting burning rafts on the enemy's fleet and encouraging people to take the heads of the enemies, for which they offered a prize. The imperial banner troops, although they sometimes fought fiercely, were ill-equipped and lacked training for warfare against the more-modern British forces. The Green Standard battalions were similarly in decay and without much motivation or good leadership. To make up the weakness, local militias were urgently recruited, but they were useless. The British proclaimed that their aim was to fight the government officials and soldiers who abused the people, not to make war against the Chinese population. And indeed there was a deep rift between the government and the people that the British could easily exploit, a weakness in Qing society that became apparent during the crisis of the war.

Elliot's successor, Henry Pottinger, arrived at Macau in August and campaigned northward, seizing Xiamen (Amoy), Dinghai, and Ningbo. Reinforced from India, he resumed action in May 1842 and took Wusong, Shanghai, and Zhenjiang. Nanjing yielded in August, and peace was restored with the Treaty of Nanjing. According to the main provisions of the treaty, China ceded Hong Kong to Britain, opened five ports to British trade, abolished the cohong system of trade, agreed to equal official recognition, and paid an indemnity of $21 million. This was the result of the first clash between China, which had regarded foreign trade as a favour given by the heavenly empire to the poor barbarians, and the British, to whom trade and commerce had become "the true herald of civilization."

The Treaty of Nanjing was followed by two supplementary arrangements with the British in 1843. In addition, in July 1844 China signed the Treaty of Wanghia (Wangxia) with the United States and in October the Treaty of Whampoa (Huangpu) with France. These arrangements made up a complex of foreign privileges by virtue of the most-favoured-nation clauses (guaranteeing trading equality) conceded to every signatory. All in all, they provided a basis for later inroads such as the loss of tariff autonomy, extraterritoriality (exemption from the application or jurisdiction of local law or tribunals), and the free movement of missionaries.

With the signing of the treaties—which began the so-called treaty-port system—the imperial commissioner Qiying, newly stationed at Guangzhou, was put in charge of foreign affairs. Following a policy of appeasement, his dealings with foreigners started fairly smoothly. But, contrary to the British expectation, the amount of trade dropped after 1846, and, to British dissatisfaction, the question of opium remained unsettled in the postwar arrangements. The core of the Sino-Western tension, however, rested in an antiforeign movement in Guangdong.

THE ANTIFOREIGN MOVEMENT AND THE SECOND OPIUM WAR (*ARROW* WAR)

At the signing of the Treaty of Nanjing, China and Britain disagreed as to whether foreigners were allowed to enter the walled city of Guangzhou. Though Guangzhou was declared open in July 1843, the British faced Cantonese opposition. After 1847 trouble rapidly grew, and, as a result of an incident at nearby Foshan, a promise was given the British that they would be allowed to enter the city in 1849. Yet troubles continued. As a result of his inability to control the situation, Qiying was recalled in 1848 and replaced with the less-compliant Xu Guangjin. As the promised date neared, the Cantonese demonstrated against British entry. Finally, the British yielded, and the antiforeigners won a victory despite the fact that the Beijing court conceded a "temporary entrance" into the city.

After the Cantonese resistance in 1841, the gentry in Guangdong began to build a more-organized antiforeign movement, promoting the militarization of village society. The city of Guangzhou was also a centre of diffusion of xenophobia, because the scholars at the city's great academies were proclaiming the Confucian theory that uncultured barbarians should be excluded. The inspired antiforeign mood also contained a strong antigovernment sentiment and perhaps a tendency toward provincialism; the Cantonese rose up against the barbarians to protect their own homeland, without recourse to the government authorities.

In the strained atmosphere in Guangzhou, where the xenophobic governor-general, Ye Mingchen, was inciting the Cantonese to annihilate the British, the *Arrow* incident occurred in October 1856. Guangzhou police seized the *Arrow*, a Chinese-owned but British-registered ship flying a British flag, and charged its Chinese crew with piracy and smuggling. The British consul Harry Parkes sent a fleet to fight its way up to Guangzhou. French forces joined the venture on the plea that a French missionary had been officially executed in Guangxi. The British government sent an expedition under Lord Elgin as plenipotentiary. The Russians and the Americans abstained but sent their representatives for diplomatic maneuvering. At the end of 1857 an Anglo-French force occupied Guangzhou; in March 1858 they took the Dagu fort and marched to Tianjin.

The Qing representatives had no choice but to comply with the demands of the British and French; the Russian and U.S. diplomats also gained the privileges their militant colleagues secured by force. During June four Tianjin treaties were concluded that provided for, among other measures, the residence of foreign diplomats in Beijing and the freedom of Christian missionaries to evangelize their faith.

In 1859, when the signatories arrived off the Dagu fort on their way to sign the treaties in Beijing, they were repulsed, with heavy damage inflicted by the gunfire from the fort. In 1860 an allied force invaded Beijing, driving the Xianfeng emperor (reigned 1850–61) out of the capital to the summer palace at Chengde. A younger brother of the emperor, Gong Qinwang (Prince Gong), was appointed imperial commissioner in charge of negotiation. The famous summer palace was destroyed by the British in October. Following the advice of the Russian negotiator, Prince Gong exchanged ratification of the 1858 treaties; in addition, he signed new conventions with the British and the French. The U.S. and Russian negotiators had already exchanged the ratification in 1859, but the latter's diplomatic performance in 1860 was remarkable.

Russian interests in the East had been activated in competition with the British effort to open China. A Russian spearhead, directed to Kuldja (Yining) by way of the Irtysh River, resulted in the Sino-Russian Treaty of Kuldja in 1851, which opened Kuldja and Chuguchak (Tacheng) to Russian trade. Another drive was directed to the Amur watershed under the initiative of Nikolay Muravyov, who had been appointed governor-general of eastern Siberia in 1847. By 1857

Muravyov had sponsored four expeditions down the Amur; during the third one, in 1856, the left bank and lower reaches of the river had actually been occupied by the Russians. In May 1858 Muravyov pressed the Qing general Yishan to sign a treaty at Aigun (Aihui), by which the territory on the northern bank of the Amur was ceded to Russia and the land between the Ussuri River and the sea was placed in joint possession by the two countries, pending further disposition. But Beijing refused to ratify the treaty. When the Anglo-French allies attacked northern China in 1860, the Russian negotiator Nikolay Ignatyev acted as China's friend and mediator in securing the evacuation of the invaders from Beijing. Soon after the allies had left Beijing, Ignatyev secured, as a reward for his mediatory effort, the Sino-Russian Treaty of Beijing, which confirmed the Treaty of Aigun and ceded to Russia the territory between the Ussuri and the sea.

The 1858–60 treaties extended the foreign privileges granted after the first Opium War and confirmed or legalized the developments in the treaty-port system. The worst effects for the Qing authorities were not the utilitarian rights, such as trade, commerce, and tariff, but the privileges that affected the moral and cultural values of China. The right to propagate Christianity threatened Confucian values, the backbone of the imperial system. The permanent residence of foreign representatives in Beijing signified an end to the long-established tributary relationship between China and other nations. The partial collapse of the tribute system meant a loss of the emperor's virtue, a serious blow to dynastic rule in China.

During the turbulent years 1858–60, the Qing bureaucracy was divided between the war and peace parties. It was the peace party's leaders—Prince Gong, Gui Liang, and Wen Xiang—who took charge of negotiating with the foreigners, though they did so not as a matter of principle but because the imminent crisis forced them to.

In 1861, in response to the settlement of the foreign representatives in the capital, the Zongli Yamen (office for General Management) was opened to deal with foreign affairs, its main staff filled by the peace party leaders. The Qing officials themselves, however, deemed this as still keeping a faint silhouette of the tribute system.

The delay and difficulty in the Qing adjustment to the Western presence may possibly be ascribed to both external and internal factors. The Chinese must have seen the Westerners who had appeared in China as purveyors of poisonous drugs and as barbarians in the full sense of the word, from whom they could learn nothing. But the Chinese staunchly held to their tradition, which also had two aspects—ideological and institutional. The core of the ideological aspect was the Confucian distinction between China and foreign nations. The institutional aspect had recently been much studied, however, and precedents in Chinese history had been found, for example, of

treaty ports with foreign settlements, consular jurisdiction, and employment of Westerners as imperial personnel; thus, the Chinese regarded the Western impact as an extension of their tradition rather than a totally new situation that necessitated a new adjustment. And at least until 1860 the Qing leaders remained withdrawn in the shell of tradition, making no effort to cope with the new environment by breaking the yoke of the past.

POPULAR UPRISING

The third quarter of the 19th century was marked by a series of uprisings, again as a result of social discontent. The most destructive of these was the Taiping Rebellion (1850–64) in southern and central China. The Nian Rebellion (c. 1853–68) was roughly contemporaneous with the Taiping in the eastern and central provinces. In addition, there were several prolonged uprisings between Muslims and Han Chinese in northwestern and southwestern China.

THE TAIPING REBELLION

In the first half of the 19th century, the provinces of Guangdong and Guangxi, the homeland of the Taiping people, had been beset with accelerating social unrest. After the first Opium War, government prestige declined, and officials lost their capacity to reconcile communal feudings. The greatest among such conflicts was that between the native settlers and the so-called guest settlers, or Hakka, who had migrated to Guangxi and western Guangdong, mainly from eastern Guangdong. The Baishangdi Hui ("God Worshippers' Society") was founded by Hong Xiuquan, a fanatic who believed himself a son of God, and his protégé, Feng Yunshan, an able organizer. Their followers were collected from among miners, charcoal workers, and poor peasants in central Guangxi, most of whom were Hakka. In January 1851 a new state named Taiping Tianguo ("Heavenly Kingdom of Great Peace") was declared in the district of Guiping in Guangxi, with Hong Xiuquan assuming the title *tianwang* ("heavenly king"). That September the Taiping shifted their base to the city of Yong'an (present-day Mengshan, Guangxi), where they were besieged by the imperial army until April 1852. At that point they broke the siege and rushed into Hunan. Absorbing some secret-society members and outlaws, they dashed to Wuhan, the capital of Hubei, and proceeded along the Yangtze to Nanjing, which they captured in March 1853, renamed Tianjing ("Heavenly Capital"), and made their capital.

The core of the Taiping religion was a monotheism tinged with fundamentalist Protestant Christianity, but it was mixed with a hatred of the Manchu and an intolerance of the Chinese cultural tradition. In the early years of the rebellion, this politico-religious faith sustained the fighting spirit of the Taiping. In the ideal Taiping vision the population was to give all of its belongings to a "general treasury," which would be shared by all alike.

While this extreme egalitarianism was rarely implemented outside the original Hakka core from Guangxi, it probably at times attracted the distressed and lured them to the Taiping cause. The origin of many Taiping religious ideas, morals, and institutions can be traced to China's Confucian tradition, but the Taiping's all-out anti-regime struggle, motivated by strong religious beliefs and a common sharing, also had precedents in earlier religious rebellions.

After the Taiping settled in Tianjing (Nanjing), village officials were appointed, and redistribution of farmland was planned in accordance with an idea of primitive communism. But in fact the land reform was impracticable. The village officials' posts were filled mainly by the former landlords or the clerks of the local governments, and the old order in the countryside was not replaced by a new one that the oppressed people could dominate.

In May 1853 the Taiping sent an expedition to northern China, which reached the neighbourhood of Tianjin but finally collapsed during the spring of 1855. After that the Yangtze valley provinces were the main theatre of struggle. Of the government armies in those years, the Green Standards were too ill-disciplined, and not much could be expected of the bannermen. The Qing government had no choice but to rely on the local militia forces, such as the "Hunan Braves" (later called the Hunan Army), organized by Zeng Guofan in 1852, and the "Huai Braves" (later called the Huai Army), organized by Li Hongzhang in 1862. These armies were composed of the village farmers, inspired with a strong sense of mission for protecting the Confucian orthodoxy, and were used for wider operations than merely protecting their own villages. The necessary funds for maintaining them were provided initially by local gentry.

The Taiping were gradually beaten down; with the capture of Anqing, the capital of Anhui, in October 1861 by the Hunan Army, the revolutionary cause was doomed. But the fall of Nanjing was accelerated by the cooperation of Chinese mercenaries equipped with Western arms, commanded by an American, Frederick Townsend Ward; a Briton, Charles George Gordon; and others. Nanjing's fall in July 1864 marked the end of one of the greatest civil wars in world history. The main cause of the Taiping failure was internal strife among the top leaders in Nanjing. Not only did they give themselves over to luxury, but also their energy was exhausted and their leadership lost by an internecine conflict that erupted in 1856. In addition, religious fanaticism, though it inspired the fighters, became a stumbling block that interfered with the rational and elastic attitude necessary to handle delicate military and administrative affairs. The intolerance toward traditional culture alienated the gentry and the people alike. Presumably, the failure of the land-redistribution policy also estranged the landless paupers from the Taiping cause.

THE NIAN REBELLION

Often in the first half of the 19th century, plundering gangs called *nian* ravaged northern Anhui, southern Shandong, and southern Henan. In mid-century, however, their activities were suddenly intensified, partly by the addition to their numbers of a great many starving people who had lost their livelihood from repeated floods of the Huang He in the early 1850s and partly because they had become emboldened by the Taiping advance north of the Yangtze. From 1856 to 1859 the Nian leaders consolidated their bases north of the Huai River by winning over the masters of the earth-wall communities, consolidated villages that had been fortified for self-defense against the Taiping. The Nian strategy was to use their powerful cavalry to plunder the outlying areas and carry the loot to their home bases.

Many influential clans, with all their members, joined the Nian cause, and the clan chiefs played an important role among the Nian leaders. Gentry of lower strata also joined the Nian. The greater part of the Nian force consisted of poor peasants, although deserters from the government-recruited militias and salt smugglers were important as military experts. The real cause of their strength was supposed to be the people's support and sympathy for their leaders, but creating a power centre proved to be difficult because the Nian's basic social unit was the earth-wall community, where a powerful master exercised autonomy. In 1856

Zhang Luoxing received the title "lord of the alliance" of the Nian, but he was far too weak to form a centre. Imperial pacification was launched by General Senggelinqin, who led a powerful cavalry into the affected area in 1862, but his pursuit was ineffective, and the general himself was killed in Shandong in May 1865. Thus, the last imperial crack unit disappeared. Zeng Guofan succeeded Senggelinqin as general and enforced a policy of detaching the earth-wall masters from their men and of employing the latter as his troops. Finally, Li Hongzhang succeeded Zeng in 1866 and set up encirclement lines along the Huang He and the Grand Canal, using that strategy to destroy the revolts in 1868.

MUSLIM REBELLIONS

Muslim rebellions in Yunnan and in Shaanxi and Gansu originated from clashes between the Chinese and Muslims in those provinces. Religious antipathy must be taken into account, but more important were social and political factors. In the frontier provinces the late-dynastic confusions were felt as keenly as elsewhere, which aggravated the problems between the Chinese and the Muslims. Yunnan had been haunted by Muslim-Chinese rivalries since 1821, but in Shaanxi small disturbances had been seen as early as the Qianlong reign. Government officials supported the Chinese, and the Muslims were obliged to rise up against both the Chinese and the authorities.

Rivalry between the Chinese and Muslim miners in central Yunnan triggered a severe clash in 1855, which developed into the slaughter of a great many Muslims in and around the provincial capital, Kunming, the following April. This triggered a general uprising of Yunnan Muslims, which lasted until 1873. Lack of a unified policy weakened the Muslims, and the rebellion was brought to an end partly through the pacifiers' policy of playing the rebel leaders off against one another.

Another Muslim uprising, in Shaanxi in 1862, promptly spread to Gansu and Xinjiang and lasted for 15 years. The general cause of the trouble was the same as in Yunnan, but the Taiping advance to Shaanxi encouraged the Muslims to rebel. The first stage of the uprising developed in the Wei River valley in Shaanxi; in the next stage the rebels, defeated by the imperial army, fled to Gansu, which became the main theatre of fighting. Encouraged by the Nian invading Shaanxi at the end of 1866, the core of the rebel troops returned to Shaanxi, and sporadic clashes continued in the two provinces. In the last phase, Zuo Zongtang, a former protégé of Zeng Guofan, appeared in Shaanxi with part of the Huai Army and succeeded in pacifying the area in 1873.

There were many independent Muslim leaders in Shaanxi and Gansu at that time, but they had neither a common headquarters nor a unified policy, nor were there any all-out revolutionaries. Pacification was delayed because the imperial camp was preoccupied with the Taiping and the Nian and could not afford the expenditure needed for an expedition to the remote border provinces.

EFFECTS OF THE REBELLIONS

The Qing authorities had to rely on local armies, financed by the provincial and local gentry class, to combat the large popular uprisings. To meet this need, a special tax on goods in transit—called the likin (*lijin*)—was started in 1853, the proceeds of which remained largely outside the control of the central government. The provincial governors-general and governors came to enlarge their military and financial autonomy, bringing about a trend of decentralization. Moreover, the locus of power shifted from the Manchu to those Chinese who had played the main part in putting down the rebellions. The Hunan Army was gradually disbanded after Nanjing had been retaken from the Taiping, but the Huai Army, after its success against the Muslims, served as a strong basis for the political maneuvers of its leader, Li Hongzhang, until its defeat and collapse in the Sino-Japanese War in 1894–95.

The rebellions brought immeasurable damage and devastation to China. Both the Taiping and the pacifiers were guilty of brutality and destruction. A contemporary estimate of 20 million to 30 million victims is certainly far less than the real number. In the course of the Taiping Rebellion, the lower Yangtze provinces lost much of their surplus population, but

thereafter the region was resettled by immigrants from less-damaged areas. Its ruined industry and agriculture had not fully recovered even by the beginning of the 20th century. The area of the Muslim rebellions too suffered catastrophic devastation and depopulation.

During the first half of the 19th century, a number of natural disasters left large hordes of starving victims who had no choice but to join the Taiping and other rebel groups. The worst calamity, however, was a drought that attacked the northern provinces of Shanxi, Shaanxi, and Henan in 1877–78 and caused hardship for perhaps as many as 13 million people. These disasters were a serious setback to China, which had just begun to promote industrialization to meet the Western challenge.

THE SELF-STRENGTHENING MOVEMENT

Upon the Xianfeng emperor's death at Chengde in 1861, his antiforeign entourage entered Beijing and seized power, but Cixi, mother of the newly enthroned boy emperor Zaichun (reigned as the Tongzhi emperor, 1861–74/75), and Prince Gong succeeded in crushing their opponents by a coup d'état in October. A new system emerged in which the leadership in Beijing was shared by Cixi and another empress dowager, Ci'an, in the palace and by Prince Gong and Wen Xiang, with the Zongli Yamen as their base of operation. The core of their foreign policy was expressed by Prince Gong as "overt peace

The empress dowager Cixi, c. 1904, late Qing dynasty, China. Courtesy of the Smithsonian Institution, Freer Gallery of Art, Washington, D.C.

with the Western nations in order to gain time for recovering the exhausted power of the state."

FOREIGN RELATIONS IN THE 1860S

The Zongli Yamen had two offices attached to it: the Inspectorate General of Customs and Tongwen Guan. The former was the centre for the Maritime Custom Service, administered by Western personnel appointed by the Qing. The latter was the language school opened to train the children of bannermen in foreign languages, and later some Western sciences were added to its curriculum; the quality of candidates for the school was not high. Similar schools were opened in Shanghai and Guangzhou.

A superintendent of trade for the three northern ports (later known as high commissioner for *beiyang*, or "northern ocean") was established in 1861 at Tianjin, parallel to a similar, existing post at Shanghai (later known as high commissioner for *nanyang*, or "southern ocean"). The creation of the new post was presumably aimed at weakening the foreign representatives in Beijing by concentrating foreign affairs in the hands of the Tianjin officials.

In 1865–66 the British strongly urged the Qing authorities to make domestic reforms and to become Westernized. Prince Gong asked the high provincial officials to submit their opinions about the proposed reforms. The consensus advocated diplomatic missions abroad and the opening of mines but firmly argued against telegraph and railway construction. Against that background, a roving mission was sent to the United States in 1868, which then proceeded to London and Berlin. This first mission abroad was a success for China, but its very success had an adverse effect on China's modernization by encouraging the conservatives, who learned to regard the Westerners as easy to manipulate.

The treaties signed in 1858 at Tianjin by the Chinese, British, and French included provisions for them to be revised in the year 1868, at which time the Qing were able to negotiate with due preparations and in an atmosphere of peace for the first time since the Opium Wars. The result was the Alcock Convention of 1869, which limited the unilateral most-favoured-nation clause of the original treaty, a sign of gradual improvement in China's foreign relations. However, under pressure from British merchants in China, the London government refused to ratify it. The resentment engendered by the refusal, together with an anti-Christian riot at Tianjin in 1870, brought an end to the climate of Sino-foreign cooperation that had prevailed in the 1860s.

The treaty arrangements made just after the Opium Wars forced China to remove the ban on Christianity, but the Beijing court tried to keep that fact secret and encouraged provincial officials to continue prohibiting the religion. The pseudo-Christian Taiping movement furthered the anti-Christian move on the part of royalists. Under such circumstances, anti-Christian riots spread throughout the country, culminating in the Tianjin Massacre in 1870, in which a French consul and 2 officials, 10 nuns, and 2 priests died and in which 3 Russian traders were killed by mistake. At the negotiating table, the French sternly demanded the lives of three responsible Chinese officials as a preventive against further such occurrences, but the Qing negotiators, Zeng Guofan and Li Hongzhang, were successful at least in refusing the demanded execution of the three (though several others were put to death). After the incident, however, Zeng was denounced for his infirm stand, and Prince Gong's political influence began to wane in the growing antiforeign climate.

Various interpretations have been given regarding the nature of the anti-Christian movement: some emphasize the antiforeign Confucian orthodoxy, while others stress the patriotic and nationalistic reaction against the missionaries' attempt to Westernize the Chinese. Still others point to the Christian support of the oppressed in their struggle against the official and gentry class. What is clear, however, is that Christianity sowed dissension and friction in the already disintegrating late Qing society and undermined the prestige of the Qing dynasty and the Confucian orthodoxy.

INDUSTRIALIZATION FOR "SELF-STRENGTHENING"

Stimulated by the military training and techniques exhibited during the Westerners' cooperation against the Taiping and supported by Prince Gong in Beijing, the Self-Strengthening Movement was launched by the anti-Taiping generals Zeng Guofan, Li Hongzhang, and Zuo Zongtang, who sought to consolidate the Qing power by introducing Western technology. The ideological champion of the movement was Feng Guifen, who urged China to "use the barbarians' superior techniques to control the barbarians" and proposed to give the gentry stronger leadership than before in local administration.

In the first period of modern industrial development (1861–72), effort was focused on manufacturing firearms and machines, the most important enterprises being the Kiangnan (Jiangnan) Arsenal in Shanghai, the Tianjin Machine Factory, and the Fuzhou Navy Yard; there were many other smaller ones. However, the output was disappointing—the shipyard at Fuzhou, for example, built 15 vessels during the half decade after 1869 as scheduled, but thereafter it declined and was destroyed in 1884 during the Sino-French War—and the weapons industry was significant not so much for its direct military purpose as for the introduction of Western knowledge and techniques through the many educational facilities that were attached to each installation.

In the second period (1872–94), weight shifted from the weapons industry to a wider field of manufacture, and the operation shifted from direct government management to a government-supervised and merchant-managed method. Leading among the several enterprises of the second period were the China Merchants' Steam Navigation Company and the Kaiping coal mines. These enterprises were sponsored by high provincial officials—the central figure was Li Hongzhang—but their management was left to joint operation by shareholders' representatives and the lower officials appointed by the sponsors.

Management, however, was beset with bureaucratic malpractices. The seat of decision making and responsibility was obscure, business was spoiled by nepotism and corruption, and the sponsors tended to use the enterprises as a basis for their regional power. The central government not only was unable to supply capital but also looked for every opportunity to exploit these enterprises as it had exploited the monopolistic salt business on which those companies were modeled. Under such circumstances, the enterprises inevitably slid into depression after some initial years of apparent success.

Compounding the problems were the compradors (Chinese agents employed by foreign firms in China) who, acting as a link between Chinese commerce and the foreign firms in the treaty ports, accumulated vast wealth from the new enterprises. Though active in supplying capital and managerial personnel to the enterprises, the compradors themselves lacked technical training and knowledge and often indulged in speculation and embezzlement. Each comprador belonged to an exclusive community by strong family or regional ties that focused his concerns on his community rather than on national interests.

These shortcomings were deeply rooted in the late Qing social conditions and more than offset efforts to construct and maintain the new enterprises. Thus, Chinese society as a whole did not change structurally before 1911.

CHANGES IN OUTLYING AREAS

With the decline of the Qing power and prestige, beginning in the early 19th century, China's peripheral areas began to free themselves from the Qing influence. Areas affected included East Turkistan to the northwest, Tibet and Nepal to the southwest, and Myanmar (Burma) and Vietnam to the south. In addition, the Japanese began asserting greater control over the islands east of the Chinese mainland, and their increasing interest in the Korean peninsula led to the Sino-Japanese War of 1894–95.

EAST TURKISTAN

To the west of Kashgaria in East Turkistan (now in western Xinjiang), a khanate of Khokand emerged after 1760 in the Fergana region and became a powerful caravan trade centre. In 1762 the Qing government countered this by establishing a presence in the Ili (Yili) River region. When Muslim rebellion spread rapidly from Shaanxi and Gansu to East Turkistan, a Tajik adventurer from Khokand, Yakub Beg, seized the opportunity to invade Kashgaria and established power there in 1865; he soon showed signs of advancing to the Ili region in support of the British in India. In Ili, rebel Muslims had set up an independent power at Kuldja (Yining) in 1864, which terrorized the Russian borders in defiance of the Sino-Russian Treaty of Kuldja in 1851. The Russians,

therefore, occupied Kuldja in 1871 and remained there for 10 years.

Having subdued the Gansu Muslim rebellion in 1873, Zuo Zongtang captured Urumchi (Ürümqi) in August 1876 and restored the whole region northward to the Tien Shan range, except for the Kuldja area, and painstakingly recovered Kashgaria at the end of 1877.

Li Hongzhang hoped to regain Ili through negotiation; however, a treaty for the restitution of Ili, signed in October 1879, was extremely disadvantageous to China. Upon returning home amid a storm of condemnation, the Chinese negotiator Chonghou was sentenced to death; the Russians considered this to be inhuman, and they stiffened their attitude. But the minister to Britain and France, Zeng Jize, son of Zeng Guofan, succeeded in concluding a treaty at St. Petersburg in February 1881 that was more favourable yet still conceded the Russians many privileges in East Turkistan.

Though at a cost of nearly 58 million taels in expedition and indemnity, the northwest was finally restored to China, and in 1884 a new province, Xinjiang, was established over the area, which had never before been integrated into China.

TIBET AND NEPAL

Qing control of Tibet reached its height in 1792, but thereafter China became unable to protect that region from foreign invasion. When an army from northern India invaded western Tibet in 1841, China could not afford to reinforce the Tibetans, who expelled the enemy on their own. China was a mere bystander during a coup d'état in Lhasa in 1844 and could not protect Tibet when it was invaded by Gurkhas in 1855. Tibet thus tended to free itself from Qing control.

The border dispute between Nepal and British India, which sharpened after 1801, had caused the Anglo-Nepalese War of 1814–16 and brought the Gurkhas under British influence. During the war the Gurkhas sent several missions to China in vain expectation of assistance. When political unrest flared up in Nepal after 1832, an anti-British clique seized power and sought assistance from China to form an anti-British common front with the Qing, then fighting the first Opium War. But this too was rejected. Jung Bahadur, who had become premier of Nepal in 1846, decided on a pro-British policy; his invasion of Tibet in 1855—which took advantage of the Taiping uprising in China—gained Nepal many privileges there. Though Nepal sent quinquennial missions to China until 1906, the Gurkhas did not recognize Chinese suzerainty.

MYANMAR (BURMA)

In 1867 the British gained the right to station a commercial agent at Bhamo in Myanmar, from which they could explore the Irrawaddy River up to the Yunnan border. A British interpreter accompanying a British exploratory mission to Yunnan was killed by local tribesmen on the Yunnan-Myanmar border in February 1875. The British minister in China, Sir Thomas Francis Wade, seized the opportunity to negotiate the Chefoo Convention with China. Negotiated and signed at the northern Shandong city of Yantai (Chefoo) in 1876, the treaty further extended the British rights by opening more Chinese ports to foreign trade and agreeing to a mission to delineate the Yunnan-Myanmar border, though the London government put off its ratification until 1885. Guo Songtao, appointed chief of a mission of apology to Britain, arrived in London in 1877. He was the first Chinese resident minister abroad, and within two years China opened embassies in five major foreign capitals.

When the last king of Myanmar, Thibaw, tried to join with France and Italy to stave off British pressure, Britain sent an ultimatum in October 1885, seized the capital of Mandalay, and annexed the country in January 1886 under the name Burma. During the final bargaining with the British, Thibaw ignored his tributary relations with the Qing, yet China proposed that the Myanmar royal court be preserved even nominally so that it could send a decennial mission to China. Britain refused, but, in a convention signed in July 1886, it agreed that the new Burmese government should send to China a decennial envoy. This outdated practice, however, was abandoned in 1900.

VIETNAM

In 1802 a new dynasty was founded in Vietnam (Dai Viet) by Nguyen Anh, a member of the royal family of Nguyen at Hue who had expelled the short-lived Tay Son regime and had unified the country, taking the dynastic name Gia Long. The Qing, under the Jiaqing emperor, recognized the new dynasty as a fait accompli, but a controversy arose as to a name for the new country. Gia Long demanded the name Nam Viet, but the Qing recommended Vietnam, reversing the two syllables. Finally an agreement was reached, and Gia Long became ruler of Vietnam.

Minh Mang, the second Nguyen emperor (reigned 1820–41), vigorously persecuted Christians in Vietnam. France resorted to arms after 1843 and, by the treaty of 1862 signed at Saigon (present-day Ho Chi Minh City), received three eastern provinces of Cochinchina, besides other privileges concerning trade and religion. In time, French attentions were focused on the Tonkin delta region into which the Red River flows, providing easy access to Yunnan. But the region was beset with many disorderly gangs escaped from China, including the Black Flags, who were under the command of Liu Yung-fu, a confederate of the Taiping. After a small French force had occupied some key points in Tongkin in 1873, a treaty was signed at Saigon in March 1874 that stipulated the sovereignty and independence of Vietnam. Though this clause implied that China could not intervene in Vietnamese affairs, the Zongli Yamen failed to file a strong protest. In 1880, however, the Qing claimed a right to protect Vietnam as its vassal state. Against the

French occupation of Tongkin in 1882–83 and France's proclamation of protectorate status for Vietnam (under the name of Annam) in the Treaty of Hue of August 1883, the Qing deployed its army in the northern frontier of Tongkin. Efforts for a peaceful settlement ended in failure, and both countries prepared for war.

In August 1884 French warships attacked Fuzhou and destroyed the Chinese fleet and dockyard there. Thereafter, however, the French navy and army were stalemated, and an armistice was reached in the spring of 1885. By the subsequent definitive treaty, the French protectorate of Vietnam was recognized, terminating the historical tributary relationship between China and Vietnam.

During the crisis the attitude of the Qing headquarters fluctuated between advocating militancy and seeking appeasement. Meanwhile, Li Hongzhang and Zeng Guoquan were reluctant to mobilize their respective northern and southern naval fleets in accordance with orders from Beijing.

JAPAN AND THE RYUKYU ISLANDS

Three years after the Meiji Restoration of 1868—which inaugurated a period of modernization and political change in Japan—a commercial treaty was signed between China and Japan, and it was ratified in 1873. Understandably it was reciprocal, because both signatories had a similar unequal status vis-à-vis the Western nations. The establishment of the new Sino-Japanese relations was supported by Li Hongzhang and Zeng Guofan, who advocated positive diplomacy toward Japan.

In 1872 the Meiji government conferred on the last king of the Ryukyu Islands, Shō Tai, the title of vassal king and in the following year took over the island's foreign affairs. In reprisal for the massacre of shipwrecked Ryukyuans by Taiwanese tribesmen in 1871, the Tokyo government sent a punitive expedition to Taiwan. Meanwhile, the Japanese sent an envoy to Beijing to discuss the matter, and the Qing agreed to indemnify Japan. In 1877, however, the Ryukyu king asked for Qing intervention to revive his former tributary relations with China; Sino-Japanese negotiations were opened at Tianjin in regard to Ryukyu's position, and an agreement was reached in 1882. However, the Qing refused to ratify it, and the matter was dropped.

KOREA AND THE SINO-JAPANESE WAR

In Korea a boy was enthroned as the Chosŏn king Kojong in 1864 under the regency of his father, Yi Ha-ŭng (called the Taewŏn'gun ["Prince of the Great Court"]), a vigorous exclusionist. In 1866 the Koreans began a nationwide persecution of Christians and repulsed the French and Americans there. The Qing, although uneasy, did not intervene.

After the Meiji Restoration, Japan made many efforts to open new and direct intercourse with Korea, but the Taewŏn'gun, citing diplomatic slights,

managed to rebuff these overtures. The Chosŏn government became more approachable after he stepped down in 1873, and a Japanese envoy began talks at Pusan in 1875. However, the parley was protracted, and Japan impatiently sent warships to Korea; these sailed northward to Kanghwa Bay, where gunfire was exchanged between the Japanese vessels and a Korean island fort. The Treaty of Kanghwa, signed in 1876, defined Korea as an independent state on an equal footing with Japan. Japan sent an envoy, Mori Arinori, to China to report on recent Korean affairs. China insisted that, although Korea was independent, China could come to the support of its vassal state (Korea) in a crisis, an interpretation that Mori saw as contrary to the idea of independence in international law.

From that time on, the Qing strove to increase their influence in Korea; they helped open Korea to the United States and supported the efforts of pro-Chinese Koreans for modernization. However, strong feelings of conservatism and xenophobia provided the basis for the Taewŏn'gun to return to power. In July 1882 he expelled Kojong's consort, Queen Min, and her clique and burned down the Japanese legation. The Qing dispatched an army to Korea, arrested the Taewŏn'gun, and urged the king to sign a treaty with Japan. Thus, the Qing claim for suzerainty was substantiated.

In December 1884 another coup was attempted by a group of pro-Japanese reformists, but it failed because of the Qing military presence in Korea. From these two incidents, Qing political influence and commercial privileges emerged much stronger, though Japan's trade in Korea far surpassed that of China in the late 1880s.

In 1860 a Korean scholar, Ch'oe Che-u, had founded a popular religion called Tonghak ("Eastern Learning"). By 1893 it had turned into a political movement that attracted a vast number of peasants under the banner of antiforeignism and anticorruption. They occupied the southwestern city of Chŏnju in late May 1894. Both China and Japan sent expeditions to Korea, but the two interventionists arrived to find the rebels at Chŏnju already dispersed. To justify its military presence, Japan proposed to China a policy of joint support of Korean reform. When China refused on the ground that this was counter to Korean independence, a clash seemed inevitable. On July 25 the Japanese navy defeated a Chinese fleet in Kanghwa Bay, and on August 1 the two sides declared war on each other. Japan gained victories in every quarter on both land and sea.

During the crisis the Qing power centre was again divided. The northern (beiyang) navy was less powerful than it appeared, lacking discipline, unified command, and the necessary equipment of a modern navy. In February 1895 Li Hongzhang was appointed envoy to Japan; he signed a peace treaty at Shimonoseki on April 17, whose main items were recognition of Korean independence, indemnity of 200 million taels, and the cession of Taiwan, the Pescadores Islands, and the Liaodong Peninsula. Six days later, however, Russia, Germany, and France forced Japan to restore the peninsula; Japan formally relinquished it on May 5, for which China agreed to pay 30 million taels. Gaining China's favour by this intervention, the three powers began to press China with demands, which gave rise to a veritable scramble for concessions.

REFORM AND UPHEAVAL

Immediately after the triple intervention, Russia succeeded in 1896 in signing a secret treaty of alliance with China against Japan, by which Russia gained the right to construct the Chinese Eastern Railway across northern Manchuria. In November 1897 the Germans seized Jiaozhou Bay in Shandong and forced China to concede them the right to build two railways in the province. In March 1898 Russia occupied Port Arthur (Lüshun; since 1984 a part of Dalian) and a small fishing village that became Dairen (Dalian; called Lüda in 1950–81) on the Liaodong Peninsula and obtained the lease of the two ports and the right to build a railway connecting them to the Chinese Eastern Railway. Vying with Russia and Germany, Britain leased Weihai in Shandong and the New Territories opposite Hong Kong and forced China to recognize the Yangtze River valley as being under British influence. Following suit, Japan put the province of Fujian under its influence, and France leased Kwangchow

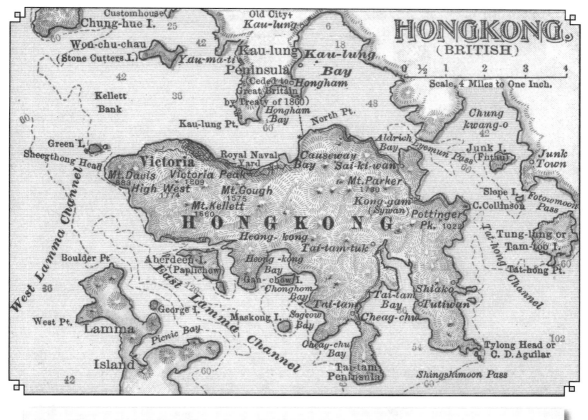

Map of Hong Kong c. 1900; from the 10th edition of Encyclopædia Britannica.

(Zhanjiang) Bay, southwest of Hong Kong, and singled out three southwestern provinces for its sphere of influence. Thus, China was placed on the brink of partition, arousing a keen sense of crisis in 1898 in which the Hundred Days of Reform was staged.

THE HUNDRED DAYS OF REFORM OF 1898

The advocates of the Self-Strengthening Movement had regarded any institutional or ideological change as needless. But after 1885 some lower officials and comprador intellectuals began to emphasize institutional reforms and the opening of a parliament and to stress economic rather than military affairs for self-strengthening purposes. For the Beijing court and high officials in general, the necessity of reform had to be proved on the basis of the Chinese Classics. Some scholars tried to meet their criteria. The outstanding reform leader and ideologist Kang Youwei used what he considered authentic Confucianism and Buddhist canons to show that change was inevitable in history and, accordingly, that reform was necessary. Another important reformist thinker, Tan Sitong, relied more heavily on Buddhism than Kang did and emphasized the people's rights and independence. Liang Qichao was an earnest disciple of Kang but later turned toward people's rights and nationalism under the influence of Western philosophy.

In April 1895, when Japanese victory appeared inevitable, Kang began to advocate institutional reform. In August Kang, Liang, and other reformists founded a political group called the Society for the Study of National Strengthening. Though this association was soon closed down, many study societies were created in Hunan, Guangdong, Fujian, Sichuan, and other provinces. In April 1898 the National Protection Society was established in Beijing under the premise of protecting state, nation, and national religion. Against this background, the Guangxu emperor (reigned 1874/75–1908) was himself increasingly affected by the ideas of reform that were broadly in the air and perhaps was also directly influenced by Kang Youwei's proposals. On June 11, 1898, the emperor began to issue a stream of radical and probably hastily prepared reform decrees that lasted for about 100 days, until September 20. The reform movement produced no practical results, however. Finally, the conservatives were provoked to a sharp reaction when they learned of a reformist plot to remove the archconservative empress dowager Cixi. On September 21 the emperor was detained and the empress dowager took over the administration, putting an end to the reform movement.

The immediate cause of the failure lay in the power struggle between the emperor and Cixi. But from the beginning, prospects for reform were dim because most high officials were cool toward or opposed to the movement. In addition, the reformist-conservative confrontation overlapped with the rivalry between the Chinese and the Manchu, who considered the Chinese-sponsored reform as disadvantageous to them. As for the reformists themselves, their leaders were few in number and inexperienced in politics, and their plan was too radical.

Among the local movements for reform, that in Hunan was the most active. After 1896, journals and schools were begun there for popular enlightenment, but Kang's radical reformism aroused strong opposition, and the Hunan movement was shattered at the end of May 1898.

Though it failed, the reform movement had a few important repercussions: it produced some degree of freedom of speech and association, furthered the dissemination of Western thought, and stimulated the growth of private enterprises. It also provided much of the substance for the "conservative" imperial reform efforts that the Manchu court undertook after the Boxer episode.

THE BOXER REBELLION

The crisis of 1896–98 stirred a furious antiforeign uprising in Shandong, aroused by the German advances and encouraged by the provincial governor. It was staged by a band of people called the Yihequan ("Righteous and Harmonious Fists"), who believed that a mysterious boxing art rendered them invulnerable to harm. The group's origin is generally supposed to have been in the White Lotus sect, though it may have begun as a self-defense organization during the Taiping Rebellion. At first the Boxers (as they were called in the West) directed their wrath against Christian converts, whom they vilified for having abandoned traditional Chinese customs in favour of an alien religion. Bands of Boxers roamed the countryside killing Chinese Christians and foreign missionaries. Developing from this anti-Christian hysteria, the Boxer Rebellion grew into a naive but furious attempt to destroy all things foreign—including churches, railways, and mines—which the people blamed for their misery and for the loss of a sacred way of life.

Some Boxer recruits were disbanded imperial soldiers and local militiamen; others were Grand Canal boatmen deprived of a livelihood by the Western-built railways. Most recruits, though, came from the peasantry, which had suffered terribly from recent natural calamities in

Drawing of a scene from the Boxer Rebellion uprising in China. Hulton Archive/Getty Images

northern China. After 1895 the Huang He flooded almost annually, and in 1899–1900 a serious drought struck the north. Vast numbers of starving people turned to begging and banditry and were easy converts to the Boxers' cause.

Many local authorities refused to stop the violence. Some supported the Boxers by incorporating them into local militias. The Manchu court, meanwhile, was alarmed by the uncontrollable popular uprising but took great satisfaction at seeing revenge taken for its humiliation by the foreign powers. As a result, it assumed at first a neutral policy. On the part of the Boxers, there emerged sometime in the autumn of 1899 a move to gain access to the court under the slogan "Support for the Qing and extermination of foreigners." By May 1900 the Qing government had changed its policy and was secretly supporting the Boxers. Cixi inclined toward open war when she became convinced of the dependability of the Boxers' art. Finally, incensed over a false report that the foreign powers had demanded that she return administration to the emperor, she called on all Chinese to attack foreigners. Within days, on June 20, the Boxers' eight-week siege of the foreign legations in Beijing began; a day later Cixi declared war by ordering provincial governors to take part in the hostilities.

An international reinforcement of some 2,000 men had left Tianjin for Beijing before the siege, but on the way it was resisted by the Boxers and forced back to Tianjin. The foreign powers then sent an expedition of some 19,000 troops, which marched to Beijing and seized the city on August 14. Cixi and the emperor fled to Xi'an.

The two governors-general in the southeastern provinces, Liu Kunyi and Zhang Zhidong, who together with Li Hongzhang at Guangzhou had already disobeyed Beijing's antiforeign decrees, concluded an informal pact with foreign consuls at Shanghai on June 26, to the effect that the governors-general would take charge of the safety of the foreigners under their jurisdiction. At first the pact covered the five provinces in the Yangtze River region, but later it was extended to three coastal provinces. Thus, the foreign operations were restricted to Zhili (present-day Hebei) province, along the northern coast.

The United States, which had announced its commercial Open Door policy in 1899, made a second declaration of the policy in July 1900—this time insisting on the preservation of the territorial and administrative entity of China. With its newly acquired territory in the western Pacific, the United States was determined to preserve its own commercial interests in China by protecting Chinese territorial integrity from the other major powers. This provided a basis for the Anglo-German agreement (October 1900) for preventing further territorial partition, to which Japan and Russia consented. Thus, partition of China was avoided by mutual restraint among the powers.

The final settlement of the disturbance was signed in September 1901. The indemnity amounted to 450 million taels to be paid over 39 years. Moreover, the settlement demanded the establishment of permanent guards and the dismantling of forts between Beijing and the sea, a humiliation that made an independent China a mere fiction. In addition, the southern provinces were actually independent during the crisis. These occurrences meant the collapse of the Qing prestige.

After the uprising, Cixi had to declare that she had been misled into war by the conservatives and that the court, neither antiforeign nor antireformist, would promote reforms, a seemingly incredible statement in view of the court's suppression of the 1898 reform movement. But the Qing court's antiforeign, conservative nationalism and the reforms undertaken after 1901 were in fact among several competing responses to the shared sense of crisis in early 20th-century China.

REFORMIST AND REVOLUTIONIST MOVEMENTS AT THE END OF THE DYNASTY

Sun Yat-sen (Sun Zhongshan), a commoner with no background of Confucian orthodoxy who was educated in Western-style schools in Hawaii and Hong Kong, went to Tianjin in 1894 to meet Li Hongzhang and present a reform program, but he was refused an interview. That event supposedly provoked his antidynastic attitude. Soon he returned to Hawaii, where he founded an anti-Manchu fraternity called the Revive China

Society (Xingzhonghui). Returning to Hong Kong, he and some friends set up a similar society under the leadership of his associate Yang Quyun. Sun participated in an abortive attempt to capture Guangzhou in 1895, after which he sailed for England and then went to Japan in 1897, where he found much support. Tokyo became the revolutionaries' principal base of operation.

After the collapse of the Hundred Days of Reform, Kang Youwei and Liang Qichao had also fled to Japan. An attempt to reconcile the reformists and the revolutionaries became hopeless by 1900: Sun was slighted as a secret-society ruffian, while the reformists were more influential among the Chinese in Japan and the Japanese.

The two camps competed in collecting funds from the overseas Chinese, as well as in attracting secret-society members on the mainland. The reformists strove to unite with the powerful, secret Society of Brothers and Elders (Gelaohui) in the Yangtze River region. In 1899 Kang's followers organized the Independence Army (Zilijun) at Hankou in order to plan an uprising, but the scheme ended unsuccessfully. Early in 1900 the Revive China Society revolutionaries also formed a kind of alliance with the Brothers and Elders, called the Revive Han Association. This new body nominated Sun as its leader, a decision that also gave him, for the first time, the leadership of the Revive China Society. The Revive Han Association started an uprising at Huizhou, in Guangdong, in

October 1900, which failed after two weeks' fighting with imperial forces.

After the Boxer disaster, Cixi reluctantly issued a series of reforms, which included abolishing the civil service examination, establishing modern schools, and sending students abroad. But these measures could never repair the damaged imperial prestige; rather, they inspired more anti-Manchu feeling and raised the revolutionary tide. However, other factors also intensified the revolutionary cause: the introduction of social Darwinist ideas by Yen Fu after the Sino-Japanese War countered the reformists' theory of change based on the Chinese Classics; and Western and revolutionary thoughts came to be easily and widely diffused through a growing number of journals and pamphlets published in Tokyo, Shanghai, and Hong Kong.

Nationalists and revolutionists had their most-enthusiastic and most-numerous supporters among the Chinese students in Japan, whose numbers increased rapidly between 1900 and 1906. The Zongli Yamen sent 13 students to Japan for the first time in 1896; within a decade the figure had risen to some 8,000. Many of these students began to organize themselves for propaganda and immediate action for the revolutionary cause. In 1902–04, revolutionary and nationalistic organizations—including the Chinese Educational Association, the Society for Revival of China, and the Restoration Society—appeared in Shanghai. The anti-Manchu tract "Revolutionary Army"

was published in 1903, and more than a million copies were issued.

Dealing with the young intellectuals was a new challenge for Sun Yat-sen, who hitherto had concentrated on mobilizing the uncultured secret-society members. He also had to work out some theoretical planks, though he was not a first-class political philosopher. The result of his response was the Three Principles of the People (Sanmin Zhuyi)—nationalism, democracy, and socialism—the prototype of which came to take shape by 1903. He expounded his philosophy in America and Europe during his travels there in 1903–05, returning to Japan in the summer of 1905. The activists in Tokyo joined him to establish a new organization called the United League (Tongmenghui); under Sun's leadership, the intellectuals increased their importance.

SUN YAT-SEN AND THE UNITED LEAGUE

Sun's leadership in the league was far from undisputed. His understanding that the support of foreign powers was indispensable for Chinese revolution militated against the anti-imperialist trend of the young intellectuals. Only half-heartedly accepted was the principle of people's livelihood, or socialism, one of his Three Principles. Though his socialism has been evaluated in various ways, it seems certain that it did not reflect the hopes and needs of the commoners.

Ideologically, the league soon fell into disharmony: Zhang Binglin (Chang

SUN YAT-SEN

Sun Yat-sen (Pinyin: Sun Yixian; b. Nov. 12, 1866—d. March 12, 1925), leader of the Chinese Nationalist Party, is known as the father of modern China. Educated in Hawaii and Hong Kong, Sun embarked on a medical career in 1892, but, troubled by the conservative Qing dynasty's inability to keep China from suffering repeated humiliations at the hands of more advanced countries, he forsook medicine two years later for politics. A letter to Li Hongzhang in which Sun detailed ways that China could gain strength made no headway, and he went abroad to try organizing expatriate Chinese. He spent time in Hawaii, England, Canada, and Japan and in 1905 became head of a revolutionary coalition, the Tongmenghui ("Alliance Society," or United League). The revolts he helped plot during this period failed, but in 1911 a rebellion in Wuhan unexpectedly succeeded in overthrowing the provincial government. Other provincial secessions followed, and Sun returned to be elected provisional president of a new government. The emperor abdicated in 1912, and Sun turned over the government to Yuan Shikai. The two men split in 1913, and Sun became head of a separatist regime in the south. In 1924, aided by Soviet advisers, he reorganized his Nationalist Party, admitted three communists to its central executive committee, and approved the establishment of a military academy, to be headed by Chiang Kai-shek. He also delivered lectures on his doctrine, the Three Principles of the People (nationalism, democracy, and people's livelihood, or socialism), but died the following year without having had the opportunity to put his doctrine into practice.

The Chinese revolutionary leader Sun Yat-Sen. Topical Press Agency/Hulton Archive/Getty Images

Ping-lin), an influential theorist in the Chinese Classics, came to renounce the Three Principles of the People; others deserted to anarchism, leaving anti-Manchuism as the only common denominator in the league. Organizationally too, the league became divided: the Progressive Society (Gongjinhui), a parallel to the league, was born in Tokyo in 1907; a branch of this new society was soon opened at Wuhan with the ambiguous slogan "Equalization of human right." The next year, Zhang Binglin tried to revive the Restoration Society.

CONSTITUTIONAL MOVEMENTS AFTER 1905

Japan's victory in the Russo-Japanese War (1904–05) aroused a cry for constitutionalism in China. Unable to resist the intensifying demand, the Qing court decided in September 1906 to adopt a constitution, and in November it reorganized the traditional six boards into 11 ministries in an attempt to modernize the central government. It promised to open consultative provincial assemblies in October 1907 and proclaimed in August 1908 the outline of a constitution and a nine-year period of tutelage before its full implementation.

Three months later the strangely coinciding deaths of Cixi and the emperor were announced, and a boy who ruled as the Xuantong emperor (1908–1911/12) was enthroned under the regency of his father, the second Prince Chun. These deaths, followed by that of Zhang

Zhidong in 1909, almost emptied the Qing court of prestigious members. The consultative provincial assemblies were convened in October 1910 and became the main base of the furious movement for immediate opening of a consultative national assembly, with which the court could not comply.

The gentry and wealthy merchants were the sponsors of constitutionalism; they had been striving to gain the rights held by foreigners. Started first in Hunan, the so-called rights recovery movement spread rapidly and gained noticeable success, reinforced by local officials, students returned from Japan, and the Beijing government. But finally the recovery of the railroad rights ended in a clash between the court and the provincial interests.

The retrieval of the Hankou-Guangzhou line from the American China Development Company in 1905 tapped a nationwide fever for railway recovery and development. However, difficulty in raising capital delayed railway construction by the Chinese year after year. The Beijing court therefore decided to nationalize some important railways in order to accelerate their construction by means of foreign loans, hoping that the expected railway profits would somehow alleviate the court's inveterate financial plight. In May 1911 the court nationalized the Hankou-Guangzhou and Sichuan-Hankou lines and signed a loan contract with the four-power banking consortium. This incensed the Sichuan gentry, merchants, and landlords who had invested in the latter line, and their anti-Beijing remonstrance grew into a province-wide uprising. The court moved some troops into Sichuan from Hubei; some other troops in Hubei mutinied and suddenly occupied the capital city, Wuchang, on October 10. That date became the memorial day of the Chinese Revolution.

The commoners' standard of living, which had not continued to grow in the 19th century and may have begun to deteriorate, was further dislocated by the mid-century civil wars and foreign commercial and military penetration. Paying for the wars and their indemnities certainly increased the tax burden of the peasantry, but how serious a problem this was has remained an open question among scholars. The Manchu reforms and preparations for constitutionalism added a further fiscal exaction for the populace, which hardly benefited from these urban-oriented developments. Rural distress, resulting from these policies and from natural disasters, was among the causes of local peasant uprisings in the Yangtze River region in 1910 and 1911 and of a major rice riot at Changsha, the capital of Hunan, in 1910. However, popular discontent was limited and not a major factor contributing to the revolution that ended the Qing dynasty and inaugurated the republican era in China.

THE CHINESE REVOLUTION (1911–12)

The Chinese Revolution was triggered not by the United League itself but by the army troops in Hubei who were urged on by the local revolutionary bodies not incorporated in the league. The accidental exposure of a mutinous plot forced a number of junior officers to choose between arrest or revolt in Wuhan. The revolt was initially successful because of the determination of lower-level officers and revolutionary troops and the cowardice of the responsible Manchu and Chinese officials. Within a day the rebels had seized the arsenal and the governor-general's offices and had gained possession of Wuchang. With no nationally known revolutionary leaders on hand, the rebels coerced a colonel, Li Yuanhong, to assume military command, although only as a figurehead. They persuaded the Hubei provincial assembly to proclaim the establishment of the Chinese republic; Tang Hualong, the assembly's chairman, was elected head of the civil government.

After this initial victory, a number of historical tendencies converged to bring about the downfall of the Qing dynasty. A decade of revolutionary organization and propaganda paid off in a sequence of supportive uprisings in important centres of central and southern China; these occurred in recently formed military academies and in newly created divisions and brigades, in which many cadets and junior officers were revolutionary sympathizers. Secret-society units also were quickly mobilized for local revolts. The antirevolutionary constitutionalist movement also made an important contribution: its leaders had become disillusioned with the imperial government's unwillingness to speed the process of constitutional government, and a number of them led their respective provincial assemblies to declare their provinces independent of Beijing or to actually join the new republic. Tang Hualong was the first among them. A significant product of the newly emerging nationalism was widespread hostility among Chinese toward the alien dynasty. Many had absorbed the revolutionary propaganda that blamed a weak and vacillating court for the humiliations China had suffered from foreign powers since 1895. Therefore, broad sentiment favoured the end of Manchu rule. Also, as an outcome of two decades of journalizing discussion of "people's rights," there was substantial support among the urban educated for a republican form of government. Probably the most-decisive development was the recall of Yuan Shikai (Yüan Shih-k'ai), the architect of the elite Beiyang Army, to government service to suppress the rebellion when its seriousness became apparent.

After the collapse of the Huai Army in the Sino-Japanese War, the Qing government had endeavoured to build up a new Western-style army, among which the elite corps trained by Yuan Shikai, former governor-general of Zhili, had survived the Boxer uprising and emerged as the strongest force in China. But it was in a sense Yuan's private army and did not easily submit to the Manchu court. Yuan had been retired from officialdom at odds with the regent Prince Chun, but, on

the outbreak of the revolution in 1911, the court had no choice but to recall him from retirement to take command of his new army. Instead of using force, however, he played a double game: on the one hand, he deprived the floundering court of all its power; on the other, he started to negotiate with the revolutionaries. At the peace talks that opened at the end of the year, Yuan's emissaries and the revolutionary representatives agreed that the abdication of the Qing and the appointment of Yuan to the presidency of the new republic were to be formally decided by a National Assembly that would be formed. However, this was renounced by Yuan, probably because he hoped to be appointed by the retiring Manchu monarch to organize a new government rather than nominated as chief of state by the National Assembly. (This is a formula of the Chinese dynastic revolution called *chanrang*, which means the peaceful shift in rule from a decadent dynasty to a more-virtuous one.) But events turned against him, and the presidency was given to Sun Yat-sen, who had been appointed provisional president of the republic by the National Assembly. In February 1912 Sun voluntarily resigned his position, and the Qing court proclaimed the decree of abdication, which included a passage—fabricated and inserted by Yuan into this last imperial document—purporting that Yuan was to organize a republican government to negotiate with the revolutionists on unification of northern and southern China. Thus ended the 268-year rule of the Qing dynasty.

CHAPTER 12

THE EARLY REPUBLICAN PERIOD

THE DEVELOPMENT OF THE REPUBLIC (1912–20)

During the first half of the 20th century, the old order in China gradually disintegrated, and turbulent preparations were made for a new society. Foreign political philosophies undermined the traditional governmental system, nationalism became the strongest activating force, and civil wars and Japanese invasion tore the vast country and retarded its modernization. Although the revolution ushered in a republic, China had virtually no preparation for democracy. A three-way settlement ended the revolution: the Qing dynasty abdicated; Sun Yat-sen relinquished the provisional presidency in favour of Yuan Shikai (Yüan Shih-k'ai), regarded as the indispensable man to restore unity; and Yuan promised to establish a republican government. This placed at the head of state an autocrat by temperament and training, and the revolutionaries had only a minority position in the new national government.

EARLY POWER STRUGGLES

The first years of the republic were marked by a continuing contest between Yuan and the former revolutionaries over where ultimate power should lie. The contest began with the election of parliament (the National Assembly) in February

1913. The Nationalist Party (Kuomintang [KMT], or Guomindang), made up largely of former revolutionaries, won a commanding majority of seats. Parliament was to produce a permanent constitution. Song Jiaoren (Sung Chiao-jen), the main organizer of the KMT's electoral victory, advocated executive authority in a cabinet responsible to parliament rather than to the president. In March 1913, Song was assassinated; the confession of the assassin and later circumstantial evidence strongly implicated the premier and possibly Yuan himself.

Parliament tried to block Yuan's effort to get a "reorganization loan" (face value $125 million) from a consortium of foreign banks, but in April Yuan concluded the negotiations and received the loan. He then dismissed three Nationalist military governors. That summer, revolutionary leaders organized a revolt against Yuan, later known as the Second Revolution, but his military followers quickly suppressed it. Sun Yat-sen, one of the principal revolutionaries, fled to Japan. Yuan then coerced parliament into electing him formally to the presidency, and he was inaugurated on October 10, the second anniversary of the outbreak of the revolution. By then his government had been recognized by most foreign powers. When parliament promulgated a constitution placing executive authority in a cabinet responsible to the legislature, Yuan revoked the credentials of the KMT members, charging them with involvement in the recent revolt. He dissolved parliament on Jan.

10, 1914, and appointed another body to prepare a constitution according to his own specifications. The presidency had become a dictatorship.

CHINA IN WORLD WAR I

JAPANESE GAINS

Following the outbreak of World War I in 1914, Japan joined the side of the Allies and seized the German leasehold around Jiaozhou Bay together with German-owned railways in Shandong. China was not permitted to interfere. Then, on Jan. 18, 1915, the Japanese government secretly presented to Yuan the Twenty-one Demands, which sought in effect to make China a Japanese dependency. Yuan skillfully directed the negotiations by which China tried to limit its concessions, which centred on greater access to Chinese ports and railroads and even a voice in Chinese political and police affairs. At the same time, Yuan searched for foreign support. The European powers, locked in war, were in no position to restrain Japan, and the United States was unwilling to intervene. The Chinese public, however, was aroused. Most of Yuan's political opponents supported his resistance to Japan's demands. Nevertheless, on May 7 Japan gave Yuan a 48-hour ultimatum, forcing him to accept the terms as they stood at that point in the negotiations.

Japan gained extensive special privileges and concessions in Manchuria (Northeast China) and confirmed its gains in Shandong from Germany. The Hanyeping mining and metallurgical enterprise in the middle Yangtze valley was to become a joint Sino-Japanese company. China promised not to alienate to any other power any harbour, bay, or island on the coast of China nor to permit any nation to construct a dockyard, coaling station, or naval base on the coast of Fujian, the province nearest to Japan's colony of Taiwan.

YUAN'S ATTEMPTS TO BECOME EMPEROR

In the wake of the humiliation of these forced concessions, Yuan launched a movement to revive the monarchy, with some modernized features, and to place himself on the throne. The Japanese government began to "advise" against this move in October and induced its allies to join in opposing Yuan's plan. Additional opposition came from the leaders of the Nationalist and Progressive parties. In December, Chen Qimei (Ch'en Ch'i-mei) and Hu Hanmin (Hu Han-min), two followers of Sun Yat-sen (who was actively scheming against Yuan from his exile in Japan), began a movement against the monarchy. More significant was a military revolt in Yunnan, led by Gen. Cai E (Ts'ai O; a disciple of Liang Qichao) and by the governor of Yunnan, Tang Jiyao (T'ang Chi-yao). Joined by Li Liejun (Li Lieh-chün) and other revolutionary generals, they established the National Protection Army (Huguojun) and demanded that Yuan cancel his plan.

When he would not, the Yunnan army in early January 1916 invaded Sichuan and subsequently Hunan and Guangdong, hoping to bring the southwestern and southern provinces into rebellion and to then induce the lower Yangtze provinces to join them. The Japanese government covertly provided funds and munitions to Sun and the Yunnan leaders. One by one, military leaders in Guizhou, Guangxi, and parts of Guangdong declared the independence of their provinces or districts. By March the rebellion had assumed serious dimensions, and public opinion was running strongly against Yuan.

A third source of opposition came from Yuan's direct subordinates, Generals Duan Qirui (Tuan Ch'i-jui) and Feng Guozhang (Feng Kuo-chang), whose powers Yuan had attempted to curtail. When he called on them for help, they both withheld support. On March 22—with the tide of battle running against his forces in the southwest, Japanese hostility increasingly open, public opposition in full cry, and his closest subordinates advising peace—Yuan announced the abolition of the new empire. His opponents, however, demanded that he give up the presidency as well. The revolt continued to spread, with more military leaders declaring the independence of their provinces. The issue became that of succession should Yuan retire. The president, however, became gravely ill and died on June 6.

Yuan's four years in power had serious consequences for China. The country's foreign debt was much enlarged, and a precedent had been established of borrowing for political purposes. Yuan's defiance of constitutional procedures and his dissolution of parliament also set precedents that were later repeated. Many were disillusioned with the republican experiment; China was a republic in name, but arbitrary rule based on military power was the political reality. The country was becoming fractured into competing military satrapies—the beginning of warlordism.

Gen. Li Yuanhong (Li Yüan-hung), the vice president, succeeded to the presidency, and Duan Qirui continued as premier, a position he had accepted in April. A man of great ability and ambition, Duan was supported by many generals of the former Beiyang Army, a powerful force based in northern China that developed originally under Yuan's leadership. Duan quickly began to gather power into his own hands. Parliament reconvened on August 1; it confirmed Duan as premier but elected Gen. Feng Guozhang, the leader of another emerging faction of the Beiyang Army, as vice president. The presidential transition and restoration of parliament had by no means answered the underlying question of where the governing power lay.

CONFLICT OVER ENTRY INTO THE WAR

In February 1917 the U.S. government severed diplomatic relations with Germany and invited the neutral powers, including China, to do the same. This brought on a crisis in the Chinese government. Li opposed the step, but Duan favoured moving toward entry into the war. Parliamentary factions and public opinion were bitterly divided. Sun Yat-sen, now in Shanghai, argued that entering the war could not benefit China and would create additional perils from Japan. Under heavy pressure, parliament voted to sever diplomatic relations with Germany, and Li was compelled by his premier to acquiesce. When the United States entered the war in April, Duan wished China to do the same but was again opposed by the president.

Duan and his supporters demanded that China enter the war and that Li dissolve parliament. On May 23, Li dismissed Duan and called on Gen. Zhang Xun (Chang Hsün), a power in the Beiyang clique and also a monarchist, to mediate. As a price for mediation, Zhang demanded that Li dissolve parliament, which he did reluctantly on June 13. The next day Zhang entered Beijing with an army and set about to restore the Qing dynasty. Telegrams immediately poured in from military governors and generals denouncing Zhang and the coup; Li refused to sign the restoration order and called on Duan to bring an army to the capital to restore the republic. Li requested that Vice President Feng assume the duties of president during the crisis and then took refuge in the Japanese legation. Duan captured Beijing on July 14; Zhang fled to asylum in the Legation Quarter, and this ended a second attempt to restore the imperial system.

Duan resumed the premiership, and Feng came to Beijing as acting president, bringing a division as his personal guard. The two powerful rivals, each supported by an army in the capital, formed two powerful factions: the Zhili (Chihli) clique under Feng and the Anhui clique under Duan. Opposed neither by Li nor by the dissolved parliament, Duan pushed through China's declaration of war on Germany, announced on Aug. 14, 1917.

FORMATION OF A RIVAL SOUTHERN GOVERNMENT

Meanwhile, in July Sun Yat-sen, supported by part of the Chinese navy and followed by some 100 members of parliament, attempted to organize a rival government in Guangzhou (Canton). The initial costs of this undertaking, termed the Movement to Protect the Constitution, probably were supplied by the German consulate in Shanghai. On September 1 the rump parliament in Guangzhou established a military government and elected Sun commander in chief. Real power, however, lay with military men, who only nominally supported Sun. The southern government declared war on Germany on September 26 and unsuccessfully sought recognition from the Allies as the legitimate government. The Constitution-Protecting Army (Hufajun), made up of southern troops, launched a punitive campaign against the government in Beijing and succeeded in pushing northward through Hunan. Sichuan was also drawn into the fight. Duan tried to quell the southern opposition by force, while Feng advocated a peaceful solution. Duan resigned and mustered his strength to force Feng to order military action; Gen. Cao Kun was put in charge of the campaign and drove the southerners out of Hunan by the end of April 1918. In May the southern government was reorganized under a directorate of seven, in which military men dominated. Sun therefore left Guangzhou and returned to Shanghai. Although his first effort to establish a government in the south had been unsuccessful, it led to a protracted split between south and north.

WARTIME CHANGES

Although its wartime participation was limited, China made some gains from its entry into the war, taking over the German and Austrian concessions and canceling the unpaid portions of the Boxer indemnities due its enemies. It was also assured a seat at the peace conference. Japan, however, extended its gains in China. The Beijing government, dominated by Duan after Feng's retirement, granted concessions to Japan for railway building in Shandong, Manchuria, and Mongolia. These were in exchange for the Nishihara loans, amounting to nearly $90 million, which went mainly to strengthen the Anhui clique with arms and cash. Japan also made secret agreements with its allies to support its claims to the former German rights in Shandong and also induced the Beijing government to consent to these. In November 1917 the

United States, to adjust difficulties with Japan, entered into the Lansing-Ishii Agreement, which recognized that because of "territorial propinquity . . . Japan has special interests in China." This treaty seemed to underwrite Japan's wartime gains.

Important economic and social changes occurred during the first years of the republic. With the outbreak of the war, foreign economic competition with native industry abated, and native-owned light industries developed markedly. By 1918 the industrial labour force numbered some 1,750,000. Modern-style Chinese banks increased in number and expanded their capital.

INTELLECTUAL MOVEMENTS

A new intelligentsia had also emerged. The educational reforms and the ending of the governmental examination system during the final Qing years enabled thousands of young people to study sciences, engineering, medicine, law, economics, education, and military skills in Japan. Others went to Europe and the United States. Upon their return they took important positions and were a modernizing force in society. Their writing and teaching became a powerful influence on upcoming generations of students. In 1915–16 there were said to be nearly 130,000 new-style schools in China with more than four million students. This was mainly an urban phenomenon, however; rural life was barely affected except for what may have been gradually increasing

tenancy and a slow impoverishment that sent rural unemployed into cities and armies or into banditry.

AN INTELLECTUAL REVOLUTION

An intellectual revolution took place during the first decade of the republic, sometimes referred to as the New Culture Movement. It was led by many of the new intellectuals, who held up for critical scrutiny nearly all aspects of Chinese culture and traditional ethics. Guided by concepts of individual liberty and equality, a scientific spirit of inquiry, and a pragmatic approach to the nation's problems, they sought a much more profound reform of China's institutions than had resulted from self-strengthening or the republican revolution. They directed their efforts particularly to China's educated youth.

In September 1915 Chen Duxiu (Ch'en Tu-hsiu), who had studied in Japan and France, founded *Xinqingnian* ("New Youth") magazine to oppose Yuan's imperial ambitions and to regenerate the country's youth. This quickly became the most popular reform journal, and in 1917 it began to express the iconoclasm of new faculty members at Peking University (Beida), which Chen had joined as dean of the College of Letters. Peking University, China's most prestigious institution of higher education, was being transformed by its new chancellor, Cai Yuanpei (Ts'ai Yüan-p'ei), who had spent many years in advanced study in Germany. Cai made the university a centre of scholarly research and inspired teaching. The students were quickly swept into the New Culture Movement. A proposal by Hu Shih (Hu Shi), a former student of the American philosopher John Dewey, that literature be written in the vernacular language (*baihua*) rather than the classical style won quick acceptance. By 1918 most of the contributors to *Xinqingnian* were writing in *baihua*, and other journals and newspapers soon followed suit. Students at Peking University began their own reform journal, *Xinchao* ("New Tide"). A new experimental literature inspired by Western forms became highly popular, and scores of new literary journals were founded.

RIOTS AND PROTESTS

On May 4, 1919, patriotic students in Beijing protested the decision at the Paris Peace Conference that Japan should retain defeated Germany's rights and possessions in Shandong. Many students were arrested in the rioting that followed. Waves of protest spread throughout the major cities of China. Merchants closed their shops, banks suspended business, and workers went on strike to pressure the government. Finally, the government was forced to release the arrested students, to dismiss some officials charged with being tools of Japan, and to refuse to sign the Treaty of Versailles. This outburst helped spread the iconoclastic and reformist ideas of the intellectual movement, which became known as the May Fourth Movement. By the early 1920s,

China was launched on a new revolutionary path.

THE INTERWAR YEARS (1920–37)

BEGINNINGS OF A NATIONAL REVOLUTION

This new revolution was led by the Nationalist Party (KMT) and the Chinese Communist Party (CCP).

THE NATIONALIST PARTY

The Nationalist Party had its origins in the earlier United League (Tongmenghui) against the Qing dynasty. The name Nationalist Party was adopted in 1912. After the suppression of this expanded party by Yuan Shikai, elements from it were organized by Sun Yat-sen in 1914 into the Chinese Revolutionary Party, which failed to generate widespread support. Sun and a small group of veterans were stimulated by the patriotic upsurge of 1919 to rejuvenate this political tradition, as well as to revive the Nationalist Party name. The party's publications took on new life as the editors entered the current debates on what was needed to "save China." Socialism was popular among Sun's followers.

The formation of an effective party took several years, however. Sun returned to Guangzhou from Shanghai late in 1920, when Gen. Chen Jiongming (Ch'en Chiung-ming) drove out the Guangxi militarists. Another rump parliament elected Sun president of a new southern regime, which claimed to be the legitimate government of China. In the spring of 1922 Sun attempted to launch a northern campaign as an ally of the Manchurian warlord, Zhang Zuolin (Chang Tso-lin), against the Zhili clique, which by now controlled Beijing. Chen, however, did not want the provincial revenues wasted in internecine wars. One of Chen's subordinates drove Sun from the presidential residence in Guangzhou on the night of June 15–16, 1922. Sun took refuge with the southern navy, and he retired to Shanghai on August 9. He was able to return to Guangzhou in February 1923 and began to consolidate a base under his own control and to rebuild his party.

THE CHINESE COMMUNIST PARTY

The CCP grew directly from the May Fourth Movement. Its leaders and early members were professors and students who came to believe that China needed a social revolution and who began to see Soviet Russia as a model. Chinese students in Japan and France had earlier studied socialist doctrines and the ideas of Karl Marx, but the Russian Revolution of 1917 stimulated a fresh interest in keeping with the enthusiasm of the period for radical ideologies. Li Dazhao, the librarian of Peking University, and Chen Duxiu were the CCP's cofounders.

In March 1920 word reached China of Soviet Russia's revolutionary foreign policy enunciated in the first Karakhan Manifesto, which promised to give up all special rights gained by tsarist Russia at China's expense and to return the Russian-owned Chinese Eastern Railway in Manchuria without compensation. The contrast between this promise and the Versailles award to Japan that had touched off the 1919 protest demonstrations could hardly have been more striking. Although the Soviet government later denied such a promise and attempted to regain control of the railway, the impression of this first statement and the generosity still offered in a more diplomatic second Karakhan Manifesto of September 1920 left a favourable image of Soviet foreign policy among Chinese patriots.

Russia set up an international communist organization, the Comintern, in 1919 and sent Grigory N. Voytinsky to China the next year. Voytinsky met Li Dazhao in Beijing and Chen Duxiu in Shanghai, and they organized the Socialist Youth League, laid plans for the Communist Party, and started recruiting young intellectuals. By the spring of 1921 there were about 50 members in various Chinese cities and in Japan, many of them former students who had been active in the 1919 demonstrations. Mao Zedong, a protégé of Li Dazhao, had started one such group in Changsha. The CCP held its First Congress in Shanghai in July 1921, with 12 or 13 attendants and with a Dutch communist—Hendricus Sneevliet, who used his Comintern name, Maring, in China—and a Russian serving as advisers. Maring had become head of a new bureau of the Comintern in China, and he had arrived in Shanghai in June

Mao Zedong. Encyclopædia Britannica, Inc.

1921. At the First Congress, Chen Duxiu was chosen to head the party.

The CCP spent the next two years recruiting, publicizing Marxism and the need for a national revolution directed against foreign imperialism and Chinese militarism, and organizing unions among railway and factory workers. Maring was instrumental in bringing the KMT and the CCP together in a national revolutionary movement. A number of young men were sent to Russia for training. Among the CCP members were many students who had worked and studied in France, where they had gained experience in the French labour movement and with the French Communist Party; Zhou Enlai was one of these. Other recruits were students influenced by the Japanese socialist movement. By 1923 the party had some 300 members, with perhaps 3,000 to 4,000 in the ancillary Socialist Youth League.

COMMUNIST-NATIONALIST COOPERATION

By then, however, the CCP was in serious difficulty. The railway unions had been

MAO ZEDONG

The Chinese Marxist theorist, soldier, and statesman Mao Zedong (b. Dec. 26, 1893—d. Sept. 9, 1976) led China's communist revolution and served as chairman of the People's Republic of China (1949–59) and chairman of the Chinese Communist Party (CCP; 1931–76). The son of a peasant, Mao joined the revolutionary army that overthrew the Qing dynasty but, after six months as a soldier, left to acquire more education. At Peking University he met Li Dazhao and Chen Duxiu, founders of the CCP, and in 1921 he committed himself to Marxism. At that time, Marxist thought held that revolution lay in the hands of urban workers, but in 1925 Mao concluded that in China it was the peasantry, not the urban proletariat, that had to be mobilized. He became chairman of a Chinese Soviet Republic formed in rural Jiangxi province; its Red Army withstood repeated attacks from Chiang Kai-shek's Nationalist army but at last undertook the Long March to a more secure position in northwestern China. There Mao became the undisputed head of the CCP. Guerrilla warfare tactics, appeals to the local population's nationalist sentiments, and Mao's agrarian policies gained the party military advantages against their Nationalist and Japanese enemies and broad support among the peasantry. Mao's agrarian Marxism differed from the Soviet model, but, when the communists succeeded in taking power in China in 1949, the Soviet Union agreed to provide the new state with technical assistance. However, Mao's Great Leap Forward and his criticism of "new bourgeois elements" in the Soviet Union and China alienated the Soviet Union irrevocably; Soviet aid was withdrawn in 1960. Mao followed the failed Great Leap Forward with the Cultural Revolution, also considered to have been a disastrous mistake. After Mao's death, Deng Xiaoping began introducing social and economic reforms.

brutally suppressed, and there were few places in China where it was safe to be a known communist. In June 1923 the Third Congress of the CCP met in Guangzhou, where Sun Yat-sen provided a sanctuary. After long debate, this congress accepted the Comintern strategy pressed by Maring—that communists should join the KMT and make it the centre of the national revolutionary movement. Sun had rejected a multiparty alliance but had agreed to admit communists to his party, and several, including Chen Duxiu and Li Dazhao, had already joined the KMT. Even though communists would enter the other party as individuals, the CCP was determined to maintain its separate identity and autonomy and to attempt to control the labour union movement. The Comintern strategy called for a period of steering the Nationalist movement and building a base among the Chinese masses, followed by a second stage—a socialist revolution in which the proletariat would seize power from the capitalist class.

By mid-1923 the Soviets had decided to renew the effort to establish diplomatic relations with the Beijing government. Lev M. Karakhan, the deputy commissar for foreign affairs, was chosen as plenipotentiary for the negotiations. In addition to negotiating a treaty of mutual recognition, Karakhan was to try to regain for the Soviet Union control of the Chinese Eastern Railway. On the revolutionary front, the Soviets had decided to financially assist Sun in Guangzhou and to send a team of military men to help train an army in Guangdong. By June, five young Soviet officers were in Beijing for language training. More importantly, the Soviet leaders selected an old Bolshevik, Mikhail M. Borodin, as their principal adviser to Sun Yat-sen. The Soviet leaders also decided to replace Maring with Voytinsky as principal adviser to the CCP, which had its headquarters in Shanghai. Thereafter three men—Karakhan in Beijing, Borodin in Guangzhou, and Voytinsky in Shanghai—were the field directors of the Soviet effort to bring China into the anti-imperialist camp of "world revolution." The offensive was aimed primarily at the positions in China of Great Britain, Japan, and the United States.

REACTIONS TO WARLORDS AND FOREIGNERS

These countries too were moving toward a new, postwar relationship with China. At the Washington Conference (November 1921–February 1922), China put forth a 10-point proposal for relations between it and the other powers, which, after negotiations, became four points: to respect the sovereignty, independence, and territorial and administrative integrity of China, to give China opportunity to develop a stable government, to maintain the principle of equal opportunity in China for the commerce and industry of all countries, and to refrain from taking advantage of conditions in China to seek exclusive privileges detrimental to the rights of friendly countries. The treaty was signed as the Nine-Power Pact on

February 6. Two other Chinese proposals, tariff autonomy and abolishing extraterritoriality, were not included in the pact but were assigned to a committee for further study. In the meantime, separate negotiations between China and Japan produced a treaty in which Japan agreed to return the former German holdings in Shandong to China—although under conditions that left Japan with valuable privileges in the province.

For a few years thereafter, Great Britain, Japan, the United States, and France attempted to adjust their conflicting interests in China, cooperated in assisting the Beijing government, and generally refrained from aiding particular Chinese factions in the recurrent power struggles. But China was in turmoil, with regional militarism in full tide. Furthermore, a movement against the Unequal Treaties began to take shape.

MILITARISM IN CHINA

During the first years of the republic, China had been fractured by rival military regimes to the extent that no one authority was able to subordinate all rivals and create a unified and centralized political structure. Southern China was detached from Beijing's control; even the southern provinces, and indeed districts within them, were run by different military factions (warlords). Sichuan was a world in itself, divided among several military rulers. The powerful Beiyang Army had split into two major factions whose semi-independent commanders controlled provinces in the Yangtze valley and in the north; these factions competed for control of Beijing. In Manchuria, Zhang Zuolin headed a separate Fengtian army. Shanxi was controlled by Yan Xishan (Yen Hsi-shan). Each separate power group had to possess a territorial base from which to tax and recruit. Arms were produced in many scattered arsenals. Possession of an arsenal and control of ports through which foreign-made arms might be shipped were important elements of power. Most of the foreign powers had agreed in 1919 not to permit arms to be smuggled into China, but that embargo was not entirely effective.

The wealthier the territorial base, the greater the potential power of the controlling faction. Beijing was the great prize because of its symbolic importance as the capital and because the government there regularly received revenues collected by the Maritime Customs Service, administered by foreigners and protected by the powers. Competition for bases brought on innumerable wars, alliances, and betrayals. Conflict was continuous over spoils, even within each military system. To support their armies and conduct their wars, military commanders and their subordinates taxed the people heavily. Money for education and other government services was drained away; revenues intended for the central government were retained in the provinces. Regimes printed their own currency and forced "loans" from merchants and bankers. This chaotic situation partly accounts for the unwillingness of the maritime powers to give up the protection that the treaties with China afforded their nationals.

THE FOREIGN PRESENCE

As a result of several wars and many treaties with China since 1842, foreign powers had acquired a variety of unusual privileges for their nationals. These became collectively known as the Unequal Treaties, and patriotic Chinese bitterly resented them. Hong Kong, Macau, Taiwan, Tibet, and vast areas in Siberia and Central Asia had been detached from China. Dependencies such as Korea, Outer Mongolia, and Vietnam had been separated. Leaseholds on Chinese territory were granted to separate powers—such as the southern part of the Liaodong Peninsula and the territory in Shandong around Jiaozhou Bay, which Japan had seized from Germany, to Japan; the New Territories to the adjacent British crown colony of Hong Kong; Macau to Portugal; and the Kwangchow (Zhanjiang) Bay area to France. Most major cities had concession areas, not governed by China, that were set aside for the residence of foreigners. Nationals and subjects of the "treaty powers" (as they became known) were protected by extraterritoriality (i.e., they were subject only to the civil and criminal laws of their own countries); this status extended to foreign business enterprises in China, which provided a great advantage in competition with Chinese firms and was enhanced when foreign factories or banks were located in concession areas under foreign protection. The Chinese had to compete with foreign ships in Chinese rivers and coastal waters, with foreign mining companies in the interior, and with foreign banks that circulated their own notes. Foreign trade also had a great advantage because there could be no protective tariff to favour Chinese products.

Christian missionaries operated many schools, hospitals, and other philanthropic enterprises in China, all protected by extraterritoriality. The separate school system, outside of Chinese governmental control, was a sore point for Nationalists, who regarded the education of Chinese youth as a Chinese prerogative. There were foreign troops on Chinese soil and foreign naval vessels in its rivers and ports to enforce treaty rights. The Chinese government, bound by a variety of interlocking treaties, was not fully sovereign in China. Past regimes had accumulated a vast foreign debt against which central government revenues were pledged for repayment. All this was the foreign imperialism against which the KMT launched its attack after being reorganized along Bolshevist lines.

REORGANIZATION OF THE KMT

The KMT held its First National Congress in Guangzhou on Jan. 20–30, 1924. Borodin, who had reached Guangzhou in October 1923, began to advise Sun in the reorganization of the party. He prepared a constitution and helped draft a party program as a set of basic national policies. Delegates from throughout China and from overseas branches of the party adopted the program and the new constitution. The program announced goals of broad social reform and a fundamental readjustment of China's international status. Its tone was nationalistic, identifying China's enemies as imperialism and militarism. It singled out farmers and labourers as classes for special encouragement but also appealed to intellectuals, soldiers, youth, and women. The program threatened the position of landlords in relation to tenants and of employers in relation to labour, and Western privileges were openly menaced.

The constitution described a centralized organization, modeled on the Soviet Communist Party, with power concentrated in a small, elected group and with a descending hierarchy of geographical offices controlled by executive committees directed from above. Members were pledged to strict discipline and were to be organized in tight cells. Where possible they were to penetrate and try to gain control of such other organizations as labour unions, merchant associations, schools, and parliamentary bodies at all levels. Sun was designated as leader of the party and had veto rights over its decisions. The congress elected a central executive committee and a central supervisory committee to manage party affairs and confirmed Sun's decision to admit communists, though this was opposed by numerous party veterans, who feared the KMT itself might be taken over. A few

communists, including Li Dazhao, were elected to the executive committee.

The executive committee set up a central headquarters in Guangzhou. It also decided to strengthen the party throughout the country by deputizing most of its leaders to manage regional and provincial headquarters and by recruiting new members. A military academy was planned for training a corps of young officers, loyal to the party, who would become lower level commanders in a new national revolutionary army that was to be created. Borodin provided funds for party operations, and the Soviet Union promised to underwrite most of the expenses of, and to provide training officers for, the military academy. Chiang Kai-shek (Jiang Jieshi), who had become a close associate of Sun, was chosen to be the first commandant of the academy, and Liao Zhongkai (Liao Chung-k'ai) became the party representative, or chief political officer.

From February to November 1924, Sun and his colleagues had some success in making the KMT's influence felt nationally; they also consolidated the Guangzhou base, although it still depended on mercenary armies. The military academy was set up at Whampoa (Huangpu), on an island south of Guangzhou, and the first group of some 500 cadets was trained. In September Sun began another northern campaign in alliance with Zhang Zuolin against Cao Kun and Wu Peifu (Wu P'ei-fu), who now controlled Beijing. The campaign was interrupted, however, when Wu's subordinate, Feng Yuxiang (Feng Yü-hsiang), betrayed his chief and seized Beijing on October 23, while Wu was at the front facing Zhang Zuolin. Feng and his fellow plotters invited Sun to Beijing to participate in the settlement of national affairs, while Feng and Zhang invited Duan Qirui to come out of retirement and take charge of the government. Sun accepted the invitation and departed for the north on November 13. Before he arrived in Beijing, however, he fell gravely ill with incurable liver cancer. He died in Beijing on March 12, 1925.

STRUGGLES WITHIN THE TWO-PARTY COALITION

After Sun's death the KMT went through a period of inner conflict, although it progressed steadily, with Russian help, in bringing the Guangdong base under its control. The conflict was caused primarily by the radicalization of the party under the influence of the communists, who organized labour unions and peasant associations and pushed class struggle and the anti-imperialist movement.

CLASHES WITH FOREIGNERS

On May 30, 1925, patriotic students who were engaged in an anti-imperialist demonstration in Shanghai clashed with foreign police. The British captain in charge ordered the police to fire on a crowd that he believed was about to rush his station. Some dozen Chinese (including some students) were killed, precipitating what came to be called the May Thirtieth Incident. This aroused a nationwide protest and set off a protracted general strike in Shanghai. A second, more serious incident occurred on June 23, when French and British marines exchanged fire with Whampoa cadets who were part of an anti-imperialist parade, killing 52 Chinese (many of them civilians) and wounding at least 117; which side had fired first became a matter of dispute. This set off a strike and boycott against Britain, France, and Japan, which was later narrowed to Britain alone. The strike and boycott, led mainly by communists, lasted for 16 months and seriously affected British trade. These incidents intensified hostility toward foreigners and their special privileges, enhanced the image of the Soviet Union, and gained support for the KMT, which promised to end the Unequal Treaties. By January 1926 the KMT could claim some 200,000 members. The CCP's membership grew from fewer than 1,000 in May 1925 to about 10,000 by the end of that year.

KMT OPPOSITION TO RADICALS

The two parties competed for direction of nationalist policy, control of mass organizations, and recruitment of new members. Under Comintern coaching, the CCP strategy was to try to split the KMT, drive out its conservative members, and turn it to an ever-more-radical course. In August 1925, KMT conservatives in Guangzhou tried to stop the leftward trend. One of the strongest advocates of the Nationalists' Soviet orientation, Liao Zhongkai, was assassinated. In retaliation, Borodin, Chiang Kai-shek, and Wang Ching-wei (Wang Jingwei) deported various conservatives. A group of KMT veterans in the north then ordered the expulsion of Borodin and the communists and the suspension of Wang Ching-wei; they set up a rival KMT headquarters in Shanghai. The left-wing leaders in Guangzhou then held the Second National Congress in January 1926, confirming the radical policies and the Soviet alliance. But as the Soviet presence became increasingly overbearing, as the strike and boycott in Guangzhou and Hong Kong dragged on, and as class conflict intensified in the south, opposition to the radical trend grew stronger, particularly among military commanders.

Chiang Kai-shek, now commander of the National Revolutionary Army, took steps in March to curb the communists and to send away several Soviet officers whom he believed were scheming with Wang Ching-wei against him. In a readjustment of party affairs, communists no longer were permitted to hold high offices in the central headquarters, and Wang Ching-wei went into retirement in France. Chiang also demanded Comintern support of a northern military campaign and the return of Gen. V.K. Blücher as his chief military adviser. Blücher, who used the pseudonym Galen in China, was a commander in the Red Army who had worked with Chiang in

1924 and 1925 in developing the Whampoa Military Academy and forming the National Revolutionary Army. Blücher returned to Guangzhou in May and helped refine plans for the Northern Expedition, which began officially in July, with Chiang as commander in chief.

THE NORTHERN EXPEDITION

During the Northern Expedition the outnumbered southern forces were infused with revolutionary spirit and fought with great élan. They were assisted by propaganda corps, which subverted enemy troops and agitated among the populace in the enemy's rear. Soviet military advisers accompanied most of the divisions, and Soviet pilots reconnoitred the enemy positions. The army was well-financed at the initial stages because of fiscal reforms in Guangdong during the previous year, and many enemy divisions and brigades were bought over. Within two months the National Revolutionary Army gained control of Hunan and Hubei, and by the end of the year it had taken Jiangxi and Fujian. The Nationalist government moved its central headquarters from Guangzhou to the Wuhan cities of the Yangtze. By early spring of 1927, revolutionary forces were poised to attack Nanjing and Shanghai.

The political situation, however, was unstable. Hunan and Hubei were swept by a peasant revolt marked by violence against landlords and other rural power holders. Business in the industrial and commercial centre of the middle

Yangtze—the Wuhan cities—was nearly paralyzed by a wave of strikes. Communists and KMT leftists led this social revolution. In January the British concessions in Hankou and Jiujiang were seized by Chinese crowds. The British government had just adopted a conciliatory policy toward China, and it acquiesced in these seizures, but it was readying an expeditionary force to protect its more important position in Shanghai. Foreigners and many upperclass Chinese fled from the provinces under Nationalist control. The northern armies began to form an alliance against the southerners.

Conservative Nationalist leaders in Shanghai mobilized against the headquarters in Wuhan. There was a deep rift within the revolutionary camp itself; the leftists at Wuhan, guided by Borodin, pitted themselves against Chiang and his more conservative military supporters, who were also laying plans against the leftists. Resolutions of the CCP's Central Committee in January 1927 showed that committee members were apprehensive about a counterrevolutionary tide against their party, Soviet Russia, and the revolutionary peasant and workers' movement; they feared a coalition within the KMT and its possible alliance with the imperialist powers. The central leadership resolved to check revolutionary excesses and give all support to the KMT leadership at Wuhan. Others within the CCP, notably Mao Zedong, disagreed; they believed the mass revolution should be encouraged to run its course.

EXPULSION OF COMMUNISTS FROM THE KMT

The climax of the conflict came after Nationalist armies had taken Shanghai and Nanjing in March. Nanjing was captured on March 23 as Beiyang troops evacuated it, and the following morning some Nationalist soldiers looted foreign properties, attacked the British, U.S., and Japanese consulates, and killed several foreigners. That afternoon, British and U.S. warships on the Yangtze fired into the concession area, allowing some of the foreign nationals to flee, and others subsequently were evacuated peacefully.

In Shanghai a general strike led by communists aroused fears that Chinese might seize the International Settlement and the French concession, now guarded by a large international expeditionary force. Conservative Nationalist leaders, some army commanders, and Chinese business leaders in Shanghai encouraged Chiang to expel the communists and suppress the Shanghai General Labour Union. On April 12–13, gangsters and troops bloodily suppressed the guards of the General Labour Union, arrested many communists, and executed large numbers. Similar suppressions were carried out in Guangzhou, Nanjing, Nanchang, Fuzhou, and other cities under military forces that accepted Chiang's instructions. The KMT conservatives then established a rival Nationalist government in Nanjing.

Wang Ching-wei had returned to China via the Soviet Union. Arriving in

Shanghai, he refused to participate in the expulsions and went secretly to Wuhan, where he again headed the government. In July, however, the leftist Nationalist leaders in Wuhan, having learned of a directive by Soviet leader Joseph Stalin to Borodin to arrange for radicals to capture control of the government, decided to expel the communists and compel the Soviet advisers to leave. The leftist government thereby lost important bases of support; furthermore, it was ringed by hostile forces and cut off from access to the sea, and it soon disintegrated.

The CCP went into revolt. Using its influence in the Cantonese army of Zhang Fakui (Chang Fa-k'uei), it staged an uprising at Nanchang on August 1 and in October attempted the "Autumn Harvest" uprising in several central provinces. Both efforts failed. In December communist leaders in Guangzhou started a revolt there, capturing the city with much bloodshed, arson, and looting; this uprising was quickly suppressed, also with much slaughter. Between April and December 1927 the CCP lost most of its membership by death and defection. A few score leaders and some scattered military bands then began the process of creating military bases in the mountains and plains of central China, remote from centres of Nationalist power.

The now-more-conservative KMT resumed its Northern Expedition in the spring of 1928 with a reorganized National Revolutionary Army. In the drive on Beijing it was joined by the National

People's Army under Feng Yuxiang, part of the Guangxi army, and the Shanxi army of Yan Xishan. In early June they captured Beijing, from which Zhang Zuolin and the Fengtian army withdrew for Manchuria. As his train neared Mukden (present-day Shenyang), Zhang died in an explosion arranged by a few Japanese officers without the knowledge of the Japanese government. Japan did not permit the Nationalist armies to pursue the Fengtian army into Manchuria, hoping to keep that area out of KMT control. By the end of the Northern Expedition, the major warlords had been defeated by the Nationalists, whose armies now possessed the cities and railways of eastern China. On October 10 the Nationalists formally established a reorganized National Government of the Republic of China, with its capital at Nanjing; Beijing was renamed Beiping (Pei-p'ing), "Northern Peace."

THE NATIONALIST GOVERNMENT FROM 1928 TO 1937

The most-serious immediate problem facing the new government was the continuing military separatism. The government had no authority over the vast area of western China, and even regions in eastern China were under the rule of independent regimes that had lately been part of the Nationalist coalition. After an unsuccessful attempt at negotiations, Chiang launched a series of civil wars against his former allies. By 1930 one militarist regime after another had been reduced to provincial proportions, and Nanjing's influence was spreading. Explained in material terms, Chiang owed his success to the great financial resources of his base in Jiangsu and Zhejiang and to foreign arms. Quick recognition by the foreign powers brought the Nationalist government the revenues collected by the efficient Maritime Customs Service; when the powers granted China the right to fix its own tariff schedules, that revenue increased.

Although the aim of constitutional, representative government was asserted, the Nationalist government at Nanjing was in practice personally dominated by Chiang Kai-shek. The army and the civil bureaucracy were marked by factional divisions, which Chiang carefully balanced against one another so that ultimate decision making was kept in his own hands. The KMT was supposed to infuse all government structures and to provide leadership, but the army came to be the most powerful component of government. Chiang's regime was marked by a military orientation, which external circumstances reinforced.

Nevertheless, the Nationalists did much to create a modern government and a coherent monetary and banking system and to improve taxation. They expanded the public educational system, developed a network of transportation and communication facilities, and encouraged industry and commerce. Again it was urban China that mainly benefited; little was done to modernize agriculture or to eradicate disease,

illiteracy, and underemployment in the villages, hamlets, and small towns scattered over a continental-size territory. With conscription and heavy taxation to support civil war and a collapsing export market for commercial crops, rural economic conditions may have grown worse during the Nationalist decade.

The Nationalist government during its first few years in power had some success in reasserting China's sovereignty. Several concession areas were returned to Chinese control, and the foreign powers assented to China's resumption of tariff autonomy. Yet these were merely token gains; the Unequal Treaties were scarcely breached. The country was in a nationalistic mood, determined to roll back foreign economic and political penetration. Manchuria was a huge and rich area of China in which Japan had extensive economic privileges, possessing part of the Liaodong Peninsula as a leasehold and controlling much of southern Manchuria's economy through the South Manchurian Railway. The Chinese began to develop Huludao, in Liaodong, as a port to rival Dairen (Dalian) and to plan railways to compete with Japanese lines. Zhang Xueliang (Chang Hsüeh-liang), Zhang Zuolin's son and successor as ruler of Manchuria, was drawing closer to Nanjing and sympathized with the Nationalists' desire to rid China of foreign privilege.

For Japan, Manchuria was regarded as vital. Many Japanese had acquired a sense of mission that Japan should lead Asia against the West. The Great

Depression had hurt Japanese business, and there was deep social unrest. Such factors influenced many army officers—especially officers of the Kwantung Army, which protected Japan's leasehold in the Liaodong Peninsula and the South Manchurian Railway—to regard Manchuria as the area where Japan's power must be consolidated.

JAPANESE AGGRESSION

In September 1931 a group of officers in the Kwantung Army set in motion a plot (beginning with the Mukden Incident) to compel the Japanese government to extend its power in Manchuria. The Japanese government was drawn step by step into the conquest of Manchuria and the creation of a regime known as Manchukuo. China was unable to prevent Japan from seizing this vital area. In 1934, after long negotiations, Japan acquired the Soviet interest in the Chinese Eastern Railway, thus eliminating the last legal trace of the Soviet sphere of influence there. During 1932–35 Japan seized more territory bordering on Manchuria. In 1935 it attempted to detach Hebei and the Chahar region of Inner Mongolia from Nanjing's control and threatened Shanxi, Shandong, and the Suiyuan region of Inner Mongolia. The National Government's policy was to trade space for time in which to build military power and unify the country. Its slogan "Unity before resistance" was directed principally against the Chinese communists.

WAR BETWEEN NATIONALISTS AND COMMUNISTS

In the meantime, the communists had created 15 rural bases in central China, and they established a soviet government, the Jiangxi Soviet, on Nov. 7, 1931. Within the soviet regions, the communist leadership expropriated and redistributed land and in other ways enlisted the support of the poorer classes. The Japanese occupation of Manchuria and an ancillary localized war around Shanghai in 1932 distracted the Nationalists and gave the communists a brief opportunity to expand and consolidate. But the Nationalists in late 1934 forced the communist armies to abandon their bases and retreat. Most of the later communist leaders—including Mao Zedong, Zhu De, Zhou Enlai, Liu Shaoqi, and Lin Biao—marched and fought their way across western China in what became known as the Long March. By mid-1936 the remnants of several Red armies had gathered in an impoverished area in northern Shaanxi, with headquarters located in the town of Yan'an, which lent its name to the subsequent period (1936–45) of CCP development.

During the Long March, Mao Zedong rose to preeminence in the CCP leadership. In the early 1930s he had engaged in bitter power struggles with other party leaders and actually had found himself in a fairly weak position at the start of the Long March campaigns, but in January 1935 a rump session of the CCP Political Bureau (Politburo) confirmed Mao in the

Mao Zedong and Zhou Enlai, two leaders of the Chinese Communist Party, during the Long March. Keystone/Hulton Archive/Getty Images

newly created post of chairman. It was also during the Long March that the CCP began to develop a new political strategy—a united front against Japan. It was first conceived as an alliance of patriotic forces against Japan and the Nationalist government, but, as Japan's pressure on China and the pressure of the Nationalist armies against the weakened Red armies increased, the communist leaders began to call for a united front of all Chinese against Japan alone. Virtually all classes and various local regimes supported this, and the communists moderated their revolutionary program and terminated class warfare in their zone of control.

Chiang was determined, however, to press on with his extermination campaign. He ordered the Manchurian army under Zhang Xueliang, now based in Xi'an (Sian), and the Northwestern army under Yang Hucheng (Yang Hu-ch'eng) to attack the communist forces in northern Shaanxi. Many officers in those armies sympathized with the communist slogan "Chinese don't fight Chinese"; they preferred to fight Japan, a sentiment particularly strong in the homeless Manchurian army. Zhang Xueliang was conducting secret negotiations with the communists and had suspended the civil war. In December 1936 Chiang Kai-shek flew to Xi'an to order Zhang and Yang to renew the anticommunist campaign. Under pressure from subordinates, Zhang detained Chiang on the morning of December 12 (this became known as the Sian Incident).

THE UNITED FRONT AGAINST JAPAN

Fearing that China would be plunged into renewed disorder if Chiang were killed, the nation clamoured for his release. The Soviet Union quickly denounced the captors and insisted that Chiang be freed (the Soviet Union needed a united China opposing Japan, its potential enemy on the east). The CCP leaders also decided that Chiang's release would serve China's interests as well as their own, if he would accept their policy against Japan. Zhou Enlai and several other communist leaders flew to Xi'an to try to effect this. Zhang Xueliang finally agreed to free his captive, with the understanding that Chiang would call off the civil war and unite the country against the invader. On December 25 Chiang was freed.

The two Chinese parties began protracted and secret negotiations for cooperation, each making concessions. But it was not until September 1937, after the Sino-Japanese War had begun, that the Nationalist government formally agreed to a policy of cooperation with the CCP. For its part, the CCP publicly affirmed its adherence to the realization of Sun Yat-sen's Three Principles of the People, its abandonment of armed opposition to the KMT and of the forcible confiscation of landlords' property, the substitution of democracy for its soviet government, and the reorganization of the Red Army as a component of the national army under the central government.

CHAPTER 13

THE LATE REPUBLICAN PERIOD AND THE WAR AGAINST JAPAN

THE EARLY SINO-JAPANESE WAR

On July 7, 1937, the Marco Polo Bridge Incident, a minor clash between Japanese and Chinese troops near Beiping (Beijing's name under the Nationalist government), finally led the two countries into war. The Japanese government tried for several weeks to settle the incident locally, but China's mood was highly nationalistic, and public opinion clamoured for resistance to further aggression. In late July, new fighting broke out. The Japanese quickly took Beiping and captured Tianjin. On August 13 savage fighting broke out in Shanghai. By now the prestige of both nations was committed, and they were locked in a war.

PHASE ONE

As never before in modern times, the Chinese united themselves against a foreign enemy. China's standing armies in 1937 numbered some 1.7 million men, with a half million in reserve. Japan's naval and air superiority were unquestioned, but Japan could not commit its full strength to campaigns in China; the main concern of the Japanese army was the Soviet

NANJING MASSACRE

The Nanjing (or Nanking) Massacre (December 1937–January 1938) was one of the most infamous events of the Sino-Japanese War that preceded World War II. Also called the Rape of Nanjing, the incident involved a series of mass killings and the ravaging of Chinese citizens and capitulated soldiers by soldiers of the Japanese Imperial Army after its seizure of Nanjing, China, on Dec. 13, 1937. The number of Chinese killed in the massacre has been subject to much debate, with most estimates ranging from 100,000 to more than 300,000.

The destruction of Nanjing—which had been the capital of the Nationalist Chinese from 1928 to 1937—was ordered by Matsui Iwane, commanding general of the Central China Front Army that captured the city. Over the next several weeks, Japanese soldiers carried out Matsui's orders, perpetrating numerous mass executions and tens of thousands of rapes. The army looted and burned the surrounding towns and the city, destroying more than a third of the buildings. In 1940 the Japanese made Nanjing the capital of their Chinese puppet government headed by Wang Ching-wei (Wang Jingwei). Shortly after the end of World War II, Matsui and Tani Hisao, a lieutenant general who had personally participated in acts of murder and rape, were found guilty of war crimes by the International Military Tribunal for the Far East and were executed.

The bodies of some of the tens of thousands of people killed during the Nanjing Massacre of December 1937–January 1938. © AP Images

Union, while for the Japanese navy it was the United States.

During the first year of the undeclared war, Japan won victory after victory against sometimes stubborn Chinese resistance. By late December, Shanghai and Nanjing had fallen, the latter city being the site of the infamous Nanjing Massacre (December 1937–January 1938) perpetrated by Japanese troops. However, China had demonstrated to the world its determination to resist the invader; this gave the government time to search for foreign support. China found its major initial help from the Soviet Union. On Aug. 21, 1937, the Soviet Union and China signed a nonaggression pact, and the former quickly began sending munitions, military advisers, and hundreds of aircraft with Soviet pilots. Yet Japanese forces continued to win important victories. By mid-1938 Japanese armies controlled the railway lines and major cities of northern China. They took Guangzhou on October 12, stopping the railway supply line to Wuhan, the temporary Chinese capital, and captured Hankou, Hanyang, and Wuchang on October 25–26. The Chinese government and military command moved to Chongqing (Chungking) in Sichuan, farther up the Yangtze and behind a protective mountain screen.

At the end of this first phase of the war, the Nationalist government had lost the best of its modern armies, its air force and arsenals, most of China's modern industries and railways, its major tax resources, and all the ports through which military equipment and civilian supplies might be imported. However, it still held a vast though largely undeveloped territory and had unlimited manpower reserves. So long as China continued to resist, Japan's control over the conquered eastern part of the country would be difficult.

PHASE TWO: STALEMATE AND STAGNATION

During the second stage of the war (1939–43), the battle lines changed only slightly, although there were many engagements of limited scale. Japan tried to bomb Free China into submission; Chongqing suffered repeated air raids in which thousands of civilians were killed. In 1940 Japan set up a rival government in Nanjing under Wang Ching-wei. But the Chinese would not submit. Hundreds of thousands migrated to western China to continue the struggle. Students and faculties of most eastern colleges took the overland trek to makeshift quarters in distant inland towns. Factories and skilled workers were reestablished in the west. The government rebuilt its shattered armies and tried to purchase supplies from abroad.

In 1938–40 the Soviet Union extended credits for military aid of $250 million, while the United States, Great Britain, and France granted some $263.5 million for civilian purchases and currency stabilization. Free China's lines of supply were long and precarious; when war broke out in Europe, shipping space became scarce. After Germany's conquest of France in the spring of 1940, Britain bowed to Japanese demands and temporarily closed Rangoon, Burma (Yangon, Myanmar), to military supplies for China (July–September). In September 1940 Japan seized control of northern Indochina and closed the supply line to Kunming. The Soviet Union had provided China its most substantial military aid, but, when Germany attacked the Soviet Union in June 1941, this aid virtually ceased. By then, however, the United States had sold China 100 fighter planes—the beginning of a U.S. effort to provide air protection.

In addition to bombing, the civilian population in Free China endured other hardships. Manufactured goods were scarce, and hoarding drove up prices. The government did not have the means to carry out rationing and price control, though it did supply government employees with rice. The government's sources of revenue were limited, yet it supported a large bureaucracy and an army of more than three million conscripts. The government resorted to printing currency inadequately backed by reserves. Inflation grew until it was nearly uncontrollable. Between 1939 and 1943 the morale of the bureaucracy and military officers declined. Old abuses of the Chinese political system reasserted themselves—factional politics and corruption, in particular. The protracted war progressively weakened the Nationalist regime.

The war had the opposite effect upon the CCP. The communist leaders had survived 10 years of civil war and had developed a unity, camaraderie, and powerful sense of mission. They had learned to mobilize the rural population and to wage guerrilla warfare. In 1937 the CCP had about 40,000 members and the poorly equipped Red Army numbered perhaps 100,000. By agreement with the Nationalist government, the Red Army was renamed the Eighth Route Army (later the Eighteenth Army Group); Zhu De and Peng Dehuai served as commander and vice commander, and Lin Biao, Ho Lung, and Liu Bocheng were in charge of its three divisions. The communist base in the northwest covered parts of three provinces with an undeveloped economy and a population of about 1.5 million. Operating within the general framework of the United Front against Japan, the leaders of the Eighth Route Army adopted a strategy that used their experience in guerrilla warfare. They sent small columns into areas of northern China that the Japanese army had overrun but lacked the manpower to control; there they incorporated remnant troops and organized the population to supply food, recruits, and sanctuaries for guerrilla units attacking small Japanese garrisons.

Early in the period of united resistance, the government permitted the New Fourth Army to be created from remnants of communist troops left in Jiangxi and Fujian at the time of the Long March. Commanded by Gen. Ye

Ting—with Xiang Ying, a communist, as chief of staff—this force of 12,000 officers and soldiers operated behind Japanese lines near Shanghai with great success. Its strategy included guerrilla tactics, organizing resistance bases, and recruitment. This army grew to more than 100,000 in 1940; by then it operated in a wide area on both sides of the lower Yangtze.

Thus the CCP revitalized itself. It recruited rural activists and patriotic youths from the cities and systematically strengthened its ranks by continuous indoctrination and by expelling dissident and ineffective party members.

RENEWED COMMUNIST-NATIONALIST CONFLICT

There were numerous clashes between communists and Nationalists as their military forces competed for control of enemy territory and as the communists tried to expand their political influence in Nationalist territory through propaganda

Chiang Kai-shek meeting with his staff during the Sino-Japanese War (1937–45). Encyclopædia Britannica, Inc.

and secret organizing. Though both sides continued the war against Japan, each was fighting for its own ultimate advantage. Bitter anticommunist sentiment in government circles found its most violent expression in the New Fourth Army Incident of January 1941.

The government had ordered the New Fourth Army to move north of the Huang He (Yellow River) and understood that its commanders had agreed to do so as part of a demarcation of operational areas. However, most of the army had moved into northern Jiangsu (south of the Huang) and, together with units of the Eighteenth Army Group, was competing with government troops for control of bases there and in southern Shandong. Ye Ting and Xiang Ying stayed at the army's base south of the Yangtze. Apparently believing that Ye did not intend to move northward, government forces attacked the base on Jan. 6, 1941. The outnumbered communists were defeated, Ye Ting and some 2,000 others were captured, Xiang Ying was killed, and both sides suffered heavy casualties. Ignoring Chiang Kai-shek's order to dissolve the New Fourth Army, the communist high command named Chen Yi as its new commander and Liu Shaoqi as political commissar.

The danger of renewed civil war caused widespread protest from China's civilian leaders. The People's Political Council, a multiparty advisory body formed in 1938 as an expression of united resistance, debated the issue and later tried to mediate. Neither the KMT nor the CCP was willing to push the conflict to open civil war in 1941. The government deployed many of its best divisions in positions to prevent the communist forces from further penetration of Nationalist-held territories and to weaken the CCP through a strict economic blockade.

THE INTERNATIONAL ALLIANCE AGAINST JAPAN

The United States had broken the Japanese diplomatic code. By July 1941 it knew that Japan hoped to end the undeclared war in China and that Japan was preparing for a southward advance toward British Malaya and the Dutch East Indies, planning to first occupy southern Indochina and Thailand, even at the risk of war with Britain and the United States.

U.S. AID TO CHINA

One U.S. response was the decision to send large amounts of arms and equipment to China, along with a military mission to advise on their use. The underlying strategy was to revitalize China's war effort as a deterrent to Japanese land and naval operations southward. The Nationalist army was ill-equipped to fight the Japanese in 1941. Its arsenals were so lacking in nonferrous metals and explosives that they could not produce effectively. The maintenance of millions of ill-trained and under-equipped troops was a heavy drain on the economy. There was no possibility that the United States could arm such numbers from its limited stocks while building up its own forces and assisting many other countries. In addition, there was a formidable logistics problem in shipping supplies along the 715-mile (1,150-km) Burma Road, which extended from Kunming to Lashio, the terminus in Burma of the railway and highway leading to Rangoon.

By December 1941 the United States had sent a military mission to China and had implicitly agreed to create a modern Chinese air force, maintain an efficient line of communications into China, and arm 30 divisions. Japan's bombing of Pearl Harbor in Hawaii brought the United States into alliance with China, and Great Britain joined the Pacific war as its colonial possessions were attacked. This widening of the Sino-Japanese conflict lifted Chinese morale, but its other early effects were harmful. With the Japanese conquest of Hong Kong on December 25, China lost its air link to the outside world and one of its principal routes for smuggling supplies. By the end of May 1942, the Japanese held most of Burma, having defeated the British, Indian, Burmese, and Chinese defenders. China was almost completely blockaded. For the moment, there was little China's allies could do other than state a willingness to offer China loans.

The solution was found in an air route from Assam, India, to Kunming, in southwest China—the dangerous "Hump" route along the southern edge of the Himalayas. In March 1942 the China National Aviation Corporation (CNAC) began freight service over the Hump, and the United States began a transport program the next month. But shortages and other difficulties had to be overcome, and not until December 1943 were cargo planes able to carry as much tonnage as was carried along the Burma Road by trucks two years earlier. This was much less than China's needs for gasoline and military equipment and supplies.

CONFLICTS WITHIN THE INTERNATIONAL ALLIANCE

China's alliance with the United States and Great Britain was marked by deep conflict. Great Britain gave highest priority to the defeat of its main enemy, Germany. The U.S. Navy in the Pacific had been seriously weakened by the Japanese air attack at Pearl Harbor and required many months to rebuild. During the winter of 1941–42, the grand strategy of the United States and Great Britain called for the defeat of Germany first and then an assault across the Pacific against Japan's island empire. China was relegated to a low position in U.S. strategic planning. The United States aimed to keep China in the war and enable it to play a positive role in the final defeat of Japan on the continent. Chiang Kai-shek, on the other hand, envisaged a joint strategy by the United States, the British Commonwealth, and China over the whole Pacific area, with China playing a major role. He demanded an equal voice in Allied war planning, which he never received, though U.S. President Franklin D. Roosevelt was generally solicitous.

From the fundamentally different outlooks of Chiang, British Prime Minister Winston Churchill, and Roosevelt and because of the divergent national interests of China, the British Commonwealth, and the United States, there followed many controversies that had powerful repercussions in China and led to frustrations and suspicions among the partners.

After Burma fell to the Japanese, a controversy developed over whether the principal Chinese and U.S. effort against Japan should be devoted to building up U.S. air power based in China or to reform of the Chinese army and its training and equipment for a combat role. Chiang advocated primary reliance on U.S. air power to defeat Japan. Several high-ranking U.S. generals, on the other hand, emphasized creation of a compact and modernized Chinese ground force able to protect the airfields in China and to assist in opening an overland supply route across northern Burma. Already in India, the United States was training two Chinese divisions from remnants of the Burma campaign, plus artillery and engineering regiments (this became known as X-Force). Also in training were Chinese instructors to help retrain other divisions in China. Both air development and army modernizing were being pushed in early 1943, with a training centre created near Kunming to reenergize and reequip select Chinese divisions (called Y-Force), and a network of airfields was being built in southern China. This dual approach caused repeated conflict over the allocation of scarce airlift space.

By the end of 1943 the China-based U.S. Fourteenth Air Force had achieved tactical parity with the Japanese over central China, was beginning to bomb Yangtze shipping, and had conducted a successful raid on Japanese airfields on Taiwan. A second training centre had been started at Guilin to improve 30 more Chinese divisions (Z-Force). The campaign to open a land route across northern Burma had run into serious difficulty. At the first Cairo Conference in November, Chiang met Churchill and Roosevelt for the first time. The Cairo Declaration issued there promised that, following the war, Manchuria, Taiwan, and the Pescadores Islands would be returned to China and that Korea would gain independence. The three allies pledged themselves to "persevere in the . . . . prolonged operations necessary to procure the unconditional surrender of Japan." These words, however, concealed deep differences over global strategy. U.S. planners realized that Japan might be approached successfully through the south and central Pacific and that the Soviet Union would enter the war against Japan after Germany's defeat; hence, the importance of China to U.S. grand strategy declined. Churchill was unwilling to use naval resources, needed for the forthcoming European invasion, in a seaborne invasion of Burma to help reopen China's supply line. Yet Chiang had demanded a naval invasion of Burma as a condition to committing the Y-Force to assist in opening his supply line. Shortly after Cairo, Churchill and Roosevelt agreed to set aside the seaborne invasion of Burma; when Chiang learned of this, he requested enormous amounts of money, supplies, and air support, asserting that otherwise Japan might succeed in eliminating China from the war. The United States did not accede, and Chinese-American relations began to cool.

PHASE THREE: APPROACHING CRISIS (1944–45)

China was in crisis in 1944. Japan faced increasing pressure in the Pacific and threats to its supply bases and communications lines in China as well as to nearby shipping. Its response was twofold—first, to attack from Burma toward Assam to cut the supply lines or capture the airfields at the western end of the Hump and, second, to capture the railway system in China from north to south and seize the eastern China airfields used by the United States.

The British and Indian army defeated the Japanese attack on Assam (March–July 1944) with help from transport planes withdrawn from the Hump. But the Japanese campaign in China, known as Ichigo, showed up the weakness, inefficiency, and poor command of the Chinese armies after nearly seven years of war. During April and May the Japanese cleared the Beiping-Hankou railway between the Huang He and the Yangtze. Chinese armies nominally numbering several hundred thousand troops were unable to put up effective resistance. Peasants in Henan attacked the collapsing Chinese armies—only recently their oppressors.

The second phase of the Ichigo campaign was a Japanese drive southward from Hankou and northwestward from Guangzhou to take Guilin and open the communication line to the India-China border. By November the Chinese had lost Guilin, Liuzhou, and Nanning, and the Japanese were approaching Guiyang on the route to Chongqing and Kunming. This was the high-water mark of Japan's war in China. Thereafter, it withdrew experienced divisions for the defense of its overextended empire, and China finally began to benefit from the well-trained X-Force when two divisions were flown in from Burma in December to defend Kunming.

Meanwhile, the Chinese government was involved in a crisis of relations with the United States, which contended that the Chinese army must be reformed, particularly in its command structure, and that lend-lease supplies must be used more effectively. There were also many subsidiary problems. Gen. Joseph Stilwell, the executor of disagreeable U.S. policies in China, had developed an unconcealed disdain for Chiang, whom he nominally served as chief of staff. Stilwell was an effective troop commander, and Roosevelt requested that Chiang place Stilwell in command of all Chinese forces. In the context of Chinese politics, in which control of armies was the main source of power, President Chiang's compliance was virtually inconceivable. He declined the request and asked for Stilwell's recall.

Roosevelt agreed, but thereafter his relations with Chiang were no longer cordial. Stilwell was replaced by Gen. Albert Coady Wedemeyer.

NATIONALIST DETERIORATION

The military weakness in 1944 was symptomatic of a gradual deterioration that had taken place in most aspects of Nationalist Chinese public life. Inflation began to mount alarmingly as the government pumped in large amounts of paper currency to make up its fiscal deficits. Salaries of government employees, army officers, teachers, and all those on wages fell far behind rising prices. For most, this spelled poverty amid growing war-weariness. Dissatisfaction with the government's policies spread among intellectuals. Inflation gave opportunities for some groups to profit through hoarding needed goods, smuggling high-value commodities, black market currency operations, and graft. Corruption spread in the bureaucracy and the armed forces. As the war dragged on, government measures to suppress dissidence grew oppressive. Secret police activity and efforts at thought control were aimed not only against communists but also against all influential critics of the government or the KMT.

COMMUNIST GROWTH

The communist armies were growing rapidly in 1943 and 1944. According to U.S. war correspondents visiting the Yan'an area in May 1944 and to a group of U.S. observers that established itself there in July, the communists professed allegiance to democracy and to continued cooperation with the Nationalist government in the war effort. There was convincing evidence that the areas under communist control extended for hundreds of miles behind Japanese lines in northern and central China.

This situation was the result of many factors. Communist troop commanders and political officers in areas behind Japanese lines tried to mobilize the entire population against the enemy. Party members led village communities into greater participation in local government than had been the case before. They also organized and controlled peasants' associations, labour unions, youth leagues, and women's associations. They linked together the many local governments and the mass organizations and determined their policies. Because of the need for unity against Japan, the communist organizers tended to follow reformist economic policies. The party experimented with various forms of economic cooperation to increase production; one of these was mutual-aid teams in which farmers temporarily pooled their tools and draft animals and worked the land collectively. In areas behind Japanese lines, some mutual-aid teams evolved into work-and-battle teams composed of younger peasants: when danger threatened, the teams went out to fight as guerrillas under direction of the local communist army; when the crisis passed, they returned to the fields. The party recruited into its ranks the younger leaders who emerged from populist activities. Thus, it penetrated and to some extent controlled the multitude of villages in areas behind Japanese lines. As the Japanese military grip weakened, the experienced communist armies and political organizers spread their system of government ever more widely. By the time of the CCP's Seventh Congress in Yan'an (April–May 1945), the party claimed to have an army of more than 900,000 and a militia of more than 2,000,000. It also claimed to control areas with a total population of 90,000,000. These claims were disputable, but the great strength and wide geographical spread of communist organization was a fact.

EFFORTS TO PREVENT CIVIL WAR

Between May and September 1944, representatives of the government and the CCP carried on peace negotiations at Xi'an. The main issues were the disposition, size, and command of the communist armies, the relationship between communist-organized regional governments and the Nationalist government, and problems of civil rights and legalization of the CCP and its activities in Nationalist areas. Suggestions for a coalition government arose for the first time. No settlement was reached, but it appeared that the antagonists were seeking a peaceful solution. U.S. Vice Pres. Henry A. Wallace visited Chongqing in June and had several discussions with Chiang,

who requested U.S. assistance in improving relations between China and the Soviet Union and in settling the communist problem.

In September 1944, Patrick J. Hurley arrived as U.S. ambassador to China and as Roosevelt's personal representative. Hurley attempted to mediate, first in discussions in Chongqing and then by flying to Yan'an in November for a conference with Mao Zedong. But the positions of the two sides could not be reconciled, and the talks broke off in March 1945. Between June and August, Hurley resumed protracted discussions, both indirect and in conferences with high-level representatives from both sides. Each side distrusted the other; each sought to guarantee its own survival, but the KMT intended to continue its political dominance, while the CCP insisted on the independence of its armies and regional governments under whatever coalition formula might be worked out.

The Pacific war (which in China became known as the War of Resistance Against Japanese Aggression) ended on Aug. 14 (Aug. 15 in China), 1945, and the formal Japanese surrender came on September 2. China rejoiced. Yet the country faced enormously difficult problems of reunification and reconstruction and a future clouded by the dark prospect of civil war.

CIVIL WAR (1945–49)

In a little more than four years after Japan's surrender, the CCP and the

People's Liberation Army (PLA; the name by which communist forces were now known) conquered mainland China, and, on Oct. 1, 1949, the People's Republic of China was established, with its capital at Beijing (the city's former name restored). The factors that brought this about were many and complex and subject to widely varying interpretation, but the basic fact was a communist military triumph growing out of a profound and popularly based revolution. The process may be perceived in three phases: (1) from August 1945 to the end of 1946, the Nationalists and communists raced to take over Japanese-held territories, built up their forces, and fought many limited engagements while still conducting negotiations for a peaceful settlement; (2) during 1947 and the first half of 1948, after initial Nationalist success, the strategic balance turned in favour of the communists; and (3) the communists won a series of smashing victories beginning in the latter part of 1948 that led to the establishment of the People's Republic.

A RACE FOR TERRITORY

As soon as Japan's impending surrender was known, the commander of the communist armies, Zhu De, ordered his troops, on August 11, to move into Japanese-held territory and take over Japanese arms, despite Chiang Kai-shek's order that they stand where they were. The United States aided the Chinese government by flying many divisions from the southwest to occupy the main eastern cities, such as Beiping, Tianjin, Shanghai, and the prewar capital, Nanjing. The U.S. Navy moved Chinese troops from southern China to other coastal cities and landed 53,000 marines at Tianjin and Qingdao to assist in disarming and repatriating Japanese troops but also to serve as a counterweight to the Soviet army in southern Manchuria. Furthermore, U.S. Gen. Douglas MacArthur ordered all Japanese forces in China proper to surrender their arms only to forces of the Nationalist government. They obeyed and thereby were occasionally engaged against Chinese communist forces.

Immediately after the surrender, the communists sent political cadres and troops into Manchuria (Northeast China). This had been planned long in advance. Gen. Lin Biao became commander of the forces (the Northeast Democratic Allied Army), which incorporated puppet troops of the former Japanese Manchukuo regime and began to recruit volunteers; it got most of its arms from Japanese stocks taken over by the Soviets.

Manchuria was a vast area with a population of 40 million, the greatest concentration of heavy industry and railways in China, and enormous reserves of coal, iron, and many other minerals. The Soviet Union had promised the Nationalist government that it would withdraw its occupying armies within 90 days of Japan's surrender and return the region to China. The government was determined to control Manchuria, which was vital to China's future as a world power. However,

Lin Biao's army attempted to block the entry of Nationalist troops by destroying rail lines and seizing areas around ports of entry. Soon the two sides were locked in a fierce struggle for the corridors into Manchuria, although negotiations were under way in Chongqing between Mao Zedong and Chiang for a peaceful settlement. The Soviet army avoided direct involvement in the struggle, but it dismantled much industrial machinery and shipped it to the Soviet Union together with hundreds of thousands of Japanese prisoners of war. By the end of 1945 the Nationalists had positioned some of their best U.S.-trained armies in southern Manchuria as far north as Mukden (present-day Shenyang), a strategic rail centre to which Nationalist troops were transported by air. The government's hold was precarious, however, because the communist Eighteenth Army Group and the New Fourth Army had regrouped in northern China, abandoning areas south of the Yangtze after a weak bid to take Shanghai. By the end of 1945, communist forces were spread across a band of provinces from the northwest to the sea. They had a grip on great sections of all the railway lines north of the Longhai line, which were vital supply lines for Nationalist armies in the Tianjin-Beiping area and in Manchuria. The Nationalist government held vast territories in the south and west and had reestablished its authority in the rich provinces of the lower Yangtze valley and in a few important cities in northern China; it had also assumed civil control on Taiwan.

ATTEMPTS TO END THE WAR

Peace negotiations continued in Chongqing between Nationalist and communist officials after Japan's surrender. An agreement reached on Oct. 10, 1945, called for the convening of a multiparty Political Consultative Council to plan a liberalized postwar government and to draft a constitution for submission to a national congress. Still, the sides were far apart over the character of the new government, control over the areas liberated by the communists, and the size and degree of autonomy of the communist armies in a national military system. Hurley resigned his ambassadorship on November 26, and the next day U.S. Pres. Harry S. Truman appointed Gen. George C. Marshall as his special representative, with the specific mission of trying to bring about political unification and the cessation of hostilities in China.

Marshall arrived in China on December 23. The Nationalist government proposed the formation of a committee of three, with Marshall as chairman, to end the fighting. This committee, with Generals Chang Chun (Zhang Qun) and Zhou Enlai as the Nationalist and communist representatives, respectively, met on Jan. 7, 1946. The two agreed on January 10 that Chiang and Mao would issue orders to cease hostilities and halt troop movements as of January 13 midnight, with the exception of government troop movements south of the Yangtze and into and within Manchuria to restore Chinese sovereignty. The agreement also called for the establishment in Beiping of an executive headquarters, equally represented by both sides, to supervise the cease-fire.

This agreement provided a favourable atmosphere for meetings in Chongqing of the Political Consultative Council, composed of representatives of the KMT, the CCP, the Democratic League, the Young China Party, and nonparty delegates. For the remainder of January, the council issued a series of agreed recommendations regarding governmental reorganization, peaceful national reconstruction, military reductions, the creation of a national assembly, and the drafting of a constitution. President Chiang pledged that the government would carry out these recommendations, and the political parties stated their intention to abide by them. The next step was meetings of a military subcommittee, with Marshall as adviser, to discuss troop reductions and amalgamation of forces into a single national army.

Early 1946 was the high point of conciliation. It soon became clear, however, that implementing the various recommendations and agreements was being opposed by conservatives in the KMT, who feared these measures would dilute their party's control of the government, and by Nationalist generals, who objected to reducing the size of their armies. The communists attempted to prevent the extension of Nationalist military control in Manchuria. On March 17–18 a communist army attacked and captured a strategic junction between Mukden and Changchun, the former Manchukuo capital; on April 18 communists captured Changchun from a small Nationalist garrison directly following the Soviet withdrawal. On that day Marshall returned to China after a trip to Washington and resumed his efforts to stop the spreading civil war.

RESUMPTION OF FIGHTING

Each side seemed convinced that it could win by war what it could not achieve by negotiation—dominance over the other. Despite the efforts of Chinese moderates and General Marshall, fighting resumed in July in Manchuria, and in northern China the Nationalists attempted massive drives in Jiangsu and Shandong to break the communist grip on the railways. The communists launched a propaganda campaign against the United States, playing upon the nationalistic theme of liberation; they were hostile because of the extensive U.S. military and financial assistance to the KMT at the very time that Marshall was mediating. The Nationalist government had become increasingly intransigent, confident of continued U.S. help. To exert pressure and to try to keep the United States out of the civil war, in August Marshall imposed an embargo on further shipment of U.S. arms to China. By the end of the year, however, he realized that his efforts had failed. In January 1947 he left China, issuing a statement denouncing the intransigents on both sides. All negotiations ended in March; the die was cast for war.

In the latter half of 1946, government forces made significant gains in northern China and Manchuria, capturing 165 towns from the enemy. Buoyed by these victories, the government convened a multiparty National Assembly on November 15, despite a boycott by the CCP and the Democratic League. The delegates adopted a new constitution, which was promulgated on New Year's Day, 1947. The constitution reaffirmed Sun Yat-sen's Three Principles of the People as the basic philosophy of the state; called for the fivefold division of powers among the executive, legislative, judicial, control, and examination *yuan* ("governmental bodies"); and established the people's four rights of initiation, referendum, election, and recall. The way was prepared for election of both central and local officials, upon which the period of Nationalist tutelage would end.

The Nationalist government struggled with grave economic problems. Inflation continued unabated, caused principally by government financing of military and other operations through the printing press: approximately 65 percent of the budget was met by currency expansion and only 10 percent by taxes. Government spending was uncontrolled; funds were dissipated in maintaining large and unproductive garrison forces. Much tax revenue failed to reach the treasury because of malpractices throughout the bureaucracy. Inflation inhibited exports and enhanced the demand for imports. The government had to import large amounts of grain and cotton, but, in the months immediately after Japan's surrender, it also permitted the import of luxury goods without effective restrictions. As an anti-inflationary measure, it sold gold on the open market. These policies permitted a large gold and U.S. currency reserve, estimated at $900 million at the end of the war, to be cut in half by the end of 1946. Foreign trade was hampered by excessive regulation and corrupt practices.

The spiraling effects of inflation were somewhat curbed by large amounts of supplies imported by the United Nations Relief and Rehabilitation Administration, chiefly food and clothing, a wide variety of capital goods, and materials for the rehabilitation of agriculture, industry, and transportation. In August 1946 the United States sold to China civilian-type army and navy surplus property at less than 20 percent of its estimated procurement cost. In spite of these and other forms of aid, the costs of civil war kept the budget continuously out of balance. Speculation, hoarding of goods, and black market operations as hedges against inflation continued unabated. The constant depreciation in the value of paper currency undermined morale in all classes who depended on salaries, including troops, officers, and civilian officials.

By contrast, it appears that the communists in their areas, which were mostly rural, practiced a Spartan style of life close to the common people. Morale remained high in the army and was continuously bolstered by indoctrination and effective propaganda. As they had during the war years, communist troops tried in many ways to win support of the masses. In newly occupied areas, social policy was at first reformist rather than revolutionary.

In Manchuria, Lin Biao was forging a formidable army of veteran cadres from northern China and natives of Manchuria, now well equipped with Japanese weapons. By 1947 the communists' Northeast Democratic Allied Army controlled all of Manchuria north of the Sungari (Songhua) River, the east, and much of the countryside in the Nationalist stronghold in the south. There the Nationalists had most of their best-trained and best-equipped divisions, but the troops had been conscripted or recruited in China's southwest, and they garrisoned cities and railways in a distant land. Beginning in January 1947, Lin Biao launched a series of small offensives. By July the Nationalists had lost half of their territory in Manchuria and much matériel; desertions and casualties, caused by indecisive Nationalist leadership and declining troop morale, reduced their forces by half. Lin Biao was not yet strong enough to take Manchuria, but he had the Nationalist armies hemmed up in a few major cities and with only a tenuous hold on the railways leading southward.

THE TIDE BEGINS TO SHIFT

Although government forces overran Yan'an in March 1947, the strategic initiative passed to the PLA during that year. In midsummer, troops under Liu Bocheng started moving toward the Yangtze; by late in the year the communists had concentrated strong forces in central China. Chen Yi operated on both sides of the Longhai railway, east of Kaifeng; Liu Bocheng was firmly established in the Dabie Mountains on the borders of Anhui, Henan, and Hubei, northeast of Hankou; and Chen Geng had another army in Henan west of the Beiping-Hankou railway. These groups cut Nationalist lines of communication, destroyed protecting outposts along the Longhai and Ping-Han lines, and isolated cities.

By the end of 1947 the government forces, according to U.S. military estimates, still numbered some 2,700,000 facing 1,150,000 communists, but the Nationalists were widely spread and on the defensive. In November, Mao Zedong established the communist headquarters at Shijiazhuang, a railway centre leading from the Beiping-Hankou line into Shanxi; this was a measure of how consolidated the communist position was in northern China. In a report to the CCP Central Committee in December, Mao exuded confidence:

> The Chinese people's revolutionary war has now reached a turning point . . . The main forces of the People's Liberation Army have carried the fight into the Kuomintang Area . . . This is a turning point in history.

A LAND REVOLUTION

One reason for communist success was the social revolution in rural China. The CCP was now unrestrained by the multi-class alliance of the United Front period. In mid-1946, as civil war became more certain, the party leaders launched a land revolution. They saw land redistribution as an integral part of the larger struggle; by encouraging peasants to seize landlords' fields and other property, the party apparently expected to weaken the government's rural class base and strengthen its own support among the poor. This demanded a decisive attack on the traditional village social structure. The party leaders believed that to crack the age-old peasant fear of the local elite and overcome the traditional respect for property rights required unleashing the hatred of the oppressed. Teams of activists moved through the villages, organizing the poor in "speak bitterness" meetings to struggle against landlords and Nationalist supporters, to punish and often to kill them, and to distribute their land and property. The party tried to control the process in order not to alienate the broad middle ranks among the peasants, but land revolution had a dynamism of its own, and rural China went through a period of terror. Yet apparently the party gained from the revolutionary dynamism; morale was at fever pitch, and, for those who had benefited from land distribution, there was no turning back.

THE DECISIVE YEAR, 1948

The year 1948 was the turning point in the civil war. In central China, communist armies of 500,000 troops proved their ability to fight major battles on the plains and to capture, though not always hold, important towns on the Longhai line such as Luoyang and Kaifeng. In northern China they encircled Taiyuan, the capital of Shanxi; took most of Chahar and Jehol, provinces on Manchuria's western flank; and recaptured Yan'an, which had been lost in March 1947. The decisive battles were fought in Shandong and Manchuria, where the forces of Chen Yi and Liu Bocheng and those under Lin Biao crushed the government's best armies. For the government it was a year of military and economic disasters.

In Shandong, despite the departure of Chen Yi's forces, communist guerrillas gradually reduced the government's hold on the railway from Qingdao to Jinan; they penned up about 60,000 government troops in the latter city, an important railway junction. Instead of withdrawing that garrison southward to Suzhou, the government left it, for political reasons, to stand and fight. Then Chen Yi's forces returned to Shandong and overwhelmed the dispirited Jinan garrison on September 24. This opened the way for a communist attack on Suzhou, the historic northern shield for Nanjing and a vital railway centre.

Beginning in December 1947, a communist offensive severed all railway connections into Mukden and isolated the Nationalist garrisons in Manchuria. The government armies went on the defensive in besieged cities, partly out of fear that demoralized divisions would defect in the field. Instead of withdrawing from Manchuria before it was too late, the government tried unsuccessfully to reinforce its armies and to supply the garrisons by air. With the fall of Jinan, Lin Biao launched his final offensive. He now had an army of 600,000, nearly twice the Nationalist force in Manchuria. He first attacked Jinzhou, the government's supply base on the railway between Jinan and Mukden; it fell on October 17. Changchun fell three days later. The great garrison at Mukden then tried to retake Jinzhou and Changchun and to open the railway line to the port of Yingkou on Liaodong Bay. In a series of battles, Lin Biao's columns defeated this cream of the Nationalist forces. By early November the Nationalists had lost some 400,000 troops as casualties, captives, or defectors.

The government's military operations in the first part of 1948 produced ever larger budget deficits through the loss of tax receipts, dislocation of transportation and productive facilities, and increased military expenditures. Inflation was out of control. In August the government introduced a new currency, the gold *yuan*, to replace the old notes at the rate of 3,000,000:1, promising drastic reforms to curtail expenditures and increase revenue. Domestic prices and foreign-exchange rates were pegged, with severe penalties threatened for black market operations. The people were required to sell their gold, silver, and foreign currency to the government at the pegged rate; large numbers did so in a desperate effort to halt the inflation. In Shanghai and some other places, the government used draconian methods to enforce its decrees against speculators, but it apparently could not control its own expenditures or stop the printing presses. Furthermore, the government's efforts to fix prices of food and commodities brought about an almost complete stagnation of economic activity, except for illicit buying and selling at prices far above the fixed levels. Some army officers and government officials were themselves engaged in smuggling, speculation, and other forms of corruption. Then came the loss of Jinan and the knowledge of the threat in Manchuria. During October the final effort to halt inflation collapsed, with shattering effect to morale in Nationalist-held cities. Prices started rocketing upward once more.

COMMUNIST VICTORY

Between early November 1948 and early January 1949, the two sides battled for control of Suzhou. Zhu De concentrated 600,000 troops under Chen Yi, Liu Bocheng, and Chen Geng near that strategic centre, which was defended by Nationalist forces of similar size. Both armies were well-equipped, but the Nationalists had a superiority in armour and were unopposed in the air. Yet poor morale, inept command, and a defensive psychology brought another disaster to the Nationalist government. One after another, its armies were surrounded and defeated in the field. When the 65-day battle was over on January 10, the Nationalists had lost some 500,000 men and their equipment. The capital at Nanjing would soon lie exposed.

With Manchuria and most of the eastern region south to the Yangtze in communist hands, the fate of Tianjin and Beiping was sealed. The railway corridor between Tianjin and Zhangjiakou was hopelessly isolated. Tianjin fell on January 15 after a brief siege, and Beiping surrendered on the 23rd, allowing a peaceful turnover of China's historic capital and centre of culture.

Thus, during the last half of 1948, the communist armies had gained control over Manchuria and northeastern China nearly to the Yangtze, except for pockets of resistance. They had a numerical superiority and had captured such huge stocks of rifles, artillery, and armour that they were better equipped than the Nationalists.

Great political shifts occurred in 1949. Chiang Kai-shek retired temporarily in January, turning over to the vice president, Gen. Li Tsung-jen (Li Zongren), the problem of holding the government together and trying to negotiate a peace with Mao Zedong. Li's peace negotiations (February–April) proved hopeless. The Nationalists were not prepared to surrender; they still claimed to govern more than half of China and still had a large army. General Li tried to secure U.S. support in the peace negotiations and in the military defense of southern China, but the U.S. government, attempting to extricate itself from its entanglement with the collapsing forces of the Nationalist government, pursued a policy of noninvolvement.

When peace negotiations broke down, communist armies crossed the Yangtze virtually unopposed; the Nationalist government abandoned its indefensible capital on April 23 and moved to Guangzhou. In succession, communist forces occupied Nanjing (April 24), Hankou (May 16–17), and Shanghai (May 25). The Nationalists' last hope lay in the south and west, but Xi'an, a longtime Nationalist bastion and the gateway to the northwest, had fallen to Gen. Peng Dehuai on May 20. During the last half of 1949, powerful communist armies succeeded in taking the provinces of southern and western China. By the end of the year, only the islands of Hainan, Taiwan, and a few other offshore positions were still in Nationalist hands, and only scattered pockets of resistance remained on the mainland. The defeated Nationalist government reestablished itself on Taiwan, to which Chiang had withdrawn early in the year, taking most of the government's gold reserves and the Nationalist air force and navy. On October 1, with most of the mainland held by the PLA, Mao proclaimed the establishment in Beijing of the government of the People's Republic of China.

CHAPTER 14

ESTABLISHMENT OF THE PEOPLE'S REPUBLIC

The communist victory in 1949 brought to power a peasant party that had learned its techniques in the countryside but had adopted Marxist ideology and believed in class struggle and rapid industrial development. Extensive experience in running base areas and waging war before 1949 had given the CCP deeply ingrained operational habits and proclivities. The long civil war that created the new nation, however, had been one of peasants triumphing over urban dwellers and had involved the destruction of the old ruling classes. In addition, the party leaders recognized that they had no experience in overseeing the transitions to socialism and industrialism that would occur in China's huge urban centres. For this, they turned to the only government with such experience—the Soviet Union. Western hostility against the People's Republic of China, sharpened by the Korean War, contributed to the intensity of the ensuing Sino-Soviet relationship.

When the CCP proclaimed the People's Republic, most Chinese understood that the new leadership would be preoccupied with industrialization. A priority goal of the communist political system was to raise China to the status of a great power. While pursuing this goal, the "centre of gravity" of communist policy shifted from the countryside to the city, but Chairman Mao Zedong insisted that the revolutionary

This undated propaganda cartoon features Chinese peasants with a poster of Chairmen Mao Zedong. AFP/Getty Images

vision forged in the rural struggle would continue to guide the party.

In a series of speeches in 1949, Chairman Mao stated that his aim was to create a socialist society and, eventually, world communism. These objectives, he said, required transforming consumer cities into producer cities to set the basis on which "the people's political power could be consolidated." He advocated forming a four-class coalition of elements of the urban middle class—the petty bourgeoisie and the national bourgeoisie—with workers and peasants, under the leadership of the CCP. The people's state would exercise a dictatorship "for the oppression of antagonistic classes" made up of opponents of the regime.

The authoritative legal statement of this "people's democratic dictatorship" was given in the 1949 Organic Law for the Chinese People's Political Consultative Conference, and at its first session the conference adopted a Common Program that formally sanctioned the organization of state power under the coalition.

Following the communist victory, a widespread urge to return to normality helped the new leadership restore the economy. Police and party cadres in each locality, backed up by army units, began to crack down on criminal activities associated with economic breakdown. Soon it was possible to speak of longer-term developmental plans.

The cost of restoring order and building up integrated political institutions at all levels throughout the country proved important in setting China's course for the next two decades. Revolutionary priorities had to be made consonant with other needs. Land reform did proceed in the countryside: landlords were virtually eliminated as a class, land was redistributed, and, after some false starts, China's countryside was placed on the path toward collectivization. In the cities, however, a temporary accommodation was reached with noncommunist elements; many former bureaucrats and capitalists were retained in positions of authority in factories, businesses, schools, and governmental organizations. The leadership recognized that such compromises endangered their aim of perpetuating revolutionary values in an industrializing society, yet out of necessity they accepted the lower priority for communist revolutionary goals and a higher place for organizational control and enforced public order.

Once in power, communist cadres could no longer condone what they had once sponsored, and inevitably they adopted a more rigid and bureaucratic attitude toward popular participation in politics. Many communists, however, considered these changes a betrayal of the revolution; their responses gradually became more intense, and the issue eventually began to divide the once cohesive revolutionary elite. That development became a central focus of China's political history from 1949.

RECONSTRUCTION AND CONSOLIDATION, 1949–52

During this initial period, the CCP made great strides toward bringing the country through three critical transitions: from economic prostration to economic growth, from political disintegration to political strength, and from military rule to civilian rule. The determination and capabilities demonstrated during these first years—and the respectable showing (after a century of military humiliations) that Chinese troops made against UN forces on the Korean peninsula in 1950–53—provided the CCP with a reservoir of popular support that would be a major political resource for years.

PLA (People's Liberation Army) troops—called Chinese People's Volunteers—entered the Korean War against UN forces in October 1950. Beijing had felt threatened by the northward thrust of UN units and had attempted to halt them by its threats to intervene. However, Douglas MacArthur, commander of the UN forces, ignored the threats, and, when UN troops reached the Chinese border, Beijing acted. By the time hostilities ended in July 1953, approximately two-thirds of China's combat divisions had seen service in Korea.

In the three years of war, a "Resist America, aid Korea" campaign translated the atmosphere of external threat into a spirit of sacrifice and enforced patriotic emergency at home. Regulations for the Suppression of Counterrevolutionaries (1951) authorized police action against dissident individuals and suspected groups. A campaign against anticommunist holdouts, bandits, and political opponents was also pressed. Greatest publicity attended Beijing's dispatch of troops to Tibet about the same time that it intervened in Korea. The distinctiveness and world reputation of the Tibetan culture was to make this a severe test of communist efforts to complete the consolidation of their power. In 1959, after a period of sporadic clashes with the Chinese, the Tibetans rose in rebellion, to which Beijing responded with force.

Under the Agrarian Reform Law of 1950, the property of rural landlords was confiscated and redistributed, which fulfilled a promise to the peasants and smashed a class identified as feudal or semifeudal. The property of traitors, "bureaucrat capitalists" (especially the "four big families" of the Nationalist Party [KMT]—the K'ungs [Kongs], Soongs [Songs], Chiangs [Jiangs], and Ch'ens [Chens]), and selected foreign nationals was also confiscated, helping end the power of many industrialists and providing an economic basis for industrialization. Programs were begun to increase production and to lay the basis for long-term socialization.

These programs coincided with a massive effort to win over the population to the leadership. Such acts as a marriage law (May 1950) and a trade-union law (June 1950) symbolized the break with the old society, while mass organizations and the regime's "campaign style" dramatized the new.

During 1949–50, policy toward the cities focused on restoring order, rehabilitating the economy, and, above all, wringing disastrous inflation out of the urban economy. To accomplish these tasks, the CCP tried to discipline the labour force, win over the confidence of the capitalists, and implement drastic fiscal policies so as to undercut inflation. These policies brought such remarkable successes that by late 1950 many urban Chinese viewed the CCP leadership as needed reformers. Indeed, numerous capitalists believed them to be "good for business."

But, beginning in 1951, the revolutionary agenda of the communists began to be felt in the cities. A Suppression of Counterrevolutionaries campaign dealt violently with many former leaders of secret societies, religious associations, and the KMT in early 1951. In late 1951 and early 1952, three major political campaigns brought the revolutionary essence of the CCP home to key urban groups. The Three-Antis campaign targeted communist cadres who had become too close to China's capitalists. The Five-Antis campaign was aimed at the capitalists themselves and brought them into line on charges of bribery, tax evasion, theft of state property and economic information, and cheating on government contracts. Finally, the thought-reform campaign humbled university professors and marked a turning point in the move from Western to Soviet influence in structuring China's university curriculum.

The pressures toward national political consolidation and the costly struggle in Korea produced significant consequences. In the several provinces of Manchuria (now called the Northeast), there was a growing concentration of industrial and military presence, as well as an increased presence of Soviet economic advisers and key elements of China's tiny corps of technicians and specialists. This was a natural development in view of the extensive economic infrastructure left behind by the Japanese in that region and its proximity to Korea. Additionally, Northeast China had long been an area of Soviet interest.

Gao Gang headed Northeast China, and, in addition to his authoritative regional position, Gao also influenced decisions in Beijing. He planned the Three-Antis campaign and took the lead in adapting Soviet techniques to Chinese factory management and economic planning. He promoted these techniques on a national basis when he moved to Beijing in late 1952 to set up the State Planning Commission. Working closely with the head of the party's Organization Department and other senior officials, Gao allegedly tried to drastically reduce

the authority of his potential competitors, notably Liu Shaoqi and Zhou Enlai, both leading members of party and state organs. The ensuing power struggle lasted more than a year, reflecting an underlying fissure in the CCP. Gao himself had long been a man of the rural base areas, while Liu and Zhou were associated far more with the pre-1949 work in the "white areas" (areas outside CCP control). After 1949, base area veterans believed that they received fewer high positions than their struggles in the wilderness had warranted. Within weeks after the National Conference of the party (March 1955) had proclaimed the defeat of the Gao clique, Beijing approved a long-delayed First Five-Year Plan (technically covering the years 1953–57). That summer, active programs for agricultural collectivization and the socialization of industry and commerce were adopted.

The period 1949–52 was marked by changes in Soviet influence in China. The officially sanctioned terms of that influence had been worked out in a visit by Mao to Moscow from mid-December 1949 until the following March and were formalized in the Treaty of Friendship, Alliance, and Mutual Assistance (signed Feb. 14, 1950). Years later the Chinese charged that Moscow had failed to give Beijing adequate support under that treaty and had left the Chinese to face UN forces virtually alone in Korea. The seeds of doubt concerning Soviet willingness to help China had been sown. Moreover, one of the errors purportedly committed by Gao Gang was his zealousness in using Soviet advisers and promoting the Soviet economic model for management. After the purge of pro-Gao elements, steps were taken to reduce direct Soviet control in China that included reaching agreement on the final withdrawal of Soviet troops from Port Arthur (Lüshun; since 1984 part of Dalian) by mid-1955. Moscow proved amenable to these changes, as the death of long-time Soviet leader Joseph Stalin had produced new Soviet efforts to end tensions with the Chinese. The applicability of the Soviet model to China and the degree to which its use might become a pretext for Soviet manipulation of China began to be questioned.

Nevertheless, these potential reductions in Soviet influence were counterbalanced by growing Soviet activity in other fields. The Chinese army was reorganized along Soviet lines, with a greater emphasis on heavy firepower and mobility. Soviet texts and propaganda materials flooded the country. The Soviet Union had earlier extended $300 million in credit (used up by 1953), which was followed by a smaller developmental loan in 1954 (used up by 1956). Under these aid programs, the Soviets supplied the equipment and technical aid for a large number of industrial projects. The Soviet Union also played a major role in Chinese foreign policy, and it appears that China accepted Moscow's leadership in the international communist movement. Coordinating with the Soviets, Beijing supported revolutionary activity throughout Asia and opposed compromise with neutralist regimes.

THE TRANSITION TO SOCIALISM, 1953–57

The period 1953–57, corresponding to the First Five-Year Plan, was the beginning of China's rapid industrialization, and it is still regarded as having been enormously successful. A strong central governmental apparatus proved able to channel scarce resources into the rapid development of heavy industry. Despite some serious policy issues and problems, the communist leadership seemed to have the overall situation well in hand. Public order improved and many saw a stronger China taking form. The march to socialism seemed to go along reasonably well with the dictates of industrial development. The determination and fundamental optimism of the communist leaders appeared justified, especially in view of the decades of invasion, disintegration, self-doubt, and humiliation that had been the lot of the Chinese people before 1949.

The First Five-Year Plan was explicitly modeled on Soviet experience, and the Soviet Union provided both material aid and extensive technical advice on its planning and execution. During 1952–54 the Chinese established a central planning apparatus and a set of central ministries and other government institutions that were close copies of their Soviet counterparts. Those actions were officially ratified by the first meeting of the National People's Congress in September 1954, which formally established the Central People's Government and adopted the first constitution of the People's Republic of China. The plan adopted Stalinist economic priorities. In a country where more than four-fifths of the population lived in rural areas, about four-fifths of all government investment was channeled into the urban economy. The vast majority of this investment went to heavy industry, leaving agriculture relatively starved for resources. The plan provided for substantial income differentials to motivate the labour force in the state sector, and it established a "top down" system in which a highly centralized government apparatus exercised detailed control over economic policy through enormous ministries in Beijing. Those developments differed substantially from the priorities and proclivities of the Chinese communist movement in the decades before 1949. Nevertheless, the First Five-Year Plan was linked with the transition of China's rural and urban economy to collective forms.

RURAL COLLECTIVIZATION

This transition was most obvious in the countryside. After land reform had been carried out, mutual aid teams allowed the communists to experiment with voluntary forms of agricultural collectivization. A campaign was launched in late 1953 to organize into small collectives, called lower-level agricultural producers' cooperatives, averaging 20 to 30 households.

Vehement debate soon broke out within the CCP concerning how quickly to move to higher stages of cooperative

production in the countryside. The debate was symptomatic of the larger tensions within the party regarding urban and rural development, Soviet influence, and the development of huge government ministries in Beijing. The strengths of Mao Zedong lay in agricultural policy, social change, and foreign relations, and in the mid-1950s he began to shift the national agenda more in the direction of his own expertise.

In July 1955 Mao, against the wishes of most of his colleagues in the CCP leadership, called for an acceleration of the transition to lower-level, and then to higher-level, agricultural producers' cooperatives in the countryside. The key difference between these two forms concerned the middle class of peasants, farmers able to live off their own land. The advanced cooperative was particularly disadvantageous to the wealthier peasants because it invested the cooperative itself with title to the land, granting no right of withdrawal, and because wages were based on labour performed, not land contributed. Middle-level peasants came to resent landless peasants, whom the party was recruiting into the new cooperatives. Also, the advanced form, modeled on the Soviet kolkhoz, brought with it the outside political controls that were necessary to extract the agricultural surpluses required to pay for China's capital equipment in its industrialization and to feed those moving into the cities to work in the growing industries. Many middle-level peasants actively resisted these changes and the measures for enforcing them, particularly grain rationing, compulsory purchase quotas, and stricter regulations on savings and wage rates. Nevertheless, Chinese agricultural organization in 1956 reached the approximate level of collectivization achieved in the Soviet Union: a peasant owned his house, some domestic animals, a garden plot, and his personal savings; by the end of 1956, some seven-eighths of China's peasant households were organized into advanced cooperatives.

URBAN SOCIALIST CHANGES

Mao combined this massive transformation of the agricultural sector with a call for the "socialist transformation" of industry and commerce, in which the government would become, in effect, the major partner. In Chinese communist fashion, this change was not simply decreed from above. Rather, extreme pressures were put on private merchants and capitalists in late 1955 to "volunteer" their enterprises for transformation into "joint state-private" firms. The results were sometimes extraordinary. For example, all the capitalists in a given trade (such as textiles) would parade together to CCP headquarters to the beat of gongs and the sound of firecrackers. Once there, they would present a petition to the government, asking that the major interest in their firms be bought out at the rate that the government deemed appropriate. The government would graciously agree.

Such actions can be understood against the background of the experiences of the capitalists in the previous few years. The Five-Antis campaign of 1952 had terrorized many of them and left most deeply in debt to the government, owing purported back taxes and financial penalties. In any case, the state sector of the economy and the state controls over banking had increased to such a degree that the capitalists relied heavily on the government for the contracts and business necessary to keep from bankruptcy. After the Five-Antis campaign, the government extended the reach of its trade unions into the larger capitalist enterprises, and the "joint labour–management" committees set up under government pressure in those firms usurped much of the power that the capitalists formerly had exercised. Thus, many Chinese capitalists saw the socialist transformation of 1955–56 as an almost welcome development, because it secured their position with the government while costing them little in money or power.

POLITICAL DEVELOPMENTS

The socialist transformation of agriculture, industry, and commerce thus went relatively smoothly. Nevertheless, such changes could not take place without considerable tensions. Many peasants streamed into the cities in 1956–57 to escape the new cooperatives and to seek employment in the rapidly expanding state-run factories, where government policy kept wages rising rapidly. China's urban population mushroomed from 77 million in 1953 to 99.5 million by 1957.

Several problems also became increasingly pressing. First, CCP leaders found that the agricultural sector was not growing fast enough to provide additional capital for its own development and to feed the workers of the cities. Until then, agricultural policy had attempted to wring large production increases out of changes in organization and land ownership, with little capital investment. By 1956–57 that policy was shown to be inadequate.

Second, Soviet assistance had been made available to China as loans, not grants. After 1956 China had to repay more each year than it borrowed in new funds. Thus, the Chinese could no longer count on Moscow for net capital accumulation in its industrialization drive.

Third, the vastly expanded governmental responsibility for managing the country's urban firms and commerce required far more experts than before. For this, the leadership tried to resolve the increasingly severe strains that had characterized the relationship between the country's intellectuals (including technical specialists) and the CCP.

The leadership's policies up to that point had been ambivalent toward the intelligentsia: on the one hand it had required their services and prestige, but on the other it had suspected that many were untrustworthy, coming from urban and bourgeois backgrounds and often having close family and other personal ties with the KMT. After 1949 and particularly during the first part of the Korean War, the Central Committee launched a major campaign to reeducate teachers and scientists and to discredit Western-oriented scholarship. In 1951 the emphasis shifted from general campaigns to self-reform; in 1955 it shifted once again to an intensive thought-reform movement, following the purge of Hu Feng, until then the party's leading spokesman on art and literature. This latter movement coincided with the denunciation of a scholarly study of the *Dream of the Red Chamber* (*Hongloumeng*), an 18th-century novel of tragic love and declining fortunes in a Chinese family. Literature without a clear class moral received blistering criticism, as did any hint that the party should not command art and literature—a theme identified with the ousted Hu Feng—and "Hu Feng elements" were exposed among intellectuals in schools, factories, and cooperatives.

The intensity of these attacks slackened in early 1956. Party leaders publicly discussed the role of intellectuals in the new tasks of national construction and adopted the line "Let a hundred flowers blossom, a hundred schools of thought contend." Because intellectuals in China included high school graduates as well as those with college or advanced professional training, the policy affected a vast number of people. The "hundred flowers" line explicitly encouraged "free-ranging" discussion and inquiry, with the explicit assumption that this would prove the superiority of Marxism-Leninism and speed the conversion of intellectuals to communism. Their response to the party's invitation for free discussion and criticism was gradual and cautious. Instead of embracing Marxism, moreover, many used the opportunity to translate and discuss Western works and ideas and blithely debated "reactionary" doctrines at the very moment Hungarian intellectuals were triggering a wave of anticommunist sentiment in Budapest.

Following this initial phase of the Hundred Flowers Campaign, Mao Zedong issued what was perhaps his most famous post-1949 speech "On the Correct Handling of Contradictions Among the People" (Feb. 27, 1957). Its essential message was ambiguous. He stressed the importance of resolving "nonantagonistic contradictions" by methods of persuasion, but he stated that "democratic" methods of resolution would have to be consistent with centralism and discipline. He left it unclear when a contradiction might become an "antagonistic" and no-holds-barred struggle. The final authoritative version of his speech contained explicit limits on the conduct of debate that had been absent in the original. According to that version, the party would judge words and actions to be correct only if they united the populace, were beneficial to socialism, strengthened the state dictatorship, consolidated organizations, especially the party, and generally helped strengthen international communism. In addition,

these textual manipulations led to an unresolved controversy concerning the initial intent of Mao's speech.

The leadership's explanation was that Mao had set out to trap the dangerous elements among the intellectuals by encouraging their criticism of the party and government. An alternative view was that the leaders used the metaphor of the trap to rationalize their reaction to the unanticipated criticism, popular demonstrations, and general antiparty sentiments expressed in the late spring, when the term "hundred flowers" gained international currency. Whatever the correct explanation for these significant textual changes, the communist leaders had encouraged free criticism of the party and its programs, and they had then turned on their critics as rightists and counterrevolutionaries. In June, noncommunists who had thrown caution to the winds reaped the full fury of retaliation in an anti-rightist campaign. The intellectuals who had responded to Mao's call for open criticism were the first victims, but the movement quickly spread beyond that group to engulf many specialists in the government bureaucracy and state-run firms. By the fall, the fury of the campaign began to turn toward the countryside, and those, especially among the rural cadres, who had remained unenthusiastic about the "high tide" of agricultural change came under fire and were removed. The spreading anti-rightist campaign then inspired fear in those who wanted a slower, more pragmatic approach to development and shifted the initiative to others who, like Mao, believed that the solutions to China's core problems lay in a major break with the incrementalist Soviet strategy and in a bold new set of distinctly Chinese ideas. International events dovetailed with that basic thrust by the winter of 1957–58.

FOREIGN POLICY

While the Chinese initially took their principal cues in shaping foreign policy from domestic developments and generally adhered to the initial pro-Soviet line, they began to act—on the basis of several important lessons gained during the Korean struggle—to reduce Beijing's militant and isolationist attitudes in international affairs. Beijing had recognized that the great costs of the war, the questionable reliability of Soviet military backing, and the danger of direct U.S. retaliation against China had come close to threatening its very existence. Although in preserving North Korea as a communist state China had attained its principal strategic objective, its leaders understood the costs and risks involved and were determined to exercise a greater caution in their international dealings. Another lesson was that the neutralist countries in Asia and Africa were not Western puppets, and it was politically profitable to promote friendly relations with them. These lessons, as reinforced by domestic considerations, led China to take a conciliatory role in the conference leading to the Geneva Accords on

Indochina in 1954 and to try to normalize its foreign relations.

Premier Zhou Enlai symbolized China's more active diplomatic role at the Bandung Conference in April 1955, held at Bandung, Indonesia, which discussed Asian-African issues. His slogan was "Unity with all," according to the line of peaceful coexistence. This "Bandung line" associated with Zhou gained worldwide attention when he told the delegates there that his government was fully prepared to achieve normal relations with all

Zhou Enlai, a leading architect of China's foreign policy. Encyclopædia Britannica, Inc.

countries, including the United States. One result of his initiative was the start of ambassadorial talks between China and the United States.

Between 1955 and 1957, however, changes in Soviet and U.S. policies caused Chinese leaders to doubt the validity of this more cautious and conciliatory foreign policy. At the 20th Congress of the Soviet Communist Party in 1956, First Secretary Nikita Khrushchev announced a de-Stalinization policy. This development angered Mao Zedong for two reasons: he thought, correctly, that it would undermine Soviet prestige, with potentially dangerous consequences in eastern Europe, and he chafed at Khrushchev's warning to other communist parties not to let a willful leader have his way unchecked. Thus, a new situation in Sino-Soviet relations began to emerge, in which antagonisms based on different national traditions, revolutionary experiences, and levels of development that had previously been glossed over broke through to the surface.

Chinese leaders—Mao foremost among them but by no means alone—now began to question the wisdom of closely following the Soviet model. Economic difficulties provided a major set of reasons for moving away from that model, and increasing mutual distrust exacerbated the situation. Nevertheless, at the end of 1957 the Soviet Union evidently agreed to provide China with the technical assistance needed to make an atomic bomb, and during 1958 the Soviet Union increased its level of aid to China. In the

final analysis, however, the spiraling deterioration in Sino-Soviet relations proved impossible to reverse.

China adopted a new, more militant foreign policy that can be traced most clearly to Mao's statement during a Moscow trip in November 1957 that the "East wind prevails over the West wind," which implied a return to militant struggle. According to some estimates, the change in line was necessitated by the U.S. buildup of anticommunist regimes to encircle China and by the lack of major gains in peaceful coexistence with Third World neutrals. Other analysts argue that Mao regarded the launching of a Soviet space vehicle (October 1957) and the Sino-Soviet nuclear-sharing agreement as indications that the balance of world forces had changed in favour of communism.

NEW DIRECTIONS IN NATIONAL POLICY, 1958–61

The pressures behind the dramatic inauguration in 1958 of "Three Red Banners"—i.e., the general line of socialist construction, the Great Leap Forward, and the rural people's communes—are still not fully known. Undoubtedly, a complex mixture of forces came into play. Mao personally felt increasingly uncomfortable with the alliance with the Soviet Union and with the social and political ramifications of the Soviet model of development. On ideological grounds and because it shifted policy away from his personal political strengths, Mao disliked the Soviet system of centralized control by large government ministries, substantial social stratification, and strong urban bias. In addition, the Soviet model assumed that agricultural surplus need only be captured by the government and made to serve urban development. This was true for the Soviet Union in the late 1920s, when the model was developed, but the situation in China was different. Chinese policy had to devise a way first to create an agricultural surplus and then to take a large part of it to serve urban growth. The Soviet model also rested on implicit assumptions about the energy and transportation sectors that were not compatible with the Chinese realities of the 1950s.

To some extent, obscure political battles also became caught up in the debates over Chinese development strategies. In the spring of 1958, for example, Mao Zedong elevated Marshal Lin Biao to a higher position in the CCP than that held by Defense Minister Peng Dehuai. At the same time, Mao initiated a critique of China's slavish copying of Soviet military strategy.

Overall, the radicalization of policy that led to the Great Leap Forward can be traced back to the anti-rightist campaign of 1957 and a major meeting of China's leaders at the resort city of Qingdao in October of that year. By the time of another central meeting—this one in Nanning in January 1958—Mao felt confident enough to launch a blistering critique of the domination of economic policy by the State Council and its subordinate ministries. The best available evidence suggests that almost all the top leaders supported Mao as he developed a series of initiatives that eventually produced the Great Leap strategy and the people's communes. The only major exceptions appear to have been Zhou Enlai and Chen Yun, a force in Chinese economic policy; both faded from the public eye in 1958 only to be brought back into active roles as the Great Leap faltered in 1959.

The general line of socialist construction and the Great Leap Forward were announced at the second session of the Eighth Party Congress (May 1958), which concentrated as much on political slogans as on specific objectives. Special emphasis was placed on political guidance by party cadres of the country's scientists and technicians, who were viewed as potentially dangerous unless they would become fully "Red and expert." The progressive indoctrination of experts would be paralleled by introductory technical training for cadres, thereby in theory transforming the entire elite into political-technical generalists. The Congress of 1958 called for a bold form of ideological leadership that could unleash a "leap forward" in technical innovation and economic output. To link the new generalist leaders and the masses, emphasis fell on sending cadres to the lower levels (*xiafang*) for firsthand experience and manual labour and for practical political indoctrination.

GREAT LEAP FORWARD

The program that came to be known as the Great Leap Forward was a failed industrialization campaign undertaken by the Chinese communists between 1958 and early 1960. Mao Zedong hoped to develop labour-intensive methods of industrialization that would emphasize manpower rather than the gradual purchase of heavy machinery, thereby putting to use China's dense population and obviating the need to accumulate capital. Rather than building large new factories, he proposed developing backyard steel furnaces in every village. Rural people were organized into communes where agricultural and political decisions emphasized ideological purity rather than expertise. The program was implemented so hastily and

zealously that many errors occurred; these were exacerbated by a series of natural disasters and the withdrawal of Soviet technical personnel. China's agriculture was severely disrupted, causing widespread famine in 1958–62. By early 1960 the government had begun to repeal the Great Leap Forward; private plots were returned to peasants, and expertise began to be emphasized again.

In 1958, during the Great Leap Forward, employees of a hotel build a small rudimentary steel smelting furnace. Jacquet-Francillon/AFP/Getty Images

The Great Leap Forward involved an enormous amount of experimentation. It had no detailed blueprint, but there were some underlying strategic principles. There was a general reliance on a combination of ideological and organizational techniques to overcome seemingly insuperable obstacles that was focused on the countryside and that drew from policies of the 1930s and 1940s. The basic idea was to convert the massive labour surplus in China's hinterlands into a huge production force through a radical reorganization of rural production. The search for the best organizational form to achieve this result led in August 1958 to popularization of the "people's commune," a huge rural unit that pooled the labour of tens of thousands of peasants from different villages in order to increase agricultural production, engage in local industrial production, enhance the availability of rural schooling, and organize a local militia force in accordance with Mao's preferred national military strategy of combining the deterrence of an atomic bomb with guerrilla warfare.

Mao believed that through these radical organizational changes, combined with adequate political mobilization techniques, the Chinese countryside could be made to provide the resources both for its own development and for the continuing rapid development of the heavy industrial sector in the cities. Through this strategy of "walking on two legs," China could obtain the simultaneous development of industry and agriculture and, within the urban sector, of both large- and small-scale industry. If it worked, this would resolve the dilemma of an agricultural bottleneck that had seemed to loom large on the horizon as of 1957. It would, however, involve a major departure from the Soviet model, which would predictably lead to increased tensions between Beijing and Moscow.

Largely because of unusually good weather, 1958 was an exceptionally good year for agricultural output. But, by the end of that year, the top CCP leadership sensed that some major problems demanded immediate attention. Initial optimism had led peasants in many areas to eat far more than they usually would have, and stocks of grain for the winter and spring months threatened to fall dangerously low. In addition, reports of sporadic peasant unrest cast some doubt on the rosy picture being presented to the leaders by their own statistical system, the accuracy of which in turn came into question.

The fall harvest of 1958 had not been as large as expected, and in February and March 1959 Mao Zedong began to call for appropriate adjustments to make policies more realistic without abandoning the Great Leap as a whole. Mao emerged as one of the most-forceful advocates of scaling back the Great Leap in order to avert a potential disaster. He faced substantial resistance from provincial CCP leaders, whose powers had been greatly increased as part of the Great Leap strategy. A meeting at Lushan in the summer of 1959 produced an unanticipated and ultimately highly destructive outcome. Defense Minister Peng Dehuai raised a range of criticisms of the Great Leap, based in large part on his own investigations. He summed these up in a letter that he sent to Mao during the conference. Mao waited eight days to respond to the letter and then attacked Peng for "right deviationism" and demanded the purge of Peng and all his followers.

The Lushan Conference resulted in several major decisions: Peng Dehuai was replaced as defense minister by Lin Biao (who would later be marked for succession to Mao's position of CCP chairman), the Great Leap Forward was scaled back, and a political campaign was launched to identify and remove all "rightist" elements. The third decision effectively canceled the second, as party officials refused to scale back the Great Leap for fear of being labeled as "rightists." The net effect was to produce a "second leap"—a new radical upsurge in policy that was not corrected until it produced results so disastrous that they called into question the very viability of the communist system.

The CCP celebrated the 10th anniversary of national victory in October 1959 in a state of near euphoria. The weather turned in 1959, however, and during the next two years China experienced a severe combination of floods and drought. Although the economy was in serious trouble by mid-1960, the Chinese leaders sharpened their debate with Moscow. In April 1960, on the occasion of Vladimir Lenin's 90th birthday, for example, Beijing published an article that contained a slightly veiled critique of Soviet foreign policy, arguing that the Soviets had become soft on imperialism. Khrushchev reacted with a rapid withdrawal of all Soviet technicians and assistance that July. (When he quietly offered to return them that November, his offer was refused.)

Despite the importance of these difficulties, China's worst problem was bad policy. The people's communes were too large to be effective, they ignored age-old marketing patterns in the countryside, and they required administrative and transport resources that did not exist. Their structure and means of allocating resources removed almost all incentive to work, and the breakdown in the statistical system meant that the top leaders had grossly erroneous ideas about what was occurring. Thus, even after many rural areas were beset by massive starvation, the orders from above continued to demand large-scale procurement of foodstuffs. The rural cadres were so afraid of being branded rightist that they followed these unrealistic orders, thus deepening the famine. By 1961 the rural disaster caught up with the cities, and urban industrial output plummeted by more than 25 percent. As an emergency measure, nearly 30 million urban residents were sent back to the countryside because they could no longer be fed in the cities. The Great Leap Forward had run its course, and the system was in crisis.

READJUSTMENT
AND REACTION, 1961–65

The years 1961–65 did not resemble the three previous ones, despite the persistence of radical labels and slogans. The Chinese themselves were loath to acknowledge the end of the Great Leap period, declaring the validity of the general line of socialist construction and its international revolutionary corollary for one and all.

Reality can be seen, however, in the increasing role of the Chinese military and security personnel. At a top-level meeting of the Military Affairs Committee in October 1960 and at one of the rare plenary sessions of the party's Central Committee the following January, the elite gave the highest priority to restoring security and national order. Party recruitment procedures were tightened, and a major thought-reform movement was launched within the cadres' ranks. The Central Committee also established six supraprovincial regional bureaus charged with enforcing obedience to Beijing and bringing the new procedures for control into line with local conditions. The army, now firmly under Lin Biao, took the lead, beginning with a "purification" movement against dissidents within its own ranks. Throughout 1961 and most of 1962, the central officials worked to consolidate their power and to restore faith in their leadership and goals.

By January 1962 Mao had, as he later put it, moved to the "second line" to concentrate "on dealing with questions of the direction, policy, and line of the party and the state." The "first line" administrative and day-by-day direction of the state had been given to Liu Shaoqi, who had assumed the chairmanship of the People's Republic of China in 1959 (though Mao retained his position of party chairman); additional responsibilities in the first line were given to Deng Xiaoping, another tough-minded organizer who, as general secretary, was the party's top administrator. By 1962 Mao had apparently begun to conclude that the techniques used by these comrades in the first line not only violated the basic thrust of the revolutionary tradition but also formed a pattern of error that mirrored what he viewed as the "modern revisionism" of the Soviet Union.

Under Liu and Deng, the CCP during 1960–61 developed a series of documents in major policy areas to try to bring the country out of the rapidly growing crisis. In most instances, these documents were drafted with the assistance of experts who had been reviled during the Great Leap Forward. These documents marked a major retreat from Great Leap radicalism. The communes were to be reduced on the average by about two-thirds so as to make them small enough to link peasants' efforts more clearly with their remuneration. Indeed, by 1962 in many areas of rural China, the collective system in agriculture had broken down completely, and individual farming was revived. Policy toward literature, art, and motion pictures permitted a "thaw" involving treatment of a far broader

Zhou Enlai and Mao Zedong pose in Bejing during a ceremony in April of 1959. AFP/Getty Images

range of subjects and a revival of many older, prerevolutionary artistic forms. The new program in industry strengthened the hands of managers and made a worker's efforts more closely attuned to his rewards. Similar policies were adopted in other areas. In general, China during 1961–65 did a remarkable job of reviving the economy, at least regaining the level of output of 1957 in almost all sectors.

These policies raised basic questions about the future direction of the revolution. While almost all top CCP leaders had supported the launching of the Great Leap, there was disagreement over the lessons to be learned from the movement's dramatic failure. The Great Leap had been intended both as a means of accelerating economic development and as a vehicle for achieving a mass ideological transformation. All leaders agreed in its aftermath that a mobilization approach to economic development was no longer appropriate to China's conditions. Most also concluded that the age of mass political campaigns as an instrument to remold the thinking of the public was past. Mao and a few of his supporters, however, still viewed class struggle and mass mobilization as core ingredients in keeping the revolutionary vision alive.

Mao personally lost considerable prestige over the failure of the Great Leap—and the party's political and organizational apparatus was damaged—but he remained the most powerful individual in China. He proved able time and again to enforce his will on the issues that he deemed to be of top priority. Claims made later, during the Cultural Revolution, that Mao had been pushed aside and ignored during 1961–65 are not supported by the evidence.

Mao was in fact deeply troubled as he contemplated China's situation during 1961–65. He perceived the Soviet socialist revolution in the years after Stalin's death in 1953 to have degenerated into "social imperialism." Mao evidently had been shocked by these developments in the Soviet Union, and the revelation made him look at events in China from a new vantage point. Mao became convinced that China too was headed down the road toward revisionism. He used class struggle and ideological campaigns, as well as concrete policies in various areas, to try to prevent and reverse this slide into revolutionary purgatory. Mao's nightmare about revisionism played an increasing role in structuring politics in the mid-1960s.

Mao was not the only leader who harboured doubts about the trends in the recovery effort of 1961–65. Others gathered around him and tried to use their closeness to Mao as a vehicle for enhancing their political power. The key individuals involved were Mao's political assistant of many years, Chen Boda, who was an expert in the realm of ideology; Mao's wife, Jiang Qing, who had strong policy views in the cultural sphere; Kang Sheng, whose strength lay both in his understanding of Soviet ideology and in his mastery of Soviet-style secret police techniques; and Lin Biao, who headed the military and tried to make it an ideal type of Maoist organization that combined effectiveness with ideological purity. Each of these people in turn had personal networks and resources to bring to a coalition. While their goals and interests did not entirely coincide, they all could unite on two efforts: enhancing Mao's power and upsetting Mao's relations with Liu Shaoqi (then the likely successor to Mao), Deng Xiaoping, and most of the remainder of the party leadership.

Mao took a number of initiatives in domestic and foreign policy during the period. At a major Central Committee plenum in September 1962, he insisted that "class struggle" remain high on the Chinese agenda, even as enormous efforts continued to be made to revive the economy. He also called for a campaign of "socialist education," aimed primarily at reviving the demoralized party apparatus in the countryside. By 1964 he began to press hard to make the Chinese educational system less elitist by organizing "part-work, part-study" schools that would provide more vocational training. Throughout this period, foreign observers noted what appeared to be some tension between a continuing thread of radicalism in China's propaganda and a strong pragmatic streak in the country's actual domestic policies.

The most important set of measures Mao took concerned the PLA, which he and Lin Biao tried to make into a model organization. Events on the Sino-Indian border in the fall of 1962 helped the PLA reestablish discipline and its image. From 1959 to 1962 both India and China, initially as a by-product of the uprising in Tibet, resorted to military force along their disputed border. On Oct. 12, 1962, a week before the Chinese moved troops into disputed border territories, Indian Prime Minister Jawaharlal Nehru stated that the army was to free all Indian territory of "Chinese intruders." In the conflict that followed, Beijing's regiments defeated Indian forces in the border region, penetrating well beyond it. The Chinese then withdrew from most of the invaded area and established a demilitarized zone on either side of the line of control. Most significantly, the leadership seized on the army's victory and began to experiment with the possibility of using army heroes as the ideal types for popular emulation.

Increasingly preoccupied with indoctrinating its heirs and harking back to revolutionary days, Beijing's leaders closest in outlook to Mao Zedong and Lin Biao viewed the soldier-communist as the most suitable candidate for the second- and third-generation leadership.

Army uniformity and discipline, it was seen, could transcend the divided classes, and all army men could be made to comply with the rigorous political standards set by Mao's leadership.

Lin Biao developed a simplified and dogmatized version of Mao's thought—eventually published in the form of the "Little Red Book," *Quotations from Chairman Mao*—to popularize Maoist ideology among the relatively uneducated military recruits. As the military forces under Lin increasingly showed

Mao Zedong at a Red Guard rally in Bejing in 1966. His followers wave their "Little Red Books," or Quotations from Chairmen Mao, *as he passes.* Keystone/Hulton Archive/Getty Images

that they could combine ideological purity with technical virtuosity, Mao tried to expand the PLA's organizational authority and its political role. Beginning in 1963, Mao called on all Chinese to "learn from the PLA." Then, starting in 1964, Mao insisted that political departments modeled on those in the PLA be established in all major government bureaucracies. In many cases, political workers from the PLA itself staffed these new bodies, thus effectively penetrating the civilian government apparatus. Other efforts, such as a national propaganda campaign to learn from a purported army hero, Lei Feng, also contributed to enhancement of the PLA's prestige.

The militancy of subsequent campaigns to learn from army heroes, or from the PLA as a whole, was echoed in international politics. In a tour of Africa in late 1963 and early 1964, Zhou Enlai startled his hosts by calling for revolution in newly independent states and openly challenging the Soviet Union for the leadership of the Third World. Simultaneously, China challenged the U.S. system of alliances by establishing formal relations with France and challenged the Soviet Union's system by forming closer ties with Albania.

Beijing's main target was Moscow. A Soviet-U.S. crisis in Cuba (October 1962) had coincided with the Sino-Indian struggle, and in both cases the Chinese believed the Soviet Union had acted unreliably and had become "capitulators" of the worst sort. For the next months,

polemicists in Beijing and Moscow publicly engaged in barbed exchanges. When the Soviet Union signed the Nuclear Test-Ban Treaty with the United States and Great Britain in August 1963, Chinese articles accused the Soviets of joining an anti-Chinese conspiracy. Confronted by this new strategic situation, the Chinese shifted their priorities to support an anti-foreign line and promote the country's "self-reliance." Mao's calls for "revolutionization" acquired a more nationalistic aspect, and the PLA assumed an even larger place in Chinese political life.

These many-sided trends seemed to collide in 1963 and 1964. With the split in the international communist movement, the party in late 1963 called on intellectuals, including those in the cultural sphere, to undertake a major reformulation of their academic disciplines to support China's new international role. The initial assignment for this reformulation fell to Zhou Yang, a party intellectual and deputy director of the Central Committee's Propaganda Department, who tried to enlist China's intellectuals in the ideological war against Soviet revisionism and in the struggle for rigidly pure political standards. (Less than three years later, however, Zhou Yang was purged as a revisionist, and many intellectuals were condemned as Mao Zedong's opponents.)

Closely connected with the concerns of the intellectuals were those relating to the party and the Communist Youth League. A drive began to cultivate what one author called "newborn forces," and by mid-1964 young urban intellectuals were embroiled in a major effort by the Central Committee to promote those forces within the party and league; meanwhile, their rural cousins were buffeted by moves to keep the socialist education campaign under the party's organizational control through the use of "work teams" and a cadre-rectification movement.

In the summer of 1964, Mao wrote a document titled "On Khrushchev's Phony Communism and Its Historical Lessons for the World," which summarized most of Mao's doctrinal principles on contradiction, class struggle, and political structure and operation. This summary provided the basis for the reeducation ("revolutionization") of all youth hoping to succeed to the revolutionary cause. This high tide of revolutionization lasted until early August, when U.S. air strikes on North Vietnam raised the spectre of war on China's southern border. A year-long debate followed on the wisdom of conducting disruptive political campaigns during times of external threat.

This period of time has come to be interpreted as one of major decision within China. One ingredient of the debate was whether to prepare rapidly for conventional war against the United States or to continue the revolutionization of Chinese society, which in Mao's view had fundamental, long-term importance for China's security. Those who argued for a postponement of the internal political struggle supported more-conventional strategies for economic development and took seriously Soviet calls for "united action" in Vietnam and the establishment of closer Sino-Soviet ties. Their position, it was later alleged, received the backing of the general staff. With the dispatch of about 50,000 logistic personnel to Vietnam after February 1965, factional lines began to divide the military forces according to ideological or national security preferences.

Meanwhile, some members tried to restore rigid domestic controls. Where Mao in May 1963 had called for an upsurge in revolutionary struggle, by the following September other leaders were circumscribing the area of cadre initiative and permitting a free-market system and private ownership of rural plots to flourish. A stifling of the revolutionary upsurge was supposedly evident in regulations of June 1964 for the organization of poor and lower-middle-peasant associations, and by early 1965 Mao could point to bureaucratic tendencies throughout the rural areas. In a famous document on problems arising in the course of the socialist education campaign, usually referred to as the "Twenty-three Articles," Mao in January 1965 stated for the first time that the principal enemy was to be found within the party, and he once more proclaimed the urgency of class struggle and mass-line politics.

It was in that period of emphasis on self-reliant struggle that China acquired nuclear weapons. Although the Soviet Union supported Chinese nuclear aims for a time, that effort was taken over completely by the Chinese after June 1959. By 1964 the costs of the program had forced a substantial reduction in other defense costs. China's first atomic explosion (Oct. 16, 1964) affected the debate by appearing to support Mao's contention that domestic revolutionization would in no way jeopardize long-term power aspirations and defense capabilities.

Mao's military thinking, a product of his own civil war experiences and an essential component of his ideology, stressed the importance of military strength through sheer numbers ("people's war") during the transition to nuclear status. He felt that preparation for such a war could turn China's weaknesses into military assets and reduce its vulnerability. Mao's view of people's war belittled the might of modern advanced weapons as "paper tigers" but recognized that China's strategic inferiority subjected it to dangers largely beyond its control. His reasoning thus made a virtue out of necessity in the short run, when China would have to depend on its superior numbers and the morale of its people to defeat any invader. In the long run, however, he held that China would have to have nuclear weapons to deprive the superpowers of their blackmail potential and to deter their aggression against smaller states.

Lin Biao repeated Mao's position on people's war, further arguing that popular insurrections against noncommunist governments could succeed only if they took place without substantial foreign assistance. To the extent that indigenous rebels came to depend on outside support, inevitably their bonds with the local populace would be weakened. When this happened, the rebellion would wither for lack of support. On the other hand, the hardships imposed by relying on indigenous resources would stimulate the comradeship and ingenuity of the insurgents. Equally important, Lin's statement also indicated a high-level decision for China to remain on the defensive.

Lin's speech coincided with yet another secret working conference of the Central Committee, in which the Maoist group reissued its call for cultural revolutionization, this time convinced that the effort of 1964 had been deliberately sabotaged by senior party and military officials. Initiated by Mao Zedong and Lin Biao, the purge first struck dissident army leaders, especially the chief of staff; as the power struggle began, China turned its back on the war in Vietnam and other external affairs. The September meeting may be taken as a clear harbinger of what came to be known as the Great Proletarian Cultural Revolution.

CHAPTER 15

CHINA SINCE 1965

THE CULTURAL REVOLUTION, 1966–76

As the clash over issues in the autumn of 1965 became polarized, the army initially provided the battleground. The issues concerned differences over policy directions and their implications for the organization of power and the qualifications of senior officials to lead. Much of the struggle went on behind the scenes; in public it took the form of personal vilification and ritualized exposés of divergent worldviews or, inevitably, "two lines" of policy. Lin Biao, in calling for the creative study and application of Mao's thought in November and at a meeting of military commissars the following January, consistently placed the army's mission in the context of the national ideological and power struggle. In these critical months, the base of operations for Mao and Lin was the large eastern Chinese city of Shanghai, and newspapers published in that city, especially the *Liberation Army Daily*, carried the public attacks on the targets selected.

ATTACKS ON CULTURAL FIGURES

The first target was the historian Wu Han, who doubled as the deputy mayor of Beijing. In a play Wu wrote, he supposedly had used allegorical devices to lampoon Mao and laud the deposed former minister of defense, Peng Dehuai. The denunciation of Wu and his play in November 1965

A Chinese communist poster commemorating the 100th anniversary of the Paris Commune in 1871. RDA/Hulton Archive/Getty Images

constituted the opening volley in an assault on cultural figures and their thoughts.

As the Cultural Revolution gained momentum, Mao turned for support to the youth as well as the army. In seeking to create a new system of education that would eliminate differences between town and country, workers and peasants, and mental and manual labour, Mao struck a responsive chord with the youth; it was their response that later provided

him with his best shock troops. As a principal purpose, the Cultural Revolution was launched to revitalize revolutionary values for the successor generation of Chinese young people.

The attack against authors, scholars, and propagandists during the spring of 1966 emphasized the cultural dimension of the Cultural Revolution. Increasingly it was hinted that behind the visible targets lay a sinister "black gang" in the fields of education and propaganda and high up in party circles. Removal of Peng Zhen and Lu Dingyi and subsequently of Zhou Yang, then tsar of the arts and literature, indicated that this was to be a thoroughgoing purge. Clearly, a second purpose of the Cultural Revolution would be the elimination of leading cadres whom Mao held responsible for past ideological sins and alleged errors in judgment.

ATTACKS ON PARTY MEMBERS

Gradual transference of the revolution to top echelons of the party was managed by a group centred on Mao Zedong, Lin Biao, Jiang Qing, Kang Sheng, and Chen Boda. In May 1966 Mao secretly assigned major responsibilities to the army in cultural and educational affairs. Another purpose of the Cultural Revolution, as then conceived, would be a "revolution in the superstructure": a transformation from a bureaucratically run machine to a more popularly based system led personally by Mao and a simplified administration under his control.

Following the May instructions, the educational system received priority. "Big-character posters," or large wall newspapers (*dazibao*), spread from the principal campuses in Beijing throughout the land. University officials and professors were singled out for criticism, while their students, encouraged by the central authorities, held mass meetings and began to organize. In June the government dropped examinations for university admissions and called for a reform of entrance procedures and a

delay in reopening the campuses. Party officials and their wives circulated among the campuses to gain favour and to obstruct their opponents. Intrigue and political maneuvering dominated, although political lines were not at first sharply drawn or even well understood. The centres of this activity were Beijing's schools and the inner councils of the Central Committee; the students were the activists in a game they did not fully comprehend.

This phase of the Cultural Revolution ended in August 1966 with the convening of a plenary session of the Central Committee. Mao issued his own big-character poster as a call to "Bombard the headquarters" ("Paoda silingbu"), a call to denounce and remove senior officials, and a 16-point Central Committee decision was issued in which the broad outlines for the Cultural Revolution were laid down and supporters were rallied to the revolutionary banner. The immediate aim was to seize power from "bourgeois" authorities. The locus of the struggle would be their urban strongholds. Now more than ever, Mao's thought became the "compass for action."

Evidently fearing that China would develop along the lines of the Soviet revolution and concerned about his own place in history, Mao threw China's cities into turmoil in a gigantic effort to reverse the historic processes then under way. He ultimately failed in his quest, but his efforts generated problems with which his successors would have to struggle for decades. Mao adopted four goals for his

RED GUARDS

The Red Guards constituted a number of paramilitary units of radical university and high-school students formed during the Chinese Cultural Revolution. Responding in 1966 to Mao Zedong's call to revitalize the revolutionary spirit of the Chinese Communist Party, they went so far as to attempt to purge the country of its pre-communist culture. With a membership in the millions, they attacked and persecuted local party leaders, schoolteachers, and other intellectuals. By early 1967 they had overthrown party authorities in many localities. Internal strife ensued as different units argued over which among them best represented Maoism. In 1968 their disruption of industrial production and urban life led the government to redirect them to the countryside, where the movement gradually subsided.

Young members of the Red Guard marching in the streets of Bejing. Central Press/Hulton Archive/Getty Images

Cultural Revolution: to replace his designated successors with leaders more faithful to his current thinking, to rectify the CCP, to provide China's youth with a revolutionary experience, and to achieve specific policy changes to make the educational, health care, and cultural systems less elitist. He initially pursued those goals through a massive mobilization of the country's urban youths—organized in groups called the Red Guards—while ordering the CCP and the PLA not to suppress the movement.

When Mao formally launched the Cultural Revolution in August 1966, he had already shut down the schools. During the following months, he encouraged the Red Guards to attack all traditional values and "bourgeois" things and to put CCP officials to the test by publicly criticizing them. These attacks were known at the time as struggles against the Four Olds (i.e., old ideas, customs, culture, and habits of mind), and the movement quickly escalated to committing outrages. Many elderly people and intellectuals were physically abused, and many died. Nonetheless, Mao believed that this mobilization of urban youths would be beneficial for them and that the CCP cadres they attacked would be better for the experience.

SEIZURE OF POWER

The period from mid-1966 to early 1969 constituted the Red Guard phase of the Cultural Revolution, and those years in turn included several important turning points. The latter half of 1966 was not only when the Red Guard mobilized (including Red Guard reviews of more than a million youths at a time by Mao Zedong and Lin Biao in Beijing) but also when key Political Bureau (Politburo) leaders were removed from power, most notably Pres. Liu Shaoqi and CCP General Secretary Deng Xiaoping. In October 1966 both Liu and Deng engaged in public self-criticism. Mao, however, rejected both acts as inadequate. At the same meeting, Mao heard bitter complaints from provincial party leaders about the chaos of the political campaign. While acknowledging the validity of much of what was said, Mao nevertheless declared that it would do more good than harm to let the Cultural Revolution continue for several more months.

In January 1967 the movement began to produce the actual overthrow of provincial CCP committees and initial attempts to construct new organs of political power to replace them. The first such "power seizure" (duoquan) took place in Shanghai and was followed by temporary confusion as to just what kind of new political structure should be established to replace the discredited municipal CCP and government apparatuses. At first, a "commune" (gongshe), reminiscent of the 1871 Commune of Paris, was set up, but the final form adopted was called a "revolutionary committee" (geming weiyuanhui); that appellation subsequently was given to

Chinese government committees until the late 1970s.

The chaos involved in the overthrow of the Shanghai authorities combined with political outrages throughout the country to lead many remaining top CCP leaders to call in February 1967 for a halt to the Cultural Revolution. During this attempt to beat back radicalism, more-conservative forces clamped down on Red Guard activism in numerous cities. The movement, dubbed the "February adverse current," was quickly defeated and a new radical upsurge began. Indeed, by the summer of 1967, large armed clashes occurred throughout urban China, and even Chinese embassies abroad experienced takeovers by their own Red Guards. The Red Guards splintered into zealous factions, each purporting to be the "true" representative of the thought of Mao Zedong. Mao's own personality cult, encouraged so as to provide momentum to the movement, assumed religious proportions. The resulting anarchy, terror, and paralysis threw the urban economy into a tailspin. Industrial production for 1968 dipped 12 percent below that of 1966.

During 1967 Mao called on the PLA under Lin Biao to step in on behalf of the Maoist Red Guards, but this politico-military task produced more division within the military than unified support for radical youths. Tensions surfaced in the summer, when Chen Zaidao, a military commander in the key city of Wuhan, arrested two key radical CCP leaders. Faced with possible widespread revolt among local military commanders, Mao tilted toward reestablishing some order.

In 1968 Mao decided to rebuild the CCP and bring things under greater control. The military dispatched officers and soldiers to take over schools, factories, and government agencies. The army simultaneously forced millions of urban Red Guards to move to the hinterlands to live, thereby removing the most disruptive force from the cities. These drastic measures reflected Mao's disillusionment with the Red Guards' inability to overcome factional differences. The Soviet invasion of Czechoslovakia in August 1968, which greatly heightened China's fears for its security, gave these measures added urgency.

THE END OF THE RADICAL PERIOD

Thus, in 1968 the society began to return to business, though not as usual. China's regular schools began to reopen, although the number of students in higher institutions represented only a small proportion of those three years earlier. In July yet another of Mao's "latest instructions" approved science and engineering education and called for the "return to production" of all graduates. In October 1968 a plenary session of the Central Committee met to call for convening a party congress and rebuilding the CCP apparatus. From that point on, the issue of who would inherit political power as the Cultural Revolution wound down became a central question of Chinese politics. (The answer came only with a coup against the radicals a month after Mao Zedong's death on Sept. 9, 1976.)

China's actions following the meeting of October 1968 suggested the degree to which fear of a Soviet invasion contributed to the closing down of the Cultural Revolution's most radical phase. Almost immediately after the meeting, China called on the United States to resume ambassadorial-level talks in Warsaw. Beijing also renewed its conventional diplomacy—it had reduced its level of ambassadorial representation abroad to a single ambassador in Egypt—and quickly sought to expand the range of countries with which it enjoyed diplomatic relations.

China's concern stemmed partly from the Soviet leadership's articulation of a policy (called the Brezhnev Doctrine) that was used to justify the invasion of Czechoslovakia on the grounds that the Soviet Union was obligated to intervene whenever the regime in a socialist country was being threatened internally or externally. To Beijing's horror, even North Vietnam came out in support of this threatening posture. Moscow had long made clear its belief that a "military-bureaucratic dictatorship" had seized power from the "true communists" in Beijing. To add to Beijing's concern, since 1966 the Soviet Union had been building up a sizable military force along the formerly demilitarized Sino-Soviet border. While the forces deployed as of late 1968 were not adequate for a full-scale invasion of China, they certainly posed a serious menace, especially given the political division and social chaos that still prevailed in much of the country.

When the Party Congress convened in April 1969, it did so in the wake of two bloody Sino-Soviet border clashes that had occurred in early and mid-March. Written into the new party constitution was an unprecedented step—Defense Minister Lin Biao was named as Mao's successor—and the military tightened its grip on the entire society. Both the Central Committee and the new party committees being established throughout the country were dominated by military men. Indeed, less than one-third of the Eighth Central Committee members elected in 1956 were reelected in 1969, and more than two-fifths of the members of the Ninth Central Committee chosen in 1969 held military posts.

Premier Zhou Enlai tried to cut back Lin Biao's power and to relieve some of the threat to China's security by engaging the Soviets in direct negotiations on the border dispute. A series of serious military clashes along the border, culminating in a limited but sanguinary Soviet thrust several miles into the Uygur Autonomous Region of Xinjiang, heightened tensions. Zhou briefly met with Soviet Premier Aleksey Kosygin at the Beijing airport in early September, and the two agreed to hold formal talks. Nevertheless, Lin Biao declared martial law and used it to rid himself of some of his potential rivals. Several leaders who had been purged during 1966–68, including Liu Shaoqi, died under the martial law regime of 1969, and many others suffered severely.

Lin quickly encountered opposition, however. Mao became wary of a successor who seemed to want to assume power too quickly and began to maneuver against Lin. Premier Zhou Enlai joined forces with Mao in that effort, as possibly did Mao's wife, Jiang Qing. Mao's assistant, Chen Boda, decided to support Lin's cause, however. Therefore, while in 1970–71 many measures were undertaken to bring order and normalcy back to society, increasingly severe strains split the top leadership.

SOCIAL CHANGES

By 1970 many of the stated goals of the Cultural Revolution had been translated into at least somewhat-operational programs. These included initiatives designed to reduce what were termed the "three major differences"—those separating intellectual from manual labour, worker from peasant, and urban from rural.

Many measures had been taken to make the educational system less elitist. The number of years at each level of schooling was shortened, and admission to a university became based on the recommendations of a student's work unit rather than on competitive examination. All youths were required to engage in at least several years of manual labour before attending a university. Within schools, formal scholarship yielded in

large measure to the study of politics and to vocational training. Examinations of the traditional type were abolished, and stress was placed on collective study. The authority of teachers in the classroom was seriously eroded. These trends reached their most extreme form when a student in the Northeast was made a national hero by the radicals because he turned in a blank examination paper and criticized his teacher for having asked him the examination questions in the first place.

Many bureaucrats were forced to leave the relative comfort of their offices for a stint in "May 7 cadre schools," usually farms run by a major urban unit. People from the urban unit had to live on the farm, typically in quite primitive conditions, for varying periods of time. (For some, this amounted to a number of years, although by about 1973 the time periods in general had been held to about six months to one year.) While on the farm the urban cadre would both engage in rigorous manual labour and undertake intensive, supervised study of ideology. The object was to reduce bureaucratic "airs."

Millions of Chinese youths were also sent to the countryside during these years. Initially, these were primarily Red Guard activists, but the program soon achieved a more general character, and it became expected that most middle-school graduates would head to the countryside. While in the hinterlands, these young people were instructed to "learn from the poor and lower-middle peasants." Quite a few were merely sent to the counties immediately adjacent to the city from which they came. Others, however, were sent over long distances. Large groups from Shanghai, for instance, were made to settle in Heilongjiang, the northernmost province in the Northeast. This rustication was in theory permanent, although the vast majority of these people managed to stream back to the cities in the late 1970s, after Mao's death and the purge of his radical followers.

The system of medical care was also revamped. Serious efforts were made to force urban-based medical staffs to devote more effort to serving the needs of the peasants. This involved both the reassignment of medical personnel to rural areas and, more important, a major attempt to provide short-term training to rural medical personnel called "barefoot doctors." This latter initiative placed at least a minimal level of medical competence in many Chinese villages; ideally, the referral of more-serious matters was to be made to higher levels. Another prong of the effort in the medical arena was to place relatively greater stress on the use of Chinese traditional medicine, which relied more heavily on locally available herbs and on such low-cost treatments as acupuncture. Western medicine was simply too expensive and specialized to be used effectively throughout China's vast hinterlands.

The Cultural Revolution was primarily an urban political phenomenon, and thus it had a highly uneven effect on the peasants. Some villages, especially those near major cities, became caught up in the turmoil, but many peasants living in more-remote areas experienced less interference from higher-level bureaucratic authorities than would normally have been the case.

Nevertheless, there were two dimensions of the Cultural Revolution that did seriously affect peasants' lives. First, the country adopted a policy of encouraging local rural self-sufficiency in foodstuffs. This policy stemmed from ideological and security considerations, and it had begun before the onset of the Cultural Revolution. Its major consequence was a stress on grain production so great that a quite irrational and uneconomical cropping pattern emerged. Second, great stress was placed on separating income from the amount of work performed by a peasant. Pressure was applied to raise the unit of income distribution to the brigade rather than the team (the former was several times larger than the latter), and an increasing share of the collective income was to be distributed on the basis of welfare and political criteria rather than on the basis of the amount of work performed.

STRUGGLE FOR THE PREMIERSHIP

As these programmatic aspects of the Cultural Revolution were being put into place and regularized, the political battle to determine who would inherit power at the top continued and intensified.

Tensions first surfaced at a meeting of the Central Committee in the summer of 1970, when Chen Boda, Lin Biao, and their supporters made a series of remarks that angered Mao Zedong. Mao then purged Chen as a warning to Lin. At the end of 1970 Mao also initiated a criticism of Lin's top supporters in the military forces, calling them to task for their arrogance and unwillingness to listen to civilian authority. The situation intensified during the spring of 1971 until Lin Biao's son, Lin Liguo, evidently began to put together plans for a possible coup against Mao should this prove the only way to save his father's position.

During this period, Zhou Enlai engaged in extremely delicate and secret diplomatic exchanges with the United States, and Mao agreed to a secret visit to Beijing by the U.S. national security adviser Henry Kissinger in July 1971. That visit was one of the more dramatic events of the Cold War era and laid the groundwork for U.S. Pres. Richard M. Nixon's trip to China the following February. At a time when the Vietnam War continued to blaze, China and the United States took major steps toward reducing their mutual antagonism in the face of the Soviet threat. Lin Biao strongly opposed this opening to the United States—probably in part because it would strengthen the political hand of its key architect in China, Zhou Enlai—and the Kissinger visit thus amounted to a major defeat for Lin.

In September 1971 Lin died in a plane crash in Mongolia in what the Chinese assert was an attempt to flee to the Soviet Union. The Chinese high military command who had served under Lin was purged in the weeks following his death.

Lin's demise had a profoundly disillusioning effect on many people who had supported Mao during the Cultural Revolution. Lin had been the high priest of the Mao cult, and millions had gone through tortuous struggles to elevate this chosen successor to power and throw out his "revisionist" challengers. They had in this quest attacked and tortured respected teachers, abused elderly citizens, humiliated old revolutionaries, and, in many cases, battled former friends in bloody confrontations. The sordid details of Lin's purported assassination plot and subsequent flight cast all this in the light of traditional, unprincipled power struggles, and untold millions concluded that they had simply been manipulated for personal political purposes.

Initially, Zhou Enlai was the major beneficiary of Lin's death, and from late 1971 through mid-1973 he tried to nudge the system back toward stability. He encouraged a revival and improvement of educational standards and brought numerous people back into office. China began again to increase its trade and other links with the outside world, while the domestic economy continued the forward momentum that had begun to build in 1969. Mao blessed these general moves but remained wary lest they call into question the basic value of having launched the Cultural Revolution in the first place. In Maoist thought it had always been possible for formerly wayward individuals to reform under pressure and again assume power.

During 1972 Mao suffered a serious stroke, and Zhou learned that he had a fatal cancer. These developments highlighted the continued uncertainty over the succession. In early 1973 Zhou and Mao brought Deng Xiaoping back to power in the hope of grooming him as a successor. But Deng had been the second most-important victim purged by the radicals during the Cultural Revolution, and his reemergence made Jiang Qing, by then head of the radicals, and her followers desperate to return things to a more radical path. From mid-1973, Chinese politics shifted back and forth between Jiang and her followers—later dubbed the Gang of Four—and the supporters of Zhou and Deng. The former group favoured political mobilization, class struggle, anti-intellectualism, egalitarianism, and xenophobia, while the latter promoted economic growth, stability, educational progress, and a pragmatic foreign policy. Mao tried unsuccessfully to maintain a balance among these different forces while continuing in vain to search for a suitable successor.

The balance tipped back and forth—nudged by Mao first this way, then that—between the two groups. The radicals gained the upper hand from mid-1973 until mid-1974, during which time they whipped up a campaign that used criticism of Lin Biao and Confucius as an allegorical vehicle for attacking Zhou and his policies. By July 1974, however, economic decline and increasing chaos made Mao shift back toward Zhou and Deng. With Zhou hospitalized, Deng assumed increasing power from the summer of 1974 through the late fall of 1975. During this time Deng sought (with Zhou's full support) to put the Four Modernizations (of agriculture, industry, science and technology, and defense) at the top of the country's agenda. To further this effort, Deng continued to rehabilitate victims of the Cultural Revolution, and he commissioned the drafting of an important group of documents much like those developed in 1960–62. They laid out the basic principles for work in the party, industry, and science and technology. Their core elements were anathema to the radicals, who used their power in the mass media and the propaganda apparatus to attack Deng's efforts.

The radicals finally convinced Mao that Deng's policies would lead eventually to a repudiation of the Cultural Revolution and even of Mao himself. Mao therefore sanctioned criticism of these policies in the wall posters that were a favourite propaganda tool of the radicals. Zhou died in January 1976, and Deng delivered his eulogy. Deng then disappeared from public view and was formally purged (with Mao's backing) in April. The immediate reason for Deng's downfall was a group of massive demonstrations in Beijing and other cities that took advantage of the traditional Qingming festival to pay homage to Zhou's memory and thereby challenge the radicals.

In the immediate wake of Deng's purge, many of his followers also fell from power, and a political campaign was launched to "criticize Deng Xiaoping and his right-deviationist attempt to reverse correct verdicts [on people during the Cultural Revolution]." Only Mao's death in September and the purge of the Gang of Four by a coalition of political, police, and military leaders in October 1976 brought this effort to vilify Deng to a close. Although it was officially ended by the 11th Party Congress in August 1977, the Cultural Revolution had in fact concluded with Mao's death and the purge of the Gang of Four.

CONSEQUENCES OF THE CULTURAL REVOLUTION

Although the Cultural Revolution largely bypassed the vast majority of the people, who lived in rural areas, it had highly serious consequences for the Chinese system as a whole. In the short run, of course, the political instability and the zigzags in economic policy produced slower economic growth and a decline in the capacity of the government to deliver goods and services. Officials at all levels of the political system had learned that future shifts in policy would jeopardize those who had aggressively implemented previous policy. The result was bureaucratic timidity. In addition, with the death of Mao and the end of the Cultural Revolution, nearly three million CCP members and other citizens awaited reinstatement after having been wrongfully purged.

Bold actions in the late 1970s went far toward coping with those immediate problems, but the Cultural Revolution also left more-serious, longer-term legacies. First, a severe generation gap had been created in which young adults had been denied an education and had been taught to redress grievances by taking to the streets. Second, corruption grew within the CCP and the government, as the terror and accompanying scarcities of goods during the Cultural Revolution had forced people to fall back on traditional personal relationships and on extortion in order to get things done. Third, the CCP leadership and the system itself suffered a loss of legitimacy when millions of urban Chinese became disillusioned by the obvious power plays that took place in the name of political principle in the early and mid-1970s. And fourth, bitter factionalism was rampant, as members of rival Cultural Revolution factions shared the same work unit, each still looking for ways to undermine the power of the other.

CHINA AFTER THE DEATH OF MAO

Perhaps never before in human history had a political leader unleashed such massive forces against the system that he had created. The resulting damage to that system was profound, and the goals that Mao Zedong sought to achieve ultimately remained elusive. The agenda he left behind for his successors was extraordinarily challenging.

During the Cultural Revolution, peasants gathered in Nanshangio, China, to recite passages of Chairman Mao's "Little Red Book." AFP/Getty Images

DOMESTIC DEVELOPMENTS

READJUSTMENT AND RECOVERY

Mao's death and the purge of the Gang of Four left Hua Guofeng, a compromise candidate elevated to the premiership by Mao following the purge of Deng Xiaoping, as the chairman of the CCP and thus the official leader of China. Hua tried to consolidate his position by stressing his ties to Mao and his fidelity to Mao's basic ideas, but many others in the top leadership wanted to move away from these issues, and Hua's position eroded over the remainder of the decade. Furthermore, Hua's successor as party chairman, Hu Yaobang, helped abolish the chairmanship in 1982 in response to concerns that one person might again become too powerful within the party; however, he remained as general secretary.

The ambivalent legacies of the Cultural Revolution were reflected in the members of the Political Bureau chosen just after the 11th Party Congress had convened in August 1977. Like Hua Guofeng, almost half of the members were individuals whose careers had benefited from the Cultural Revolution; the other half were, like Deng Xiaoping, the Cultural Revolution's victims. While a balance between the two groups would be reached only after a period of years, in the short run the tide quickly shifted in favour of the latter group.

ECONOMIC POLICY CHANGES

In the late fall of 1976, the CCP leadership tried to bring some order to the country through a series of national conferences. They moved quickly to appeal to workers' interests by reinstating wage bonuses. The economy had stagnated that year largely because of political turmoil, and Mao's successors were anxious to start things moving again. Despite some uncertainty, Deng was rehabilitated and formally brought back into his previous offices in the summer of 1977.

Lacking detailed information on the economy, the leaders adopted an overly ambitious 10-year plan in early 1978 and used the government's resources to the limit throughout that year to increase investment and achieve rapid economic growth. Much of that growth consisted of reactivating capacity that had lain idle because of political disruption. Future growth would be harder to achieve, and long-term trends in matters such as capital-output ratios made it increasingly clear that the old strategies would be less effective.

One of the major changes of 1978 was China's sharp turn toward participation in the international economy. While in the 1970s there had been a resumption of the foreign trade that had been largely halted in the late 1960s, along with far-more-active and Western-oriented diplomatic initiatives, the changes during and after 1978 were fundamental. China's leaders became convinced that large amounts of capital could be acquired from abroad to speed up the country's modernization, a change in attitude that elicited an almost frenetic response from foreign bankers and entrepreneurs.

These several strands came together in late 1978 at a major meeting of the CCP leadership, when China formally agreed to establish full diplomatic relations with the United States. China's leaders also formally adopted the Four Modernizations as the country's highest priority, with all other tasks to be subordinated to that of economic development. This set of priorities differed so fundamentally from those pursued during the Cultural Revolution that the implications for future policy and for the interests of various sectors of the population were profound.

The opening of China's economy to the outside world proceeded apace. In the late 1970s the country adopted a joint-venture law, and it subsequently enacted numerous other laws (such as one governing patents) to create an attractive environment for foreign capital. An initial experiment with "special economic zones" along the southern coast in the late 1970s led in 1984 to a decision to open 14 cities to more intense engagement with the international economy. The idea was to move toward opening ever larger sections of the country to foreign trade and investment.

Within the domestic economy, numerous experiments were undertaken in finance, banking, planning, urban economic management, and rural policy. Of these, by far the most important were the series of measures taken toward the roughly four-fifths of the population that lived in the countryside at the time. Prices paid for farm products were sharply increased in 1979, thus pumping significant additional resources into the agricultural sector. The collective farming system was gradually dismantled in favour of a return to family farming. At first, families were allowed to contract for the use of collective land for a limited period of time. Subsequently, the period of those contracts was extended, and subcontracting (essentially, allowing one family to accumulate large amounts of land) was permitted.

Peasants were also allowed far greater choice in what crops to plant, and many abandoned farming altogether in favour of establishing small-scale industries or transport companies and other services. Thus, rural patterns of work, land leasing, and wealth changed markedly after 1978. Exceptionally good weather during the early 1980s contributed to record harvests.

The reforms in the urban economy had more-mixed results, largely because the economic system in the cities was so much more complex. Those reforms sought to provide material incentives for greater efficiency and to increase the use of market forces in allocating resources. Problems arose because of the relatively irrational price system, continuing managerial timidity, and the unwillingness of government officials to give up their power over economic decisions, among other difficulties. In the urban as well as the rural economy, the reformers tackled some of the fundamental building blocks of the Soviet system that had been imported during the 1950s.

Reforms have continued in the rural and urban areas. Rural producers have been given more freedom to decide how to use their earnings, whether for agricultural or other economic activities. Private entrepreneurship in the cities and the rationalization, privatization, and, in some cases, dismantling of state-owned enterprises have gained speed. At the same time, the central government has moderated the pace of change—primarily to avoid increases in social unrest resulting from rising unemployment—and constructed a social safety net for those who lose their jobs.

POLITICAL DEVELOPMENTS

The reformers led by Deng Xiaoping tried after 1978 to reduce the level of political coercion in Chinese society. Millions of victims of past political campaigns were released from labour camps, and bad "class labels" were removed from those stigmatized by them. This dramatically improved the career and social opportunities of millions of former political pariahs. To a considerable extent, moreover, the range of things considered political was narrowed, so that mundane elements such as style of dress and grooming and preferences in music and hobbies were no longer considered politically significant. More importantly, criticizing policy no longer triggered political retaliation against the critics. Overall, the role of the Public Security (police) forces was cut back substantially.

The reformers also tried to make preparations for their own political succession. This involved first rehabilitating cadres who had been purged during the Cultural Revolution (most of which was accomplished in the late 1970s). These cadres in many cases were old and no longer fully able to meet the demands being made on them, and they were encouraged to retire. Younger, better-educated people committed to reform were then brought into prominent positions. Deng proved masterful at maintaining a viable coalition among the diverse forces at the top. By the end of 1981 he had succeeded in nudging Hua Guofeng and others of the more-rigid Maoists out of high-level positions. Although he refused to take the top positions for himself, Deng saw his supporters become premier (Zhao Ziyang and then Li Peng) and general secretary of the CCP (Hu Yaobang, Zhao, and Jiang Zemin), and he worked hard to try to consolidate and maintain their hold on power.

In early 1982 the CCP leadership made a concerted attempt to restructure the leading bodies in both the government and the party, and much was reorganized, with the appointment of many new officials. This general effort continued, with the focus increasingly on the bloated military establishment, but progress slowed considerably after the initial burst of organizational reformism.

Throughout 1982–85 the CCP carried out a "rectification" campaign designed to restore morals to its membership and weed out those who did not support reform. This campaign highlighted the increasing difficulties inherent in maintaining discipline and limiting corruption at a time of rapid change, when materialistic values were being officially propagated.

By the mid-1980s, China was in transition, with core elements of the previous system called into question while the ultimate balance that would be struck remained unclear even to the

On June 5, 1989, a lone protester stands down a column of tanks at the entrance to Tiananmen Square in Bejing. CNN/Getty Images

top participants. The reform movement began to sour in 1985. Financial decentralization and the two-price system combined with other factors to produce inflation and encourage corruption. China's population, increasingly exposed to foreign ideas and standards of living, put pressure on the government to speed the rate of change within the country.

These forces produced open unrest within the country in late 1986 and again on a much larger scale in the spring of 1989. By 1989 popular disaffection with the CCP and the government had become widespread. Students—eventually joined by many others—took to the streets in dozens of cities from April to June to demand greater freedom and other changes. Government leaders, after initial hesitation, used the army to suppress this unrest in early June (most visibly in Tiananmen Square), with substantial loss of life. China's elderly revolutionaries then reverted to more-conservative economic, political, and cultural policies in an attempt to reestablish firm control. In 1992, however, Deng Xiaoping publicly criticized what he called the country's continuing "leftism" and sought to renew the efforts at economic reform. Economic growth had been especially remarkable in southern China, which had developed the highest concentration of private-sector enterprise. Since the mid-1990s the CCP has worked to drastically accelerate market reforms in banking, taxes, trade, and investments. These reforms have continued apace, and the party has attempted to increase public support by conducting energetic anticorruption campaigns that rely in part on high-profile prosecutions and occasional executions of high-level officials accused of corruption.

Jiang proved to be a capable successor to Deng. He replaced Zhao Ziyang as general secretary in 1989 after the Tiananmen incident and also was named chair of the Central Military Commission (1989) and president of the National People's Congress (1993). He combined a pragmatic, reform-minded economic policy with an insistence that the party maintain strong control over the government. Jiang consolidated his power after Deng's death in 1997 to become China's paramount ruler but gradually relinquished his posts to Hu Jintao in 2002–04.

EDUCATIONAL AND CULTURAL POLICY CHANGES

In education, the reformers gave top priority to training technical, scientific, and scholarly talent to world-class standards. This involved re-creating a highly selective and elitist system of higher education, with admission based on competitive academic examination. Graduate study programs were introduced, and thousands of Chinese were sent abroad for advanced study. Large numbers of foreign scholars were also used to help upgrade the educational system. Somewhat ironically, the value the reformers attached to making money had the unintended consequence of encouraging many brilliant people to forgo intellectual careers in favour of more-lucrative undertakings. The range of cultural fare available was broadened greatly, and new limits were constantly tested. Few groups had suffered so bitterly as China's writers and artists, and policies since the 1980s have reflected the ongoing battle between cultural liberals and more-orthodox officials.

INTERNATIONAL RELATIONS

True reintegration of the People's Republic of China into the international community can be said to date to 1971, when it replaced Taiwan (Republic of China; ROC) as China's representative to the United Nations. With that event, many countries that formerly had recognized the ROC established relations with the People's Republic. The normalization of diplomatic ties with the United States, which began in 1973, culminated in 1979.

China's foreign policy since the mid-1970s generally has reflected the country's preoccupation with domestic economic development and its desire to promote a peaceful and stable environment in which to achieve these domestic goals. Except for its disagreement with Vietnam over that country's invasion of Cambodia in 1978, China has by and large avoided disputes and encouraged the peaceful evolution of events in Asia. China adopted a policy of "one country, two systems" in order to provide a framework for the successful negotiation with Great Britain for the return of Hong Kong and adjacent territories in 1997 and with Portugal for the return of Macau in 1999; both were given special administrative status. Furthermore, China became an advocate of arms control and assumed a more-constructive, less-combative stance in many international organizations.

The bloody suppression of the demonstrations in 1989 set back China's foreign relations. The United States, the European Community (European Union since 1993), and Japan imposed sanctions, though by 1992 China had largely regained its international standing with all but the United States. But by the mid-1990s both sides had taken steps toward improved relations, and China retained its most-favoured-nation status in U.S. trade—subject to annual review by the U.S. Congress until 2000, when Congress made the status permanent.

The collapse of communism in eastern Europe beginning in mid-1989 and the subsequent disintegration of the Soviet Union deeply disturbed China's leaders. While hard-liners used these developments to warn about the dangers of reform, Deng Xiaoping and Jiang Zemin were able to minimize such backsliding and move China closer to becoming a major world power. The country's admission into the World Trade Organization in 2001 was considered a significant step in its further integration into the global economy. Added to that was the international prestige that accompanied Beijing's selection to host the 2008 Summer Olympic Games.

RELATIONS WITH TAIWAN

A major unresolved issue in the region has been the status of Taiwan. Since 1949 the regimes on both the mainland and Taiwan have agreed that Taiwan is a province of China—the principal difference being that each has asserted it is the legitimate government of the country. Tensions were especially high between the two entities in the first decades after the split, marked by periodic artillery duels between batteries on the Taiwan-controlled islands of Matsu and Qemoy, just off the coast of Fujian province, and those opposite them on the mainland. The ROC's claim of legitimacy was dealt a serious blow after 1970 with its loss of UN representation and diplomatic recognition by most of the world's countries. Still, Taiwan has remained viable and has emerged as a global economic powerhouse, its security guaranteed by a commitment from the United States and backed by U.S. military presence in the region. The continued American involvement in Taiwan affairs has at times been a source of friction in U.S.-China relations.

Through all this, economic ties have improved considerably between the mainland and Taiwan. Taiwan has become one of China's major trading partners, and large numbers of people from the island live and work on the mainland. Beijing has continued to press for reintegrating Taiwan as a province of China under mainland administration. However, a growing movement on Taiwan has advocated that the island become an independent sovereign state and not continue to be considered a part of China. Tensions escalated after the pro-independence Chen Shui-bian was elected president of the ROC in 2000. Nonetheless, discussions have continued between the two sides, and in 2005 high-ranking Nationalist Party (KMT) officials traveled to the mainland, the first such visits since 1949. In addition, tensions between China and Taiwan eased significantly after the Nationalists regained control of both Taiwan's legislature and the presidency in 2008.

CONCLUSION

In anticipation of the 2008 Olympic Games, Beijing underwent a huge makeover that China used to show how fast change could happen in a country of 1.3 billion people. New subway lines were completed, and more and more skyscrapers were added each month to the landscape to replace the fast-disappearing traditional housing (*hutongs*). As the

world's third largest economy and also the third largest trading country, China accounted in 2007 for approximately 5 percent of world GDP and had recently graduated in status to a middle-income country. Beijing was also emerging as a key global aid donor. In terms of production, China supplied more than one-third of the world's steel, half of its cement, and about a third of its aluminum.

China's achievements in poverty reduction from the post–Mao Zedong era, in terms of both scope and speed, were impressive; about 400 million people had been lifted from poverty. The standard of living for many Chinese was improving, and this led to a widespread optimism that the government's goal of achieving an overall well-off, or *xiaokang*, society, was possible in the near future.

The figures that illustrated China's remarkable economic achievements, however, concealed huge and outstanding challenges that, if neglected, could jeopardize those very same gains. Many local and foreign-development analysts agreed that China's unsustainable and reckless approach to growth was putting the country and the world on the brink of environmental catastrophe. China was already coping with limited natural resources that were fast disappearing. In addition, not everyone was sharing the benefits of growth—about 135 million people, or one-tenth of the population, still lived below the international absolute poverty line of $1 per day. There was a huge inequality between the urban and rural population, as well as between the poor and the rich. The increasing number of protests (termed mass incidents in China) was attributed to both environmental causes and experiences of injustice. If these social problems remained, it could imperil the "harmonious development," or *hexie fazhan,* project of the government and eventually erode the Communist Party of China's continued monopoly of political power.

China consumed more coal than the U.S., Europe, and Japan combined and in 2007 was about to surpass, or had already surpassed, the U.S. as the world's biggest emitter of greenhouse gases. Beijing was also the biggest emitter of sulfur dioxide, which contributes to acid rain. Chinese scholars blamed the increase in emissions on rapid economic growth and the fact that China relied on coal for 70% of its energy needs. More than 300,000 premature deaths annually were attributed to airborne pollution. The changing lifestyle of the increasing number of middle-class families also contributed to the problem. In Beijing alone, 1,000 new cars were added to the roads every day. Seven of the 10 most polluted cities in the world were located in China.

The UN 2006 Human Development Report cited China's worsening water pollution and its failure to restrict heavy polluters. More than 300 million people lacked access to clean drinking water. About 60 percent of the water in China's seven major river systems was classified as being unsuitable for human contact, and more than one-third of industrial wastewater and two-thirds of municipal

wastewater were released into waterways without any treatment. China had about 7 percent of the world's water resources and roughly 20 percent of its population. In addition, this supply was severely regionally imbalanced—about four-fifths of China's water was situated in the southern part of the country.

The Pearl River Delta and Yangtze River Delta, two regions well developed owing to recent export-oriented growth, suffered from extensive contamination from heavy-metal and persistent organic pollutants. The pollutants emanated from industries outsourced from the developed countries and electronic wastes that were illegally imported from the U.S. According to an investigation of official records conducted by the Institute of Public and Environmental Affairs (IPE), a domestic environmental nongovernmental organization, 34 multinational corporations (MNCs) with operations in China had violated water-pollution-control guidelines. These MNCs included PepsiCo, Inc., Panasonic Battery Co., and Foster's Group Ltd. The IPE's data were based on reports by government bodies at local and national levels.

China was beginning to realize, however, that its growth path was not cost-free. According to the State Environmental Protection Administration and the World Bank, air and water pollution was costing China 5.8 percent of its GDP. Though the Chinese government carried the responsibility for fixing the overwhelming environmental consequences of China's breakneck growth, help, if offered, from the transnational companies and consumers from industrialized countries that benefited greatly from China's cheap labour and polluting industries could also be utilized in the challenging cleanup task.

When the Chinese government in 2004 began setting targets for reducing energy use and cutting emissions, the idea of adopting a slower growth model and the predictions about the looming environmental disaster were not received with enthusiasm at first. By 2007, however, targets had been established for shifting to renewable energy, for employing energy conservation, and for embracing emission-control schemes. The target was to produce 16 percent of energy needs from alternative sources (hydro and other renewable resources) by 2020.

Inside China in 2007, people were more concerned about issues related to the problem of widespread inequality than they were about showcasing the upcoming Olympics. The Gini coefficient (which indicates how inequality has grown in relation to economic growth) had increased in China by 50 percent since the late 1970s. Less than 1 percent of Chinese households controlled more than 60 percent of the country's wealth. This inequality was more pronounced when seen in urban versus rural per capita income. In the countryside, life was harsh, and people were poor. The ratio of urban versus rural per capita income grew from 1.8:1 in the early 1980s to 3.23:1 in 2003. (The world average was between 1.5:1 and 2:1.) Added to the problem of low income, Chinese rural residents also

shouldered disproportionate tax burdens while having less access to public services, such as education and health care. Recently, the government abolished a number of taxes to help address poverty in the countryside.

The temporary migration from rural areas to the cities of 100 million–150 million Chinese peasants was not an easy transition. The rural migrant workers who kept factories and construction sites running were denied access to urban housing and to urban schooling for their children. Women migrant workers faced triple discrimination for being poor unskilled labour, female, and rural in origin. The anger and bitterness that set off riots and protests (reportedly more than 80,000 in 2006) in the countryside was not so much about poverty as it was about fairness. Agricultural land in China was communally owned. (In theory, each village owned the land around it, and each family held a small tract of land on a long-term lease.) In the past 20 years, however, urbanization had claimed some 16 million acres (about 6.5 million hectares) of farmland; people saw their land being taken from them and then turned into homes that were sold to the new rich for several million dollars, and they witnessed local officials lining their own pockets. Meanwhile, they received little compensation in return and spent years away from home to live tenuous hand-to-mouth existences as factory or construction workers. Many were cheated of their wages by unscrupulous bosses. Given the reports of mass public

A portrait of former Chinese Communist Party leader Mao Zedong displayed during National Day celebrations in Beijing on October 1, 2009. Frederic J. Brown/AFP/Getty Images

protests, it was evident that many in China were clamouring for a more equitable distribution of China's bounty from its two-decades-long growth.

On October 1, 2009, China's communist government celebrated its 60th anniversary with a huge military parade featuring tanks and marching soldiers. This display demonstrated China's growing military might. It was just one symbol of how far China has come from its weak and devastated state when the government was founded in 1949. China has experienced many bewildering changes in fortune. It has been both conquered and conqueror, shattered and united. Yet, longer than any other nation in the world, it has retained its essential character through all of its many incarnations. China faces many challenges as it looks to the future. But with its wealth of history, resources, and people, it is likely to be able to adapt to whatever may come.

GLOSSARY

assay Analysis of components in an ore to determine quantity of each component.

bourgeois According to Marxist doctrine, a capitalist, or a person who owns property.

cash crop Any crop grown specifically to be sold.

cell A small entity that acts as a unit within a larger political organization.

censorate Body of government officials responsible for supervising the conduct of other officials and rulers.

Collective A business or farm organized under the political idea of centralized economic control.

Comintern An international association of communist parties from different countries, started in the Soviet Union in 1919.

communism A system of social organization based on the idea of holding all property in common and of workers being organized to labor for the community rather than for themselves.

corvée Unpaid labour for a feudal lord.

dowager A widow with a title or property from her deceased husband.

eunuch A male who has been castrated, often for the purposes of serving as a palace official or guard.

feiqian "Flying money"; a type of paper credit used to transmit funds.

fief Area of land given to select individuals, usually relatives of the ruler.

filial piety The Confucian virtue of devotion to and respect for one's parents and ancestors.

gongsuo Trade guild.

guozijian State academy.

herrenvolk A master race.

jia Family.

khan A ruler, often of a Central Asian country.

khanate The area over which a khan presides.

microlith Small stone artifact.

mingjiao The "doctrine of names"; a combination of Confucian and Legalist ideas forming a doctrine emphasizing social duty, ritual, law, and human traits.

prefect An official appointed to govern a prefecture, often with a limited range of authority.

prefecture system Division of land into localities governed by appointed officials (prefects).

primogeniture The eldest son's right to inherit all the property of his parents.

revisionism A strain of Marxism in which certain classic Marxist principles have been abandoned.

sanjiao "Three teachings"; the major Chinese philosophies: Daoism, Confucianism, and Buddhism.

scapulae Shoulder blades, often used in divination.

sinecure A position or title with few responsibilities, if any, and usually, some form of income.

soviet A governmental council, particularly of the former Soviet Union.

triad A fraternal secret society, often built around kinship, work, or native-place ties, with its own set of rules, rituals, and lore.

vassal An individual who serves a feudal lord.

FOR FURTHER READING

Abramson, Marc S. *Ethnic Identity in Tang China*. Philadelphia, PA: University of Pennsylvania Press, 2008.

Bell, Daniel A., ed. *Confucian Political Ethics*. Princeton, NJ: Princeton University Press, 2008.

Bol, Peter K. *Neo-Confucianism in History*. Cambridge, MA: Harvard University Asia Center, 2008.

Clark, Paul. *The Chinese Cultural Revolution: A History*. New York, NY: Cambridge University Press, 2008.

Fenby, Jonathan. *Modern China: The Fall and Rise of a Great Power, 1850 to Present*. New York, NY: HarperCollins, 2008.

Feng, Li. *Bureaucracy and the State in Early China: Governing the Western Zhou*. New York, NY: Cambridge University Press, 2008.

Gascoigne, Bamber. *The Dynasties of China*. New York, NY: Carroll & Graff, 2003.

Gelber, Harry G. *The Dragon and the Foreign Devils: China and the World, 1100 B.C. to the Present*. New York, NY: Walker & Company, 2007.

Graff, David A., and Robin Higham. *A Military History of China*. New York, NY: Westview Press, 2002.

Hansen, Valerie. *The Open Empire: A History of China to 1600*. New York, NY: W.W. Norton, 2000.

Kieschnick, John. *The Impact of Buddhism on Chinese Material Culture*. Princeton, NJ: Princeton University Press, 2003.

Kohn, Livia. *Daoism and Chinese Culture*. Cambridge, MA: Three Pines Press, 2001.

Kuhn, Dieter. *The Age of Confucian Rule: The Song Transformation of China*. Cambridge, MA: Harvard University Press, 2009.

Lewis, Mark Edward. *China Between Empires: The Northern and Southern Dynasties*. Cambridge, MA: Harvard University Press, 2009.

Liu, Li. *The Chinese Neolithic: Trajectories to Early States*. New York, NY: Cambridge University Press, 2004.

Pan, Philip P. *Out of Mao's Shadow: The Struggle for the Soul of a New China*. New York, NY: Simon and Schuster, 2008.

Rowe, William T. *China's Last Empire: The Great Qing*. Cambridge, MA: Harvard University Press, 2009.

Schneewind, Sarah. *A Tale of Two Melons: Emperor and Subject in Ming China*. Indianapolis, IN: Hackett, 2006.

Tanner, Harold M. *China: A History*. Indianapolis, IN: Hackett, 2009.

Thorp, Robert L. *China in the Early Bronze Age: Shang Civilization*. Philadelphia, PA: University of Pennsylvania Press, 2006.

Weatherford, Jack. *Genghis Khan and the Making of the Modern World*. New York, NY: Random House, 2004.

N